Radical Philosophy of Law

RADICAL PHILOSOPHY OF LAW

Contemporary Challenges to Mainstream Legal Theory and Practice

Edited by

DAVID S. CAUDILL

and

STEVEN JAY GOLD

HUMANITIES PRESS
NEW JERSEY

First published 1995 by Humanities Press International, Inc.
165 First Avenue, Atlantic Highlands, New Jersey 07716

This collection © 1995 by Humanities Press
Individual articles © 1995 by the authors

Library of Congress Cataloging-in-Publication Data
Radical philosophy of law : contemporary challenges to mainstream
  legal theory and practice / edited by David S. Caudill and Steven
  Jay Gold.
       p. cm.
    Includes index.
    ISBN 0–391–03861–3 (cloth).—ISBN 0–391–03862–1 (pbk.)
    1. Sociological jurisprudence. 2. Law—Philosophy.
  3. Radicalism. I. Caudill, David Stanley. II. Gold, Steven Jay.
  K370.R33 1995
  340'. 115—dc20   94–18238
                                                        CIP

A catalog record for this book is available from the British Library.

Printed in the United States of America.

10 9 8 7 6 5 4 3 2

CONTENTS

Preface and Acknowledgments   vii

Introduction: Philosophy with a Focus
    David S. Caudill   ix

PART I: THEORY

1   The Legacy of Marxist Jurisprudence
       Raymond A. Belliotti   3

2   The Analytic Defense of Functional Marxism and Law
       Steven Jay Gold   32

3   Postmodern Law and Subjectivity: Lacan and the
    Linguistic Turn
       Dragan Milovanovic   38

4   Re-returning to Freud: Critical Legal Studies as
    Cultural Psychoanalysis
       David S. Caudill   45

5   A Theory of Social Injustice
       Thomas W. Simon   54

6   Feminist Legal Critics: The Reluctant Radicals
       Patricia Smith   73

7   Rethinking the Language of Law, Justice, and
    Community: Postmodern Feminist Jurisprudence
       Bruce A. Arrigo   88

PART II: APPLICATIONS

8   The Marxian Critique of Criminal Justice
       Jeffrey Reiman   111

9   Legitimation Crisis in Contract Law: A Test Case for
    Critical Legal Studies and Its Critics
       David Ingram   140

10   Constituting the Modern State: The Supreme Court,
    Labor Law, and the Contradictions of Legitimation
       Carl Swidorski   162

11   The Chaotic Indeterminacy of Tort Law: Between
      Formalism and Nihilism
            Denis J. Brion   179

12   Perversions of Justice: Examining the Doctrine of
      U.S. Rights to Occupancy in North America
            Ward Churchill   200

13   Marriage, Law, and Gender: A Feminist Inquiry
            Nan D. Hunter   221

14   Disembodiment: Abortion and Gay Rights
            Ruth Colker   234

15   Hate Speech, Freedom, and Discourse Ethics in
      the Academy
            Patricia S. Mann   255

Notes   272
Contributors   333
Index   335

PREFACE AND ACKNOWLEDGMENTS

Most of the papers in this volume were collected by Steven Jay Gold on behalf of the Radical Philosophy Association (RPA), a nonpartisan and nonsectarian forum for the philosophical discussion of fundamental social change. The present volume derives its strength from the disciplinary diversity of the RPA, as the contributors come from the fields of law, criminology, sociology, and political science as well as philosophy. Consistent with the eclectic interests of the RPA, this collection deals with a wide range of perspectives within the radical tradition. Most of the papers were written especially for the volume, many by RPA members; the four articles previously published (Ingram, Reiman, Belliotti, and Hunter—the latter two were modified for this volume) were chosen to round out the diversity of issues presented. Credit to the journals that published these four articles, and to the journals and books in which the initial ideas (developed in this volume) of some of the other contributors were introduced, appear in the notes to this volume. The editors are grateful for the permissions granted by all such publishers, in every case without cost.

The editors are especially grateful to Keith Ashfield, President and Publisher of Humanities Press, for his advice and assistance throughout the publication process; to Chad Graddy for proofreading and for ensuring uniformity of citation styles; and to the Frances Lewis Law Center, Washington & Lee University, for providing research funds to support Graddy's efforts. Finally, and most importantly, we are grateful to the scholars who contributed papers to make this book possible.

D.S.C.
S.J.G.

vii

Introduction:
Philosophy with a Focus

DAVID S. CAUDILL

The term "radical philosophy of law" has various connotations; thus a clarification of the purpose and organization of this volume is in order. Those in law departments might think immediately of the contemporary Critical Legal Studies (CLS) movement[1] among legal scholars; though the perspectives associated with CLS are represented and/or discussed by various contributors to this collection (see, e.g., the chapters by Belliotti, Caudill, Ingram, Swidorski, and Brion), this volume is decidedly not a CLS reader (though several exist).[2] Outside the field of law, radical jurisprudence calls to mind the Marxian and neo-Marxian traditions; again, while those perspectives are critically explored in several contributions (see, e.g., the chapters by Belliotti, Gold, Milovanovic, and Reiman), the influence of Marxism is indirect in most of the essays that follow. Finally, the term "philosophy" might suggest a narrow disciplinary approach distinct from politics or sociology, but the term is here employed to capture foundational reflections on legal processes and institutions from various disciplinary perspectives.

This volume represents a cross section or sampling of work in contemporary left legal theory. Readers will immediately notice that the critique of law is inherently interdisciplinary—it does not "belong" to radical lawyers, to Marxian social critics, to feminist scholars, or to language theorists. Unfortunately, disciplinary fragmentation persists among those engaged in critical legal theory; this volume was designed to bring together philosophers, legal scholars, sociologists, and political theorists at work on common tasks. Moreover, this volume introduces a variety of theoretical models (including Marxian analysis, psychoanalytic social criticism, semiotics, and feminism—and feminist theology) and develops those models (*i*) in specific subfields of law (criminal justice, contracts, labor law, family law, torts); (*ii*) in the critique of racism, sexism, and gender bias in law; and (*iii*) in several contemporary constitutional and public policy controversies (including the controversies over abortion and hate speech). While no single volume in radical legal philosophy could be claimed to be comprehensive, the essays collected here are more than mere "samples"—together they identify, and apply in various practical contexts, most of the major theoretical currents in today's left legal thought. Each essay invites, sometimes explicitly, reflection beyond the issues considered, on new theoretical models and/or other pragmatic localities.

I must concede that the division between theory (Part I) and applications (Part II) imposed by the editors is artificial; the contributors did not intend to be so categorized, and the division certainly implies neither that the later essays are less theoretically "sophisticated" than the earlier ones nor that the earlier essays are impractical. Rather, the organization reflects only the fact that the essays in Part I describe theoretical paradigms, while the essays in Part II address particular problems in contemporary law. A brief summary of the essays will clarify that (initially misleading) distinction.

Part I, Theory, begins with Raymond Belliotti's superb overview of Marx's theories of alienation, exploitation, base/superstructure, ideology, the dialectic, fetishism, and liberal-capitalist domination. Belliotti includes a critical reassessment of Marxism for law, summarizes the influence of Marxism on legal realism, feminism, CLS, and critical race theory, and concludes that Marxian theory is less jurisprudence than an unmasking of law's participation in oppression. Co-editor Gold's essay on "analytical Marxism" then defends functionalism and revitalizes a form of Marxian critique of criminal law. Milovanovic, also working from a Marxian base, evaluates the weaknesses in traditional Marxian theory (especially with respect to subjectivity) that are overcome in the turn to supplemental perspectives such as that of psychoanalysis. Co-editor Caudill next shifts the focus from the Marxian tradition to its heir, the Critical Legal Studies movement in American law schools; Jacques Lacan's return to Freud, Caudill argues, is significant for the cultural (psycho)analysis attempted by critics of legal ideology. Stepping back from the presumption among radical philosophers that justice is a clear goal, Thomas Simon asks (in his essay) whether the concept of injustice is not easier to grasp and apply in critical social theory. Patricia Smith's introduction to the feminist critique of law highlights a persistent injustice within legal processes and institutions; Smith also raises the question of whether feminism is properly a mainstream liberal or a radical critique of law, and she concludes that its strength is in the latter. Part I ends with Bruce Arrigo's appropriation of postmodern language theory, especially that of Kristeva, as an empowering paradigm for feminist legal criticism.

Jeffery Reiman's opening essay in Part II, Applications, is a return to Marxian theory as a perspective on the fundamental ethical categories of criminal justice; like Belliotti, Reiman succinctly summarizes the terminology and foundational theories of Marxism, but Reiman's attention to the major subdiscipline of criminal law places Marxism in

a practical context. David Ingram, shifting the theoretical focus from
Marxism to Critical Legal Studies, both credits and criticizes the CLS
critique of liberalism as a legitimating ideology; contract law, as well
as labor regulation and welfare legislation, provides exemplary contexts for Ingram's critique of liberal ideals of pluralism and his revision of radical legal theory. A deep analysis of labor law is then sustained
in Carl Swidorski's essay, which builds upon the understanding by
CLS scholars of how the institutions and processes of law, and even
attempts at legal reform, typically support existing social orders; the
CLS critique of labor law, Swidorski argues, provides a model for legal
criticism in other arenas, such as property law and the critique of racism
in law. A more critical assessment of CLS appears in Denis Brion's
analysis of tort law, which employs insights from chaos theory and
semiotics in a revisitation of the conflict between traditional formalists
and CLS indeterminists in contemporary legal theory. Ward Churchill's examination of the treatment of Native Americans in U.S. history both confirms and calls into question the use of legal processes in
acts of domination and oppression; the legitimacy of U.S. property claims
in North America is also questioned in light of traditional and contemporary international law. Nan Hunter's essay on marriage law
exemplifies the feminist critique of gender bias in terms of the contemporary controversy over "gay and lesbian marriage." Ruth Colker
then brings a uniquely theological perspective (unique in radical legal
philosophy) to her analyses of abortion and gay rights. Another contemporary controversy, hate speech on college campuses, is reconsid-
ered by Patricia Mann in her essay, which emphasizes the collective,
and not just individual, nature of speech acts.

While the above summary of this collection of essays reveals a thematic
unity amongs its authors—each attempts to critically assess the potential of law to create injustices—these radical scholars are characterized
as well by their diversity. Marxism, as well as Critical Legal Studies,
is inspirational for some and a target for others; feminism, as well as
critical race theory, is not a unitary doctrine; and constitutional "rights"
are as often claimed for protection as they are rejected for their tendency to mislead critics of law. Just as it is difficult to classify the
contributors to this volume as belonging to a particular disciplinary
tradition or critical movement, it is difficult to think of the radical
philosophy of law as a set of predictable positions on contemporary
controversies. The boundaries of left legal theory are dynamic, and its
proponents unfaithful to anything that might appear to them as doc-
trinaire. As a whole, this representation of critical approaches to law
should, in the conversation imposed on readers, also represent the
necessary self-critical aspect of sociolegal theory and critique.

PART I

Theory

1

The Legacy of
Marxist Jurisprudence*

RAYMOND A. BELLIOTTI

Rather than advancing a refined theory of judicial decision-making or puzzling over the nature of law, Marxist jurisprudence offers a critique of liberal-capitalist conceptions of law. As part of its general undermining of bourgeois consciousness, Marxism aspires to manifest the legitimating functions of law as a contributor to ideological distortion and as a solidifier of the political status quo. Accordingly, there is not so much a Marxist theory of law as there is a Marxist unmasking of law's alleged unsavory participation in domination and oppression.

GENERAL MARXISM

In order to understand the Marxist critique of law, we must first attend to a few general themes in Marxist thought. I do not intend to advance an innovative or especially controversial interpretation of these general themes. Rather, I will adumbrate a standard description of those themes in order to set the stage for the critique of law.

ALIENATION

According to Marxists, alienation results from market forces and the capitalist production process, especially capitalist relations of production, which disenfranchise workers from decision making. Lacking a voice in the productive process, workers toil merely to satisfy survival and sustenance needs. As the insipid routinization of capitalist production and its suffocating division of labor overwhelm workers'

3

creative and imaginative capacities, workers are reduced to semihuman extensions of productive machinery. Workers are thereby estranged from their labor, their employers, their fellow workers, the product, and ultimately from themselves.[1]

Although Marx was not a proponent of a fixed, universal human nature, he viewed alienation as estrangement from historically created human possibilities. His minimalist view of species-being included the conviction that human fulfilment is intimately connected with the imaginative, unshackled use of productive capacities. Labor is a distinctively human activity and possesses central normative significance. Humans presumably shape their social world and forge their personal identities through interaction with their material work and its dominant productive process. It is only through free and creative activity that a person realizes unalienated being.[2] For Marx, the conditions and reality of alienation are not dependent on workers' subjective reports. Regardless of whether workers self-consciously announce the requisite feelings of estrangement, the objective social condition of the proletariat is pervaded by alienation.[3]

In sum, capitalist social and economic institutions prevent the actualization of workers' potential and thereby disconnect workers from their species-being because they stifle workers' voice, creativity, and imagination; transform labor power itself into a commodity; incline workers to seek the false consolations offered by ideological superstructure; fail to mediate the social aspect of labor by cooperation and solidarity; and produce the ironic and pernicious consequence that the more diligently and more intensely the proletariat class works the more surplus value is produced, and the greater becomes the class and power disparity between workers and capitalists. In this fashion, through mystification and exclusion and with the connivance of its economic ideology, capitalism nurtures workers' desperation for material possessions, not their sense of creative expression.

EXPLOITATION

In its most general Kantian-Marxist sense, "exploitation" occurs when someone uses another person as merely an object for her own benefit without regard for the humanity of that person. In its more particular Marxist sense, exploitation occurs when one class, the proletariat, produces a surplus whose use is controlled by another class, the capitalists.[4] Moreover, the capitalist economic mode differs from other economic modes in that this kind of exploitation occurs absent the use of explicit duress, physical threat, or other noneconomic force. It is through the capitalists' vastly superior economic bargaining power over workers, their ownership of the means of production, and the lack of real alternatives for workers that exploitation flourishes in a capitalist regime. Finally, capitalism, shrouded by its pretensions to neutral, economic processes, is especially pernicious in that it is thereby able to mask the nature and effects of the exploitation of workers.[5]

Capitalists exploit workers by siphoning the surplus value produced by the labor of the proletariat class. Capitalists purchase workers' labor power at its value, which is equivalent to a subsistence wage, and sell products at their value. Because the value workers create is greater than the value of labor power itself, surplus value results. The exploitive nature of the relationship is reflected in the fact that workers do not receive the labor equivalent of what they produce.[6] Moreover, workers' labor is "forced" in the sense that only limited and equally debilitating alternatives are available for workers seeking to satisfy their subsistence requirements.[7]

Although there is considerable dispute as to precisely which set of necessary and sufficient conditions captures the meaning of Marxist exploitation, the following elements are relevant: workers benefit capitalists; capitalists economically force, in the relevant Marxist sense of that term, workers to supply that benefit; and capitalists wrongfully fail to supply reciprocal benefits to workers.[8]

ECONOMIC SUBSTRUCTURE AND IDEOLOGICAL SUPERSTRUCTURE

One of Marx's most intriguing and baffling pronouncements concerns the relationship between a society's economic substructure ("the base") and its ideological superstructure ("the superstructure"). A society's mode of economic production includes its forces of production (natural resources, instruments and means of production, workers and their skills, raw materials) and its relations of production (the formal and informal organization of relations among people, or among people and commodities, in the productive process). The base consists, strictly speaking, of the relations of production. The superstructure consists of our political and legal institutions, and our forms of social consciousness (what we think and believe, how we understand and experience the world).

Marx's clearest and best known passage about the relationship between the base and superstructure is the following:

> In the social production of their life, humans enter into definite relations that are indispensable and independent of their will, relations of production which correspond to a definite stage of development of their material productive forces. The sum total of these relations of production constitutes the economic structure of society, the real foundation, on which rises a legal and political superstructure and to which correspond definite forms of social consciousness. The mode

of production of material life conditions the social, political, and intellectual life process in general. It is not the consciousness of humans that determines their being, but, on the contrary, their social being that determines their consciousness.[9]

It is clear that for Marx the development of the forces of production results in changes in the relations of production. Moreover, there will come a time when the existing relations of production no longer effectively and efficiently allow the growth of productive forces. This internal contradiction divides society and will result in the fall of the obsolete set of productive relations: "At a certain stage of their development, the material productive forces of society come in conflict with the existing relations of production. . . . Then begins the epoch of social revolution."[10] New relations of production will triumph because they have the capacity to facilitate the continued growth of society's productive forces. Thus Marx provides an economic explanation for political revolution.

It is less clear precisely what Marx means by the passage, "It is not the consciousness of humans that determines their being, but, on the contrary, their social being that determines their consciousness." He surely distances himself here from philosophical idealists who hold that reality consists in or depends on minds and ideas; or that the engine of social change is human agency fueled by ideas. Marx clearly wants to deny the autonomy and explanatory primacy attributed to ideas and forms of consciousness. But what is his precise meaning about the relationship of the base and superstructure? There are at least three candidates: economic determinism, economic limitation, and economic practice.[11]

Economic determinism holds that the base causes the superstructure, in the sense that our forms of consciousness and the institutions which embody them are the effects of the economic processes of material production. This view suggests that the base is independent of and logically prior to superstructure. There are, however, at least three major difficulties with this interpretation.

First, it marginalizes human freedom to the point of fetishizing impersonal economic processes as the animating forces of history. Second, it is clear that the base is not independent of superstructure. On the contrary, a superstructure of property rights and legal categories is essential for the coherent functioning and sanctioning of productive processes:

Plamenatz contends that it is impossible for a set of relations of production to be described without reference to legal rules, and furthermore that many modes of production like capitalism are actually dependent upon the legal system for the creation of their basic economic relations.[12]

Absent the requisite superstructure the base simply cannot take hold. Thus it is misleading to declare the independence of the base.

Third, Engels rejected the crude reductionism reflected in economic determinism by stressing the "ultimate supremacy" of or "determination in the last instance" by the base, which passages concede that elements of the superstructure can produce effects and react on the base:[13] "... political, legal, philosophical theories, religious ideas and their further development into systems of dogma—also exercise their influence upon the course of the historical struggles."[14] Moreover, Marx suggested that the relationship of the base and superstructure was historical and complex, and that the superstructure was not merely the passive reflector of productive processes: "If material production itself is not conceived in its *specific historical* form, it is impossible to understand what is specific in the spiritual production corresponding to it and the reciprocal influence of one on the other."[15] Regardless of the success of persuasiveness of such passages, they do allow sympathetic interpreters to liberate Marx and Engels from charges of economic determinism and crude reductionism.

Economic limitation asserts that the base sets limits on social consciousness. That is, a society's dominant ideologies are constrained in the sense that numerous possible parts of a society's superstructure will not be actualized because those possibilities are incompatible with the society's base.[16] The productive process thus narrows the range of ideas and practices that can gain currency in a society. This interpretation has the advantage of removing the burden of economic determinism from Marx and Engels—it does not insist that the base is the cause of and logically prior to the superstructure. But this gain is purchased at a stiff price: it weakens the Marxist claim about the relationship of the base and superstructure to a point at which many centrists could agree with Marx and Engels. Portrayed in this fashion, Marxism loses its political bite and becomes too domesticated.

Moreover, it seems clear that Marx and Engels aspired to more than the economic limitation view: "The ruling ideas are nothing more than the ideal expression of the dominant material relationships, the dominant material relationships grasped as ideas."[17] Accordingly, economic limitation is both untrue to Marx's original motivation and too insipid to distance Marx from the centrist philosophers he disdained.

The economic practice interpretation has been defended most recently by Richard Schmitt.[18] Under this view, the base is not conceived as consisting of "impersonal economic processes that unfold independent of human wishes and desires, and independent of human thinking and understanding."[19] Rather, the base must also include "what humans do":

By [the base] Marx means also what human beings *do*—that is, he refers to their material activities or "production and reproduction." But those, like all human activities, are thinking activities, because it is the essence of human beings to think about what they do. The distinction between base and superstructure is not one between matter that does not think and thinking that is not material. The base consists of human activities. . . .[20]

Given this refined understanding of the base, the superstructure is viewed as describing, codifying, and defending extant social practices:

The practices that constitute the base may well be understood—people generally know what they are doing—without having been put into words. At some time in the history of a group, the practices are put into words, described, codified, and defended—and those . . . form the superstructure. *The base is what we do; the superstructure is how we talk about it.*[21] . . . It seems eminently plausible that the base determines the superstructure: Our practices determine how we describe and justify them.[22]

The economic practice interpretation expands the constituents of the base to include social practices, at least those in the areas of human "production and reproduction." Moreover, it distances Marxism from those philosophical idealists who privilege consciousness and from the crude reductionism of economic determinism.

People talk about their lives in the way they do because their daily practices are what they are. But the relationship is not a causal one in the sense in which the lit match is the cause of the explosion. In the latter situation, we can predict the explosion if we know the conditions. In observing how people act, we can venture some guesses about their ideologies, but we cannot make firm predictions.[23]

This interpretation renounces willingly the predictive power of the base-superstructure relationship as the price Marxism must pay in order to avoid worse problems. It still seems to suggest that the base is logically prior to the superstructure, and this suggestion is troubling. But the economic practice view has demonstrable advantages over its two main competitors, and it need not be committed to the position that the base is *always* logically prior to correspondent intellectual activity in the superstructure. The economic practice view is also compatible with the Marxist position that a superstructure is needed to organize and stabilize the very base from which it arose.

FALSE CONSCIOUSNESS

The term "false consciousness" suggests an inverted representation of reality that is systematically misleading and socially mystifying in that it misrepresents what are in fact the interests of the ruling class as the natural, common interests of society. This misrepresentation, which flows from superstructure, justifies, stabilizes, and reinforces the social and political status quo. A person who holds a view that is the result of false consciousness is unaware of the underlying motives and causal processes by which she came to accept that view.[24]

The term "false consciousness" is used specifically when oppressed classes adopt the dominant prevailing ideology and perceptual prism. When these dominant ideas do not truly correspond to the experience of the oppressed classes, ideological distortion occurs.[25] Such distortions have a functional explanation: they legitimate the ruling classes' monopoly on power by depicting current social relations as natural, appropriate, or inevitable. In this fashion, the interests of the ruling class misrepresent themselves as universal human interests. Thus, a particular class perspective comes to prevail on the members of subordinate classes. There is often a tension, which can intensify into contradiction and eventually revolution, between the ideological prism acquired through socialization and the experience of the subordinate class accumulated in productive activity.

A belief is ideological only if it would perish upon the revelation of its causal origins. Because the relationship between false consciousness and nonideological perception cannot be interpreted validly as a species of the general relationship between illusion and truth, ideological distortion cannot be overcome solely by *intellectual* criticism. Ideological distortion is not the opposite of truth, but is, instead, a narrow or one-sided rendering of truth that functions to preserve the practices of the ruling class.

Accordingly, false consciousness dissolves only when the internal contradictions of an economic system—especially evident when relations of production can no longer efficiently make use of developing technology—are *practically* resolved.

Marxism is not committed to the simplistic position that all members of subordinate classes, or all subjects generally, are *necessarily* victims of the mystifying effects of ideological distortion. It should be obvious that at least some (and perhaps all) of the people some of the time will be able to pierce through the smokescreen that is false consciousness:

> Marx gave the title "Critiques" to successive versions of his economics in order to suggest that he was trying to separate out the ideological distortions from genuine insights in the existing economic theories. He thereby recognized the strong influence of ideology in the self-understanding of capitalist society *and* the possibility of unmasking these ideological distortions.[26]

DIALECTICAL METHOD

Although I can scarcely begin to do justice to the complexities of Marx's dialectical method in a few paragraphs, it is important to at least sketch a few characteristics of it. The method stresses the process of conflict, antagonism, and contradiction as necessary for progress. Truth is reached, or approximated, by the conflict of ideas, and social change occurs because of class conflict and contradictions in a society's economic substructure. The conflict of opposite views is necessary because each position, taken by itself, contains a partial or one-sided insight into a larger truth. As a thesis (a starting point) evolves into its antithesis (opposite) and then into a synthesis (a balance), earlier stages of the dialectic prefigure and are transformed by later stages. Each stage provides what was lacking in the preceding stage, while developing what was of value:

> The dialectic is conceived as a process of struggle between opposite views that are nevertheless connected, because each is merely a partial view.... Out of these struggles emerges something new that combines what was true and worth saving in the two opposites and discards what deserved to be lost.[27]

The dialectical method contrasts with the more conventional notion of progress: slow refinement of earlier perspectives, discarding what was wrong while retaining what was correct, and supplementing for completeness. The dialectic has more dramatic shifts and less stable points of equilibrium. It underscores the mutual dependence of opposites, and the partiality and provisionality of current conceptions. It is purported to apply not merely to intellectual progress, but also to how humans evolve social life under specific material conditions. Conceiving societies as organic wholes, Marx reiterates that social change results from contradictions within society's base. However, a sympathetic reading of Marx allows that he did not intend that the dialectic be viewed as a logic that superseded formal logic: "When Marx and Engels use the term 'contradiction,' they are referring to oppositions, conflicts, and incoherences of all kinds but not to logical contradictions in the strict sense ... [They] are not accepting ... irrationalism."[28]

CRITIQUE OF LIBERAL-CAPITALIST NOTIONS OF LAW

Marxists refuse to construct elaborate jurisprudential theories because they insist that to do so reduces them to participants in the liberal-capitalist fetishism of law.

THE FETISHISM OF LAW

The term "fetishism" connotes an unnecessary and distracting obsession. Fetishism involves conferring specific characteristics on objects or concepts, which characteristics take on the aura of being inherent, while in fact these traits are present because of the prevailing social and economic arrangements:

[F]etishism signifies that the general ideological perception of things and social relations is to a certain extent misleading. In particular, Marx used the word to refer to occasions when there is a common tendency to reduce variegated aspects of social life into a single conceptual framework.[29]

The fetishism of law in liberal-capitalist regimes is alleged to be manifest in at least three ways: (a) the necessity of law; (b) the autonomy of law; and (c) the desirability of the rule of law.[30]

(a) The necessity of law: Encomiums to law flow freely in the rhetoric of liberal-capitalist regimes. Law is seen as the body of rules and principles that preserve what is best about humans and protect us all from what is worst. Apologists portray a refined legal system as that which holds a community together, facilitates the progress of civilization, and redeems us from the anarchy of a Hobbesian state of nature.[31]

Marxists deny the inevitability of law. First, they place greater trust than do liberal-capitalists in the informal, customary prescriptions and prohibitions that hold a culture together. Second, and more important, they view the necessity of law as emanating from pre-socialist historical and economic situations. Liberal-capitalists may be correct that law is necessary in the kinds of regimes they have known. But Marxists are committed to the rise of a new set of social relations in which claims of legal necessity ring hollow.

The inevitable collapse of capitalism—due to the failure of its relations of production to make effective, efficient use of its forces of production—will pave the way for the elimination of the conditions which nurture class division. The elimination of class division speeds along the end of capitalist alienation and exploitation, which, in turn, will permit socialist relations of production to facilitate economic growth. The more rational allocation of resources in production and distribution, and the radical decentralization of decision making to self-managed public enterprises and to relatively small privately owned businesses will presumably culminate in economic abundance, which will realize the famous slogan "from each according to ability, to each according to need."

The transformation of the relations of production and the elimination (or near elimination) of the conditions of scarcity bring about the context from which societal relations can be reimagined and remade. Human social relations and experience will no longer be tyrannized by the pernicious antinomy of self versus others. The perplexing tension between individuality—our felt need to maintain our specialness and uniqueness when confronted by others—and community—our felt need for intimacy, connection, and bonding—will be radically transformed. Because Marxists believe generally that the state and ideological superstructure function to maintain and legitimate class domination and exploitation, the elimination of class division allows much (perhaps most) of the superstructure to "wither away." Marx's mature position was that law was fundamentally superstructural—a reflection of the ruling class's dominant needs and interests as developed from the conditions of the base. Accordingly, Marxists view with suspicion liberal-capitalists' claims of the necessity of law.

(b) *The autonomy of law:* Liberal-capitalists allegedly herald the independence and uniqueness of law in order to add to law's mystique. Hugh Collins describes the autonomy of law as consisting of three dimensions:

> First, there are regular patterns of institutional arrangements associated with law such as the division between a legislature and a judiciary. Second, lawyers communicate with each other through a distinctive mode of discourse, though the exact nature of legal reasoning remains controversial. Third, legal systems are distinguished from simple exercises of force by one group over another; for legal rules also function as normative guides to behaviour which individuals follow regardless of the presence or absence of officials threatening to impose sanctions for failing to comply with the law. Together these three features of law, its institutional framework, its methodology, and its normativity, are considered to make law a unique phenomenon.[32]

Marxists scoff at liberal-capitalist claims of law's uniqueness. True to the primacy it places on economic substructure, Marxism is reluctant to champion law as a separate aspect of social life. Rather, Marxists are more likely to underscore law's complicity in "the manipulation of power and the consolidation of modes of production of wealth."[33] Law is taken to be another part of the superstructure which tends to mask the reality of the base and which contributes to the illusions of false consciousness. Furthermore, although law is superstructural, it functions in the economic base as the definer of productive and property relations.

(c) *The rule of law:* Liberal-capitalist systems consistently extol the allegedly formal and necessary rule of law virtues: like cases must be decided alike; there can be no *ex post facto* (retroactive application of) law; there must be notice to citizens of the laws' requirements; laws must be crafted generally and impersonally; and the most fundamental aim of a legal system must be the impartial application of law and the principled restraint of the power of legal officials.

Marxists view the rule of law as a primary culprit in the liberal-capitalist legitimation of the status quo. The seductions of paeans to due process and to the principled restraint on the power of legal officials function to defend the naturalness and appropriateness of existing social arrangements. Behind the rule of law's mask of formal neutrality lies a conglomeration of processes, doctrines, and structures that serve generally to advance certain class interests and to defeat or marginalize other class interests. The formal equality of the rule of law places an imprimatur on substantive inequality. Yet the individualistic presuppositions and intoxicating effects of rule of law rhetoric impede the development of class consciousness. Thus, Marxists tend not to praise the rule of law, but to interrogate it: not to offer a set of necessary and sufficient conditions for the existence of the rule of law, but to ask what functions the rule of law has served and whose interests it has advanced.

> [Marxists portray law] as a dialogue with the background dominant ideology on the basis of the formal constraints of coherence and consistency. . . the source of law and legal developments lies in the ideology of the dominant class. The judge's aim may be to treat like cases alike, but we can be sure that definitions of similarity and difference are determined by criteria supplied by that dominant ideology. Formal justice is not so much hollow justice but another style of class domination.[34]

THE CRITIQUE OF LAW

It should be clear by now that the Marxist critique of law has two primary elements: (a) a functional explanation of the legal system and (b) a firm conviction concerning the contingency of law.

(a) Functional explanation of law: To avoid participating in the fetishism of law, Marxists cannot treat law as if it is unique and independent. Thus, when they examine the functions of law they take their object to be that which is conventionally perceived as law.[35]

We have already sketched Marxism's reductionist explanation of the function of law: law serves the dominant interests of the ruling class. But Marxists have come to see this reductionist explanation as too crude to portray accurately the machinations of the modern capitalist state. The ruling class, the owners of the means of production, have much less direct control over the workings of government than they did in the days of Marx and Engels. Moreover, there seem to be numerous examples of the intervention of the government and the legal system which have enfranchised workers and the underclasses at the expense of the narrowly conceived interests of the owners. When confronting the myriad of changes capitalism has undergone, which alterations have prevented the collapse of capitalism that early Marxists insisted was imminent, modern Socialists advance the notion of the relative autonomy of law in order to reduce the reductionism of their predecessors:

> ultimately the dominant class determines the direction of political initiatives and ensures that the legal system serves to perpetuate the mode of production . . . there is in reality less direct manipulation of

political power by the dominant class in modern society than there
was in earlier social formations ... The appearance of autonomy
conceals deep structural constraints upon the powers of the State
apparatus which ensure that it faithfully pursues the interests of
the ruling class.[36]

Under this view, one of the most important functions of law is ideological. Law plays the fundamental role of preserving the status quo.
Not only is there a conservative bias built into law by rule of law
doctrines such as the observance of precedent and faithfulness to the
intentions and policies of the past; law also assumes a paramount
educative role. Law interprets and resolves social conflicts and relationships, mediates the potentially disruptive tensions in economic
substructures and issues authoritative proclamations which purport to
be the product of an objective, neutral, rational process. As such, the
dominant ideology is filtered through a series of legal surrogates, pu-
rified of direct contamination by the ruling class, sanctified as the
outcome of eminently fair procedures, and solidified as part of society's core commonsense normative beliefs. As citizens further internalize the decrees of law, and come to accept these judgments as their
own, they are further victimized by the ideological distortions of false
consciousness and are thereby less likely to vent the rage necessary
for meaningful social transformation. Marxists contend that in this manner the dominant ideology secures the "consent" of the oppressed in
their own oppression. To put a finer point on it: because of the power
of its educative function, law is in part the instrument by which the
disenfranchised become accomplices in their own subordination.

I must stress, however, that Marxists are not contending that state
officials are engaged in a self-conscious, grand conspiracy that seizes
law as its bludgeon. Legal doctrines and processes are not simply the
product of the economic base:

Some legal rules are the product of non-instrumental and discrete
modes of discourse ... The fundamental principles of law are materially determined, but within these constraints legal reasoning selects
solutions to particular concrete problems ... the dominant ideology
produces the basic standards of justice, the underlying categories
and values of the legal system, but through a logical process judges
articulate the precise implications of these norms.[37]

The educative role of the law is not a linear, relentless indoctrination by the dominant ideology. Because contradictions in the economic base give rise to counterpart tensions in ideological superstructure,
legal officials can be viewed as mediators not merely of particular
disputes among citizens, but also of potentially disruptive economic
and ideological disharmony. The dominant ideology itself is not a

fully coherent, monolithic whole. Moreover, there are usually competing ideologies, articulate to varying degrees, that confront the dominant ideology:

> Hard cases are . . . not crises of [logical] inconsistency . . . they occur when no legal expression of the dominant ideology has been established or during periods of ideological transition when there are competing background ideologies. Ultimately the material determination of the content of law in these hard cases is ensured because the dominant ideology is itself the source of the conflict between legal rules; it defines the issues to be discussed and delimits the range of possible solutions. What can never be accepted by a Marxist is the view that each legal rule is not the product of a dialogue with the background ideology.[38]

(b) The contingency of law: As has been noted previously, the Marxist denial of the necessity of law is closely linked with its exposition of the functions of law. Because Marxists deny that those legitimating, educative, and mediating functions will be required in the "final form" of society, law will wither away along with other superstructural elements.

Lenin is credited with being "the first to subscribe explicitly to the thesis that law will wither away in a Communist society."[39] But even he conceded that a communist society would require customary normative rules and principles to guide social life. The emphasis here is on less formal action by fellow citizens—ranging from social disapproval up to sanctions administered by "comrades' courts"—and away from highly institutionalized dispute resolution conducted primarily by state officials. This difference in emphasis manifests that a society lacking class division has no need for and cannot logically sustain institutionalized forms, such as law, that promote primarily the interests of one class. In a society where the antinomy between individual and community is transformed the entire society will affirm and protect its normative foundation:

> . . . law defined as an instrument of class oppression will disappear with the demise of the class system. Yet, both Engels and Lenin recognize that some norms will remain. There will be both rules for the administration of a planned economy and elementary rules of social life. They cannot be law, however, because they do not support a system of class oppression.[40]

There is another reason why Marxists deny the necessity of law. Often, perhaps usually, liberal-capitalists argue that law is necessary to constrain humans who are by nature self-interested, motivated by material incentives, and competitive. It is claimed that law is required to enforce the social contract that itself is required to mediate our baser strivings and selfishness. But Marxists deny any thick and substantial notion of human nature. They insist that liberal-capitalists have such a notion because their economic base encourages, sustains, and rewards the very traits that come to be seen as natural. The familiar processes and products of legitimation and fetishism, not human inherent attributes, give rise to our commonsense belief that law is necessary in order to save us from ourselves. Once humans are liberated from the productive relations and other material vestiges that nourish this commonsense conviction, they will be empowered to transcend those traits hitherto thought of as inherent and untransformable. Marxists believe generally in the plasticity of human nature and subscribe only to a thin notion of inherent human attributes: our "species being" consists of our collective ability to change our traits along with our material circumstances, and our general predisposition to find fulfilment in unalienated labor. Accordingly, the fall of capitalism and the emergence of communism provide the presuppositions for a classless society, unalienated labor, collective human transformation, and the end of law.

CRITICISMS OF MARXIST JURISPRUDENCE

There are several general criticisms of Marxism that generate specific questions about Marxism's musings on law. I address each in turn with the exception of comments directed at Marxism's denunciation of the rule of law, which I have examined thoroughly elsewhere.[41]

NECESSITY AND CONTINGENCY

Marxism begins by castigating liberal-capitalist claims of necessity and inherency in the areas of human nature, social relations, and the legal order. Ironically, Marxism itself ends with a series of necessitarian claims: the inevitable fall of capitalism and rise of communism, the apodictic withering away of law, and the incontestable metamorphosis of the human species. Infatuated by a particular, distorted view of the natural sciences, Marxists peer back at the past and assert confidently the existence of historical and economic laws.

But the evidence that is the past does not come so unambiguously packaged. This data underdetermines any particular theory and admits to numerous interpretations. Those who look back and who try to harness this data into a coherent whole usually find what they seek: they begin with an intuition or hypothesis about the future, project this vision onto the indeterminate meanderings of history, and selectively embrace past events that are consistent with their original vision. They put the rabbit in the hat, pull it out, and then proclaim their insights to the world. Unfortunately, their claims of necessity ring at least as hollow as those of their philosophical rivals. Post-Marx history has not revealed the working class as the vanguard of communist revolution; has not manifested a pattern of revolutionary activity in advanced capitalist countries; and, instead, has witnessed capitalism maintaining its basic structure while incorporating numerous marginal adjustments, which has permitted it to mediate its alleged internal contradictions.

Marxists appear to have been trapped by their own presupposition that only an objective analysis of the social order, an examination based on their simplistic view of the natural sciences, could claim persuasively to have eluded the mystification of liberal-capitalist false consciousness. While liberal-capitalist ideology may well be hostage, to one degree or another, to social practices and material conditions, so too, Marxist ideology may well be a pawn to this simplistic view of the natural sciences.

FALSE CONSCIOUSNESS

Sneers of "false consciousness" often resound when liberal-capitalist thinkers encounter Marxists. When philosophical adversaries report conclusions or arguments that deny Marxism's central aspirations, they frequently are accused of promulgating the ideological distortions of false consciousness. In effect, Marxism charges that liberal-capitalists *verify* certain Marxist tenets by the very way these liberal-capitalists try to *refute* Marxism.

This is not to say that the notion of false consciousness is without currency. There is much truth to the observation that certain views may be the unconscious, conditioned reflection of economic and social oppression; and that subordinate classes often become accomplices in their own torment by internalizing the very dominant ideologies that contributed to their mistreatment.

But if applied relentlessly, the notion of false consciousness loses much of its critical bite. If the notion is advanced as a nonrefutable thesis, if all denials of Marxism are taken to be affirmations of the doctrine of false consciousness, then the notion of false consciousness is trivial. Any subjective report that denies any basic Marxist conclusion seems too easily and automatically to stigmatize itself. Marxists dismiss the content of a view because it allegedly can be explained by its determinants. Moreover, such a posture demeans the experiences, and not merely the ideologies, of Marxism's philosophical rivals. In fact, subjective reports of one's inner condition or of one's ideological commitments are neither incorrigibly true nor self-refuting. The challenge for a Marxist is to delineate without begging the question under what circumstances such reports and commitments do and do not reflect veridical perceptions correlated to wider experience.[42]

BASE AND SUPERSTRUCTURE

There is persuasive force in the pronouncement that economic relations and material conditions "determine" our ideological superstructure. But it is not easy to delineate precisely the nature of "determine" and to make such delineation compatible with Marxism's scientific pretensions.

We have seen already the difficulties with the economic determinism and the economic limitation interpretations of the relationship between the base and superstructure: the former unrealistically marginalizes human freedom and serendipitous possibilities, and is untrue to the reciprocal interaction between base and superstructure that Marx and Engels sometimes acknowledged, while the latter is too weak to facilitate Marx's materialistic purposes. A third interpretation, the economic practice interpretation, seemed preferable to the others.

The strength of the economic practice interpretation lies in its realism and resonates with common sense: our social practices, what we do, affect greatly how we explain and justify them.[43] Furthermore, there is some textual evidence from Marx that supports this interpretation: "The chief defect of all hitherto existing materialism . . . is that . . . reality . . . is conceived only in the form of the object, or of *contemplation*, but not as *human sensuous activity, practice.*"[44]

But this interpretation is not without problems. First, it brings a loss of predictive power that may be anathema to a general theory, such as Marxism, that exalts the scientific inevitability and certitude of numerous future events. Second, it expands the elements of the base to include what many Marxists would regard as superstructural elements because not all of our social practices seem at first blush to have the requisite materialist connection. Third, it radically threatens the very distinction between base and superstructure: describing, explaining, and justifying our social practices are themselves social practices; describing, explaining, and justifying our first-order descriptions, explanations, and justifications are also social practices, and so it goes. Because talking about what we do is itself inexorably a doing, we may question whether the economic practice interpretation sanctions any clear or useful distinction between base and superstructure. Rather, it is arguable that the economic practice interpretation artificially distances the bulk of our social practices from other, specific social practices: our theoretical, introspective reflections on and examinations of all of our social practices.

Put this way, the economic practice interpretation may be true, but trivial: our social practices, some of which are describing, explaining, and justifying, determine how we describe, explain, and justify! But how could it be otherwise? Alternatively, the economic practice interpretation can salvage a distinction between base and superstructure by showing some principled way to distance (*i*) the social practices of describing, explaining, and justifying our various social practices from (*ii*) all other social practices that do not describe, explain, and justify our various social practices. This must be accomplished in a non-question-begging fashion that rescues Marxism's scientific pretensions and materialistic aspirations. My suspicion is that the end product of this mission will be eviscerated historical materialism that lacks the flair and dramatic appeal of "base determines superstructure."

All of this is complicated further when applied to the law. Because the law seems to function in both the base and superstructure, however they are conceived, Marxists have distanced themselves from relentless use of the base/superstructure model when discussing law:

> [The] Marxist explanation of the form of modern law ... avoids attempts to establish direct links between the material base and all aspects of law. On the contrary, it is claimed that distinctive attributes such as formal justice and autonomy of legal reasoning depend upon complex legitimating ideologies, which are themselves derived from political practices within the relatively autonomous state not directly concerned with the capitalist relations of production.[45]

Accordingly, whatever the general persuasiveness of its base/superstructure model, modern Marxists wisely acknowledge that this model has a more limited specific utility when applied to analyses of law.

FUNCTIONS OF LAW

At times, Marxism flirts with a crudely instrumental portrayal of law that perceives law as the minion of ruling class interests. The problems of this position are obvious and numerous: do the "owners" of the means of production truly constitute a ruling class? If so, how do individual capitalists solidify into a class and spin out a shared vision of their collective interests? Even if there are collective interests, how do all (or the bulk of) individuals within that class become conscious of those interests? Even if the bulk of individuals do become conscious of those interests, how do they act in accordance with them? How does the "conscious behaviour of the ruling class always ... coincide with their best material interests"?[46]

Marxism is not well served by crude instrumentalism. Fortunately, Marxism can elude many of the aforementioned problems by reminding us of the hegemonic role played by dominant ideologies:

> ... ideologies arise from and are conditioned by social practices in the relations of production. Since the class of owners of the means of production share similar experiences and perform approximately the same role in the relations of production, there emerges a dominant ideology which permeates their perceptions of interest. Laws are enacted pursuant to this ideology.[47]

The legitimating and educative functions of ideology grant Marxists the ability to transcend crude instrumentalism and permit them to underscore the fashion in which certain ideas become entrenched as common sense:

> There is no need . . . to suggest that the ruling class is aware of its class position and deliberately sets out to crush opposition. Instead, its perceptions of interest will appear to be the natural order of things since they are confirmed by everyday experiences . . . Laws enacted according to the dictates of a dominant ideology will appear to the members of that society as rules designed to preserve the natural social and economic order. The ruling class will not have the oppression of other classes in mind, but simply the maintenance of social order.[48]

The mediating role of ideology allows Marxism to refine crude instrumentalism, but at a price. What passes for a "dominant ideology" in liberal-capitalist regimes is hardly a solidified, fixed body of doctrine from which specific, determinate conclusions must be drawn. Moreover, specific laws and their justifications are not easily linked, clearly and inexorably, to material conditions in the economic base. Because specific laws themselves admit to interpretation and their genesis is rarely unambiguous, Marxism seems to have two choices. It can downplay the link between the material base and the content of law, highlight the relative autonomy of law and the superstructure, and soften its depiction of dominant ideology. Such concessions to plasticity make Marxism more plausible, but attenuate and domesticate the radical panache of historical materialism and scientific socialism.

Alternatively, Marxism can give ad hoc analyses of specific laws, which analyses purport to show how the dominant ideology provides an indirect linkage of the material base to those laws. This approach aspires to preserve the integrity of historical materialism and scientific socialism, but it is highly improbable that its piecemeal explanations would ever constitute a coherent whole. As such, this approach could be seen as circular apologetics: Marxists have a theory that says the material base B is indirectly linked to law by dominant ideology I; here is a given law L; L is linked to B by I in the following way W, but W may be quite different from (and perhaps incompatible with) the other Ws by which other Ls are linked to B. The main difficulty with circular apologetics is that its various explanations are so elastic that they do not admit of possible refutations and thus trivialize themselves.

This unappealing journey between the Charybdis of servility and the Scylla of triviality results from the tensions in Marxism's understanding of the relationship between base and superstructure, its acknowledgment of relative autonomy, its commitment to scientific socialism, its understanding of the role of ideology, and the reality of law. All is not lost: Marxism is left with several general, plausible claims about the structure and form of law, but these lack the explanatory specificity and political acuteness to which Marxism originally aspired.

CONTINGENCY OF LAW

Some non-Marxists have argued that the flair of the slogan "law will wither away" is misleading for two reasons. First, Marxists concede that even under communism, the final form of society, "[t]here will be both rules for the administration of a planned economy and elementary rules of social life."[49] But these are not termed "Laws" because under communism they would not function as instruments of class oppression; in the final form of society differentiated classes, and thus class struggle itself, have vanished. Accordingly, it may well appear that "[t]he whole thesis of the withering away of law rests upon the dubious definitional fiat that rules which serve any other purpose than class oppression cannot be law."[50] Second, there seem to be functions of law that go beyond class struggle: "It is hard to connect laws concerning abortion, drugs, homosexuality, and rape with the instrumental pursuit of their interests by the ruling class."[51] There is reason to believe that such laws would not pass from sight even if communism was realized.

There is merit to both points, but neither is totally devastating to Marxism's aim. The first remark raises the question of whether the radicality of claims about the contingency of law rests on a mere tautology: "law" is stipulated as that which serves class oppression; there is at least one society in which class oppression is not necessary, or even possible; therefore, law is not necessary, or even possible, in all societies. While it is true that stipulative definitions generally produce uninteresting conclusions, we should not take this semantic quibble as fatal to Marxism's goals. Indeed, its main purpose here is to undermine liberal-capitalist dogma that law is what necessarily holds any society together, what preserves the best and discourages the worst in us. Seen in this light, the thrust of Marxism is that eliminating class division, effacing the distinction between individual and community, and facilitating opportunities for unalienated labor are the more fundamental ways to bind a society and to actualize our species being. The prime error of legal fetishism is that by privileging law by proclaiming law's necessity, it deflects attention from the more essential conditions required for human progress. Thus, Marxism perceives the unwavering commitment to the necessity of law as an ideological obstacle to societal transformation.

The second remark seems unassailable. In a communist society there would be deviants to whom the structure must respond. Moreover, even within a class or within a classless society, personal relations among members admit to regulation. Furthermore, contemporary socialist doctrine has seemingly acknowledged this: even prior to *glasnost* and *perestroika*, we have witnessed an increase in the importance of law in socialist societies. Thus, Eugene Kamenka writes that

> [Law] is said to ensure stable and predictable social life, to organize production and to protect the individual and his rights. Law is now seen as the regular, necessary, fair and efficient means of steering society in conditions of social ownership. Like the state, it is allegedly a fundamental element in human affairs, which has been captured and distorted in the class interest in class societies, but which will not wither away when class disappears and which has elements of a non-class nature within it.[52]

But, again, Marxism is not defenseless. It would probably try to account for the nature and extent of deviant behavior in our time by pointing to economic scarcity, alienated relations of production, and ideological distortions. A truly communist society would presumably ameliorate such conditions and the concomitant behavior. Moreover, we must also note that

> while law has grown into an indispensable principle of social organization in the civilization of the West due to the particular historicity of that civilization, that is not the case with other civilizations . . . wherein law and its concomitant principles, such as equality of humans, are deemed, as in China and Japan, as dehumanizing.[53]

Still the critics' point seems powerful: not all law is eliminable even in a communist paradise. But remember that Marxism acknowledges the need for elementary rules governing social life, and for community pressure as a response to destructive behavior. It is not as if Marxism was or is blind to the critics' point.

In sum, it is not so obvious, although it is probable, that critics are correct in thinking that in a communist society not all of that which is conventionally described as "law" can disappear. Even if taken *literally*, it has not been proved that Marxism's claim that the law will wither away is either plainly false or trivially (tautologically) true. Moreover, taken less strictly, the claim serves several Marxist purposes: it highlights the fundamental changes required for human progress, which changes are allegedly retarded by paeans to law's necessity; it insists that numerous layers of institutionalized legal mechanisms must be viewed as unessential; it reveals the allegedly reactionary implications of our sanctification of law; and it challenges us to reconceive a nonlegal response to the polarity of self and others. All these theses, whether ultimately convincing, retain much vibrancy and provide difficult challenges to conventional wisdom.

Although Marxism's depiction of law seems at times reductionist or simplistic, and at other times does not hang coherently with general Marxist theory, much remains about it that resonates in history. Marxist themes about the contingency, relative autonomy, and functions of law are refined in later movements such as legal realism, Critical Legal Studies, and feminist jurisprudence.[54] Mark Tushnet captures this sentiment well when he says that

> in one sense Marxism is the only remaining secular view that is committed to fighting domination wherever it occurs. . . . Law may be taken as a metaphor for all those facets of our social relationships that seem to us necessary for us to get along in the world and that also seem somehow imposed on us. Marxism is then a metaphor for a world of radical contingency, in which we know that social regularities are constructed by our own actions, have no life of their own, and may be challenged and reconstructed whenever and however we want.[55]

This, then, is Marxism's ultimate irony: despite its original pretensions to scientific objectivity and historical necessity its greatest legacy may be its challenge to those very pretensions and its affirmation of radical contingency. Seen in this light, Marxism's own internal contradictions dialectically generate its most profound contribution.

THE LEGACY OF MARXIST JURISPRUDENCE

The power of the Marxist theme of the radical contingency of law reverberates historically in both legal theory and political practice.

LEGAL REALISM: JEROME FRANK

The legal realists emerged in the 1920s and remained a formidable force through the early 1940s. Insisting on the inadequacy of formal logic as an explanation of judicial decision making and carefully unmasking the conflict and contradiction that permeated court decisions, the legal realists hurled a strident challenge to legal formalists and natural law theorists, the dominant modes of legal debate at the time.

The best known and most uncompromising legal realist was Jerome Frank.[56] In Frank's judgment, there are no politically neutral meanings embedded in the texts and words of legal materials; no interpretation or application of language can be logically required by preexisting legal materials; and thus a judge's private motives and values are fundamental in understanding the true basis of her legal conclusions. Frank, himself a judge, did not perceive a vast judicial conspiracy aimed at consciously venerating the interests of the powerful at the expense of the relatively disadvantaged; instead, he saw most judges, along with the general populace, as captives of the dominant formalist ideology that proclaimed the determinacy, objectivity, and vitality of language, logic, and morality. Accordingly, although judges often took themselves to be deriving necessary conclusions from preexisting legal materials, they in fact were thinking and acting under the mystifying spell of the dominant ideology.

As a result, Frank concluded that a judge's argument, no matter how carefully crafted and assiduously supported, is merely a rationalization and not the true explanation of her decision. The true explanation consists of a complex series of psychological factors, many elements of which would remain shrouded even from the most introspective judges and the most effective psychological therapists. A judge's legal conclusions are ultimately *choices*, and the phenomenology of choice is intricate and not completely accessible to us.

The basic elements of Frank's jurisprudence were clearly prefigured in Marxist thought: the indeterminacy of language, logic, and bourgeois morality; the mystifying effects of the dominant ideology; the relationship between political outcomes and the distribution of political power; and the self-delusions of those who subscribe to the formalists' pretension of achieving the aspirations of the rule of law. While it is now commonplace to assert that today we are all realists—as a way of identifying the overwhelming number of theorists who accept in some form the realist attack against formalism and mechanical jurisprudence— it might be more accurate historically to assert that today we are all Marxists. This slogan, however, accompanied as it is by a host of other political baggage, is obviously unlikely to sweep the academy.

When compared with the virulence of their widespread critical attacks on formalism, the constructive programs of realists appear insipid or fatuous. Animated by hopes of liberal reform, some realists took refuge in toothless judicial deference to legislators; other realists advocated self-conscious judicial implementation of liberal political values; still others, such as Frank, concluded that judicial decision-making should be grounded on empirical data accumulated by social scientists rather than on inherently manipulable legal concepts. Such realists identified the emerging social sciences and newly founded federal administrative agencies as the appropriate instruments of liberal social reform.

Many aspects of Frank's sweeping critique of mainstream jurisprudence are vulnerable: Did he wrongfully conflate the distinction between "the context of discovery" (how judges arrive at legal conclusions) and "the context of justification" (how judges explain and defend those conclusions)? Does Frank's view begin with a compelling, robust attack that becomes so relentless and pervasive that it disintegrates into a rabid skepticism that precludes the consistent development of *any* constructive political program? Did Frank implicitly and unwittingly buy into one of formalism's major dubious assumptions: either legal reasoning is determinate, rational, and applied mechanically or it is radically indeterminate, nonrational, and fully subjective? Did Frank replace formalism's effete idolatry of logical abstraction with an equally noxious worship of the social sciences?

In any event, a clear but often overlooked corollary emerges from the legal realist attack on formalism: although social reformers have historically accepted the radical contingency of law as a way of unsettling the political status quo, the acceptance of the radical contingency of law does not logically imply the ratification of a leftist political agenda. Thus, the radical contingency of law tends to eviscerate conservatism in the sense of "status quo preserving," but it does not necessarily upset conservatism as a descriptive and prescriptive world vision.

FEMINIST JURISPRUDENCE: CATHARINE MACKINNON

Contemporary feminist jurisprudence also owes much to Marxist thought. Accepting and refining the central Marxist themes of radical contingency, critique of conceptual abstraction, and attention to the actual social effects wrought by legal decision making, feminists add an important ingredient to the mix: the centrality of sexuality and gender.

Catharine MacKinnon[57] provides one of the fuller feminist accounts of law. Her fundamental precept is that the law is yet another domain where the ideological assumptions and power of men are wrongly cloaked with the honorific myths of objectivity and necessity. Although such assumptions are socially constructed from the situation of male domination and female subjugation, and such power is seized contingently, sex differences come to be viewed as the justification for male prerogatives rather than the result of them. MacKinnon thus views the aggregate injustices of sexism as not merely the result of a few mistakes made at the margins of legal doctrine, but as an integral part of an entire social system geared for the advantage of men at the expense of women.

MacKinnon claims that dominant legal analyses place women in a double bind: on the one hand, if the law uses a single standard and "neutrally" invokes similar treatment for men and women, then women are measured according to their correspondence with men and to a standard whose default position registers male images; on the other hand, if the law uses a special protection rule for women, thereby making allowances for the real differences between men and women, then women are measured according to their lack of correspondence with men and by their distance from male standards. Either way, MacKinnon argues that the law inadvertently contributes to the hegemonic process that reinforces hierarchy and presupposes men as the measure of all things.

A truly feminist jurisprudence must consist of at least the following: an understanding and acceptance of the critique of objectivity and abstraction; an awareness of the centrality of sexuality and the pervasiveness of gender hierarchy; a final relinquishment of the vestiges of formalism; and a good faith effort by (male) judges to structure and perceive legal questions from a (female) point of view different from their own. MacKinnon's feminism is fueled by the commitment to take women's narratives and experiences seriously, especially when those narratives and experiences conflict with the perceptions of women held by the dominant culture.

Accordingly, a feminist approach to law is grounded in at least three general themes: (1) consciousness raising—a collective reconstruction of the meaning and measure of women's social experience; (2) result orientation—such that appropriate remedial legal measures to gender oppression are constructed by reference to sex; and (3) acceptance and appreciation of paradox—for example, the legitimacy of the phenomenon of women's consent to assume certain social roles is unsettled by the limited alternatives available to women, and thus the reality of women's oppression may be neither demonstrable nor empirically refutable.

Once again, we see the enduring ubiquity and the plasticity of the Marxist theme of radical contingency. Part of the excitement of the Marxist legacy of jurisprudence is that its boundaries are not antecedently circumscribed and its themes need not be crystallize into tired dogmas. For example, feminists, such as MacKinnon, acknowledge the debt they owe Marxist thought but ultimately distance themselves from what they take to be the vestiges of patriarchal oppression within Marxism. From MacKinnon's perspective, Marxists often advance invigorating analyses of class oppression, but they too often ignore gender oppression. From this feminist standpoint, the battle is waged over which type of oppression, class or gender, is fundamental and paramount.

Interestingly, disparate political proponents of the theme of radical contingency, although seemingly voyaging on different seas, often end up greeting the same obstacles and dangers. For example, MacKinnon arrives at a classic dilemma confronted by numerous advocates of radical contingency. On the one hand, she has a persuasive point: the preferences of a subordinate class are, at least partly, the result of established social rules and practices that were initially established predominantly by the privileged classes. Thus those rules and practices cannot be justified by appeals to those very preferences. On the other hand, MacKinnon is guilty of philosophical imperialism if she automatically stigmatizes all who contest her legal prescriptions as unwitting victims of the dominant consciousness.

Here feminism comes full circle and confronts questions that Marxism has struggled with for decades: How can the notion of false consciousness retain its seductive critical bite yet not disintegrate into question-begging dogma? How can a self-consciously deviant discourse, such as radical feminism or Marxism, preserve and extend its revolutionary implications yet still engage the dominant discourse of the oppressors?

CRITICAL LEGAL STUDIES: ROBERTO UNGER

Critical Legal Studies emerged in the late 1970s sounding three familiar themes: (1) the radical indeterminacy of law (there is no pure method of analysis that is capable of yielding a determinate answer to legal questions); (2) the use of law in political legitimation (traditional jurisprudential theories mystify and often deny the value choices inevitable in the selection and application of legal rules, suggest that such rules correspond to a transcendentally appropriate standard or result from an inherently fair process of choice, and thereby help confer a deeper legitimacy on the status quo); and (3) law as ideology (law can be manipulated, based on the conflicting ideological assumptions embedded in preexisting doctrine, to "justify" numerous rationalizations for various outcomes).

Roberto Unger[58] has produced what is by far the most innovative constructive program arising from the Critical Legal Studies genre. Unger grounds the predicaments of law in a deeper vision of human personality. He argues that the animating drive of human passion is to transcend the cultural contexts that are provided by the established forms of personal relations, intellectual inquiry, and social arrangements. We face, however, an existential dilemma: a simultaneous yearning and fear when in the presence of others. Human passions are thus centered around the duality of our undeniable need for others and our felt danger at their approach. Moreover, there is only one noncontingent fact of human personality: contingency itself—the capacity of human personality to transcend the limits of the culturally determined possible and impossible. While we cannot transcend all contexts at once and experience contextlessness itself, we can transcend any particular context at any particular time. Unger concludes that to advance self-understanding and to mediate our existential dilemma, we must open ourselves to a full life of personal encounter, thereby giving full expression to our need while accepting the accompanying danger.

To avoid the charge of contentlessness (for what can truly follow from claims about the plasticity of human nature?) Unger claims that there are four main images of personality reflected in literature and philosophy: the heroic ethic; fusion with an impersonal absolute; Confucianism; and the Christian-Romantic ideal. Unger argues that if we take these four images and cleanse them of aspects that deny the infinite quality of human personality, the remaining theoretical ideas converge and yield similar answers to our most important normative questions. Unger thus insists that the concept of infinite personality permits us to avoid abject relativism, while the phenomenon of convergence provides a substantive conception of human personality.

Unger acknowledges that the act of context-smashing creates a new context; we are never unencumbered and unsituated. However, we progress as we ascend to looser contextual structures that encourage their own destabilization, thereby giving currency to human personality. Although we never discover the Archimedean point that might arrest all future context smashing and we never create a nontranscendable context that is indisputably superior to all competitors, some conditional contexts are superior to others based on their flexibility and acceptance of destabilization.

His perceptions of human personality trigger Unger's legal and political prescriptions. Social arrangements, rather than being depicted classically as a set of concrete institutions defining a fixed and closed structure, should incorporate destabilization mechanisms. Such mechanisms would undermine existing social arrangements and unsettle hierarchical relations before these firmly solidify into entrenched power. Unger's goal is to recognize the contingency of our institutional and social arrangements and open them to transformation.

Accordingly, we see yet another variation on the classical Marxist theme of radical contingency: rather than advocating a particular substantive political situation, such as socialism, liberalism, republicanism, or communism, to which all societies should aspire, Unger concentrates on the process and necessity of recurring social change. His project can be viewed as grafting the framework of radical contingency onto the classical method of arriving at normative conclusions from a conception of human nature.

Unger's project thus realizes two immediate theoretical advantages over other radical projects: he can easily engage the dominant political discourses while seemingly retaining the radical implications of his main theses, and he need not get bogged down in the elusive subtleties embodied by the notion of false consciousness. As such, he can act as an insider but preserve an outsider's transformative panache.

Some radicals, however, will be unconvinced. They will insist that Unger's is a romantic and ultimately impotent vision. Fueled by the background assumption that rational argument can raise social consciousness and liberate us from the chains of dominant ideology, Unger renounces violent revolution as the instrument of social change. Yet, some will argue, true and enduring change is not produced by better rational demonstrations or more comprehensive social theories; instead, it springs from widespread alterations in the perceptual grids through which humans view and understand their daily activities. Such sweeping upheavals, they will argue, only follow in the wake of class struggles and successful violent revolution.

CRITICAL RACE THEORY

Emerging in the 1980s and gaining great momentum in the 1990s, critical race theory is a self-consciously eclectic movement that borrows from and refines numerous traditions: Marxism, classical liberalism, feminism, poststructuralism, critical legal theory, pragmatism, and nationalism.

In a recent work[59] Mari Matsuda, Charles Lawrence, Richard Delgado, and Kimberle Williams Crenshaw identify and describe six common themes of this genre: (1) the pervasiveness of racism in the United States (critical race theory aspires to understand how traditional institutions and dominant normative discourses facilitate and systematize racial subordination); (2) critique of neutrality, objectivity, and meritocracy (such notions mask the reality of racism by suggesting that racial subordination results from "a series of randomly occurring, intentional, and individualized acts")[60]; (3) contextual and historical analyses of law (beginning from the presumption that all current identifiable racial inequalities stem at least in part from institutionalized racism); (4) primacy of the collective experiential wisdom of subordinated people of color (the critical reflection of those who have suffered from racism requires special attention, especially when we analyze law and societal institutions); (5) an interdisciplinary and eclectic outlook (critical race theory appropriates from a variety of traditions methodological and theoretical suppositions that empower hitherto disenfranchised races and thereby facilitate racial justice); (6) an overall goal of ending all oppression (critical race theory recognizes that racism is often found intertwined with other forms of political oppression: "the interests of all people of color necessarily require not just adjustments within the established hierarchies, but a challenge to hierarchy itself").[61]

Critical race theorists are now addressing a host of legal issues from the perspective adumbrated broadly above: First Amendment issues related to assaultive speech, special issues pertaining to feminists of color, the implementation of affirmative action policies, and the nuances of equal protection law, among others. Such theorists abrogate all pretensions to political neutrality and perspectival objectivity: "we used personal histories, parables, chronicles, dreams, stories, poetry, fiction, and revisionist histories to convey our message."[62]

Critical race theorists must grapple with numerous difficult questions: Why and how, if at all, do experiences of subordination translate into special collective knowledge? What is to be said about members of subordinate classes, such as Clarence Thomas, Thomas Sowell, and Randall Kennedy, who seemingly cannot be classified plausibly as victimized dupes yet whose perceptions and judgments vary radically from this genre's preferred political conclusions? Must whispers of "false consciousness" reenter the radical agenda? Can one subordinate group, consciously or inadvertently, contribute to the further subordination of other groups through intraracial conflict? Are there truly intellectual grounds for granting white, male scholars less standing to engage in race-related legal discourse than scholars of color? Will critical race scholars merely invert, rather than eliminate, the perniciousness of "insider/outsider" classifications? Do critical race scholars begin by excoriating dualism yet continue by implicitly analyzing normative matters in "black" (representing the racially oppressed, the experiential, the subjective, the historical, the valuable) or "white" (representing the racial oppressors, the abstract, the objective, the ahistorical, the imperialistic) terms? Can critical race theory circumvent the danger of compromising their revolutionary aspirations as well as the danger of no longer engaging the dominant discourses?

As it attends to the answers to such questions, critical race theory will prove a refreshing and important addition to the literature of the politics of challenge that can trace most of its origins to Marxist thought. Although critical race theory admits straightaway its debt to other traditions, the most fundamental themes of those traditions—the enthusiastic acceptance of radical contingency, the levying of strident challenges to the objectivity of the superstructure, the unmasking of the complicity of power and knowledge—find their most influential and forceful early articulation in Marxism.

In fact, even less radical intellectual movements such as legal and political versions of pragmatism[63] are influenced greatly by those same fundamental themes. Although such movements tend more toward liberal incrementalism rather than radical political transformation, they share attenuated versions of contingency, nonobjectivity, and suspicion of the knowledge of the privileged with the more radical traditions. The attraction of these themes lies in their empowering possibilities: by forcefully exposing the status quo as contingent they open social life to reimagination and reinvention.

Accordingly, once we note the important jurisprudential exceptions (the Chicago school of economics, the remaining originalists, the enduring subtle versions of formalism and natural law) it is no exaggeration to chant, "Most philosophers of law are Marxists now." This may seem a peculiar refrain at a time when capitalistic democracies have self-declared their technical knockout of socialist regimes, but once we understand the theoretical and practical legacies of Marxist jurisprudence it may be unfair and inaccurate to hum any other melody.

2

The Analytic Defense of Functional Marxism and Law

STEVEN JAY GOLD

One need not look far to the left in social science to find the phenomenon I like to call "Parsonophobia," or the irrational fear of functional
explanation. Talcott Parsons, and the bourgeois school of sociology known
as structural functionalism, has done more to trash the good name of
functional methodology than Pete Rose has done for the good name of
professional betting. The reactionary nature of structural functionalism
makes functionalism *simpliciter* seem an unlikely partner for Marxian
social theory—and then along comes G. A. Cohen. In this paper I will
defend Cohen's use of functional explanation and show how this methodological interpretation of Marxian social theory, as it applies to law
and the state, can be a useful explanatory guide to empirical research.

For Cohen, the basic categories of historical materialism can only be
expressed in functional terms, that is, in terms of a "consequence law."
He writes, "IF it is the case that if an event of type E were to occur at
t_1, then it would bring about an event of type F at t_2, THEN an event
of type E occurs at t_3."[1] The dispositional attribution of E-type events
to cause F-type events is expressed in this conditional format. Thus,
functional explanation, so Cohen tells us, is a distinctive form of causal
explanation, in that institutions exhibit causal tendencies toward producing effects that are beneficial to the mode of production.

Functional explanation, at first, made many uneasy—by expressing
a tendency, it seemed to explain a prior event by a later occurrence.
When we say that, for example, a Bonapartist leader like Hitler came
to power because he was best suited to meet the needs of a desperate
bourgeoisie, it may seem that we are claiming that the phenomenon

32

(Hitler's rise to power) occurred because of, or was caused by, the effect (the benefit of saving the economy). Hence, proponents of functional explanation have often been accused of "backwards causation." Cohen deals with this, as was said, by claiming that functional explanation is a particular form of causal explanation. For Cohen, a consequence law explains something in terms of a preexisting disposition to produce a particular outcome—hence the consequence law that some form of Bonapartism will have a tendency to be produced at times of extreme capitalist crisis.

The most important thing that needs to be dispelled with respect to functional analysis is any necessary connection to Talcott Parsons and the school of thought known as structural functionalism. The structural functionalists attempted to construct a general social ontology where social structures were explained by their beneficial effects for the stability of the social whole. Each element of the society was considered to exist *because* it contributed to the stability of that totality. Hence, the model was static and ahistorical. Beyond this, the claim is then made that functionalism is essentially conservative: if everything serves a useful and necessary purpose for the whole, then meaningful social change is impossible. Aside from seeking a favorable balance of institutions, any revolutionary restructuring of the social cannot, on this picture, be imagined.

Cohen tells us, however, that it is simply absurd to take the substantive theses of structural functionalism and impute them to the very nature of functional explanation, let alone Marxian functionalism. The fact that structural functionalism is seen as conservative comes from the conception that each part of the institution exists to maintain society only. However, in Marxism the primary, or *first-order*, functionality of social structures lies in their ability to reproduce a mode of production that is functional for developing the productive forces. These productive forces eventually become at odds with the social structure and transform the very nature of society. Class struggle reconstructs, often violently, the social structure itself. And it is through this dynamic class struggle that social change, radical social change, occurs. So while the social and political superstructure does serve to maintain the class structure, this social formation will inevitably be transformed by its inability to functionally develop expanding productive forces. Hence, according to Cohen, a functional formulation of historical materialism is dynamic, historical, and above all, revolutionary.

A third objection to Cohen's functional interpretation of historical materialism can be seen in the work of writers like Levine and Wright.[2] They suggest that Cohen's functional argument is "fatally mitigated" since historical counterexamples exist where nonoptimal relations are produced. However, the problem that often dysfunctional social formations are produced does not cause any serious difficulty for functional Marxism.

Explanation by reference to tendential structures does not entail determinism. Milton Fisk does an excellent job of explaining why functional explanation "is not intended to tell us that if an institution exists because it is needed to perform a certain function it will infallibly perform that function once it exists. . . . [The] most that is required is that the functional institution be endowed with a tendency that left to itself would perform appropriately."[3] Of course, Fisk tells us, no institution is ever "left to itself," and such a tendency is always surrounded by other tendencies and contradictions.

The capitalist state, for example, has within its institutions the tendency to foster the accumulation of capital. Often in contradiction with that tendency, however, is the tendency toward state independence and legitimation. The struggle for autonomy and legitimacy often counteracts the tendencies of the state toward maximizing surplus extraction. And this interplay of tendency and countertendency, the conflict between legitimacy and economic reproduction, has as its foundation the class struggle.

The importance of a functional account in Marxian social theory is nowhere more evident than in the way it helps us defend against the charges of reductionism. In a provocative article, Levine, Sober, and Wright (LSW)[4] make two suggestions about macrosociological explanation that are consistent with Cohen's understanding of historical materialism in terms of objective social functions and show how this method is nonreductionistic.

In refuting the charge of reductionism, LSW make use of common concepts in the philosophy of mind. The type/token distinction, where tokens are particular instances of a type claim, is used to show how token instances can be reduced to the choices and behavior of individuals, while macrosocial categories, like those in historical materialism, cannot. Some type claims, however, are reducible to microproperties. To deal with this, LSW show that Marxian macrosocial type claims (and I would add, of course, social functions) are *supervenient* on the microprocesses of social life. Contrasted with the type "water," which is reducible to H_2O since the effects of water can always be reduced to the effects of aggregates of H_2O molecules, macrosociological phenomena have no single microproperty and are hence not straightforwardly reducible. Like the concept "fitness" in biology, there are many token instances where the microprocesses involved are radically different or even incompatible. LSW explain that, in biology, there is no one microproperty that all "fit" animals share beyond this supervenient type. Similarly, macrosociological phenomena, and I would add the objective social functions Marx refers to, cannot be reduced to any one microcontextual social phenomenon.

Given that functional explanation is defensible, I would suggest that the appropriate Marxian project then is to answer both the "why" and "how" functional questions. By the "why" question I mean to refer to the task of understanding the nature of a particular macrosociological function and identifying token instances of it. By the "how" question I mean to refer to the genetic aspect of the explanation. Let's take each in turn.

Looking at the "why" questions, when institutions within the state and legal system serve to maintain and facilitate the extraction of surplus value, we call it a *first-order* function of the state, for example, regulating labor relations, strike breaking, protecting property from theft, and so on. Political and legal institutions also function to reproduce state power itself or legitimate and develop the autonomy of the state and legal apparatuses via *second-order* functions, for example, the suppression of political dissent, taxation, and especially war itself.

We can also talk in terms of repressive and ideological functions of the state. First-order repressive legal functions are exhibited when parts of the legal system are used to forcibly maintain the system of surplus extraction. As a police reform activist I have observed numerous ways the police are used to harass homeless people and keep them out of the way of the tourist industry vital to the city in which I used to live. For example, excessive bail, where "dog-at-large" or "open container" fines would be boosted to several hundred dollars and selectively enforced against homeless people, has been used to keep the homeless in jail, typically for four days, since they would be picked up on a Thursday and be unable to make bail until Monday night, such that this intolerable harassment would "encourage" them to move on down the road.

First-order ideological functions of the legal system can be seen, for example, in how the state defines the notion of crime itself.[5] A crime *should* be the sort of thing that represents a harm to the community and its members. And yet, if you ask your average American what a crime is you will get the racist picture of violent crime committed by an African-American in an inner-city area, usually associated with drugs. However, it is statistically rather uncontroversial to suggest that one has an infinitely greater chance of being injured or killed in the workplace, where safety issues are barely criminalized, than meeting the same fate on the streets.

Second-order repressive functions obtain when the legal system flexes its muscles to maintain its own power. The obvious example of political prisoners comes to mind here. When the U.S. government pompously and hypocritically rails about political prisoners in other countries, it is worth reflecting not just on the McCarthyism of old, but on how the U.S. government consistently harasses and oppresses left activists who oppose our imperialist policies abroad and our exploitative system at home.

Nowhere are second-order ideological functions of the criminal justice system seen better than in the so-called war on drugs. The draconian expansion of police, prosecutorial, and correctional power so typical of the Reagan/Bush (and we can include Thatcher) tyranny capitalizes on the public's fear of street crime such that the criminal justice system can grow at a rate that strains public coffers, even when we openly admit that this system is entirely incapable of even denting the drug trade.

While the "why" question really does not seem to pose any serious philosophical problems, the "how" question is quite another matter. One main reason often advanced for rejecting historical materialism lies with the charge of what I have elsewhere called crude functionalism.[6] Crude functional analysis in Marxism entails the assumption that citing the beneficial consequences of the explanandum for the development and maintenance of the mode of production is in itself adequate to explain the phenomenon. Of course this view neglects the possibility that the benefits may arise accidentally, or that they may not be accidental but be nonexplanatory, or that there may be a third variable that accounts for both the *explanandum* and the benefit. Jon Elster, for one, has made much of how Marxism has suffered from such crude functional explanation.[7]

However, this problem is not unique to functional explanation. Cohen tells us that the fact that F preceded E does not guarantee that F caused E, and does not disqualify all causal explanations any more than the fact that G's tendencies are beneficial does not guarantee that G is explained by those tendencies. What it does tell us, though, is that functional explanation is only a partial form of explanation. In biology, the fact that a certain trait is functional for the survival of a particular organism only becomes explanatory when we come to understand how chance variation and natural selection make clear the way in which the usefulness of these characteristics account for their existence. The problem in social theory, then, is that no such comparable mechanism is known.

We must ask ourselves, then, does the person advancing a functional explanation need to have an account of the connection between the phenomenon and its function? Jon Elster, Cohen's leading critic, argues that absent a genetic theory, functional explanations are worthless. However, Cohen argues that in light of suitable evidence, but in advance of an elaborating theory, it is very important for social science and history that we see these functional explanations as explanatory. As long as we are uncertain about the microprocesses, we must be cautious, but that is true of all forms of explanation.[8]

For Cohen, we seek a fuller explanation and a more precise specification of the functional fact within a longer story. And Cohen does make an attempt to point out numerous ways a Marxian functional explanation can be confirmed genetically. He discusses purposive elaborations in terms of industrial decision makers; Darwinian elaborations in terms of competition, chance variation, scarcity, and natural selection; Lamarckian elaborations in terms of individual adaptation; as well as others. These types of explanatory mechanisms and others may be found, he suggests, throughout Marx's complex historical narratives as well as in his theoretical works on economics.[9] As far as elaborating theories are concerned, Cohen is right to suggest that we are at the same stage now that biologists were prior to Darwin's discovery of chance variation and natural selection. The difference, I think, is that in social science we are dealing with multiple supervenient categories. Hence, I do not believe that we will find one particular method of elaborating functional claims. Instead, I think we must return to Marx's method of detailed historical narrative. Describing the nature of class conflict, and hence integrating agency into structure, Marx spelled out how a given institution came to be functional in concrete terms.

Michel Foucault, whose relationship to Marxism is, in my view, not as tenuous as most think, describes his genealogical method in a fashion that, to me, seems quite similar to what I am advocating here. He says that

> We need to see how . . . [micro] mechanisms of power, at a given moment, in a precise conjuncture and by means of a certain number of transformations, have begun to become economically advantageous and politically useful . . . [; how] all the micro-mechanisms of power, that came, from a certain moment in time, to represent the interests of the bourgeoisie.[10]

Like Foucault, I see the essential method for elaborating just how certain phenomena came to be functional for the social system in concrete historical terms—from the bottom up, as it were. Historical narrative and interdisciplinary study, something abhorred by most analytic philosophers, at differing levels of generality, must be engaged in order to understand the genetic aspects of Marxian functional claims.

In conclusion, I would suggest that the best way to understand the U.S. political and legal system is through detailed empirical study that seeks to identify and elaborate first-order and second-order repressive and ideological functions with an eye toward generalized elaborating mechanisms. In fact, I am not sure that this is not exactly what most Marxist social scientists, admittedly or not, in effect actually do.

3

Postmodern Law and Subjectivity: Lacan and the Linguistic Turn

DRAGAN MILOVANOVIC

INTRODUCTION

The postmodern approach to law has ushered in a new legal paradigm. Its contours are only recently taking form. In many ways it is a response to the shortcomings of some aspects of Marxian and neo-Marxian critical theory, which has failed to offer a bona fide conception of the active human subject. The central figure in the revival of human agency has been Jacques Lacan (1901–1981), who offered a compelling account of the desiring subject inseparably linked to discourse.

This article will first briefly outline the major perspectives in Marxist sociology of law. I then briefly explain the Lacanian subject. Finally, I offer some suggestions based on the work of current thinkers developing a Lacanian informed critical legal theory.

MARXIAN THEORY IN THE SOCIOLOGY OF LAW AND THE QUESTION OF AGENCY

Marxist theory in the sociology of law is a misnomer. In truth we have Marxist *theories*. Interested theorists must comb through Marx's voluminous writings and construct a consistent theory of law—there exists no systematized theory of law within his treatises.[1] Accordingly, as a starting point, we can distinguish between the instrumental Marxist perspective and the structural Marxist perspective (see Figure 1). Within the structural Marxist perspective there is an additional division: the structural interpellation perspective and the commodity-exchange perspective. I will argue that the structural interpellation perspective is

FIGURE 1. MARXIST PERSPECTIVES

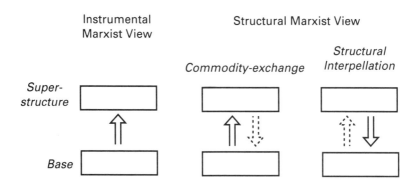

best situated to offer a convincing conceptualization of the desiring subject, and therefore to offer the best hope of reviving agency. It offers the best "fit" with Marxist theory, postmodern theory, and the constitutive perspective in law.[2]

The instrumental Marxist theory was dominant in the 1960s and 1970s. Its main claim was that a ruling class existed that was homogeneous, secretive, and conspiratorial in nature. The legal order was merely an instrument of control, domination, and a method of maximizing surplus value. Here the notion of agency was inconsequential. Subjects were merely determined by the mode of production (the "base") and the class in control of the ideological and repressive state apparatus (the "superstructure").

The structural Marxist perspective developed in the early 1980s, became further refined in the later 1980s, and now is the dominant position within critical legal theory. (Of course, we still witness the old guard hanging on tenaciously to the conspiratorial theory of instrumental Marxism.) The key thinker for this recent transition to the structuralist position was Pashukanis (1891–1937), a legal theoretician who ascended to power after the October 1917 Russian Revolution. His main contribution, spelled out in *The General Theory of Law and Marxism* (1924), was to become the dominant legal position in postrevolutionary Russia until about the early to mid-1930s, when its main arguments concerning the prospects of the "withering away of the state, law, lawyers and the juridic subject" gave way to Stalin's call for further consolidating the powers of the "dictatorship of the proletariat." Hence, Pashukanis was executed and his theory purged. Vyshinski, Stalin's right-hand man, then introduced his crude instrumental Marxist position.

Pashukanis' complex theory of law, which pointed out a homology between the legal and the juridic form (commodity fetishism was paralleled by legal fetishism), was to be named the commodity-exchange theory of law. Notions of the abstract legal subject with universal rights (i.e., to equality, freedom, and proprietorship) could be traced, Pashukanis claimed, directly to commodity exchange taking place in the competitive capitalist marketplace.

Pashukanis' commodity-exchange perspective was to lie dormant with his purge until the late 1970s and early 1980s, when a number of theoreticians were to discover his works.[3] This discovery fundamentally transformed critical theory in law (and criminology). Rather than a ruling class, the commodity-exchange perspective offered the notion of a hegemonic group, or the power bloc. Rather than seeing a direct nexus between the political-legal and the economic institutions, the new perspective looked at the totality of the structural configuration of a political economy in dynamic, dialectical movement and argued for a relative autonomy. That is, relatively independent spheres—the political, economic, political, ideological—existed and appeared historically articulated in particular configurations. Both the capitalists and the proletariat were subject to the effects of these articulations. Here, the notion of control and domination became much more problematic. Rather than instrumental control, this structural position held that the exploited often participated actively, albeit inadvertently, in their own oppression by maintaining the form of control. Hence, hegemony appeared in much more complex ways than outright gestapo control.

The early structural Marxist position, while offering a considerable improvement over the instrumental Marxist position, ultimately retained the economy as primarily determinative—"in the last instance." Subjects, too, were but "supports" of the structures of capitalist institutions.[4] Here, apart from the important contribution of how in fact hegemonic rule takes place with the active consent of the dominated, the subject was still relegated to a deterministic role.

In the late 1980s a second variation of the structural Marxist position was offered, the structural interpellation perspective.[5] From this viewpoint, "late" capitalism, or the state-regulated form, was different from the early competitive, laissez-faire form of the twentieth century. The state, it was argued, had to intervene more actively in the social formation to offset crisis tendencies.[6] The "balancing interest" form of resolving legal disputes had become more prevalent in the judiciary. Thereafter, the importance of the notion of a homogeneous juridic subject was to give way to the notion of "status" (i.e., prisoner, mental patient, free citizen, juvenile, employer, alien, homeless, etc.) once again being determinative of rights.[7]

Just as important, the notion of the subject and agency was to become more important in Marxist theorizing. That is, the subject was said to be "interpellated" by the dictates of the superstructural forces. In other words, the particular historically specific articulation of instances (political, economic, ideological, legal) was to generate structuring influences on the subjects in the social formation. As Althusser would have it, subjects are constituted by ideological state apparatuses directing certain messages their way. A subject is "hailed" by these forces and in acknowledging their existence (i.e., by the very act of paying attention to their call) is inserted in certain subject-positions which then structure background relevancies and the immediate "life world" of the subject. In cinema theory the constituted or the interpellated subject is now referred to as the *spoken subject*.[8]

What was missing in all this, of course, was the mechanism that underlies the process. Surely, Althusser was on the right track in indicating that subjects are in fact interpellated by forces that they themselves help inadvertently to maintain (i.e., hegemony). But the transmitter of these messages needed to be explicated. The notion of specifying the "ideological state apparatus" (school, media, family) as the culprit was a beginning. But much more needed to be said. The postmodern position, which has gained much ground in the 1990s, was to offer such an answer.

Postmodern thought, in turn, rested in part on the work of Jacques Lacan, who offered a number of seminars from the 1950s through the 1970s that were attended by many of the most notable intellectuals of Europe at the time. It was this group and Lacan's writings that were to have a profound influence on the development of postmodernist thought. These theoretical insights offered a key link in the construction of subjectivity and in offering a more compelling argument as to agency.[9] In the next section, I highlight some of the central ideas of Lacan and then introduce some of those in law who are currently offering syntheses of Lacan and critical perspectives on law.

LACAN, PSYCHOANALYTIC SEMIOTICS, AND CRITICAL THEORY

Jacques Lacan has offered a conception of the desiring subject as being inherently linked to discourse. Lacan, a revisionist Freudian, implied that Freud was really a linguist who articulated how the subject embodied desire, first in dreams through "dream work," and then in signifiers and discursive chains that represented the subject in its absence. Rather than a subject, Lacan offered the idea of a "speaking being" (*parlêtre*, or *l'être parlant*).

For Lacan, three orders exist, which together are the determinants of the speaking-being: the Real, Imaginary, and Symbolic. The Real Order is the domain of directly lived experience; it is beyond any possibility of congruent representation. The Imaginary Order is the domain of images, of imaginary constructions of self and others. The Symbolic Order is the domain of language and the unconscious—the

FIGURE 2. SCHEMA L

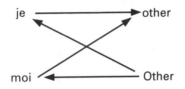

Other, with a capital *O*, from which the subject speaks. The Symbolic Order is structured by the semiotic tropes of metaphor and metonymy. In other words, unconscious processes were to account for much of the activity of the speaking-being. Desire finds embodiment in signifiers which then represent the subject in discourse as the subject fades from the scene. It is to this understanding of the Other and its relationship with the Imaginary and Real Orders that one must look in order to understand agency and the subject. Of course, Lacan's theory on its own is lacking. But as an element in a more comprehensive critical theory, it provides tools for critical inquiry and the potential for the development of a more humanistically based replacement discourse.

Lacan's desiring subject was represented in Schema L. This schema indicates the quadrilateral nature of the subject. The more dynamic form was represented in the *Graphs of Desire* and *Schema R*.[10]

In Schema L (see Figure 2) we find two axes: *je*-Other, *moi*-other— the former being unconscious in nature, the latter imaginary. The *moi* represents the illusions of self gained through the eyes of the other. It is essentially specular. The *other* is the imaginary construction of the one to whom one speaks. The *Other* is the domain of the unconscious, the sphere where a "treasure-house of signifiers" float, unique to the person's idiosyncratic being in the world. The *je*, as a signifier, represents the subject. It is the filled-in *I* of discourse, the representative of the being her/himself. The interaction between these two axes produces the manifestation of embodied desire. The speaking-being, then, is but the effect of these processes.

What mobilizes the psychic apparatus is periodically felt lack, a lack-in-being. This essential lack has its source in the inauguration of the child into the Symbolic Order. The subject thereafter continuously attempts to *suture*, that is, to "stitch over" a series of existential gaps-in-being. Objects of desire (*objet petit a*) offer the potential for experiencing fulfillment or a sense of completeness. Words can be conceptualized as one operationalization of *objet petit a*. In order to suture, the speaking-being must insert her/himself into some relatively stabilized discursive subject-position (i.e., client, patient, defendant, prosecutor, etc.) within a circumscribed discourse (a linguistic coordinate system) and there embody desire in signifiers.[11]

Note that the nature of desire can be described in more conservative, homeostatic terms (i.e., Hegel, Freud) or in a more dynamic manner (i.e., rooted in Nietzsche).[12] It is the latter that offers the potential for a transformative praxis to develop. As Lecercle has it: "desire can also be conceived as a forward movement, a flight towards an object which always eludes our grasp, the attempt, never successful but never frustrating, to reach the unattainable by exploring the paths of the possible."[13] Much of postmodern writing, however, is embedded within the tension between these two diametrically opposed conceptions of desire.

In law, narrative coherence is a function of subjects embodying desire within legal categories and within acceptable semantic and syntagmatic structures.[14] To be in the law is to insert oneself in these discursive subject-positions and to confine oneself to the dominant discourse of the courts. Accordingly, some voices are heard in court; many, however, are not—the marginal, oppositional, disenfranchised, minorities, those engaged in alternative styles in living, those with alternative sexual preferences, etc. Women, too, are denied a full voice. They are, according to Lacan, relegated to *pas-toute*.[15] The upper limits of the illusory perception of completeness (*jouissance*) exist within a phallocentric symbolic order and hence man, or a person assuming this discursive subject-position, may be *tout*, but a woman, or a person assuming this discursive subject-position, is *pas-toute*. This is the fundamental insight that the French postmodernist feminists have been embracing in making suggestions for genuine changes in the male-dominated Symbolic Order.[16] No, Lacan was not an apologist for the male-dominated Symbolic Order as some critics suggest. Rather, he was offering a descriptive analysis of how this order dominates. It is the reformer's task to draw out the implications of this insight in any prescriptive analysis.

DOING CRITICAL LAW

I now turn to what Lacan has offered for critical theory in law. It is my view that Lacan's findings of the subject's relation to discourse are the most convincing statement concerning the notion of agency, and, for critical theorists, the most important element in any development of a more comprehensive analysis of law, ideology, the subject, agency, hegemony, reification, and so forth. Much recent work has brought this out.

The key contemporary thinkers in integrating Lacan with a critical analysis of law have been Caudill,[17] Cornell,[18] Goodrich,[19] and Arrigo;[20] my own work, as well, reflects this emphasis.[21] Each theorist has dealt with different aspects of Lacan's psychoanalytic semiotics and has brought it to bear on some issue in law. Feminist analysis has been particularly important in explaining how gender construction takes place in language[22] and how an alternative vision may arise.[23] The notion of the law-of-the-father being the basis of much of legal ideology has been developed quite poignantly.[24] Lacan's psychoanalytic semiotics has also been applied to the contract.[25] The development and stabilization of certain ideological and imaginary constructions in law have been addressed.[26] The debate concerning *essentialism* versus the relative or the contingent nature of the subject, particularly the gendered subject in law, has been the basis of much fruitful debate.[27] The notion of the dialectics of struggle and hegemony is especially well illuminated by the tools offered by this line of inquiry.[28] And the offering, by constitutive theory in law, of the notion of the codeterminous construction of reality[29] provides insights as to how the oppressed themselves inadvertently construct and reconstruct the dominant symbolic order. This is especially noteworthy with activist lawyers before our courts.[30] Here, for example, politicized defense lawyers realize very quickly that resigning themselves to constructing narratives and the "story" (the "what happened?") within legal discourse perhaps contributes to "winning" the case but also contributes to giving further legitimacy to the rule of law ideology as well as to the dominant symbolic order.

Most important, perhaps, is that the tools of inquiry that postmodernist analysis has offered, particularly the tools that can be traced to many of the insights of Jacques Lacan, promise to pave the way to a transformative politics. This transpraxis has, as an essential element, the call for the development of the wherewithal of a humanistically based replacement discourse within which subjects may embody desire in more liberating ways. The challenge, then, is not to develop a revolutionary praxis based on the dynamics of reaction and negation, but to develop one based on an affirmative transformative practice, a transpraxis. Too much energy on the left has been consumed on hate politics, political correctness, "us versus them," and other forms of schmarxism.[31]

4

Re-returning to Freud: Critical Legal Studies as Cultural Psychoanalysis*

DAVID S. CAUDILL

The very existence of the Critical Legal Studies (CLS) "movement" is in question nowadays. Evidence of a "school" of thought persists, both in the form of a loose organization (with members, or at least a mailing list; with a newsletter, the appearance of which is irregular; and with occasional conferences) and in legal scholarship, where any survey of contemporary perspectives on law will likely include a reference to CLS (and perhaps a citation to a canonical essay or two). In actuality, theorists and practitioners who identify in some degree with CLS include those who also identify, in their critiques of legal processes and institutions, with critical race theory, feminism, postmodern literary theory (e.g., deconstruction), or some version of neo-Marxism.

In the literature commonly associated with CLS, one often reads that the movement, in part, employs Freudian ideas. The same is said of the Frankfurt School, but one can easily point to the writings of Herbert Marcuse and Erich Fromm for unambiguous developments and revisions of Freud's work. The connection between Freud and CLS is not so clear. The purpose of this essay is to explore briefly the use and potential of Freudian conceptions in CLS.

CLS AS A CRITIQUE OF LEGAL IDEOLOGY

While there is no central or core theory shared by all scholars associated with CLS, conceiving the eclectic movement as a form of ideology-critique helps to explain the methodology and terminology of many CLS adherents. Ideologies, in the sense of worldviews or cultural belief systems, can be said to establish and direct communal life and thought. When an ideology is hidden (or *unconscious*), its power to obscure alternatives and to create false necessities is greatest. The critique of ideology seeks to disclose belief systems not only to enhance understanding and meaningful communication within a community, but to challenge and change social processes.

"Ideology," however, does not have a clear meaning. In some Marxian formulations, the term has pejorative connotations—ideology as false consciousness—and refers to that which masks social contradictions and thereby legitimizes oppressive institutions. "Ideology" can also be a descriptive reference to the coherent set of collective beliefs of any social group.[1] In CLS literature, the term "ideology" often refers descriptively "to the beliefs that individuals hold about law or to the set of beliefs, ideas, and values embodied in the legal institutions and legal materials . . . of a particular society." However, ideologies also operate, according to some CLS scholars, to marginalize alternatives and to distort social knowledge—a pejorative sense of the term.[2]

Adding to the confusion, some theorists have questioned the assumption that members of a society share a common set of beliefs that constitutes common sense or that legitimizes asymmetrical relations of power. David McClellan argues that a dominant ideology will generally be accepted by the ruling class, but that lower classes may be ignorant of or indifferent to the dominant ideology.[3] John Thompson remarks that societies are more likely "stabilized by virtue of the diversity of values and beliefs and the proliferation of divisions between individuals and groups." Ideology, for Thompson, is not grounded in consensus, but in everyday language, where "meaning is mobilized in defense of [relations of] domination." The study of ideology is therefore construed as an investigation into the ways in which meaning legitimates, hides, and neutralizes power in society.[4]

Even if a workable definition of ideology is established, as a common set of beliefs or as a set of limitations on thought and power embedded in everyday language, questions remain as to how legal ideology works—how is "the population in general or some particular section . . . influenced by the ideological products of the legal process?"[5] Moreover, how do critics account for their own ideological presuppositions or, in another formulation, their own given, limiting framework? Critical legal theorists can escape neither belief nor language in their analyses of legal culture.

The foregoing problems, together with the recurring accusations that CLS literature is incomprehensible and impractical, plague critical legal research. My thesis is that psychoanalytic theory offers insights with which to confront some of the problematical aspects of CLS—insights that are already contained within the radical traditions on which CLS draws.

FREUD AND SOCIETY

While psychoanalysis is often viewed solely as an explanatory model for individual human behavior,

> it also contains the possibilities for an approach that analyzes the mechanism by which the social world enters into the experience of each individual, constructing the human "subject" and reproducing itself through the perpetuation of particular patterns of ideology.[6]

Just as the individual represses himself or herself, society represses the individual. Just as the individual seeks to control powerful instincts, "civilization is built upon a renunciation of instinct."[7] Freud thus believed that the primordial and dangerous passions of the individual must be controlled by inherently oppressive social structures. Such a view, however, invites pessimism and provides the basis for an implied conservatism rather than for a radical or utopian critique of the status quo.

Freud's views on sexuality, however, imply that "normal" sexuality is not biological—that is, (*i*) in anthropological terms, different societies will have different views of normality, and (*ii*) in critical terms, alternatives to socially acceptable sexuality are imaginable. More important to the present study is

> the recognition that what Freud describes is the way society enters into the essence of the human individual, organizing the instincts where usually we consider that we are most privately ourselves.[8]

In the radical Freudian scheme, it is *not* that an already established individual consciousness is conditioned or shaped by social interaction, but rather that sociality has an unconscious and formative effect on individual experience and perception of oneself and others. That is, our social relations are "themselves only available because of the particular ideological structures that dominate within a society." The impulses and feelings that appear to be so much part of our "selves" are, in this view, actually products of our sociality.[9]

The radical tradition inherited from Freud the promise of power to analyze,

> to display the unconscious roots of personal and social action, to make this material open to awareness and hence to make ideology open to inspection and change imaginable.[10]

Freud's preoccupation with illusions, despite his descriptive and positivistic ("scientific") goals, could not help but suggest the possibilities for emancipation and demystification.

Critical Theory and structuralism, the two extralegal traditions most often identified as the forerunners of CLS, both signal a latent role for psychoanalysis in social theory.

FREUD AND CRITICAL THEORY

Erich Fromm, for a time, helped to reconcile Marx and Freud, although he later disassociated himself from both the Frankfurt School and orthodox Freudianism. Fromm's identification of "psychoanalytic mechanisms as the mediating concepts between individual and society" established for the neo-Marxists a Freudian component in social criticism. Horkheimer welcomed the growing psychological supplement to Marxian theory, as did Adorno, yet both grew dissatisfied with Fromm's revision of Freud's work.[11] It was not Fromm, but Herbert Marcuse, who finally rescued for Critical Theory the revolutionary Freud.

Marcuse's *Eros and Civilization* (1955) plays several roles for those inspired by Critical Theory and enamored of Freud. First, the book is a criticism of Freudian revisionism. Second, Marcuse did not accept Freud's pessimism (concerning society) and implied conservatism, finding instead a critical and liberating tendency, or "hidden trend," in psychoanalysis. Third, Marcuse argued that "Freud's individual psychology is in its very essence social psychology."[12]

In the preface to the first edition of *Eros and Civilization*, Marcuse immediately identifies the psychological with the political:

[Formerly] autonomous and identifiable psychical processes are being absorbed by the function of the individual in the state—by his public existence.... [P]rivate disorder reflects more directly the disorder of the whole, and the cure of personal disorder depends more directly than before on the cure of the general disorder.[13]

External repression, Marcuse continues, is internalized as self-repression; in Freudian categories, the repressions of the ego ("in the service and at the behest of the superego")[14] became "unconscious, automatic as it were." Rather than simply accommodating reality, the superego now enforces *past* reality, the status quo.

Stephen Frosh is ultimately disappointed in Marcuse's individualistic and libertarian analysis, wherein "social relations are reduced to pure, unproblematic and unmediated encounters between totally unalienated individuals." A genuinely radical psychoanalysis, Frosh argues, needs to concern itself with social structures as well as specific others, "themselves carriers of social and ideological messages."[15]

FREUD AND STRUCTURALISM

Lévi-Strauss' discovery in myths of universal and unifying structures was a type of cultural psychoanalysis, analogous to bringing the unconscious into consciousness.[16] Freudian conceptions of the unconscious later appeared in the writings of Althusser, Ricoeur, Foucault, and, less directly, Derrida. The most obvious integration of psychoanalysis and structuralism, however, is found in the work of Jacques Lacan.

Lacanian theory is best known, perhaps, for its complexity and for the elusive style of Lacan's seminars. The difficulties experienced by readers of Lacan are not unusual, however, in light of the challenges of (for example) French or German philosophical discourse, and Lacan is almost popular in American literary theory (or "cultural studies") circles. While Lacan claimed (merely) to return to Freud—Lacan's seminars are anchored in Freudian texts—the framework of Lacanian psychoanalysis is unfamiliar; Lacan's rejection of neo-Freudian revisionism is even stronger than Marcuse's. Everyday thought and clinical disorders are rearticulated by Lacan in terms of desire and lack, of others and the Other, and of his three orders of subjectivity: the imaginary realm of identificatory images, the symbolic order of (highly determinative) language, and the real—not our "reality" but the unknowable "real." The self, which only appears to be (at times) unified, is splintered among conscious and unconscious relations with images, language, others, and the Other (the ambiguous place of unconscious "language," of Law, of the outside-within-us).[17]

Lacan, in an effort to introduce the "imaginary order," identified the "mirror-stage" in every child's development, roughly the child's initial awareness of itself before the experience can be verbalized or understood.[18] This first impression or *image* becomes the basis for construction of a "self" and for all relationships to come. Thereafter, the child becomes aware of the mother (the "other body"), of the father (the "Law") and sexual differences, and of gender roles; concurrently the child discovers language itself. The imaginary order is thus interrupted by the symbolic order, Lacan's term for "the pre-given structure of social and sexual roles and relations which make up the family and society." With the passage into the symbolic, however, the child loses direct access to the imaginary possession of reality and emerges into the restless world of language and repressed desire.[19]

The unconscious, for Lacan, is structured like a language[20]—in Terry Eagleton's paraphrase, the unconscious exhibits "a constant fading and evaporation of meaning, a bizarre 'modernist' text which is almost unreadable and which will certainly never yield up its final secrets to interpretation." The ego, or consciousness, represses the turbulence by "provisionally nailing down words onto meanings," but articulation is always an approximation of truth. The "imaginary" thus reappears in the conscious and necessary attempt to view oneself as reasonably unified and coherent.[21]

Lacanian clinical analysis, which (following Freud) seeks verbalization of the patient's unconscious, is an attempt to escape "normal" (or civil, coherent, and rational) communication between analyst and analysand, and thereby to discover another logic. In Schneiderman's account, the controversial "short session" (Lacan's repudiation of the traditional 50-minute analytic hour) serves to keep the analysand off balance—"the analysand did not have time to get his bearings, to establish his sense of being in control of the situation, to get his thoughts in order." In Freudian terms, the short session frustrates the ego's censorship and explanatory functions:

> Almost by definition, the ego can never be the master of the short session. . . .
>   This ego, however, . . . asserts itself with a vengeance, not only in trying to control the situation but in offering interpretations. . . . This mode of interpretation is eventually revealed to be the system that holds the neurosis in place.

The analyst, in this conception, ignores the intentions of the ego, and "hears the discourse of the other . . . that slides through the gaps of intentionality."[22]

Appropriation of Lacan for social theory is problematical at best. Critics of Freudian approaches dismiss Lacan as hopelessly psychoanalytic, while neo-Freudians accuse Lacan of postmodernizing Freud, especially in the primacy accorded to the symbolic. Postmodern critics, on the other hand, often view Lacan as a traditional structuralist metaphysician. Such labels seem particularly inappropriate in the case of Lacanian theory, which to its credit or to a fault constructs bridges between the extremes in the debates over Freud and over postmodern conceptions of language.

GABEL: CONTOURS OF A SOCIOLEGAL PSYCHOANALYSIS

References to Freud appear now and then in CLS literature, but Freudian terminology abounds—law is a denial of contradictions, a repressive structure, a distortion of reality, a defense mechanism for uncomfortable realities, a symptom, and so forth. Peter Gabel, whose work is associated with CLS scholarship, clearly employs such psychoanalytic language and concepts. He focuses on the social and intersubjective nature of desire, and the need for those involved in progressive politics to understand the desire for social confirmation.

"Desire" is nowadays associated with the instinctual forces of the id that must be controlled. The desire for mutual recognition that we experience and perceive in others

> is resisted and even opposed by those around us who have learned ...
> to deny this desire in themselves. The medium of this opposition is
> well-captured by what ... Lacan called "misrecognition," a process
> by which the parent, instead of confirming the infant in his or her
> being, "throws" the infant and later the child into a series of roles
> that ... alienate the child ... from the centered desire that is the
> social dimension of the child's soul.

The split between the child's desire and his or her social self will be reproduced in others through familial and social contacts; moreover, the desire may be repeatedly repressed in an effort to maintain the validity of the internalized role.[23]

Legal culture tends to reinforce the collective denial identified by Gabel. Lawyers and judges, and legal reasoning itself, are "disembodied" and elevated in our society:

> [Law] is made to appear as an authoritative system of thought outside of and above everyone ... rather than as a contingent and developing expression of social and political meaning that we actively create and interpret.[24]

Legal discourse is thus an embodiment of the dynamic projection of an externalized source of social authority.

CONCEPTUAL ENRICHMENT OF LEGAL *IDEOLOGIEKRITIK*

The suggestive remarks that follow are but further "traces" of the potential for psychoanalytic concepts in critical legal research.

Roles. Freud's interpretation of childhood teaches that "the organization of everyday life by the social institution of the restricted family [leaves] a clear imprint on the course of [the] childhood experience." However, Freud tended to view the child's psyche as a primary function and the social environment as a secondary influence. By contrast, as John Brenkman points out,

> Lacan's project has been the attempt to give language and
> intersubjectivity primacy.... He recognizes that the *Umwelt*, the
> environment or outer world, of the infant is preeminently social.
> From birth, the human being is affected by actions, gestures, wishes
> and intentions that are already imbued with the symbolic and that
> occur within the constraints of specific, historically determined
> institutions.

That is, the subject is "radically dependent on the field of the other" for identity and for the language that eventually makes interaction

possible. Recall that Althusser (following Lacan) sees the family configuration as an ideology that waits for each of us to be born and
assigns our respective places or roles. The family as social and social-
izing institution "limits the possibilities of interaction which emerge
in the experience of speech."[25] Note, however, that Althusser's appropriation of Lacan invites criticism by students of Lacan; at times Althusser
implies a subject in control of desire and language,[26] and at times
Althusser removes the subject's flexibility within the determinative
symbolic order;[27] in either case, Lacanian theory is reduced in the service
of a Marxian notion of the subject.

CLS identifies legal institutions and processes as arrangers of everyday life, shaping and constraining the situations and interactions we
experience. Furthermore, critics of legal ideology can be conceived as
cultural analysts who disclose or bring to the surface hidden or unconscious belief systems concerning the law. However, while such
metaphors are perhaps inspirational, they represent an impoverished
conception of psychoanalysis. Peter Gabel's recent reflections on collective desire provide a richer analogy between the critical-legal and
the social-psychoanalytical projects.

Desire. Gabel posits a collective desire for social confirmation and
mutual recognition. He suggests that the social self is often alienated
or blocked from such real desire by our *privatization* of desire and by
collective *denial* of that social dimension. The alienation or blockage is
reproduced (by repetitive repression of desire to maintain social roles)
and maintained (by deference to "phantom" social structures for identity and by reciprocal projection of that "given" world) in a circle of
denial and desire. Legal culture exemplifies role-based interaction wherein
political or moral desire is privatized in subjection to an externalized
social authority.[28]

John Brenkman's psychoanalytic theory of culture, another attempt
to employ and go beyond Freud and Lacan, is similar in several respects
to Gabel's approach. Freud, in his neglect of the social constitution of
the ego and the social organization of "reality," grants to the ego only
the ability to adjust to reality.[29] Lacan's restatement of Freudianism in
social and cultural terms (as a theory of the subject's constitution by
and through language) initiates an immanent critique of psychoanalysis that Brenkman incorporates into his own neo-Marxian critique:

> The critical theory of society and culture requires a theory of subjec-
> tivity and lived experience, and in turning to psychoanalysis to de-
> velop that, it discovers another task as well: to disclose those points
> in psychoanalytic theory where historical forms of domination—prin-
> cipally the social division of labor and the social organization of
> sexual difference—have to become integral and primary elements
> of that theory itself.[30]

Brenkman's reassessment of psychoanalysis also inspires a hope for social change. Repression of desire, which blocks the "subject's access to his or her own history," is a response of the ego to the conflict between desire and present reality. If reality, however, is essentially social, then a third orientation "toward the future and toward another reality" appears. This critical orientation implies the possibility of renouncing reality "not in the mode of repression, which hampers the possibilities of the present under the impact of an unlived and untold past, but in the mode of a liberation which, comprehending the past and demanding a new future, condemns the present."[31]

Gabel's recognition of the need to reconstitute legal culture by challenging "given" roles and contingent social structures provides an example of Brenkman's "third orientation." Moreover, the problematical questions of the existence and operation of legal ideology is directed by Gabel into a reflection upon the division between desire (experienced and perceived in others) and collective denial, between our privatized ideals and our social selves, and between contingent realities.

Cultural Self-Criticism. The psychoanalytic project inspired by Lacan's Freud also provides a model of self-criticism for the critic of legal ideology. Althusser's Lacanian conception of the eternity of ideology at least provides a contrast with the Marxian notion of ideology as *false* consciousness, a term which suggests that the critic is outside ideology. Indeed, the critic, at best, encourages cultural self-awareness, hence the significance of the early Habermas' picture of psychoanalysis as fundamentally self-reflective as well as his analogy between a patient's self-consciousness and social liberation. In Brenkman's construction:

> Human knowledge cannot, especially when it pretends to be a scientific knowledge of the forms of everyday cognition, detach itself from the lived experiences out of which genuine subjectivity emerges.
>
> *   *   *
>
> This problematic, in which science is inseparable from politics in the development of an understanding of human social, psychological, and cultural life, never becomes visible in Freud and never completely breaks into the clear in Lacan.[32]

Gabel, I think, would agree, as he links his social theory directly to politics.

I would go farther, avoiding the reduction to politics, and maintain that *all* theoretical and everyday thought is inseparable from ideology in the sense of belief systems, open hidden (or unconscious) but subject to self-critical disclosure and discourse. Informed by the psychoanalytic tradition, such belief systems can now be seen to include changeable social desire, repression, and reality.

5

A Theory of Social Injustice

THOMAS W. SIMON

INTRODUCTION

> White teenagers, screaming racial insults, beat a 12-year-old Hispanic boy and smeared him with white paint today as he awaited a bus to school in the Bronx, police said. It was the second such attack in a week.[1]

For most people, this example invokes a "sympathetic reaction of outrage, horror, shock, resentment, and anger"[2] as well as moral condemnation, "an indissociable blend of reason and empathy."[3] Reason and emotion combine in the evocative phrase "an injustice." The injustice label seems to fit the situation well. The incident qualifies as an injustice, in part, because the boy's only "wrong" lies in his group identity, which he cannot control.

Racial insults and slurs, all too commonplace today, pale in comparison to other forms of suffering that involve groups. Blacks brutalized at Soweto, Jews mutilated at Dachau, the disabled left to rot in Rumania; hundreds of thousands of "communists" slaughtered in East Timor.[4] The list of horrors, easily compiled, continues its regressive march. Despite the prominence of injustices throughout the world and in the United States, injustice does not occupy the foreground of the more prominent political theories. While political theorists do not entirely ignore injustices, they tend to do little in terms of even cataloguing the different types of injustices. Instead political theorists concentrate on the notion of justice. Emphasizing justice over injustice may seem like nothing more than a difference in emphasis. Making an issue out of the different emphasis may seem as important as chastising the economist who chooses to talk more of employment than unemployment. The divergence of justice from injustice, or lack thereof, serves as a primary issue for this study. I will explore the ways in which a theory of injustice takes on a very different character from a theory of justice.

Recently, a few writers, most notably Judith Shklar in *The Faces of Injustice*[5] and Elizabeth Wolgast in *The Grammar of Justice*,[6] have challenged the preoccupation that political theorists have had with the concept of justice. Their work promotes the centrality of the concept of injustice. This study extends their work by providing a systematic analysis of injustice. The study has the further goal of exploring the relationship between injustice and democracy. In order to connect democracy and social injustice, I first need to develop a theory of a particular kind of injustice, that is, social injustice. I will largely confine the sense of social injustice to group injustice. I will argue that the struggle for democracy includes the fight to eradicate social (group) injustice. Before turning to these tasks we first need to examine ways in which a theory of injustice differs from its much more well-known kin, a theory of justice.

JUSTICE AND INJUSTICE

Theories of justice come in many varieties. It would require an additional book just to disentangle the many competing conceptions of justice. Generally speaking, the theorists define justice in terms of something else: libertarians define justice in terms of liberty; socialists, in terms of equality; liberals use a combination of liberty and equality; and communitarians see justice in terms of the common good.[7] I want to show how a theory of injustice cuts across and, in some senses, comes before the justice projects.

To resort to a bad pun: the following comparison will not do justice to all the theories of justice. In order to find a niche for injustice, thereby placing it more centrally on the political theory agenda, it will prove helpful to make some general comparisons between theories of injustice and justice. Before elaborating on the more concrete and contextual nature of injustice and showing the ways in which injustice has priority over justice, we first need to establish at least the separability of the two notions. If justice and injustice cannot be disentangled, then it makes little sense to talk about the priority of one over the other.

SEPARABILITY

Injustice and justice seem inseparable since justice typically provides the standard by which to assess injustice.[8] While I recognize the critical interplay between injustice and justice, the theories of injustice and justice also diverge in important ways. One can make invaluable judgments about injustice without having a full-blown positive theory of what justice is. A few analogies should help establish the separation between injustice and justice.

Someone can have a very clear understanding of hell without the foggiest idea of heaven. One could have a clear-cut, well-developed theory of wrongs with only a weak intuition of what is right. The environmentalist may have an elaborate theory about industrial production that causes widespread and harmful pollution without a clue as to what constitutes good production. Judgments regarding bad, polluting production can be separated from those about good production.

A person can clearly condemn the hell of child abuse without having any idea as to the best and most heavenly way to raise children. Agreement comes more readily over the condemnation of abuse than over the best child-rearing practices. Moreover, effective use of condemnation is least likely to raise typically libertarian or liberal objections when the parent's liberties become violated. Jailing parents for failure to properly inculcate moral virtues in their children falls in a category entirely different from that of jailing them for child abuse. Parents deserve having their liberties restricted for engaging in child abuse. Courts would readily dismiss a lawsuit seeking to restrict parental liberties for their failure to educate their children in a politically correct manner. In short, a theory of injustice does not require a fully explicated theory of justice.[9]

The separation of injustice from justice poses more than an interesting academic exercise. Separating injustice from justice has important consequences. A theory of injustice sets a research agenda different from that of a theory of justice by posing and emphasizing different questions. Another analogy should prove helpful.

For decades positivists and Popperians fought over whether confirmation or falsification characterized scientific methodology. Did (or should) scientists try to confirm or to disconfirm hypotheses? Whatever the outcome of the debate, it at least became clear to most observers and participants that the two sides had very different research programs. They asked different questions about science and saw the history of science differently. For example, the positivists emphasized the normal aspect of science, whereas the Popperians (and later, Kuhnians) put the spotlight on the more unusual phases of science. Analogously, a theory of justice gives priority to the positive, whereas a theory of injustice roots out the negative, the bad. Thus, while both theories of injustice and justice may cite instances of injustice, the injustice theory must provide a means of cataloguing and comparing the various forms of injustice, whereas the justice theory can go on to other concerns. Saddled with classificatory tasks, a theory of injustice may appear far less foundational than a theory of justice. A theory of injustice catalogues like a taxonomist; a theory of justice provides the underlying explanatory principles of the evolutionist.

Rawls, a prominent foundationalist and political theorist, makes a distinction between his strict compliance theory of justice and a partial compliance theory that "studies the principles that govern how we are to deal with injustice."[10] Rawls claims that the former constitutes the "only basis for the systematic grasp of these more pressing problems."[11] Yet, a theory of injustice, while failing to provide the political equivalent of an all-encompassing, unified field theory in physics, does at least enhance understanding and informs political action. A theory of injustice occupies an important middle range between the lofty abstractions of the principles of justice and the concrete examples of human suffering and misery.[12]

The foundationalist's quest for unifying political principles may be an idle one. The twentieth century has produced a number of severe challenges to those who propose all-encompassing unified systems. Einstein's unified field theory met the Heisenberg uncertainty principle. Frege's hopes to uncover the foundation stones of logic were dashed by the Gödel proof. These developments in the more solid reaches of the sciences and the clearer domains of logic should give pause to the hope of establishing foundational political principles.

If a partial compliance theory provides the "principles that govern how we are to deal with injustice," that is no small achievement. Eradicating injustice poses a monumental challenge. We need not be concerned with the purportedly strong conservative implications of merely correcting the wrongs inflicted on others and thereby sustaining the status quo.[13] While a theory of injustice, compared to a fully worked out theory of justice, has a minimalist agenda, a theory of injustice, at least the version proposed here, would be very disruptive of the status quo. Moreover, a theory of injustice does not preclude the quest for a theory of justice. A theory of injustice can open the door wider in terms of shedding light upon a theory of justice.

In any event, a theory of injustice pleads for people to first get straight on what is wrong.

CONCRETENESS VERSUS ABSTRACTION

Justice seems most akin to an abstract concept like perfection. Perfection is seldom, if ever, found in the real world. Yet it serves an important role by guiding action. The same might be said of justice.[14] Specific instances of justice do not come readily to mind. People talk of a just distribution of resources when relief workers find an equitable means of distributing food during a crisis. When these examples of justice do arise, they appear often in the wake of injustice. The just distribution follows on the heels of conditions of deprivation and injustice.

Whereas justice is most easily described in the abstract, injustice is usually perceived within a fully contextualized, concrete situation. Injustices are often glaring and demand an immediate response.[15] To take just one of many examples, the beatings of the Freedom Riders in 1961 in Rock Hill, South Carolina, and Montgomery, Alabama, invoked a sense of injustice in many people. Television made people eyewitnesses to the injustice. Injustice stood before the viewers in a way that moved many to action.

Ostensive definitions ("Look, there it is") that define by pointing out their actual instantiations fit some terms better than others. Injustice seems particularly amenable to ostensive definitions. Instances of injustice can be sensed immediately, pointed to, and seen relatively clearly. People may disagree about some purported cases of injustice, but seeing certain kinds of pain and suffering, especially those that could have been avoided, brings a relatively quick consensus.

Instances of injustice occur in specific settings. Descriptions and depictions of injustice occur in the more "nonintellectual" media formats that portray at least some aspects of the context. Talk of justice more often takes an intellectual form, in which context is of less importance, as in the academy.[16]

PRIORITY

Separating out the different questions asked by injustice and justice proves a far easier task than establishing a priority of one over the other. The question of priority places the theorist on shakier but nonetheless interesting grounds.

Injustice could take priority over justice in three senses: empirically, psychologically, and morally. Empirical priority, where injustice occurs temporally before justice, refers to a point raised above in the discussion on the concrete nature of injustice. Concerns for justice often arise out of specific cases of injustice. "Justice appears... as an indefinite corrective to injustice rather than something definable in its own right."[17] Generally, instances of injustice accumulate or predominate before the justice corrective is administered. So, injustice generally precedes justice, at least temporally.

Psychologically, a sense of injustice has deep and passionate roots. Manifestations of injustice give rise to moral indignation, which, in turn, lies at the heart of morality. Injustice causes anger,[18] whereas justice has a more tenuous grip on the emotions. I would not go so far as Shklar in claiming that "Justice radiates no emotional appeal."[19] Visions of a more just world order convince and arouse considerable passion in many individuals. However, the passions aroused by injustice need little introduction or explanation. The responses to the pain and suffering

A videotape, played on national news programs across the country, of the notorious beating of Rodney King provided ample evidence to identify the Los Angeles police officers who inflicted the torture.

Recognizing the human causal agent behind instances of injustices provides a new perspective on so-called natural disasters. Despite the intuitive appeal of the distinction, the line between natural cause and human agency begins to blur upon a closer analysis. For example, nature, regarded by some as the cause of drought, appears to others as a false surrogate for humans engaging in overgrazing with their cattle. So, injustice may well encompass a broad array of so-called natural afflictions. What may initially look like a natural disaster may turn out, upon closer examination, to be an instance of injustice. Success in labeling it as an instance of injustice depends, in part, on the ability to uncover human causal agents.

Finding the human agent or agents behind the event proves difficult in many cases. The spotlight does not always reveal a single human causal agent behind the episode. Injustices seem to result even without any readily apparent human agency. A homeless man in the District of Columbia dies from hypothermia near the White House. The cold serves as the immediate, natural cause, but few would stop the analysis there. Yet, the search for a human causal agent will probably not reveal any single human being responsible for the victim's demise. The cynic may reply that no one forced the man to remain out on the street during the cold snap. Undoubtedly, unlike the Rodney King case, the search for the culprit in the homeless case will not uncover a video incriminating specific individuals.

The initial failure to find the human cause does not end the matter. Human agency plays a role, however obliquely. In the example of the homeless man, let us suppose that this particular man had a mental illness and that the government failed to provide him with treatment. Human agency lies hidden behind the morass of legislation and bureaucracy. At some points in the legislative/bureaucratic process people made decisions affecting this man's homeless condition and ultimate death.

Instead of linking the cause of injustices directly to human agency, I propose to use the term "sociopolitical cause" to cover those cases where a causal link can be made to social and political institutional structures and rules. Injustices could have been avoided in a way that naturally caused misfortunes could not have been averted, for injustices involve the sociopolitical realm, subject to human whim and open to human reason and morality. An injustice has not been committed when the victim has responsibility for the act. Injustice, then, has an external sociopolitical cause, which, as will become apparent later, gives it a connection to democracy.

SUFFERING

One of the four noble truths in Buddhism recognizes suffering in the world. "People suffer" serves as a simple but easily forgotten or ignored truth.[23] Whatever its noble status, the proposition seems beyond dispute. Even a quick glance at the world far and near reveals suffering on a massive scale.

Some claim that suffering has a single nature and that "general opposition to human suffering constitutes a standpoint that both transcends and unites different cultures and historical epochs."[24] I shall not pretend to bring the many different forms of suffering under one theoretical roof. Instead, I shall concentrate on the social aspect of each form of suffering, particularly the physical and psychological kinds of suffering, which too easily get separated from the social realm.

PHYSICAL SUFFERING

The most easily recognizable form of suffering is physical. Everyone has experienced physical pain in one form or another. Initially, pain may seem like a highly individualized phenomenon, one that has little to do with the political world. An individual's fractured arm hurts. Experiencing the pain from the hurt hardly constitutes a political act. Cutting my hand with a knife in the kitchen does not have the ingredients of an injustice. Now, add the following information: the accident occurred while in an unsafe work environment. A case for claiming an injustice begins with situating the pain outside of the individual and in the social-political realm.

PSYCHOLOGICAL SUFFERING

Suffering need not exist only on the physical plane. Clinical evidence demonstrates the separation of the physiological sensation of pain from the psychological dimension. Intractable pain patients, after receiving a prefrontal lobotomy, report that "My pain is the same, but it doesn't hurt me now."[25] Conversely, some patients report pain sensations in their phantom limbs. Interestingly, the psychological states respond to social influence as in "Kolb's observation that pain in the phantom limb could be induced by bringing problematic features of the patient's life and adjustment, such as occupation or sexual attractiveness, to the patient's attention."[26] The psychosocial dynamics of suffering has a special relevance to a theory of injustice, for it edges suffering toward the political realm, where a theory of injustice operates.

Often, suffering is most brutal and, simultaneously, most subtly manifested in the psychosocial realm. Susan Brownmiller describes rape not only in its gruesome physical details but also as "nothing more or less than a conscious process of intimidation by which *all men* keep *all women* in a state of fear."[27] Any analysis of suffering should include the case of members of a particular group being placed in a constant state of fear.

However odd it might seem to claim that someone suffers in the absence of any overt physical or psychological manifestations, that oddity has some truth to it. Even if a caged individual such as Nelson Mandela had most of his physical and psychological needs met while in prison (and I am not claiming that he did), we would still rightfully attribute suffering to Nelson Mandela. Mandela had his freedom wrongly curtailed while in prison. However humane his treatment, restricting his movement may well be enough to justify ascribing suffering to him. Mandela does not need to try to break free from the prison walls in order to suffer. He does not need to experience any immediate physical or psychological harm in order to suffer. He simply needs to have his interests thwarted in a certain way. When an individual has his or her interests thwarted, an injustice may well result.

SOCIAL SUFFERING

Replace the physical bars and barriers with social ones. In the social scenario an individual has her or his interests thwarted by social forces. Social forces can restrict, literally and figuratively, the mobility of a black woman in the labor force since she cannot obtain certain kinds of jobs because of her race and gender. Her group status has socially imprisoned her in a way that could prove far more harmful than the physical barriers that surrounded Nelson Mandela. Since Mandela's imprisonment qualifies as one of suffering, the social thwarting of interests qualifies as well.

In certain cases, people are born into the conditions of suffering. People are not born onto a social tabula rasa—a blank slate. Rather, they come into the world with labels already attached to them. People are born with racial, gender, and ethnic tags socially attached to them. Many times the newborn quickly get religious classifications as well. Soon after birth the children are divided into the normal and abnormal with respect to bodily and mental functioning. Well before a child can even talk, the child has already acquired a social identity.

Labeling a person along any one of these dimensions—race, gender, ethnicity, etc.—does not induce immediate suffering. The labeling itself seems rather innocuous—and, for certain labels, such as sex at birth, the labels appear unavoidable. Despite their initial innocence, the classifications are not made along purely scientific and value-neutral lines. Labeling begins to take on a new form when we consider that for most of the labels, the individual had no choice or input over the label. Obviously, the newborn cannot choose from among the labels.

Furthermore, the labels come complete with a value-laden, political and historical baggage. Racial classifications are not entirely biological ones. Placing the label "black" upon a newborn socially and historically situates that individual.

While the labeling does not itself induce suffering, it does partially set the conditions of vulnerability to suffering. In order for an individual to suffer because of her or his group identity, the group label must first attach. Shklar highlights the dangers of group identity: "There is nothing just about a communal identification that one may not leave at will and that may doom one to social inferiority or to an unwarranted social identity."[28] However, unlike Shklar we should not condemn group difference too quickly or paint it with too broad a brush.[29] Group identity, along just the dimensions mentioned, has its positive aspects as well as its negative ones.[30] Identifying oneself as an Afro-American, as a woman, as a Jew, etc., can enhance self-worth and self-development while providing "a standpoint from which to criticize prevailing institutions and norms."[31]

A theory of injustice does not deny the "positivity of group identity," as Young calls it. It applauds a vision of a "democratic cultural pluralist" world where "there is equality among socially and culturally differentiated groups, who mutually respect one another and affirm one another in their differences."[32] The theory of injustice proposed here has a far more limited task. It condemns the negativity of group identity, primarily those externally imposed aspects of group identity that cause or set the conditions for social suffering. Certain forms of suffering have a firm connection with the social in the sense that social stratification helps to create a greater vulnerability to suffering. The external social grouping of an individual because of skin color, facial features, body type, or name helps to establish conditions of vulnerability.

Susan Estrich, a white, identified her rapist as a black man she did not know, a "crow" in the police social stratification scheme.[33] Her skin color helped to make her rape "real" (as distinguished from a technical or simple rape); his skin color helped to make him more vulnerable to prosecution. According to Estrich, "white women are not required to resist black men, but black women are."[34] As this example demonstrates, social stratification affects vulnerability to suffering.[35]

So, the physical, the psychological, and, of course, the social forms of suffering have social aspects. When group status has set the conditions of vulnerability to physical, psychological, and social suffering, the ingredients are in place for social injustice. At this stage, the analysis has highlighted the sociopolitical cause of and the suffering due to injustice. Now let us turn to the response of powerlessness.

POWERLESSNESS

A focus on injustice forces the negative to the foreground. Emphasizing the negative runs against certain currents of debate within political theory. Instead of concentrating on power, empowerment, and community, the theory of injustice pays closer attention to their opposites—powerlessness, disempowerment, and negative community. Injustice forces the cameras in the direction of the negative, constructing a different research agenda than the one set for a theory of justice. To explore this more fully consider the theories of power and contrast them with the phenomenon of powerlessness.

Lukes developed a highly influential classification of power involving three dimensions.[36] A one-dimensional view conceives of power in terms of the actual decision-making process.[37] Taking democracy and voting as nearly synonymous, many discussions of democracy focus on decision making.[38] Those who succeed at the polls wield the power.

Yet, this focus assumes a limited view of power, for decision making represents only a small portion of the dynamics of power. A two-dimensional view broadens the one-dimensional one so as to include covert ways of affecting decision-making.[39] For example, power manifests itself not only in the actual decision-making process but also in other nondecision areas such as agenda setting, normally controlled by the leaders of an organization. Those who control the items that appear on the agenda certainly exercise some degree of power.

The three-dimensional view, favored by Lukes, expands power one step further. While the actual observable decision process (one-dimensional) as well as the more covert agenda setting (two-dimensional) are important, Lukes claims that power operates at even more insidious levels that have little immediate connection with conscious decision making. "The bias of the system can be mobilized, recreated and reinforced in ways that are neither consciously chosen nor the intended result of particular individuals' choices."[40] A three-dimensional analysis of power includes the "many ways in which *potential issues* are kept out of politics, whether through the operation of social forces and institutional practices or through individuals' decisions."[41] The third dimension of power operates at the level where covert activities keep issues away from decision-making forums. The question as to whether or not to place certain items on the agenda never gets asked in the third dimension.

As an example of the third dimension of power Lukes cites Crenson's 1971 study of urban responses to the air pollution crisis. United States Steel effectively kept the issue from decision-making forums by not addressing the issue in Gary, Indiana. The political institutions of Gary, dominated by U.S. Steel, promoted a selective perception and articulation of social problems that excluded air pollution. U.S. Steel exercised power over the citizens of Gary by making them believe that something that is really harmful to them was not actually so. Therefore, power operates on three dimensions: formal decision making, agenda setting, and belief formation.

In each dimension power is characterized as a dyadic relationship between two entities *A* and *B*. Wartenberg offers a trenchant criticism of power as a dyadic relation.[42] According to Wartenberg, power often exists beyond multiples of two. *A* may well exhibit power over *B* but only with the aid of *C* and others. Moreover, power has spatial and temporal dimensions overlooked by the formulation of it as a dyadic relation. Power exists throughout a spatial field. Power does not confine itself to the space between two agents. Power often reverberates throughout a social field, affecting and being affected by a number of structures and agents. And it does not simply appear as an episode; power often has an ongoing, recurrent dynamic to it.

Powerlessness may seem to simply reside on the opposite side of the coin from power. Using the original dyadic formulation, *A* has power over *B*. Therefore, *B* is powerless with respect to *A*. Now apply Wartenberg's analysis of power to powerlessness. The dyadic relationship does not adequately capture powerlessness. An individual may well be powerless not simply in relationship to a specific individual but also relative to a number of individuals and institutions. Rephrasing Wartenberg's formulation of power in terms of powerlessness, an agent's powerlessness alters the social space for acting that is occupied by social agents who have power over her.[43] Similarly, powerlessness does not simply manifest itself in a single instance. Rather, powerlessness persists over time.

Powerlessness persists over space as well as over time. Powerlessness often slithers along beneath a network of situations. If found in education, powerlessness will probably also be found in employment and housing. One reinforces the other, creating an interconnectedness of disadvantaged conditions.

The picture provided thus far paints powerlessness with far clearer strokes than an accurate representation seems to warrant. A messy fingerpainting, without a power focal center, more accurately depicts powerlessness. For powerlessness takes its toll even in the absence of another with power. Powerlessness arises in the context of discipline, opinion, custom, culture, etc.[44] It finds its most parasitic niche internally, with the powerless thinking and feeling themselves unworthy.

Powerlessness can operate at a psychological level through the use of language. An adult woman called "girl" or an adult black male called "boy" can internalize that label in a way that would effectively mold subsequent action. Power can manifest itself internally as well as externally. An individual or a group may act or not act according to how an external threat is perceived or misperceived. The internalization may or may not be conscious. The symbol of power as the big boot stamping on the helpless individual paints a very incomplete and misleading picture of the forces of powerlessness at work.

Powerlessness has its own dynamic; it does not need the immediate stimulus of power in order to manifest itself. Powerlessness can operate as a malaise that hovers over an entire group of people. It can take the form of self-destructiveness. Socially disadvantaged groups often engage in self-destructive behavior, as exemplified by drug use among urban blacks. Powerlessness, ironically, can also invoke power in the form of rage, where an individual inflicts harm on another, often innocent, victim. Paradoxically, the powerless often exhibit a simultaneous fear and envy of the powerful: "The native is an oppressed person whose permanent dream is to become the persecutor."[45]

Powerlessness makes up an important component of injustice. The powerful can certainly suffer at the hands of an external sociopolitical agent, thereby incorporating the first two ingredients of injustice. Yet, a reluctance to label their affliction as a case of injustice seems justified, since the powerful, by definition, lack the third ingredient of injustice, powerlessness. The injustice of a situation seems to reside not only in the victim's suffering but also in the victim's not fighting back, especially if the victim's powerlessness can be traced to factors that the victim has little control over, such as group stereotyping.

Injustice, then, consists of a victim's suffering that humans could have or should have done something to avoid and that the victim did not avert, in part, because of her or his powerlessness. Social injustice includes those instances of injustices linked to group identity.

DEMOCRACY AND INJUSTICE

For Shklar, the relationship between democracy and injustice is one of democracy providing the forum to allow victims of injustice to express their grievances.[46] Victimology recommends democratic responses such as providing victims with compensation, restitution, and social services for the wrongs that have been suffered. However important it is to listen to complaints of victims in a democracy, the relationship between democracy and injustice operates at an even more fundamental level. Before unearthing the more fundamental connections between democracy and group injustice, attempts to minimize the tie between democracy and injustice deserve some mention.

Democracy may seem to have relatively little connection to injustice, except insofar as democratic institutions establish just procedures. On a proceduralist account injustice consists of unfair procedures. At best, democracy guarantees a fair set of procedures.[47] Beyond the set of procedures, democracy does not make any substantive claims.

Yet, injustices may well arise with respect to differing groups' access to the procedural mechanisms. Democracy would then have an immediate concern about injustices that might prevent group access to the political process. Gerrymandering blacks out of access to political power through the electoral process exemplifies the interface between democratic procedures and group injustice.

Any democratic theory should address the welfare of social groups as well as that of the individual. Physical and psychological torture of individuals at the hands of the state characterizes tyranny, the antithesis of democracy. Any democratic system must address and redress injustices perpetrated on individuals. The protection afforded the individual in a democracy should not swamp the importance of group injustice. Democracy involves constructing institutional structures for governance among individuals.

Nevertheless, democracy also involves establishing means for governance between groups. Even the etymology of the word *democracy* shows the group aspect of democracy. One root of *democracy* is *deme*, the geopolitical units established by the Greek Cleithenes in order to begin to break up and thereby equalize the tribal powers in the Athenian state. Cleithenes wanted to prevent certain tribal groups from amassing too much power. Historians generally label the way Cleithenes redrew the political boundaries between groups as a democratic response. Since its inception in the Athenian city-state democracy, group status has been a democratic concern.

Democracy involves at least three key elements: citizenship, freedom, and rule. As demonstrated below, each element independently connects injustice to democracy.

DEMOCRACY, CITIZENSHIP, AND POLITICAL CAUSES

Democracy entails citizenship. Even the most confining sense of democracy allows for participation of those individuals annointed as citizens. A democratic theory must address the political causes of injustice, particularly to the extent that the political causes of injustice undermine an individual group member's capacity for citizenship. Ascribing a political cause to injustice means that something could have been done about the cause since, at some point, the cause was by human design. It also means that something political could possibly be done about the injustice once the political cause has been revealed.

Minimally, democracy involves the freedom to participate in the activities of ruling. Democracy has a close negative link to social injustice in that one of the consequences of social injustice is the exclusion of certain groups from citizenship. Democracy should not tolerate the wholesale exclusion of certain groups from rule. South Africa under apartheid did not deserve the honorific title of democracy, simply because the state excluded otherwise deserving groups from participation. The exclusion of blacks from the activities of the state in South Africa represented a flagrant case of social injustice, complete with political causes, social suffering, and powerlessness. Other cases of social injustice are not as blatant, but to the extent that they involve the effective exclusion of groups from the *polis*, they constitute a major democratic concern.[48]

The de jure (formal, political) exclusion of blacks from the South African *demos* presents a relatively easy case for connecting democracy to social injustice. Other forms of (primarily de facto) exclusion— economic, social, etc.—operate at a level that seems removed from the immediate grasp of democracy. The critical issue is the extent to which the forms of exclusion are convertible to de jure, political exclusion.

Even if other forms of exclusion connect directly to the political, it seems that some groups do not deserve inclusion within the *demos*, and therefore their status should not concern a democracy, at least immediately. Robert Dahl, a leading contemporary democratic theorist, arrives, after considerable analysis, at the following principle of inclusion: The *demos* must include all adult members of the association, except transients and persons proved to be mentally defective.[49] According to Dahl, the *demos* should exclude children, aliens, and the mentally defective. These groups should not be allowed to vote, etc., since they do not meet minimum standards of competency. While Dahl would not countenance any harm to individual members of these groups, the group harm would not occupy the attention of democratic theory, even though it might preoccupy a theory of justice (or, in my terms, a theory of injustice). Hence, following Dahl's analysis here, democracy and injustice begin to part company.

Dahl's inclusion principle holds as long as the concepts of competency and citizenship remain unchallenged. However, competency does not stand as a wholly neutral, objective, static standard, as history proves. "The category of incompetent persons once included married women and sailors and—for some purposes—aliens, persons born out of wedlock, servants, wards, Jews, Quakers, villains, monks, clergy, excommunicants, lepers, and civil servants."[50] A democracy should always remain open to having its citizenship exclusions challenged.

Just as we should send up a red flag of caution when incompetency attaches to certain groups, so the notion of citizenship remains open to challenge.[51] Citizenship is often narrowly confined to acts of voting. As soon as nonvoting activities, such as attempts to influence government in other ways, come under the banner of citizenship, then more groups, including children, may qualify. However, even given a narrowing of citizenship to voting and admitting the incompetency of certain groups does not foreclose the issue. While members of Dahl's category of "mental defectives" may not have the competency to vote, democratic theory does not thereby preclude representatives of the mentally defective from voting for them. Whatever the many problems that would confront this scheme, it does at least illustrate the need for a democratic theory to address group injustice. Injustices inflicted upon a group do not lie outside of the purview of democratic theory simply because the democracy has deemed the group to be noncitizens because of their alleged incompetency.

DEMOCRACY, FREEDOM, AND SOCIAL SUFFERING

Democracy might seem to have little connection with the prevention of suffering, except, by some accounts, for the link between a democratic system of governance and the well-being of its citizens. However, democracy has a direct link to social suffering, particularly to the extent that suffering can be said to be social. Democratic theory needs to address the type of thwarting of an individual's interest that can be traced to that individual's group identity. Social suffering affects—positively and negatively—the group member's ability to democratically participate. Social suffering may actually mobilize a group politically. However, the need for group mobilization indicates that there is something amiss with the democratic structure as it stands.

Social injustice seems to reside largely in the social realm, as the name implies, and democratic theory appears to operate in the political sphere. However, the social and the political can be linked. To illustrate the importance of the social-political overlap consider one of Japan's major minority groups, the *burakumin*, who perform laboring tasks other Japanese refuse to engage in. In Japan, few formal political mechanisms exist for excluding the *burakumin* from political activity. In 1871, the Meiji government formally abolished the caste system that treated the *burakumin*, easily identified as those residing in a specific area, the *buraku* (the wrong *deme*), within each community, as the lowest on the social hierarchy. Yet, in 1992 strong social forces persist in sharply curtailing the effective political participation of the *burakumin*, who rate well above the national average for unemployment, birth defects, alcoholism, etc.[52] The social suffering of groups like the *burakamin* should be a primary concern of any democratic theory. A democracy must politicize certain forms of social suffering.

If the spotlight goes from the excluded groups to the included ones, another connection between democracy and injustice appears. Democracy has to do with how citizens, in the narrow sense of those who can vote, treat other groups. Any moral system should address how one group treats another. No one group should treat another group unjustly. This may seem to be within the purview of social ethics and not of democratic theory. Yet, the mistreatment of one group by another can have serious repercussions for a democracy. Citizenship carries responsibilities with it, one of which would be not to use the power associated with citizenship to inflict suffering on other groups, particularly those with less power. And if the mistreatment results in the mistreating group attaining political power at the expense of the mistreated group, a democratic concern is created.

DEMOCRACY, RULE, AND POWERLESSNESS

Democracy involves rule by the people. Powerlessness undermines an individual's and, sometimes, an entire group's ability to participate in ruling activities. The powerlessness associated with social injustice, that is, powerlessness related to group membership, seriously undermines democracy in the following manner. Democracy can accept powerlessness as long as it has some degree of fluidity. Different organized groups attain power while others lapse into states of powerlessness at different times. Witness the rise and fall of organized labor in the United States and Britain. At one time, organized labor commanded a relatively high degree of power when compared to management. Today, its power has devolved to a rather low ebb. Any democracy would welcome the fluctuating power dynamics between groups.[53]

However, when the powerlessness of a group becomes deeply entrenched, then democracy should take notice. When group powerlessness cuts across generations, when it becomes an inescapable and effectively defining feature of the group, it should receive top priority on the democratic agenda. At that point powerlessness no longer can be fairly characterized as part of the give and take of politics.

Democracy needs to address political causes of social suffering that result in entrenched group powerlessness. Democracy, in effect, must confront the problems of social injustice. As the discussion has shown, a great deal of the linkage between democracy and social injustice depends upon another tie, that is, that between the political and the social.

CONCLUSION

The various political theories of justice may try to deal with the problems of injustice, but political theory needs to confront injustice head-on if it expects to make any progress. Political theory must directly confront the many forms of human misery. Injustice provides political theory with that opportunity. By turning directly to injustice, political theory will find it to have a different character from its close kin, justice. The simple framework of cause, effect, and response provides the beginning tools for unraveling the complexities of injustice.

Paradoxically, by emphasizing the negative, a theory of injustice brings out the positive. The human dimension of the cause and effect of injustice places it in the realm where something can be done about it. The powerlessness of others can well lead to the humanitarian use of power by others. Perhaps through a better understanding of what wrongs infect the world, we can begin building the rights.

A full-blown theory of injustice needs many more pieces than I have provided. I have developed an important section—the social or group aspect of injustice. When the cries for democratic reform in other countries, such as those in Central and Eastern Europe, go out, the call for the eradication of social injustice should rise to an equally audible level. Democratic theory needs to fully address group status, abroad and at home.

"Thus the sense of injustice equips a human being to increase progressively the ambit of his own career and to survive and grow in an expanding community of experience. Without it, he is locked in the walls of his psychic cell; with it he can become a spiritual congener."[54] Perhaps nothing quite as grandiose follows from the study undertaken in this paper. Given the tentative nature of many of the conclusions and the exploratory focus of much of the paper, the study may not deserve the title "theory." If injustice takes on a new importance, if the study helps remove some human misery, then the project has been worthwhile.

6

Feminist Legal Critics: The Reluctant Radicals

PATRICIA SMITH

Feminist legal criticism began not as a radical critique, but as a liberal argument for the universal application of traditional legal categories.[1] The early campaigns for universal suffrage are the first obvious examples. The arguments for women's suffrage were radical only in the limited sense that they tended to restrict traditional patriarchal power and to equalize the political power of women in a very limited way. Women's suffrage was in that sense socially radical, but this fact was hardly recognized at the time. That is, giving women the vote was not widely expected to change the social, legal, or political situation of women in any radical way at all.

And conceptually, the arguments for women's suffrage were not radical in any sense; they were liberal. It was not necessary for them to be radical. This was because of an interesting contradiction between universal liberal rhetoric and patriarchal social structures that depended for its resolution on ultimately unsustainable factual assumptions about the differences between the basic nature of men and women. These assumptions were explicitly built into law in the form of overt prohibitions against the participation of women in various aspects of public life.

In the case of voting, for example, the prohibition against women voting was most generally based on the view that women were incapable of understanding political issues. Incompetence (along with danger, including moral danger) has been the most common argument throughout all of history against women doing almost everything. The incompetence argument has struck contemporary feminists as ironic in the face of apparently powerful counterexamples, such as Cleopatra and

73

Queen Elizabeth, to name only two powerful female leaders who seemed to understand not only political issues but political strategy quite as well as any man. But human beings have never allowed powerful but inconvenient counterexamples to stand in the way of powerful and convenient theories, and we still do not. We call them exceptions, and early political thinkers called them exceptions too. Queens didn't count. But eventually, as women gradually became more generally educated, the exceptions overpowered the rule of incompetence as to voting, and the prohibition was overcome. This development was based on a liberal rather than a radical view. The liberal view is that all human beings are presumptively entitled to equal treatment, or equality before the law. Eighteenth-century political rhetoric speaks this way about human rights, often referred to as the "rights of man." Now, the fact is that a significant portion of the human population was excluded from these "human" rights. Apparently you had to prove you were human. Native Americans, Chinese immigrants, and African-American slaves had no more rights than women; and the justification was that these groups of individuals were different. (What they were different from was left unspecified, but the assumption was that they were different from the norm, which was taken as given, and which in this country had the characteristics of white, male, heterosexual Christians of European heritage.) The presumption of equality was overridden when it came to the rights of others or did not apply to them because of "intrinsic" differences of race and sex.

Thus, the great liberal debate of the nineteenth and twentieth centuries has been over who gets included in the ranks of personhood, citizenship, and humanity. Over time the circle was expanded to include more and more groups that had previously been considered unfit for rights: non-property owners, working men, different nationalities, different races, and finally even women. In all of these cases the decision to include these groups was based on the conclusion that differences that were previously thought significant were not significant after all. For purposes of law it was decided that differences between the excluded groups and the included group were largely irrelevant. What never changed was the norm—the standard of evaluation or the standard of comparison. That standard was based on the status quo founded in the assumptions of those in power. The standard was never questioned because it was assumed to be necessary, neutral and universal—simply a description of the world. Thus, the great liberal debate was over which classes of people are factually or materially (as opposed to morally) equal. If you could prove (or convince those in power) that you were materially equal (that is, psychologically, dispositionally, and intellectually equal to the norm), then and only then were you entitled to formal equality or equality before the law.

That was the forum entered by liberal feminists, and it is in fact the forum of greatest advance in the cause of women's rights. One thing that shows is that much of the liberal ideal is correct—most differences between groups of people should be considered irrelevant to law. But in recent decades women have discovered that the liberal program has certain serious limitations, and that discovery has led many feminist to a more radical evaluation of law and to the greatest intellectual contribution that feminists have made to legal analysis, namely the critique of traditional discriminatory norms. Nowadays, feminists are asking why, as a matter of justice, those in power are entitled to formulate standards that favor themselves by which to measure all others. As a matter of power this is easily understood. As a matter of justice it is quite puzzling. The answer to the puzzle is that the norms formulated by those in power are not characterized as favoring themselves, but as neutral descriptions of necessary features of the world. So the current challenge for feminist scholars is to show how norms traditionally considered neutral are actually biased. The feminist critique of equal protection law provides the clearest illustration of both the liberal approach and its limits, while some recent work of feminist legal critics in this area and others demonstrates the new and radicalized challenge feminism now presents to previously unexamined discriminatory legal norms. In the next two sections I consider each of these to illustrate the development of feminist legal analysis as a certain form of radical legal critique.

The Evolution of Sex Discrimination in Equal Protection Law

The 1950s and 1960s marked the first serious consideration among the American people of the possibility that a legal system overall might be biased against an entire class of people, and in particular an entire race of people. (Of course, the Marxists had been making the class argument for years, but it had very little impact in the United States.) With the struggle for civil rights for American blacks came the realization that law itself was at least sometimes used systematically to disadvantage an entire group with no apparent justification, because by the 1960s it had become embarrassing to argue that blacks are not human beings, or not human "in the relevant sense."

It is interesting that it took more than a decade for any serious analogies to be drawn between the legal treatment of blacks and the legal treatment of women, but at least by the 1970s effective arguments were being made that sexism was in some sense analogous to racism. In 1971 the Supreme Court struck down for the first time a sex-based classification as a violation of the equal protection clause of the Fourteenth

Amendment.[2] The arguments made in this case and others of the time were analogous to the liberal arguments being made against race discrimination. For example, in 1973 ACLU counsel Ruth Bader Ginsberg argued in *Frontiero v. Richardson* that sex-based classifications, like racially based classifications, should be recognized as constitutionally suspect on three grounds. First, historically women have been subjugated and restricted as a class. Second, women ought to be judged on their individual merits rather than on the basis of stereotypes that are often inaccurate, and even if accurate in general may be inaccurate as applied to a particular individual. (In other words, if an individual woman meets the standard norm she ought not to be eliminated by a blanket prohibition against women as a class.) Third, sex is an immutable characteristic that often bears no relation to the ability to perform or contribute.[3]

Thus, the typical argument for the advancement of women's rights in the early 1970s was the liberal argument that challenged the dominant power to make good on its universal claims for impartiality and justice by opposing historical oppression, recognizing the value of individuality, and avoiding the individual unfairness of frequently inaccurate stereotypes. This argument worked well initially, at least in blatant cases of overt discrimination, and well it should since it employs the dominant ideology of the classical liberal tradition, which is central to western legal thought. However, it did not take long for problems to crop up.

Since the basis of sex discrimination claims was the traditional idea of similarly situated persons being differentially treated on irrelevant grounds, the Court saw no basis for deciding cases in which persons were not similarly situated. Thus, when *Roe v. Wade* was decided shortly after *Frontiero*, the woman's right to choose abortion was based on the right to privacy, with no mention of a foundation in equal protection law based on sex.[4] Similarly, when mandatory unpaid maternity leaves for schoolteachers were challenged in *Cleveland Board of Education v. LaFleur*, the Court avoided the sex discrimination claim by striking down the policy on other grounds.[5] Having thus hemmed itself into an analysis of sex discrimination based only on the differential treatment of similarly situated persons, when the Court was faced squarely and unavoidably with the sex discrimination claims of pregnant women in *Geduldig v. Aiello* in 1974, it reached the stunning conclusion that discrimination based on pregnancy does not involve a sex-based classification.[6] *Geduldig* does not represent one of the Court's shining hours. It generated an enormous wave of critical commentary. The extension of the reasoning in *Geduldig* to a Title VII case prompted a swift amendment (the Pregnancy Disability Act) by Congress, repudiating the Court's reasoning. And the Court itself in more recent decisions has backed away from this holding, though it has not changed its general rationale for sex discrimination under the equal protection clause.[7]

The problems caused by the general rationale that bases a discrimination claim solely on the differential treatment of similarly situated persons show that it cannot deal with questions of fair treatment where differences are real. There is something so obviously wrong with the idea that where differences are real equal protection of the law cannot apply, that a raft of critical commentary has been generated which has led to a more radical feminist critique of law. What feminists have realized is that equal protection law itself, while claiming to be neutral, in fact assumes a male standard of what is normal. For example, the average working woman will be pregnant twice during her working career. Pregnancy is abnormal only for a working man. Thus, the standard of normality that discounts pregnancy for working persons is male. The question, of course, is why should that be the standard?

Christine Littleton has summarized the feminist critique of current equality analysis in the following three points that demonstrate its male bias. First, it defines as beyond its scope precisely those issues that women find crucial to their concrete experience as women (such as pregnancy). Second, it construes difference (which is created by the relationship of women to particular, contingent social structures, such as home and work responsibilities) as natural (that is, unchangeable and inherent) and as located solely in the woman herself (women are naturally domestic). Third, it assumes (without evidence) the gender neutrality of social institutions, as well as the notion that practices must distinguish themselves from "business as usual" in order to be seen as unequal.[8]

More briefly put, equality analysis is biased against women in three respects: (1) it is inapplicable once it encounters a "real" difference from men; (2) it locates the difference in women, rather than in relationships; and (3) it fails to question the assumption that social institutions are gender neutral, and that women and men are therefore similarly related to those institutions.

This analysis made many feminists acutely aware of the arbitrariness of norms and of the fact that the inability of the courts to deal with sex discrimination in many cases is directly related to the inability to evaluate biased norms. And some feminists reasoned that if the liberal presumption of neutral legal processes retards the ability to evaluate norms as biased, then the liberal approach is sharply limited in its ability to correct systematic injustice, such as that which grows out of systematic patriarchal norms.

THE DEVELOPMENT OF FEMINIST LEGAL CRITIQUE AS RADICAL REFORM

Feminists have recognized that a significant part of law is the legitimation of the dominant ideology and that a significant part of the dominant ideology of most societies is patriarchal. This is the focus of some recent feminist legal critique. It is the embodiment of the observation that norms are often systematically biased in ways that reinforce the subordination of women to men by assuming a male standard of what is normal, or a male perspective of what is real, and then entrenching these assumptions by characterizing them as neutral. A number of feminists have developed this position in a variety of ways.

Perhaps the best known are the views of Catharine MacKinnon. In a recent book, MacKinnon sets out a radical feminist thesis of law and jurisprudence.[9] She is concerned with the transformation of belief into reality. Law, she points out, is a crucial factor in that transformation. Virtually all societies, she notes, are organized in social hierarchies that subordinate women to men on the basis of sex, as well as subordinating certain people to others on the basis of race and class. These facts of social organization which institutionalize social power are embodied in the organization of states as law. That is, through law, social domination is made both legitimate and invisible. It becomes reality—just the way things are. Liberal legalism or positivist jurisprudence buries the embodiment of patriarchal dominance even further by insisting that the proper domain of jurisprudence is descriptive, not evaluative or normative. As she puts it:

> Liberal legalism [i.e., legal positivism] is thus a medium for making male dominance both invisible and legitimate by adopting the male point of view in law at the same time as it enforces that view on society.... Through legal mediation, male dominance is made to seem a feature of life, not a one-sided construct imposed by force for the advantage of a dominant group. To the degree it succeeds ontologically, male dominance does not look epistemological: control over being produces control over consciousness.... Dominance reified becomes difference. Coercion legitimated becomes consent.... In the liberal state, the rule of law—neutral, abstract, elevated, pervasive—both institutionalizes the power of men over women and institutionalizes power in its male form.[10]

There are many variations on this theme. Quite a number of feminists have suggested that legal standards often uncritically reinforce social disadvantages imposed on women. For example, Deborah Rhode[11] and Christine Littleton[12] have both suggested moderate versions of the radical thesis that recognize the need to address structural problems of patriarchy that entrench inequality, but argue for addressing them in terms of disadvantage rather than domination. Both are examples of feminist theories that call for accepting diversity in all its forms, using law to ensure that diversity is not penalized. Both require the equal acceptance of cultural differences and concentrate on eliminating the unequal consequences of sex differences, whatever their origin or nature. One of the attractive features of this approach is that it makes no particular assumptions about the intrinsic psychological nature of men or women. It does not presume that we can know what the intrinsic differences or similarities might be, or what the sexes would be like if social conditioning were different. It holds only that no cultural position should be penalized—it should not be a disadvantage to be one sex or race or nationality rather than another. The idea, as Littleton puts it, is to embrace diversity and make difference costless.

In another interesting proposal from a rather different direction, Nadine Taub and Wendy Williams[13] have suggested one way in which the courts could formulate in legal doctrine the ideal that difference should not be penalized. Taub and Williams advocate the expansion of what the Court has called the *Griggs* doctrine of discriminatory impact.[14] Very generally speaking, the *Griggs* doctrine says that if a norm or practice has a disproportionate impact on a suspect class (such as a race or sex) then that norm or practice is subject to reevaluation. Unfortunately, the Court has chosen to restrict rather than expand the *Griggs* doctrine, but suggestions like that of Taub and Williams show that equal protection could be made an effective device for the protection of disadvantaged classes if the dominant class saw fit to develop it in that direction.

Whether these critiques are formulated in terms of disproportionate impact, the domination of women or their disadvantage, all represent a shift from liberal claims for inclusion in traditional norms to a radical critique of those norms as fundamentally biased. Martha Minow[15] has generalized this position to a critique of the inability of courts (and particularly the Supreme Court's inability) to deal with the problem of differences in a pluralistic society. Unexamined assumptions create what Minow calls dilemmas of difference for the courts. Minow points out that the Supreme Court is often faced with the apparent dilemma of reinforcing disadvantage no matter which choice it makes. If it recognizes a disadvantage so as to correct it, it may reinforce stereotypes that perpetuate it. On the other hand, if the Court ignores the difference so as to counter the stereotypes associated with it, then there is no way to address the disadvantage attached to the difference.[16] This is a serious problem for all classes that are systematically disadvantaged, since the "neutral" (that is, disinterested and detached) application of biased standards simply reproduces systematic disadvantage, thus calling into question the very meaning of neutrality. Minow suggests that courts could defuse these dilemmas by recognizing the unexamined assumptions that generate them.

First, she points out, we commonly assume that differences are intrinsic rather than relational or comparative. Women are considered intrinsically different rather than different as compared to men. Jews are intrinsically different rather than different as compared to Christians, and so forth. As Minow points out, men are as different from women as women are from men; Christians are as different from Jews as Jews are from Christians. The question is why the norm should be male and Christian? Second, we typically adopt an unstated norm as a point of reference in evaluating others. This norm is not neutral or inevitable, but it seems so when left unstated and unexamined. It is taken as given rather than recognized as chosen. It is assumed universal rather than recognized as particular. Third, we treat the perspective of the person doing the judging as objective, even though in fact no one can see fully from someone else's point of view or without a point of view. Fourth, we assume that the perspective of those being judged is either irrelevant or already covered by the supposedly objective and universal perspective of the judge. Fifth, it is assumed that the status quo—the existing social and economic arrangement—is natural, neutral, inevitable, uncoerced, and good. So departures from the status quo risk non-neutrality and interference with individual freedom. Minow believes that making these assumptions explicit will require judges to examine the foundations of their own perspectives, which are often not recognized as perspectives at all. Once recognized as perspectives, the views must be defended as compared to other perspectives rather than being erroneously assumed as universal.[17]

The above examples illustrate that many feminists today recognize that a significant part of law is the legitimation of the status quo (which is to say, the dominant power or ideology) and that a significant part of the dominant ideology of our society (and most others) is patriarchal. Thus, standard traditional norms must be examined and defended in terms of the interests of all people rather than assumed as inevitable and neutral.

However, a fact that many feminists do not mention but most presume is that patriarchy is not the only or the entire dominant ideology of this society. Our society is also individualist, committed to justice and freedom, committed to the ideals of impartiality, the rule of law, and equality before the law. These are not patriarchal ideals as such.[18] They are universal, humanistic ideals. In fact, they are not particularly compatible with patriarchy; and this contradiction between what is often called liberal ideology (but what might be called humanist ideology) and patriarchy can still be exploited in the cause of justice for women.

That is, the contradiction between patriarchy and humanistic liberal ideals that are both embodied in Anglo-American law enables even radical feminists to advocate reform rather than revolution. Thus, even radical feminists are radical only in the sense of advocating far-reaching reforms. They need not advocate the overthrow of government, or even the amendment of the Constitution. On the other hand, a commitment to the elimination of patriarchy is a commitment to revolutionize fundamental social and legal institutions.

The view of Taub and Williams illustrates this clearly. On the one hand, the proposal they make is very moderate—a simple and reasonable extension of a doctrine already formulated by the Court and regularly used in one form in Title VII cases. In another respect the proposal is a radical one because the effect of it would be to counteract the disadvantages imposed on certain classes of people by social organization itself. Yet, the rationale is perfectly compatible with humanistic liberal ideals verbally expressed in the Anglo-American legal tradition for two hundred years.

Similarly, Minow's suggestions would have a radical impact on the process of judging itself, yet on the other hand, all she is really arguing is that those in power should be accountable to the point of examining their own assumptions. This is so reasonable a requirement that one wonders how anyone committed to rational thinking could argue against it. Certainly, liberals would not.

Even MacKinnon, one of the most radical of feminists, utilizes the distinction between humanistic liberal rhetoric and patriarchal practices. In her recent analysis of equality, MacKinnon argues that the law of equality provides a peculiar opportunity for challenging the inequality of law on behalf of women, since law does not usually guarantee rights to something that does not exist. Equality in law is understood formally, and so it is presumed that by and large women already have it. Many, if not most, formal legal barriers for women have been dismantled. Women can now own property, execute contracts, attend universities, and engage in businesses and professions without formal prohibition. But, as many feminists have observed, this formal equality does not eliminate informal discrimination, nor does it provide equal opportunity in fact. MacKinnon argues that it is up to feminists to make equality law meaningful for women by defining it in terms of the concrete experience of women's lives, and challenging the male forms of power that are affirmatively embodied as rights in law. MacKinnon recognizes that equality is not about character traits or even human nature. It is not about "sameness and difference," as it is so often construed, but about domination and subordination. Equality and inequality are about the distribution of power. To confront that distribution of power directly, recognizing it for what it is, and to remove the mask of legitimacy raised by its legalization is the critical task of feminist jurisprudence, according to MacKinnon.[19]

These positions recognize implicitly or explicitly that there are serious contradictions between the universal values that we profess and the patriarchal institutions that structure our lives. This is a consistent factor in feminist legal analysis that connects recent work with early liberal feminist views. But early liberal feminist criticism was effective only while it was directed at explicitly patriarchal legal doctrines. These patriarchal legal doctrines made the contradiction explicit and clear.[20]

However, feminists today recognize that the form of the contradiction has changed. It is no longer an explicit contradiction between two clearly articulated legal rules. At least much of the time the contradiction is now between two (or more) rather vaguely understood legal norms that are the embodiment of traditional social standards. Thus, traditional standards cannot simply be taken as given. Rebutting false claims of factual difference between men and women is not enough. The contradictions between universal values and patriarchal practices cannot be effectively utilized for freedom and justice for women until the bias of certain norms is recognized.

These problems are far from over, and a major aggravating factor in their solution is the common claim that they have already been solved.[21] I believe that the remaining problems can be usefully characterized in the form of two remaining hurdles.

The first hurdle is simply a development of the original liberal battle: how to keep the discrimination that used to come in overtly through the front door from sneaking covertly through the back door. Old stereotypes die hard, and despite our best efforts to combat unfounded and untestable assumptions about differences between men and women, these assumptions seem able to reinstitute themselves like chameleons in new forms.

The second hurdle is how to get those who occupy positions of power to see that the norms they use are, after all, just the norms they choose, and that many traditional norms in fact benefit men at the expense of women and/or reinforce traditional social arrangements that restrict the freedom of women. Negotiating this hurdle requires a more radical approach to challenging basic norms. Such an approach is not incompatible with classical liberal ideals of justice and equality, but it does set up serious tensions with traditional presumptions of neutral legal processes.

The case of *EEOC v. Sears*[22] provides a good example of the issues involved in the first hurdle. This case involved a Title VII class action lawsuit charging Sears Roebuck and Co. with employment discrimination against women in hiring and promotion. The charge was based on statistical evidence that women were greatly underrepresented in higher-paying commission sales positions although the pool of applicants was more or less equal, and lower-paying jobs were predominantly filled by women. This approach relied on a typical focus of Title VII class action suits which utilizes statistics that indicate a disproportionate impact from facially neutral practices as presumptive evidence of discrimination. In other words, if a disproportionate impact is shown, Title VII presumes that discrimination is the reason for it. This, then, shifts the burden of proof to the defendant to provide nondiscriminatory reasons for the differences shown by the statistics.

To meet this burden of proof, Sears argued successfully that women were not underrepresented in the high-paying commission sales jobs because of discrimination, but because women as a class really are not interested in such jobs.[23] Ironically, Sears used the language of certain feminist scholars to support its claim that women dislike competition and value good relationships more than money. According to this view, women tend to sacrifice monetary advancement for less stressful working conditions and more limited hours that enable them to meet their responsibilities at home. So disparities in high-paying jobs are not due to discrimination but to women's own choices. This argument was accepted by the court, even in the face of contradicting testimony from women who had actually applied to Sears for commission sales positions.[24]

Joan Williams[25] has done a good job of pointing out that this reasoning simply re-enshrines old stereotypes of women as passive, domestic, and self-sacrificing. These old stereotypes are powerful and entrenched. It is always easier to fall back into them than it is to get rid of them. What is particularly distressing about the *Sears* case is that it inserts sexist stereotypes into precisely the legislation that was enacted to counteract them. Even if the stereotypes are true as generalizations, Title VII was designed to protect those women who do not fit that generalization, specifically those women who applied for the commission sales positions at Sears. Sears simply discounted these women and so did the court. That is, Sears assumed that those women who applied for commission sales and supervisory positions did not really want those jobs. They were padding their applications to increase their chances of getting hired, it was claimed.[26] Since most women applied for low-level clerking positions, Sears reasoned, that must be what all women prefer. That outrageously invalid argument is the argument that the court accepted as the basis of its interpretation of Title VII. This will disadvantage all future claimants. Furthermore, if actual testimony cannot rebut the Sears argument that women are not interested in competitive work, how could any plaintiff overcome that argument on the part of any employer? One wonders how any woman can ever win a Title VII claim based on disproportionate impact again. Cases like *Sears* show how easy it is to go backward, even with regard to the old liberal argument that we are all human and are entitled to equal treatment based on our individual merits. We have far to go before men and women will be presumed equal, and discriminatory assumptions about the "intrinsic" differences in male and female disposition and intellect are overcome.

There are no easy examples of the issues connected with the second hurdle, because in the evaluation of traditional norms what seems normal is what everyone is used to, and that is the status quo. The challenge always carries the burden of persuasion, always seems at least initially less plausible than the norm, and that is true whether or not the norm is just.[27] Feminists have found that norms are most difficult to challenge where the differences (physical or social) between men and women are real, and where the interests of men and women are perceived to be at odds. In such cases it is the status quo itself that disadvantages women, and it cannot be corrected unless the norm is changed. This involves new evaluations at very fundamental levels.

Consider, for example, the formulation of harm or injury. What constitutes an injury is central to legal action. It has long been a truism that justice and law require interpersonal respect, at least to the extent that we may not intentionally harm, defraud, or interfere with the freedom of other individuals. We are not entitled to cause injury. Virtually all moral and legal theories agree that this is the core of interpersonal responsibility. One person's freedom ends with the freedom and bodily integrity of another. Any individual's rights are limited by the basic rights of all other persons. Thus, coercion, intimidation, fraudulent deception, and bodily injury are prohibited by justice and law without question. That is the settled core of our moral tradition, but it does not specify what counts as harm or injury, or what qualifies as coercion, intimidation, or deception at a level that can be prohibited.

Somehow injury does not apply the same way to women, at least with respect to men who are related to them or even who know them. If assault is prohibited, why are husbands so often not prosecuted for beating their wives? If exploitation is wrong, why are employers so often not prosecuted for pressuring their employees into sexual relations? If rape is illegal, why are men so often not prosecuted if they are acquainted with the women they coerce into sex? If bodily integrity is a fundamental right, how could decisions regarding pregnancy rest ultimately with anyone other than the woman whose body is involved? All of these are areas that involve real differences between men and women, and they are areas in which the interests of men and women can now be interpreted as possibly conflicting.

As Minow has pointed out, contrary to assumptions of universality, all law is formulated from a perspective. So we can hardly be surprised if it turns out to be the perspective of those who formulated it, which is to say, the perspective of powerful men—the traditional patriarchs. It is difficult to assume the perspective of someone else. It takes a level of self-awareness that is truly rare. Nor is it more common for people in power to recognize the limits of their own views and the value of understanding and accommodating the views of others.

Until almost the twentieth century, women were not considered to have interests or views of their own. Women were not independent or free. In fact, they were not separate individuals legally. A woman could not have an interest that conflicted with the interests of her husband or father. Thus, she could not be harmed or injured by her husband or father (unless he killed her). The man to whom she was related was responsible for her and in charge of her.

So it is hardly surprising that wife-beating was construed as discipline, which is not a harm. It is not surprising that rape, unlike any other crime, was defined from the perspective of the perpetrator rather than the victim. Nor is it surprising that until recently sexual harassment simply did not exist, and procreation (both in terms of contraception and abortion) was controlled by government rather than by women. Women did not have separate interests; their interests were defined by men, from the perspective of men, in terms of the interests of men, because that is who formulated the law. This was not a commitment of liberalism. It is not even compatible with liberalism. It was an assumption of patriarchy that was left unexamined because it was the norm (a) that women had no interests separate from their husbands or fathers, and (b) that the law should not intrude into family matters. The challenge for feminists is then how to change such norms and others like them, which have been taken as given—as normal—for hundreds or even thousands of years.

The very fact that such issues are now being addressed, that such topics are being publicly discussed is the first sign of social progress. Yet we have far to go before women are recognized as entitled to bodily integrity that cannot be coercively usurped by men who know them and by legislators who presume to define their interests. The great divide between the protection of women from strangers and the nonprotection of women from men who know them reflects old and deeply embedded notions of male supremacy, domination, and the ownership of women. Until recently these views were supported by overt acceptance of male authority and supremacy. Today, many people say that these old presumptions of patriarchy no longer hold. Today we say that women are entitled to determine their own physical integrity by their own voluntary choices.

Yet these abstract ideals have serious concrete limits. Powerful forces have mobilized to oppose reproductive freedom for women on the assumption that women are not entitled to make such choices. The physical integrity of women does not include the right to control their reproductive capacities. Pregnancy is not a harm; it is a blessing. Thus, the norm is still that women are essentially mothers, first and foremost. The choice not to be a mother (i.e., to be in actual control of one's reproductive capacities), while formally acknowledged in law, is still highly controversial and is flatly rejected by many. The long-standing commitment to individual autonomy is a fundamental norm of our society that has never been and still is not applied equally to men and women. That is because (a) men and women are different, so deciding what an equal commitment to autonomy means is not a simple matter; (b) autonomy was never considered important for women in the past; and (c) those who decided legal, moral, and religious policy about motherhood and procreation were not the same people who were subject to the disadvantages of such policies. So the fight over who should be in control of women's bodies is still far from settled.

And old patterns of social interaction based on norms that subordinate women are perpetuated, largely by denial and by blaming the victim. If a woman is raped or beaten not by a stranger but in the course of normal life, then she must have brought it on herself. If she is harassed by her employer she must have led him on. And anyway, date rape has to be rare. Wife battering is surely uncommon. Sexual harassment must be largely imaginary. We do not want to hear about these problems.

Statistical surveys clearly indicate that women are harmed much more often by men who know them than by any other cause. For example, 4 million women are battered in their homes in the United States each year. Women are harassed, beaten, raped, and killed by men who know them far more often than by strangers. Yet these offenses, with the exception of killing, are still largely unprosecuted. Why? Because we the people excuse the abuse of women as a form of control or an outlet for frustration ("If you can't beat your wife who can you beat?"). This behavior is a hangover from an earlier and more overtly sexist day, and we don't want to know about it. So we pretend that it is a rarity committed by a few outlaws like ordinary crimes. But it is not.[28]

The pervasiveness of these abusive practices attests to the worst features of the continuing sexism of our society. Old norms die hard. Physical coercion and violence remain an option for male domination in personal relations as a last resort. The more women struggle for freedom and equality, the more some men will respond with violence. The more women compete, the more they will be harassed by those who feel threatened or offended by the changing status quo.

And the failure to prosecute attests to the continuing sexism of our law.[29] This will not change significantly until traditional norms are changed that condone it. Until police and prosecutors, judges and juries recognize such injuries as serious harms and stop making excuses for them, women will not be protected. But police and prosecutors, judges and juries by and large reflect the attitudes of the general public.

So long as overpowering your date is not the same as raping a stranger, and beating your wife is not as serious as assaulting someone on the street, and pressuring your secretary into sex is just the way life is, and pregnancy is characterized by Supreme Court justices as an inconvenience, the physical integrity of women will not be determined by their own voluntary choices. Thus, many women today are still dominated by physical force and restrictive legislation, denied the most basic protections of justice by a society and a legal system that pretends that some physical coercion is not real harm, and in any case that women can avoid it by "proper behavior," by understanding their limits. Such a view is not compatible with the liberal commitment to freedom and equal treatment, as liberal feminists have argued for many years. It can only be made compatible by assuming the normative commitments of patriarchy as a fact of life. And that is not actually hard to do (in fact it is actually harder not to do) since patriarchal assumptions have set the standard of normal social relations, religious ideals, moral expectations, and legal standards for thousands of years. Patriarchy is the norm—or more accurately, it is an enormously complex network of norms. It is challenging those norms and that network that constitutes the radical agenda of modern feminists. It is an agenda that does not conflict with liberal values; it does not require overthrow of the government, or even amending the Constitution, but it does require the eventual transformation of our most fundamental institutions, including extensive legal reform.

7

Rethinking the Language of Law, Justice, and Community: Postmodern Feminist Jurisprudence

BRUCE A. ARRIGO

INTRODUCTION

In the postmodern age, speculation about women's ways of knowing has spawned some fascinating scholarship addressing our limited understanding of many important topics in social theory and practice. A brief review of the literature includes contributions on such issues as the feminine voice,[1] subjectivity,[2] mind,[3] and body.[4] Underscoring much of the research is the fundamental question of desire in language[5] and its corresponding link to sexual politics.[6]

Most recently, several groundbreaking studies have emerged that apply these insights in feminist philosophy and psychology to the areas of law and society,[7] legal theory,[8] and feminist jurisprudence.[9] Clearly, each project has demonstrated the vitality and versatility of postmodern feminist analysis. In addition, some works have extended the postmodern women's agenda to the realm of praxis[10] and critique.[11] These projects represent a concerted effort to comprehend more fully the dynamics of power, truth, and knowledge, and their inexorable connection to that desire in language, that *jouissance* that announces an *ecriture feminine*.[12]

Within the current scholarship on feminist sociolegal studies, forging a jurisprudence for and about women continues to be a source of debate. In particular, questions remain about the misogynous role that language assumes, invalidating feminine ways of knowing[13] and, consequently, denying women access to the juridico-linguistic communicative market.[14] Most significantly, critics contend that traditional "male speak" underpins the Anglo-American system of law and justice, producing a phallocentric discourse. It is precisely because women's ways of knowing are denied in the law that further theoretical examination on the nature of the feminine is required. Put another way, in order to establish a fundamental feminist jurisprudence, not only must the concepts of justice and law be deconstructed, but the conditions under which women engage in truth or sense-making must be explored.

The philosophical quest for feminist jurisprudence entails a criticism of the very tools utilized by legal scholars and practitioners in their assertions concerning the nature of truth. The essentialism of the legal method and its attendant features—boundary definition, defining relevance, and case analysis—must be abandoned because they are founded on a theory of the subject that carries with it a demand for a unitary morality. This project is a deliberate attempt to reframe and shift the analysis of jurisprudence away from legal positivism and to supplant it with a more meaningfully lived account of diverse and intimate situations. A search for ways of being that are as different from each other as possible is vital to dethroning law's normalizing power.

Elsewhere, I have referred to this model of jurisprudence as "experiential feminism."[15] This model destabilizes the essence of the masculine system of justice which celebrates the logical, rational, sequential, and, by its proponents' own deductive reasoning, therefore reliable and ethical form of judgments. The offering of an "experiential" feminism is not made here so much for purposes of determining which approach, as a recipe, more authentically interprets human experience. Instead, the aim is to acknowledge that the masculine code alone is insufficient and often inapplicable in rendering juridical decisions concerning the voice of women.

As a point of departure, a review of the writings of Michel Foucault and his symbiotic treatment of power/knowledge will ground our understanding of how each society presupposes a regime of truth.[16] His rejection of power operating on the basis of restrictive commandments or laws, colonized by the complex network of normalizing, disciplinary systems, helps to inform us of how our system of jurisprudence, in claiming to speak the truth, effectively discounts other discourses like experiential feminism. Carol Smart, moreover, contends that law's unique method and language extend into most aspects of social life, always remaining legal and retaining for itself the mantle of legal power.[17] This juridical imperialism is constituted through law's claim to truth manifested in its lofty vision of itself—even more striking than exercising power in concrete effects (judgments) is its ability to disqualify other nonlegal experiences or knowledge, or to relegate them to second-class status. This brings Smart to the issue of deconstructing jurisprudence. But where she opts to forgo grand theorizing and instead to pursue feminist postulates on specific laws (rape, pornography, child sexual abuse, etc.), challenging the core of jurisprudence is the aim of this paper.

As mentioned earlier, this concern entails a radical reconstitution of both justice and law, constructs now cast in phallocentric terms. Irigaray provides the first step toward a women's discourse that successfully disputes and displaces male-centered structures of both language and thought.[18]

By critiquing both Freudian and Lacanian psychoanalytic theory, which defines female sexuality in masculine meanings, Irigaray understands the feminine in terms of deficiency or atrophy or in its absence. Her poetic prescription for "coming out of" misogynous language, by which women are freed from masculine categories, signifies the birth of a feminine language that contains tremendous implications for the reformulation of knowledge in general and for the discipline of jurisprudence in particular. Irigaray's pronouncements ostensibly stand in opposition to Husserlian intersubjectivity, which posits that in order for truth to be "objective" it must not merely be personal or subjective but must be taken up in the same way that others experience it.[19] Additionally, what is universally "given" assumes that the human subject maintains a particular stance with respect to the world. It is this stance that Irigaray questions. Although something is given to the subject (language and thought), the attitude by which it is lived is undeniably male oriented. If this be so, how can an experiential feminism help to inform our understanding of juridical truth as intersubjective?

On a more pragmatic level, the insights of both Carol Gilligan and Catharine MacKinnon contextualize and legitimize the feminine experience in the areas of justice and law.[20] Each in her own way has exercised the power of revaluing and revalidating feminine discourse. Where Gilligan's construction of the development of ethical and moral values of women provides a theoretical framework for a feminine psychology, MacKinnon's rejection of male-dominated, politically conceived, hierarchical power structure anticipates a legal praxis that more genuinely represents the concerns of women. Finally, in returning to Foucault's methodology,[21] we learn that the eternal, unitary self is an illusion, a product of disciplinary practices and discourses like science and law. Uncertainty, indeterminacy, and multiplicity are the cornerstones of an ethic (systemic jurisprudence) that resists whatever form totalitarian power might take. His suggestion for an aesthetic of daily life offers some hope for a new order that does not itself become oppressive. When coupled with Murray's general, but compelling, description of the imagination's power to express discourse, especially through metaphorical, symbolic, and narrative modalities,[22] we discover that a feminist jurisprudence must construct alternative images that more authentically portray one's relationship to organized society.

This relationship, however, implies a reframing of community—one that acknowledges a necessary return to practices that are primitive, primary, and therefore healing to the human condition. A rediscovery of ritual, not law, constituted by neighbors, not judges, informs this "village" aesthetic as personally meaningful. The metaphors of experience and storytelling displace the language of rules and facts. A communal gathering of residents preempts the calculated courtroom trial. The concernful search for "authentic" justice replaces the mental exercise of legal manipulation.

Taken together, these authors (Smart, Irigaray, Gilligan, MacKinnon, Foucault, and Murray) make possible the deconstruction of our present system of jurisprudence. Indirectly, they also speak to the important issue of community and, as a consequence, allow for some insightful reconceptualization. In my effort to criticize the prevailing paradigm, I hope as well to marginalize its sovereign status rather than to reaffirm its exalted position. Clearly there are juridical themes that govern basic principles of justice, rights, freedom, and equity. It is to these themes, expressed through the legal method, that objection is raised. My critique is rooted in a particular appreciation of knowledge, and it is to that understanding that I now turn.

KNOWLEDGE AND POWER

Foucault draws a marked distinction between classical and contemporary theories of power. Although his interests are in the mechanisms of power rather than who regulates it, his analysis implies a class structure that rules out the functional use of this commodity for some. The established economic construction of power suggests that it is a juridical right. When a criminal breaks a law, the violator is punished. In this regard, power is oppressive and negative. Foucault contends, however, that society has become transformed. In the modern era the growth of new knowledges (epidemiology, psychology, criminology, forensics, etc.) has fostered the development of the disciplinary society. As a constellation of truths, this "modern episteme" brings with it alternative avenues by which people and their behavior are regulated. Rather than imposing retributive measures on norm violators, modes of surveillance need to be carefully implemented so that the individual becomes depathologized and normalized. The disciplinary systems or new technologies of medicine, education, psychology, and the like make possible this transformation of the spirit. Power, then, is inventive, technical, and productive. Its mechanisms forge dialectical resistances that produce new expressions of knowledge, which further enhance society's capacity to wield greater surveillances of control.

Foucault's insistence that truth does not exist without power and his rejection of the idea that power functions merely through restrictive laws refocus our attention on the complex disciplinary systems that dictate what particular truths or knowledges are accepted and esteemed. He asserts that these modern technologies of normalization will increasingly colonize traditional power, the outcome of which will be law's diminished force. In discussing the concept of truth, Foucault refers to the grouping of rules that separate the true from the false in which specific effects attach to the true. He is concerned with exposing what particular discourses claim to speak the truth, exercise power accordingly, and reaffirm that version of truth which society values. In a culture where respect is afforded science, scientific assertions are an exercise of power that reduce the merit of other knowledge claims (like belief and experience) as less rigorous and, therefore, less valid.

Law as a normalizing discipline only modestly fits into Foucault's analysis. It is not until Carol Smart that his theory concerning power-truth-knowledge is applied more fully in the area of jurisprudence.[23] Her contention that law possesses its own language, method, testing ground, and system of results distinguishes it from other disciplines. Although she is careful not to elevate it to the level of esteemed science, she accurately submits that law sets itself apart from other discourses, as does science.[24] In this way, law is master over other disciplines. Like science, law's claims to truth are indivisible from the exercise of its power. Through its legal method, law sets itself outside the social order, rendering sound, rational judgments concerning complex and contradictory life circumstances occurring within this arena. In this way, our system of jurisprudence functions as a force, believing that it has the power to right wrongs.

Smart rejects law's apparent omnipotence. She cites the adversarial system's inability to secure true findings of guilt or nonguilt because appellate courts frequently overrule lower courts' decisions. Moreover, law's claim to truth as a form of the expression of power disqualifies other knowledge that cannot fit into legal theorems. Common sense, everyday experience, intuition, feelings, etc., are routinely discounted because they cannot be adequately condensed into legal dictums. Entire fields of knowledge like psychology, sociology, anthropology, etc., are given lower-class status because they fail to meet the legal standard of juridical rigor. Her point is that we ascribe so much value to the discipline of jurisprudence that it does not matter if in practice cases are overturned, guilty persons go free, or that innocent persons are convicted.

Law's truth outweighs other truths. The principal culprit in this re-

alization is the legal method. Presumed to be neutral, it is this phenomenon which evades the feminist challenge. As Bottomley observes,
the question is not only whether the practice of law oppresses wom-
en's styles of existence and conversely privileges those of men, "but
whether the very construction . . . of legal discourse [and the] representation of the discourse in the academy . . . [are] the product[s] of
patriarchal relations at the root of society."[25] Smart recoils from any
deep and direct examination of the legal method, choosing to adopt
Mossman's position that it is "probably impervious to the feminist challenge."[26] This is surprising, especially since she admits that law can be
deconstructed at its point of origin, namely, law schools across the
country. In support of this position, Smart cites Stang Dahl and the
Women's Law Movement at the University of Oslo Law School.[27] Dahl's
work suggests a legal praxis that encourages the use of custom and
public opinion regarding law. Admittedly, this sanctions empirical (experiential) evidence about women and their understanding of intimate
situations as a mechanism for shaping law's role in society. Additionally, the juridical system becomes more grounded in the everyday experiences of people, relinquishing control of its own internal imperatives.
The problem with this approach, however, is that it maintains the ascendancy of the legal method. By her own admission, Dahl contends
that the prescribed methodology of legal doctrine should retain for
itself the tools of its craft.[28] Both Dahl and, because of her affinity for
Dahl's work, Smart succumb to the seduction of systemic law. Although
the Oslo paradigm promulgated by Dahl acknowledges the dilemma
with judge-dominated legal practice—that abstract norms are applied
to a particular case in which a judge must be persuaded in the rigidly
prescribed legal fashion—her model only further affirms the power of
the prevailing methodology. Ostensibly demoting the importance of
formal law (presenting cases before judges) by ignoring the heart of
its construction (legal method), Dahl focuses on law in practice. Arguing that major legislation and precedent law have little to no relevance
for the situation of women, she calls for a governmental, administrative impact in the areas of welfare benefits, the operation of private
law of maintenance, and the formulation of guidelines for decision
making at the level of bureaucratic operation. This strategy, encased
in a careful avoidance of legal method, amounts to altering the form
of juridical truth that is sought, but not its substance. What we are left
with is a constellation of legal practices pursued by feminists (money
law, housewives' law, and waged labor law), but on law's (and therefore a masculine) standard. Rather than demoting the pristine omnipotence of law's misogynously constructed status, Dahl's evasive strategy
enhances the purity of our juridical system's claim to truth and, by
extension, its unbridled power.

Smart's conclusion on Dahl's maneuvering is that feminism must sustain its challenge to law's power to define women in its terms. While Smart asserts that feminism has the power to contest prevailing subjectivity and to alter women's consciousness,[29] she settles for a new form of legal practice that maintains traditional methods of legal reasoning. I contend that much of her dilemma is based in the language and thought that limit our way of being to unitary dimensions, effectively prohibiting a genuine feminine discourse. This matter is dealt with extensively by Luce Irigaray in her accounts of female sexuality as multiplicity and of discourse's power to subordinate the feminine.

LANGUAGE AND THOUGHT

Irigaray posits that psychoanalytic discourse on female sexuality is the discourse of truth.[30] Like Foucault she acknowledges that this language system is an expression of power. In order to determine what models (and laws) feminine discourse occurs in, Irigaray returns to the writings of Freud. She retraces Freud's formulation of penis envy in which the little girl, in the beginning, is nothing but a little boy. Castration signifies for her an acceptance that she does not possess a male sex organ. She turns away from the mother, hates her, because she discovers that the mother does not have the valorizing organ the daughter believed the mother had. Not only is the mother rejected, so too are all women, including herself, and for the same reason (the lack of the phallus); and so she turns toward the father to possess what neither she nor any woman can: the penis. The desire to give birth to a child signifies, for a woman, the desire to possess finally the equivalent of the phallus.

This phallocentric theme pervades the writings of Jacques Lacan.[31] In his treatment of the castration complex and the symbolic order, Lacan contends that what is at issue is not so much the real organ (the penis) but the phallus as the signifier of desire. The locus of castration for the boy child must reside in the mother if the child is to flee from the imaginary domain of maternal desire and be returned to the law of the father, possessor of the phallic emblem.

Irigaray submits that the problem with such truth assertions is that woman herself is never of concern—"the feminine is defined as the necessary complement to the operation of male sexuality."[32] Moreover, she argues that female sexuality is never defined with respect to any sex but the masculine, "a sex which interprets sexual difference by giving *a priori* value to Sameness."[33] It is this Sameness that lays down the law. It is this Sameness that creates an economy that subjugates women. And it is this Sameness with its power of discourse that Irigaray disrupts.

In her discussion of woman and feminine pleasure, Irigaray maintains that if we subscribe to traditional conceptions, the lot for this sex is that of lack. Women exist in their absence of and desire for the sexual male organ. But this is foreign to a woman's intrinsic, natural pleasure—pleasure removed from the dominant phallic economy. Irigaray illustrates this point in her discussion of male versus female autoeroticism. For men some form of mediation is required: his hand, a woman's body, language. Women touch themselves all the time without the intrusion of an instrument. Her genitals are formed by two contiguous lips, caressing each other without proscription. Within herself, woman is two lips—but not divisible into ones—that enfold each other.[34]

This autoeroticism is disrupted violently by the intrusive penis, which separates the two lips and distracts woman from this self-caressing, announcing the disappearance (oppression) of her own pleasure in sexual relations. The feminine dilemma is complicated by these alternatives (defensive virginity versus male objectification) and must endure in a climate that applauds the masculine imperative. The prevailing sexual imagery (who has the "biggest," "strongest," "stiffest" penis?) relegates woman's role to that of an obliging prop in male fantasies. The fact that female sexuality is obscured in these transactions should come as no surprise, argues Irigaray. Rediscovering its origins would require a return to an ancient civilization constituted by a different culture and a different language.[35]

Irigaray attempts to describe this uncultivated discourse. Touching rather than looking would signal female eroticism. The female genitalia, which are misogynously depicted as masked, sewn up inside, signify the importance of a form. This organ lacks an identifiable form of its own, and phallomorphically privileges the *one* inexorable form—the male sexual organ. In a culture that inventories everything, woman is an anomaly. Is she one? Is she two? And what of her sexual organ? She is constituted by two lips and compared to the only visible, designatable organ (the penis) and therefore counted in its absence: none.

This disruption is intended by Irigaray. The feminine is multiplicity! A woman's sexual pleasure does not reside *either* in clitoral activity *or* in vaginal passivity, as Freud maintained. Female eroticism is diversified; fondling the breasts, touching the vulva, spreading the lips constitute only a fraction of the geography of women's pleasure.[36] Contrary to what is typically imagined, sameness does not speak the feminine language. Irigaray contends that the feminine consciousness is undecidedly other in its meanings. Woman sets off in all directions employing contradictory, incomprehensible words that constitute her *logos* and obliterate masculine constructs of coherence. This is her reason—unintelligible for those who find comfort in exact definition and structure. What the feminine consciousness desires is nothing and everything, always at the same time even in moments of silence.

Irigaray's deconstruction of female sexuality and psychoanalytic thought and language lead her to an interpretive rereading of the texts that define the history of philosophy. This is significant for purposes of understanding the discourse of jurisprudence because she challenges the conditions under which the systematization of disciplines originated. As in psychoanalytic theory, a pivotal theme in this enterprise is the teleological construction of sameness. This reductive mechanism operates unconsciously as well in the works of each philosophy, which prompts Irigaray to call for a close rereading of the "grammar of each figure of discourse, its syntactic requirements, its imaginary configurations, its metaphoric networks and . . . its silences."[37]

Irigaray admits that linguistic psychoanalysis alone cannot solve the plight of female sexuality in discourse. Her prescription for a working against or disruption of the discursive phallomorphic mechanism is a plea for reconstituting the issue of woman. Rather than raising the question "What is woman?" (a question that seduces us into thinking in masculine language constructs), she posits that reflexivity (mimicry)— repeating and interpreting how, within discourse, the feminine finds itself negatively and oppressively defined—is the fundamental task of a deconstructive praxis. Irigaray cautions that a balance between this disruptive process as excessive needs to be maintained with the feminine style of simultaneity. Resisting form, thesis, position—all of which are masculine, all of which are unity—requires an adherence to feminine fluidity. Thus, what is posited must also be reversed only to loop around again as a supplement to the reversal. As Irigaray states it: "we need to proceed in such a way that linear thinking is no longer possible . . . there would no longer be either a right side or a wrong side of discourse."[38] This language work would thwart any attempt of masculine discourse to cast its shadow upon the feminine, allowing for the experience of a different language in which the masculine was not everything—all truth or all power.

Irigaray's injunction for disrupting the masculine language, thought, and understanding of female sexuality, all manipulated by men, seemingly defies the Husserlian notion of truth as intersubjective.[39] Interpersonal truth maintains that the locus of the "real" or the "objective" resides in the potential that what one is experiencing can be similarly experienced by others. The event is further understood as intersubjectively real when one makes an aspect of the world stand before the human subject. Another way of saying this is that my experiences are always from a perspective. The validity of Irigaray's assertions concerning the phallocratic systematization of the history of philosophy as intersubjectively objective rather than mere personal opinion stems in part from the breadth of poststructuralist authors who critique civilization similarly.[40] Moreover, the attitude by which individuals consider what is given to them (language, thought, etc.) is not regarded in a less involved, merely present way. Their perspective is decidedly concernful. In order to see objectively what is given to her, Irigaray assumes a disruptive attitude, an attitude others maintain, therefore affirming her stance as intersubjectively real.

Following Irigaray, reconstitution of the issue of woman is precisely the appeal that Carol Gilligan and Catharine MacKinnon make.[41] Each acknowledges (in her own way) the patriarchal power of law in feminist discourse. Because each introduces us (in her own way) to the importance of revaluing the feminine code as a model of justice dismissed, their treatments of this issue will be explored concurrently in the next section.

WOMEN, LAW, AND JUSTICE

Like Irigaray before her, Gilligan reexamines Freudian formulations regarding the nature of woman. Where Irigaray posits a biological nexus that accounts for women's "anti-Oedipal" consciousness, Gilligan addresses the ethical implications of Freudian theory for women. More than reestablishing that his psychoanalytic theory concerning the masculine code unalterably compares the feminine to and by this standard, Gilligan asserts that this paradigm functions as the recipe for sound moral judgments and cultural expectations of justice. The masculine system is sacred and the feminine register is dismissed. Acknowledging that there are real physiognomic differences between genders, Gilligan sets out to rediscover the feminine experience, grounded in the psychosocial development of adolescent girls. Her work, *In a Difference Voice*, begins this investigatory process. She uncovers the feminine in consciousness as other than, different from, the masculine code. Women's experiences are situated in relationship maintenance and networking. Relationally caring about others, their intimate involvement with situations, their world, and their own voices, constitutes a feminine moral code and justice model, argues Gilligan. This theme is renewed in her collaborative work, *Making Connections*. Here, Gilligan et al. listen to the ways in which juvenile girls touch (connect with) and separate from one another. From this study we learn that the feminine code experiences the other interpersonally. Through the Emma Willard School students (the subjects of the project of Gilligan et al.), we discover that women respond to the feelings of others with feelings of their own. In addition, we discover that, for women, challenging the *reasons* for acts of violence is less important than *imagining* how these acts occur, how they can be stopped, and what role one can play to limit them.[42] Perhaps more illuminating than these revelations is the painful acknowledgment that in a society where masculine constructions of reality dominate, this form of expression will inevitably meet its death. As Gilligan et al. put it: "As the river of a girl's life flows into the sea of Western culture, she is in danger of drowning [or] disappearing."[43]

Gilligan's ideas are appealing because they offer a sort of putty by which the feminine code is apparently framed without a reliance on the masculine model. However, her language choice, namely to conceive of the feminine as "different" from the masculine, has been staunchly criticized by MacKinnon as ignoring the phallocratic power structure that subtends women's experiences. MacKinnon's argument is that Gilligan fails to consider that this moral register ascribed to women is "what male supremacy has attributed to [this sex] for its own use."[44] For MacKinnon, women's moral reasoning is to speak in terms of what the misogynous gender system says the feminine code of ethics or justice is, because the real social relationship between the sexes is organized male dominance and subordination of women. MacKinnon further posits that feminism lacks a method and is regarded as a loose collection of issues that describe rather than explain women's victimization. Her solution is to erect an elaborate methodology that attends with specificity to the central issue of unmodified feminism, particularly the issue of sexuality.

What is most interesting about both perspectives is what they contribute to feminism and concede in the process. Gilligan reminds us of Irigaray's search for an uncultivated, feminine language and culture. Gilligan's metaphor of connection and relational experience is a more lived, more practical account of Irigaray's fluid touching. We also discern from Gilligan that the interpersonal (the intersubjective) is relational. When asked to complete a sentence beginning with the phrase: "Rules are. . . .," Gilligan et al. find that the response from at least one adolescent participant was, "Rules are supposed to be the *guidelines* of life and the way to live it, but I can't say frankly that I'm convinced of that."[45] This allows Gilligan to query, if the traditional description of women is that they are "unruly," by whose rules are they being judged? What is understood as authentic justice, then, depends on who raises the question, to whom it is raised, for whom it is about, and how each interprets the description from their own unique perspective and experience. This reading of Gilligan leads to the realization that justice is many things for many people, a concept many sober legal scholars and practitioners dismiss as undisciplined.

Yet Gilligan, as MacKinnon accurately points out, does not reconcile the obvious power differential implied in the notion of gender difference. The problem with the language of difference is that it falsely presumes gender equity. Men and women are not equal, not if we accept as a premise that the world is phallocratically constructed. This is why MacKinnon is quick to challenge Gilligan, and it is the insight that she offers feminism. That men's voices speak through women's bodies is again reminiscent of Irigaray. Here, however, MacKinnon constructs an action-oriented praxis built around consciousness-raising in which, through discourse, women can better understand their personal sexuality and the implications this holds for others, systematically forging an altered situational politics for women.

In her zealous pursuit of an unmodified feminism, MacKinnon succumbs to the belief that a methodical, rigorous, and driven (?) approach will in time yield a more enlightened consciousness. But this is the shadow of the masculine infiltrating her being. Her imperative is decidedly unidimensional—there can be only *one* feminism, hereinafter referred to as "unmodified feminism." This belies the feminine consciousness understood as multiplicity. The systematic reconstitution of the feminine experience is a masculine endeavor. It implies an elemental inventory of characteristics, a checklist, that forms a unitary set of guiding principles. A significant strength of feminism is its polymorphism—that it is a disunity holding many meanings for different people.

The project of "relanguaging" jurisprudence as experiential feminism entails the use of imaginative discourse. Rediscovering the signification of metaphor, symbol, and myth as ingredients of storytelling (the unfolding of one's life) helps to inform this process as a meaningful expression of one's reality. This notion is likened to Foucault's philosophical ethos or aesthetic of daily life, in which we search for alternative styles of existence to avoid law's normalizing and unitary power.[46] Implicated in this process is the awareness that there is no such phenomenon as the individual self. We are always, in some respect, of the Other. Much of this holds salient meanings for the reformulation of justice and community, as we shall see shortly. But it is to the matter of grasping the importance of imaginative discourse in experiential feminism that I now turn.

IMAGINATIVE DISCOURSE

Murray argues that culture is the way in which people imagine their lives and that, in living one's life, one is imagining life in the way that it has already been imagined for that person.[47]

The implications of this perspective remind us of Heidegger's person/world dialectic and his treatment of the Other.[48] Heidegger posits that there is no sense of person without world and that there is no sense of world without person. This inexorable connection makes possible certain assertions regarding truth, knowledge, power, law, and the like. Moreover, this existential relationship signifies that living out what others have bequeathed to us, the culture (language and thought) of our ancestors, is illustrative of the Other's value in human life, and of its paramount role in informing one's own becoming: "The Other is those of whom one is a part and who conversely are part of the person."[49]

This understanding is not to suggest that we are somehow hopelessly condemned to the limitations of our culture. Having embodied its traditions we can imaginatively distance ourselves from its values, mores, and customs; begin to challenge them; even repudiate them. This entails sufficient time and experience wherein we employ what has been bestowed to us (language and thought) to critique what has been so bequeathed. This hermeneutical recounting of experience is an authentic movement toward "transcending what has been given to us so that we may from within it rethink what has been given to us and perhaps even better it."[50]

These ancestral imaginings of life are precisely what need to be disrupted if jurisprudence is to be situated in experiential feminism. Integral to this creative enterprise is the use of metaphor, symbol, and myth in altering the prevailing social reality. Ricoeur asserts that the strategy of discourse in metaphorical language is to "shatter and to increase our sense of reality by shattering and increasing our language."[51] Ricoeur's pronouncement is an elaboration upon I. A. Richards' tension theory. In his treatise *Philosophy of Rhetoric*, Richards maintains that entire sentences convey metaphorical meanings.[52] In propositions, there is a purposeful semantic discrepancy that is created. This impertinence fosters a tension between what was previously understood as reality and what, through the metaphor, constitutes a redescription of reality. Simultaneously, there is an enunciation of sameness amidst difference. An example of this notion is a line from Jonathan Swift's "Polite Conversation," in which justice is described as follows: "What's sauce for a goose is sauce for a gander."[53] Immediately, there is an intuitive likeness (justice as egalitarian) and a perplexing incongruity (justice compared to the sauce for a goose/gander?).

The importance of metaphor is that it touches, reaches, us in ways that defy traditional understanding. The metaphorical in language resituates our experiences in ambiguity, multiplicity, uncertainty, and contradiction. As Murray concludes, "[it is] as a lie that tells the truth, a confusion that clarifies, a detour that puts one directly on the road, a blindness that enables one to see all the better."[54]

This interpretation of metaphor ushers in a metamorphosis of both language and reality. As an ingredient of experiential feminist discourse, the metaphor resonates throughout one's body as an invitation to venture forward into a previously unknown realm. As experiential feminism uncovers metaphorical expressions that more authentically describe the feminine in consciousness, a more meaningfully lived account of one's story will unfold.

In addition to the integral role metaphor assumes in redefining the feminine in conscious experience is the related concept of symbols. Susan Langer describes the two symbolic modes that ground our human responses to experience as constructive and active.[55] One idea of symbols is their ability to express the logical as a function of scientific knowledge and certainty. The other notion attends to the world of emotion, fantasy, and dreams. This latter reference to symbolism characterizes the human subject's experiences in the *lebenswelt*. This is the realm that is beset by plurisignification, multiple meanings, and ambiguity rather than the antiseptic, calculating, dispassionate realm of logic.

In his work *Metaphor and Reality*, Wheelwright elaborates upon the symbolic as lived world.[56] He unpacks the various levels at which the symbol can be discerned, revealing five such grades. One of the more interesting symbolic levels is the cultural, where images extend to an entire community or people. They possess the capacity to instantly reveal and touch the traditions of a society and its individuals, while at the same time they can effect a transformation of both.[57] This rebirth is rooted in our imagination and its ability to contextualize experience in ways that more intimately announce our own life stories.

The project of experiential feminism, in its reconceptualization of juridical truth, entails dismantling the prevailing phallocratic symbols—the courtroom, the legal method, the reasonable man standard, burdens of proof, a demand for factual evidence, case precedent, etc.—and replacing them with a gathering of communal residents, storytelling, perspectivity, experiential discourse, interpersonal truth as relational, the historicity of one's own existence, etc. This is not to suggest that this alternative is itself a methodology. As Irigaray reminds us, the systematization of every discipline implies a unity that results in the oppression and victimization of people.[58] The plea of experiential feminism through symbols is an acknowledgment and acceptance of diversity. Our present system of jurisprudence does not permit such cultural heterogeneity and is therefore inadequate in speaking to the experience of the feminine in consciousness as lived.

The relevance of myth in informing our understanding of a fundamental, experiential feminist jurisprudence is equally profound. Like both metaphor and symbol, myth and myth-making are critical ingredients in the imaginative discourse process. As Murray acknowledges, through myth a world is established where the customs, beliefs, and even institutions of a culture are mirrored.[59] In this way, myth is linked to ritual; the two manifest a delicate interdependence illuminated by language where the spoken narrative is transformed into lived action. The myth, then, announces a particular style of language or a unique understanding of a people's thought, just as much as ritual enacts that language or thought. This wording returns us to the symbolic and metaphorical orders that each, in turn, informs our culture's choice of mythology and/or myth-making.

Because the myth is always and already of a language, the form that it takes is that of the narrative.[60] These stories are imbued with a sense of character, situation, and time; describe the unfolding and enduring drama of one's existence; and point to the dissonance and ambiguity of one's decisions. We are forever living our stories with all their incompletenesses, inconsistencies, and inevitabilities. We touch and are touched by those of others because there is something of our own narrative there—intimate yet shared, personal yet public.

Acknowledging that the myths of our lives are, in some fashion, commonly shared stories is not to imply that they are a static constellation of events. Precisely because the myth is a story its beginnings are born in the imagination's capacity to conceive of and describe ongoing, lived experience in intimately meaningful ways. Myth-making is that practice where we invent, through language, those stories that depict our own unique encounters with the world. That there is an element of familiarity for us in the imaginings of others should come as no surprise, given that narration (language) is a critical dimension of our existence. In this regard, we recognize that the wording of life is intrinsic to its being lived and that institutional expressions of our culture (in this case jurisprudence) originate through the instrumentality of language promulgated by the selected mythology that we create through it.

Experiential feminism is the process whereby one authors one's life. This chronicling is a personal recounting of the journey of one's lived experience. The work of experiential feminism through myth is to render the telling of narratives that more authentically depict the experience of women and the situations in which they find themselves. As alluded to earlier, Catharine MacKinnon, through her action-oriented praxis of consciousness-raising, does much in the way of grounding this process.[61] But here, the plea is for a reflective, concernful, imaginative discourse where the feminine in consciousness ushers in and reveals the myths of one's life.

Earlier the suggestion was made that the imagination possesses an affinity for ritual and that it announces the culture of a community or people. If experiential feminism is to be transformative in its rendering of law and justice, a brief examination of community or neighborhood is necessary to contextualize how this metamorphosis might occur.

COMMUNITY CULTURE

Recent studies on the concept of community draw a parallel to the study of organizations and the particular images or metaphors that describe these structures' operation.[62] One paradigm that offers some interesting insight into the nature of organizations or neighborhoods is the cultural perspective.[63] Admittedly, there is a great deal more to a community's make-up than its culture. Ecological determinants, demographic composition, infrastructure management, inter- and intragroup relationships, as well as a host of other factors contribute to the functioning of a neighborhood. But the notion of culture, informed as it is by a people's languaged imagination (metaphors, symbols, myths), does much in the way of telegraphing the character of a community's system of justice.

Elsewhere, I have described how neighborhoods can minimize instances of social deviance and crime by drawing a relationship between these factors and the extent to which these residents participate in their neighborhood's social designing.[64] I suggested that the more people naturally involve themselves in the construction of their environment, the greater the level of their investment in their community's well-being, the greater the likelihood of compositional stability, and the smaller the likelihood of crime occurrences. What is important in this understanding of community, as it relates to experiential feminism and jurisprudence, is the acknowledgment that individual diversity and cultural heterogeneity promote neighborhood stability, *provided* that neighbors are afforded the opportunity to construct their own reality.

Roberto Unger has also assessed this phenomenon of promoting a self-actualized society in his discussion of an empowered democracy.[65] Unger's point is that far-from-equilibrium conditions in the form of diversity, multiplicity, and heterogeneity must govern the operation of institutions (e.g., schools, the media, the press, the law) if cultural sedimentation and stasis are to be neutralized. This is precisely the form of existence that Foucault urges if we are to resist society's normalizing, unitary power.[66] It is an aesthetic of daily living in which we are the architects of our lives—not submitting to a singular ethic, morality, or law.

Experiential feminism is an invitation to us all to unpack the meanings of our community's metaphors, symbols, and myths. Moreover, it is the project of reconstituting, through our imagination, those enchanting images that more intimately reveal the feminine in consciousness, and to incorporate these significations into the culture of one's community through storytelling and ritual. This process leads to a reconceptualized and more authentic understanding of justice, not only because it discloses how such requirements as burdens of proof, a weighing of evidence, and a presentation of facts have come to be coded as the essence of juridical truth, but because it readies the way for styles of existence that are as different from one another as possible. These styles, through the imagination, bring with them multiple meanings, plurisignifications, uncertainties, ambiguities, contradictions, indeterminacies, and a variety of other experiences that defy the singularity of law's normalizing claim to truth.

This philosophical ethos shows us not only how much our legal culture affects our formulation of sound and informed judgments about people, but how much it excludes from consideration ways of being that do not fit law's unitary imperative. At this juncture, a preliminary application of the ideas discussed herein is necessary to demonstrate the manner in which individuals and communities might take up the issue of crime or harm against citizens. One poignant issue where outrage seems to be most evident is in the example of rape. The question, then, is how would experiential feminism regard this phenomenon and what implications would this position hold for the parties involved and for society at large?

EXPERIENTIAL FEMINISM AND PRAXIS

In order to interpret the experience of rape as authentically as possible, it is necessary to examine its relationship to both power and sexuality. This task entails an investigation of the apparent universality of patriarchal domination as well as the specific form (sexual) this domination takes in our present society. Foucault maintains that power is diffused throughout the social order: "Power is everywhere, not because it embraces everything, but because it comes from everywhere."[67] In the same text, he demonstrates how sexuality is a domain saturated with power whose processes produce particular forms of socially constructed sexuality that encode our understanding of the "proper" relationship between the sexes as well as what types of pleasure are socially sanctioned. Winifred Woodhull contends that Foucault's analysis shifts power's emphasis away from its oppressive function to its productive function.[68] Beyond power's ability to pronounce which forms of sexual expression are permissible is its capacity to "generate new forms of pleasure and new positions from which to resist."[69]

This interpretation of power is not meant to imply that sexuality is somehow outside of its normalizing purview. Effective resistance to power is flawed if sexuality is understood as the avatar of freedom—poised outside and against power's oppressive rule. An effective resistance to our contemporary understanding of sexuality, with all of its gender-constructed, power-differential relationships, is the Foucaultian strategy of desexualizing sexuality. This neutralization of sexuality entails a proliferation and diffusion of various forms of sexual pleasure so that the prevailing paradigm of sexuality is disrupted.

When this orientation is brought to bear on the issue of rape, it becomes evident that this phenomenon, as a sexual act, is understood as a grand transgression inexorably linked and fundamentally opposed to the law.[70] In desexualizing rape, law's claim to power is unalterably diminished, provided we acknowledge that juridical truth presupposes a unitary code of sexually acceptable behavior. The greater the construction and acceptance of diverse sexual pleasures, the greater the reduction of law's normalizing grip on what constitutes sanctioned and proscribed sexual conduct and, more importantly, law's claim to truth. But this analysis one is not to infer that rape is experienced as devoid of inflicting harm. It is a physical attack with a multitude of psychological implications, brought about by real or imagined power, with injurious results.

The desexualization of rape as a productive form of resistance to power must be interpreted in such a way that our present system of jurisprudence is not affirmed. To do otherwise would be to acquiesce to the prevailing power differential in sexual relations, as well as to discount other experiences that do not conform to our singularly prescribed code of ethics. The work of experiential feminism in unveiling the meaning of rape for particular individuals so harmed is threefold. It must: (1) unpack how the vagina has come to be coded as a place of emptiness and vulnerability, the penis as a weapon of potential harm, and the act of rape as violation;[71] (2) disrupt these images by inventing, through imaginative discourse, interpretations that more authentically describe the many meanings our sexual bodies hold for us rather than accepting and announcing descriptions that our misogynous language and thought have permitted us; and (3) usher these resituated interpretations into our culture, so that language, thought, and reality can be transformed.

As we discover the unfolding significations sexuality holds for individuals, and desexualize and recommunalize it by granting that sexual pleasure abounds in multiplicity, the experience of rape is neutralized to the extent that it does not affirm the power of the law. Rape is no longer understood as a grave infraction undermining society. This is not to argue that the meaning of rape for persons so harmed is not injurious. The jurisprudential questions that are posed here for further review are as follows: What metaphors, symbols, and myths have come to constitute the situation in this way? Do these language constructs genuinely speak for a woman's experience of this phenomenon? How would a community's culture look when informed by imaginative discourse where its citizens seek ways of being that reflect communal participation, individual diversity, and cultural heterogeneity?

And what impact would these altered realities have in redefining our system of jurisprudence?

SUMMARY AND CONCLUSIONS

The task of establishing a fundamental feminist jurisprudence simultaneously entails decentering our phallocratically constituted legal reality and reframing the notion of justice as authentically lived experience. In terms of disrupting the given juridical system, both Foucault and Smart inform us of law's claim to knowledge (therefore power) and how this version of truth effectively eliminates entire bodies of knowledge that cannot fit the legal, unitary imperative. Irigaray, through her careful rereading of the history of psychoanalytic philosophy, makes evident that within the systematization of entire disciplines, masculine constructions are deeply embedded. Language and thought reflect the misogynous culture. Her psycholinguistic treatment of the feminine indicates that the feminine in consciousness is multiplicity—touched by and touching the world through multiple meanings, plurisignifications, contradictions, and indeterminacies. Carol Gilligan and Catharine MacKinnon contextualize the profound insights of Irigaray. Through her studies of adolescent girls, Gilligan ostensibly reveals to us the unadulterated feminine moral code. This register embraces others relationally, is more concerned with the intimacy of relationship maintenance, and values the interconnectedness that women share with others and their lived experiences. MacKinnon moves us onward to the level of praxis. Through consciousness-raising, the meanings situations hold for women, the significations others engender for women, and the awareness one experiences regarding oneself disclose the intimate, interiorized world of women, thereby informing them and us of their situational politics.

Having sufficiently described the limitations of the masculine code's capacity to speak the feminine language, an examination of the imagination's role in shaping human experience ushers in a reformulation of justice. Through metaphor, symbol, and myth we discover the tremendous power the imagination possesses in creating culture. Experiential feminism must reveal those enchanting images that more intimately describe one's encounter with the *lebenswelt*. Only in this way can we witness a metamorphosis of language and reality in which people are the architects of their lives. This transformation is a rediscovery of a "village" aesthetic in which community members co-shape their culture through storytelling and ritual. Informal community gatherings, perspectivity, narration, lived experience, the historicity of one's existence, and the interpersonal as relational are all ingredients of this philosophical ethos or systemic jurisprudence, provided they do not function collectively or individually as an oppressive methodology.

The product of experiential feminism is a code of justice that applauds personal diversity, esteems cultural heterogeneity, experiences situations contextually, acknowledges individual/collective competency and fallibility, encourages communal participation, and invites imaginative discourse. In short, the juridical transformation constituted by experiential feminism is a spiritual revalidation of one's freedom to imagine the world in all its possibilities—an invitation to touch the transcendent in all of us.

In applying these principles to rape, we discover that an authentic interpretation of this experience must consider its relationship to power and sexuality. Because power comes from everywhere, we understand that sexuality is already infused with a particular form of sanctioned pleasure. In order to disrupt this normalizing, unitary paradigm, sexuality must be desexualized. By manufacturing and then dispersing other expressions of sexual pleasure, not only is the guiding principle of sexuality undermined but so too is law's claim to socially sanctioned sexuality.

When rape is recommunalized we reinterpret the meanings our bodies hold for us and the significations this act announces to us in relationship to others. Moreover, through imaginative discourse, we are called to describe our experience in individually felt and interiorized ways that have an impact on our understanding of personal harm and of society at large. The point is not that rape is not injurious but how it is that this is the way in which it is coded. More importantly, does this wording speak the feminine-in-consciousness experience of it, given our misogynous understanding of the vagina and phallocratic understanding of the penis?

Throughout this paper I have attempted to demonstrate the inadequacy of the masculine language to speak the feminine voice, especially as it relates to issues of law, justice, and community. This has not been a plea for an elimination of the masculine register as much as for an acceptance and validation of the feminine code in describing experience. Imaginative discourse has been the cornerstone of the theory—a theory whose implications for jurisprudence make possible the revaluation and revalidation of women's ways of knowing.

PART II

Applications

8

The Marxian Critique of Criminal Justice*

JEFFREY REIMAN

My assignment in this chapter is to present the Marxian perspective on the fundamental ethical concepts of criminal justice, such as guilt and punishment. In this introductory section, I want to sketch out my view of the kind of theory that Marxism is, so that the reader will be able to understand the approach I take toward this assignment in the material that follows.

Before all else, I should say that I regard Marxism not as a moral theory about how societies should be organized but as a scientific theory about how societies—especially capitalist societies—do function. To my way of thinking, then, Marxism has no distinctive ethical position on criminal justice. It has a theory (at least implicitly) of what criminal justice (primarily in capitalist societies) *is*, and thus an account of the source and social function of the concepts that make it up. Only by adding to this account certain ethical views that Marxists commonly hold do we reach what may be called characteristic Marxian moral judgments about criminal justice. But these judgments are, in my view, a matter separate from Marxian theory itself. Incidentally, my view also implies that Marxism as a scientific theory must be distinguished from the moral commitment to socialism which Marx had and Marxists, generally, have. Moral preference for socialism does not follow automatically from Marxism the scientific theory. For that, there must be added at least, some suitable moral premise, and, even then, preference for socialism depends on the soundness of the belief that real, humane, and liberating socialism (as distinct from the rather grim imitations currently on the world market) is possible—a belief which

I think is yet to be verified. I point this out because I believe that if the separability of Marxism from commitment to socialism were more widely understood, many more inquirers would be willing and able to see and to profit from the power of the Marxian scientific theory. Accordingly, it is to this that I shall attend. The major portion of this essay will be addressed to determining what criminal justice under capitalism *is* according to Marxian theory. At the close, we shall have occasion to reflect on the moral judgments—particularly about criminal guilt and punishment—that are appropriate on this account.

Whatever else criminal justice is, it is an organized practice in which some human beings carry out the task of protecting an ongoing social system by preventing or discouraging behavior that deviates from the patterns of behavior constitutive of the social system. As such, criminal justice has a concrete reality comprising police, prisons, courts, guns, and the rest. However, what is most important for our purposes is the particular shape that this concrete reality takes in capitalism. That shape is governed according to certain principles that spell out what shall count as violations, what shall be done to violators, and so on. (For simplicity's sake, I shall use the term *criminal justice* as shorthand for the principles that normally govern criminal justice practices and practitioners in capitalism, and use *criminal justice system* as shorthand for the concrete reality of the practices and practitioners so governed.) It is to the governing principles that Marxian analysis is in the first instance directed. And, since these principles are, or at least appear to be, products of reason, that analysis takes the unique form of *critique*. Hence, "the Marxian critique of criminal justice." It will be helpful to suggest briefly what is meant here by *critique*.

Like Kant, Marx called his major works "critiques." In addition to "A Contribution to a Critique of the Hegelian Philosophy of Right," *The Holy Family or Critique of Critical Critique, The German Ideology: Critique of the Most Recent German Philosophy . . ., Outline of a Critique of Political Economy* (known as the *Grundrisse*), and "A Contribution to a Critique of Political Economy," there is, of course, *Capital*, whose subtitle is: *A Critique of Political Economy*. Also like Kant, Marx understood critique as an enterprise that is not exclusively negative. For Kant, critique involved tracing the illusions to which reason is vulnerable, and the knowledge which reason achieves, to their source in reason's own activity. Kant's critiques show both the limits of human reason and the power of reason within those limits. Marx retains this double-edged sense of critique, while altering it in one profound way. With Marx, critique becomes *materialist*. The achievements and errors of reason are traced to a source outside of reason, namely, to the existing social arrangement for the production and distribution of the means of material existence—what Marx calls the "mode of production." Reason's complicity is largely reduced to the hubris of taking itself as autonomous, claiming authorship for its products without seeing its own dependence on the material setting in which it occurs.

In the most general terms, then, Marxian critique aims to show products of reason to be *in reality* products of the mode of production that *appear* to be products of reason functioning independently of the mode of production. This is what makes the products of reason *ideological*. The interplay of reason's real dependence on the mode of production and its apparent independence enables the products of reason to confer legitimacy on the mode of production: If, unbeknownst to us, we get our principles from existing arrangements *and* think that those principles are products of independent reason, we shall think that existing arrangements embody the requirements of rationality itself. Believing that we are evaluating our mode of production by an independent standard, we shall in fact measure it by a standard that it provides. And, of course, since it provides the standard, it will naturally measure up well.

Engels writes that

> the jurist imagines he is operating with *a priori* principles, whereas they are really only economic reflexes; so everything is upside-down. . . . And it seems to me obvious that this inversion . . ., so long as it remains unrecognized, forms what we call *ideological conception*.[1]

These remarks suggest what we should expect from the Marxist critique of criminal justice. Such a critique will not show that the governing principles of criminal justice are simply false or illusory. Rather, it will show those principles to be a more or less faithful reflection of aspects of the capitalist mode of production—but not recognized as such. They are seen instead as products of independent reason, so capitalist criminal justice appears to be an expression of the requirements of rationality itself. As a consequence of this "inversion," criminal justice embodies and conveys a misleading and partisan view of the reality of the whole capitalist system. In particular, it obscures features of that system that undermine the normal ethical claims of criminal justice. Thus the Marxian critique sets the stage for critical moral judgments about the ethical status of criminal justice.

This said, it must be added that setting forth the Marxian critique of criminal justice is no obvious or uncontested matter. Neither Marx nor Engels developed a systematic theory of law or criminal justice. Rather, their works are peppered with observations about law, crime, and justice which defy easy systematization. Moreover, and this is a point all too often overlooked by Marxist writers, even if remarks by Marx and Engels on law could be rendered into an unambiguous, coherent whole, we would not thereby have what we need. What we need is not a theory of what Marx or Engels thought about law—that is a matter for their biographers. What we want to know is what Marxism—the theory—implies about law. And this we cannot find simply by gathering quotations. The reason is that a Marxian theory of law will be a theory of its *necessary tendential* structure under capitalism, that is, a theory of the structure toward which criminal justice systems will necessarily tend in capitalism. I shall say more shortly about the notion of a "necessary tendential structure." For the moment, note that the structure is a kind of skeleton that can be fleshed out in various ways. The structure sets limits to the diversity of practices that can occur, but it doesn't determine which of the possible ones in particular will occur. That will be a matter of particular historical circumstances and opportunities and even personalities. (This will seem odd to those who ascribe to Marx some caricatured version of "economic determinism"; to those familiar with Marx's historical writings, such as *The Eighteenth Brumaire*, it will come as no surprise at all.) Since some of Marx's or Engels' observations about the law relate to the necessary structure and others to ways it happens to be fleshed out, we cannot find the Marxian theory of law simply by collecting quotations. We will need the theory in order to know how to classify the quotations.

An example of failure to come to terms with this problem is found in the all-too-common confusion of Marxism with what should better be called "radicalism."[2] I take radicalism to be the view that the defining feature of capitalism is that capitalists more or less intentionally use their great power to feather their nests at the expense of workers and others. Marx never doubted that capitalists do often use their power this way. His (and Engels') writings document numerous examples. However, Marx's theory of capitalism is not based on the assumption (or expectation) that capitalists selfishly abuse their power. Rather it is a theory of the necessary structure that sets limits to what capitalists can do—and stay capitalist. Those limits are not subject to intentional modification by capitalists. And Marx's theory of capitalism is indifferent as to whether—within those limits—capitalists use their power selfishly or act with the most laudable intentions. Failing to see this, one is likely to take Marx's comments about capitalists' abuse of power as if they were the theory (when they record what some capitalists in fact do but need not do according to Marxian theory per se). Likewise, Marx's writings contain many references to capitalists cheating their workers and their customers. But Marx's theory of capitalism (in particular, the systemic and crisis-prone self-regulation of capitalism according to the labor theory of value) is based on assuming that capitalists do not cheat but buy labor (actually "laborpower") and sell products at their real value. Accordingly, Marx's remarks about cheating are observations about how capitalism can and sometimes does work but not about how it must work according to Marxian theory per se.

The confusion of Marxism with radicalism is only the most visible sign of two larger and interrelated problems that haunt Marxian theorizing. Since no one can write about Marxism for long without staking out positions on these problems, it will serve clarity to identify the problems and locate in advance the positions that will be taken on them here. The first of the problems we can call "the structure-versus-agency" problem, and the second, "the theory-versus-empiricism" problem.

The structure-versus-agency problem reflects the fact that there seem to be two Marxisms. There is the Marxism of *Capital*, in which Marx speaks of economic actors as mere personifications of roles in the capitalist mode of production, individuals who play out necessities built into the structure of capitalism.[3] And there is the Marxism of *The Communist Manifesto*, in which Marx speaks of economic systems as forms of class struggle, where social behavior seems not so much the product of structural necessities as of conflicts between more or less conscious agents with competing class interests.[4] The first Marxism seems to emphasize economic determinism and to downplay the capacity of free actors to shape history, and the second does the reverse.

The theory-versus-empiricism problem reflects the fact that what Marx describes in *Capital* as the laws of capitalism are the laws of pure and perfect capitalism.[5] Consequently, actual capitalist systems seem in myriad ways to diverge from the laws, inviting the conclusion that Marx's laws are belied by the facts. Since I shall try to spell out the necessary tendential structure of criminal justice, it should be clear that I understand Marxism primarily in terms of structure rather than agency, and since I aim to bring out that structure as an implication of Marx's theory of capitalism, I give pride of place to theory over empirical observations. Nonetheless, I think the rightful claims of agency and empiricism can be accommodated in this view, as follows.

The necessary tendential structure of capitalist criminal justice stands to actual capitalism as, say, the orthodox economist's model of perfectly rational consumer behavior stands to actual consumption. It is the shape that criminal justice tends to take to the extent that the conditions of capitalism (open markets, smooth information flow, absence of political or traditional constraints on investment decisions or on labor mobility, and so on) are realized. This is what I mean by calling it a *tendential* structure. But, as many things can block the perfect realization of the conditions of capitalism, many things can block the perfect realization of the tendential structure. And many of these things will be the result of human action. Moreover, while theories of capitalism (Marx's and others') are generally theories of how it operates when it is the only economic system, actual capitalist societies are not pure or perfect cases of capitalism. They are generally mixed up with holdovers from the precapitalist past, say, feudal landholding patterns, or modern additions, say, socialistically organized public sectors. A capitalist society is not a purely capitalist society, but one in which capitalist relations (namely, labor hired for wages to produce for private profit) predominate. Consequently, the actual functioning of capitalism will be distorted by the effect of noncapitalist forms, much as rational market behavior is distorted by irrational practices such as racism.

Nonetheless, there is according to Marxism a basic structure of capitalism that sets limits to the range of human actions that are compatible with the functioning of the capitalist system. Since, within capitalism, it is generally within people's interests (at least as perceived) to support this functioning (at least in the short run), actions within these limits will tend to be supported and recur, and actions beyond them will tend to be opposed and disappear. Thus, where capitalist relations predominate, precapitalist economic relations will tend to decline, and socialistic arrangements will always be hanging on for dear life. In presenting his theory of capitalism, Marx portrays capitalism in perfect form. He does so not to claim that that is how it actually exists anywhere but rather to show the shape to which it tends everywhere. Actual systems will be a product of the force of that tendency versus the force of all those factors that block the perfect development of capitalism. Likewise, the necessary tendential structure of criminal justice is the perfect realization of the criminal justice system that supports the perfect functioning of capitalism. Thus the actions that constitute such a criminal justice system will receive support and tend to recur, and actions contrary to such a system will meet opposition and tend to disappear. But these are tendencies. As a result of the complex interactions of human actions and of the existence of noncapitalist economic forms, actual criminal justice systems will be approximations of this tendential structure.

If this is correct, actual criminal justice systems will clearly be shaped by human actions, and often substantially so. No Marxist need deny that criminal justice in the capitalist United States is quite a different thing from criminal justice in capitalist Chile. What he must claim, rather, is that as capitalism develops in both, their criminal justice systems will increasingly take on the shape of the necessary tendential structure that the theory implies. Moreover, this also implies that Marxian theory is no less hospitable to empirical testing than any other theory that spells out tendencies. The ideal depiction of rational consumer behavior must be confirmed not by showing that the facts match the outcomes, but by showing that the actual outcomes tend to gravitate around the outcomes predicted by the ideal depiction. The Marxian theory of capitalism and of capitalist criminal justice must be tested in the same way. The tendency among certain Marxist writers to shy away from such tests and take refuge in dialectical mumbo-jumbo and other epistemological obscurantism does Marxism little good. Marxism claims to be a scientific theory of capitalism. If so, it must at some point make good its claim by showing that the real world is the way Marxian theory says it is. There is no way to show that outside of empirical confirmation. If Marxism is not rightly subject to such testing, then it should give up its claim to science.

The foregoing remarks are not meant to settle the deep disputes that currently divide Marxist writers. Rather, they are meant to clear the way sufficiently to allow some theorizing that many readers are likely to regard as quite abstract. To be sure, it is. I shall try to show how Marxism leads to a theory of the structure that criminal justice systems necessarily tend to have under capitalism, while at the same time not claiming that any existing criminal justice system is more than an approximation to this structure. In order to give the reader as complete a picture as possible (in this short space) of the whole of Marxian theory—from general theory of capitalism to particular theory of criminal justice, and from there to ethical evaluation—I shall necessarily sacrifice much detail. Moreover, I shall largely ignore the differences that individual actions may make in determining the shape of actual systems. I hope I have said enough to suggest that this in no way implies either that human actions are irrelevant to historical outcomes or that Marxian theory is beyond empirical confirmation.

I shall proceed in the following way. In the first section, "Marxism and Capitalism," I shall sketch out enough of Marx's theory of the capitalist mode of production as is necessary to lay the foundation for a Marxian theory of law. Since law is, for Marxism, a form of ideology, we shall have to see how ideology works in capitalism. I take this up in the second section, "Capitalism and Ideology." In the third section, "Ideology and Law," I shall try to construct the Marxian theory of law and, from it, the Marxian theory of criminal justice. And then in the fourth section, "Law and Ethics," I shall consider the characteristic Marxian moral judgments about criminal justice—particularly about guilt and punishment—that are appropriate in light of the Marxian account.

MARXISM AND CAPITALISM

Marx says of capitalism that it is a system of "forced labor—no matter how much it may seem to result from free contractual agreement." Here is both the truth that Marx asserts about capitalism and the legal ideology that shrouds that truth. To understand precisely how this works, we must consider the nature of the coercion that Marx discovered in capitalism.

For Marx, the value of any commodity is equivalent to the average amount of labor-time necessary to produce it.[6] Under capitalism, the worker's ability to labor—Marx calls this *labor-power*—is sold to the capitalist in return for a wage. Since labor-power is also a commodity, its value is also equivalent to the average amount of labor-time necessary to produce it. Producing labor-power means maintaining a functioning worker. The value of labor-power then is equivalent to the labor-time that on the average goes into producing the goods (food, clothing, shelter, and so on) necessary to maintain a functioning worker at the prevailing standard of living, which Marx understood to differ among countries depending on their respective histories.[7] The worker receives this in the form of a wage, that is, in the form of the money necessary to purchase these goods.

The capitalist obtains the money he pays as a wage by selling what the worker produces during the time for which he is employed. But if the worker produced an amount of value equivalent only to his wage, there would be nothing left over for the capitalist and no reason for him to hire the worker in the first place. Labor-power, however, has the unique capacity to produce more value than its own value.[8] That is, the worker can work longer than the labor-time equivalent to the value of the wage he receives. The amount of labor-time that the worker works to produce value equivalent to his wage, Marx calls *necessary labor*. The additional labor-time that the worker works beyond this, Marx calls *surplus labor*, and the value it produces, Marx calls *surplus value*. It, of course, belongs to the capitalist and is the source of his profit.[9]

Profit then rests on the extraction of unpaid surplus labor from the worker. To see this, one need only recognize that while all products in the economy are produced by labor, only a portion of those products are wage-goods. The workers, then, produce it all and receive back for their troubles a part of what they have produced. The rest belongs to their bosses, and is effectively uncompensated. "This expenditure of labor-power," Marx writes, "comes to [the capitalist] gratis." And thus, "The secret of the self-expansion of capital [that is, the secret of profit] resolves itself into having the disposal of a definite quantity of other people's unpaid labor."[10]

But, for Marx, capitalism is not only a system in which unpaid labor is extracted from workers, it is a system in which workers are *forced* to provide this unpaid labor. Workers are not merely short-changed, they are enslaved. Capitalism is "a coercive relation."[11] The coercion, however, is not of the direct sort that characterized classical slavery or feudal serfdom. It is rather an indirect force built into the very fact that capitalists own the means of production and laborers do not. Lacking ownership of means of production, workers lack their own access to the means of acquiring a livelihood. *By this very fact* workers are compelled to sell their labor to capitalists for a wage, since the alternative is (depending on conditions) either painful or fatal: relative pauperization or absolute starvation.

This compulsion is not in conflict with the fact that the terms upon which the worker works for the capitalist are the result of free contractual agreements. Indeed, the compulsion works *through* free agreements. Since the agreements are free, each side must offer the other a reason for agreeing. If workers offered capitalists only as much labor as went into the wage-goods they will get back in return from the capitalists, the capitalists would have no reason to purchase their labor. It follows that, no matter how free the wage contract is, as long as it occurs in a context in which a few own all the means of production, those who do not own means of production will be compelled to give up some of their labor without compensation to those who do. Thus Marx describes the wage-worker as a "man who is compelled to sell himself of his own free will."[12] And the compulsion of the worker operates through the structure of property relations: "The dull compulsion of economic relations completes the subjection of the laborer to the capitalist. Direct force, outside economic conditions, is of course still used, but only exceptionally."[13]

The very existence of the social roles of capitalist and worker—defined by ownership and nonownership of means of production, respectively— is what coerces the worker to work without compensation. It coerces in the same way that a social structure that allotted to one group ownership and thus control of all the available oxygen would coerce. Beyond what was necessary to defend this group against challenges to its ownership of the oxygen, no additional force would be necessary for the coercion to operate. Indeed, it would operate quite effectively by means of bargains freely struck in which the non-oxygen-owners had to offer something to the owners to get the chance to breathe. They too would be compelled to sell themselves of their own free will. The same can be said of capitalism. Once its structure of social roles is in place, all that is necessary is that individuals choose, from among the alternatives available to them in their roles, the course of action that best serves their self-interest, and the extraction of unpaid surplus labor is enforced without further need for overt force except in unusual circumstances.

As with the oxygen-owning society, so too with capitalism, overt force is used or threatened to defend owners against challenges to their ownership. That is just another way of saying that, in capitalism, the state uses overt force to protect private property. But this differs crucially from the way in which overt force is exercised in social relations like slavery. In slavery, the use of overt force is part of the normal exercise of the master's power. In capitalism, overt force is used to defend everyone against forceful interference with their right to dispose of whatever property they happen to own, be it means of production or labor-power. Accordingly, such force is not part of the capitalist's power, but left to a third party which is neutral toward all owners—the state.

With both capitalists and workers protected in their capacity to dispose of what they own, the process by means of which workers are forced to work gratis can proceed apace. Note that this effect can be achieved with the state functioning neutrally. While the state does normally favor the interests of capitalists over workers,[14] it can serve the process of forced extraction of unpaid labor by protecting capitalists and workers alike in their freedom to dispose of what they happen to own. It just turns out that what capitalists happen to own is means of production, and what workers happen to own is the muscles in their arms. Capitalism, then, naturally appears as a system of free exchange between people with equal rights. This brings us to the phenomenon of ideology.

CAPITALISM AND IDEOLOGY

Of the study of social revolutions, Marx writes:

In considering such transformations a distinction should always be made between the material transformation of the economic conditions of production, which can be determined with the precision of natural science, and the legal, political, religious, aesthetic or philosophic—in short, ideological forms in which men become conscious of this conflict and fight it out.[15]

The legal, then, is an ideological form. This is not to say that it is merely mental. It has a material reality in the form of police and prisons and guns and courts and legislators and lawbooks and the rest. What is crucial is how this material reality is shaped, and for that we must understand how ideology is shaped. Consequently, our attempt to formulate the Marxian theory of law must detour through a discussion of the Marxian theory of ideology.

As its etymology suggests, *ideology* means the science of ideas, where science can be taken in the ordinary sense as the study of causal connections.[16] In the context of Marxian theory, ideology comes to mean the caused ideas themselves, and, equally important for Marxism, the caused ideas are in some important way false. Thus understood, for Marxism, the study of ideology denotes the study of how the mode of production gives rise to people's false beliefs about society. In *The German Ideology*, Marx writes,

> If in all ideology men and their circumstances appear upside down as in a *camera obscura*, this phenomenon arises just as much from their historical life-process as the inversion of objects on the retina does from their physical life-process.
>
> ... The phantoms formed in the human brain are also, necessarily, sublimates of their material life-process, which is empirically verifiable and bound to material premises.[17]

As this statement makes clear, the study of ideology requires that both the existence and the falsity of ideological beliefs be given a *materialist* explanation. To understand this requirement, consider that Marxian materialism is the conjunction of two distinct claims, an ontological claim and a social scientific one. The *ontological* claim is that what exists is material, that is, physical objects in space. Mind or spirit in any immaterial sense is a chimera. ("From the start the 'spirit' is afflicted with the curse of being 'burdened' with matter, which here makes its appearance in the form of agitated layers of air, sounds, in short, or language.")[18] The *social scientific* claim is that the way in which a society is organized for the production of the material conditions of its existence and reproduction ("the mode of production") plays the chief (though by no means the only) causal role in determining the nature and occurrence of social events. ("The mode of production of material life conditions the social, political and intellectual life process in general.")[19] The notion that societies are shaped primarily by their members' attitudes, or, likewise, that history is shaped by the progressive development of knowledge or ideals, is rejected as a misapprehension. Rather, it is primarily the organization of production which shapes people's attitudes, and the progressive development of modes of production which shapes history.

> That is to say, we do not set out from what men say, imagine, conceive, nor from men as narrated, thought of, conceived, in order to arrive at men in the flesh. We set out from real, active men, and on the basis of their real life-process we demonstrate the development of the ideological reflexes and echoes of this life-process.[20]
>
> It is not the consciousness of men that determines their being, but, on the contrary, their social being that determines their consciousness.[21]

Of these two claims, the social scientific is more restrictive than the ontological. The ontological claim requires only that we attribute ideology to material realities, be they brains or agitated layers of air or modes of production. The social scientific claim requires that among these material realities, pride of place be given to the mode of production as the primary cause of ideological beliefs. This means that the *main* source of false ideology is to be looked for not in the perceiving subject but in the perceived objects. It is not a "subjective illusion," the result of erroneous perception by individuals of their material conditions, but an "objective illusion," the result of more or less accurate perception of those conditions.[22] Viewing ideology this way has the added benefit of leaving the door open just wide enough so that the theory of ideology does not exclude the possibility of all true beliefs—and thus of the very science upon which it is based.[23] A materialist theory of ideology, then, must show that false ideology is an *objective illusion* arising primarily from more or less accurate perception of the organization of material production rather than from some subjective error.[24] Bear in mind that this is a matter of placing primary emphasis on objective factors, not of absolutely excluding subjective ones.

We can fix the idea of an objective illusion by considering a very common example of one, namely the illusion that the sun goes around the earth. Any illusion, any erroneous belief that an individual holds, can be *stated* as a subjective error—but not every erroneous belief arises primarily *because* of a subjective error. A person who believes that the sun rises above a stationary horizon in the morning makes a mistake. However, this sort of mistake differs crucially from, say, the mistake of believing that the light is green when it is red that a colorblind person might make, or the mistake of believing that a number is 4 when it is 2 that a person balancing his checkbook might make. In these latter cases, the mistaken beliefs are not merely held by the individuals; they arise in the individuals primarily as the result of a defective perceptual faculty or misuse of a sound one. These are subjective illusions. In these cases, correcting the defect in or the use of the perceptual faculty should undo the mistake. The mistaken belief that the sun goes around the earth, by contrast, arises as a result of a sound perceptual faculty properly exercised. This is an objective illusion. Neither healthier vision nor looking more carefully is likely to enable an individual to correct this mistake and see that what occurs at dawn is not the sun rising above the horizon, but the horizon tipping down before the sun.

The illusion that capitalism is uncoercive is a mistake of the same type as the illusion that sun goes around the earth. What corresponds in capitalism to the movement of the sun seen from earth is the free exchange of wages and labor-power between capitalists and workers. That the sphere of exchange is the objective basis of ideology[25] is recognized in effect by Marx when he writes that this sphere, within whose boundaries the sale and purchase of labor-power goes on, is in fact a very Eden of the innate rights of man. There alone rule Freedom, Equality, Property . . . . Freedom, because both buyer and seller of a commodity, say of labor-power, are constrained only by their free will.[26]

The normal perception of what goes on in exchange gives rise to the ideological illusion that capitalism is uncoercive. And this is not because the freedom in exchange is an illusion. The fact is that, for Marx, capitalism only works because the moment of exchange, through which the circuit of capital continually passes, is truly free.

> For the conversion of his money into capital, therefore, the owner of money must meet in the market with the free laborer, free in the double sense, that as a free man he can dispose of his labor-power as his own commodity, and that on the other hand, he has no other commodity for sale, is short of everything necessary for the realization of his labor-power.[27]

That the second of these senses of freedom is the worker's "freedom from" ownership of means of production does not deny the reality of the first sense without which we would have slavery or serfdom rather than capitalism. In fact, it is a precondition of the labor theory of value that, in exchange, parties are free in the sense that neither can use force to bring the other to terms. If one person could use violence to compel the other to buy or sell his commodity at a price he would not voluntarily agree to, there is no reason why the selling price of a commodity would have to cover the cost of the labor that went into it, and thus no reason why commodities should exchange in proportion to labor-time, indeed, no reason why commodities should exchange in proportion to anything other than the relative physical strength of buyer and seller.

In exchange, the power that capitalists have over workers recedes from view. If we distinguish two sorts of power—the power to withhold one's commodity until offered something preferable, and the power to command obedience and back this up with violent force—then it is clear that in the sphere of exchange, the latter power is suspended and all that remains is the former power. And this former power is a power that all parties to the exchange have equally. Thus the unequal power of capitalist and worker appears as their equal power to withhold from exchange what they happen to own, and their social inequality appears as the difference between the things that they happen to own. To use the celebrated words of Marx's analysis of the fetishism of commodities, a "social relation between men . . . assumes, in their eyes, the fantastic form of a relation between things."[28] However unequal or even unfree they really are, the parties to the exchange transaction appear as free and equal persons who just happen to own different things.

But if this accurate perception of what goes on in exchange is to explain how capitalism appears uncoercive, we need to understand how the sphere of exchange—which is only a part of capitalism—should be the source of beliefs about the whole of capitalism. Why should the experience of freedom in exchange—rather than, say, the experience of taking orders on the production line—determine the beliefs that members of capitalist societies come naturally to have? How is the representation of exchange *generalized* into a view of capitalism as a whole?

Marx offers a clue to the answer to this question when he says that the fetishism of commodities results because "the producers do not come into contact with each other until they exchange."[29] Exchange transactions are the salient points of social contact for economic actors in capitalism. They literally punctuate capitalist social relations. Every social interaction between individuals playing roles in the capitalist mode of production begins with such a transaction (say, the signing of a wage contract, exchanging labor-power for money) and can be ended with such a transaction (say, the dissolution of the wage contract). Each of these beginnings and endings is characterized by the absence of either party having the power to command the other's obedience and use violence to get it. Each party knows that he can enter or withdraw from any capitalist social interaction without being subject to the command or the overt force of the other. What constraint either feels is just a matter of what he happens to own, which naturally appears as a feature of his own good or bad fortune rather than a condition coercively imposed by the other. Thus *all* capitalist social interactions, *not just the exchanges themselves*, appear as voluntary undertakings between equal people who happen to own different things.

By means of an agreement in which no party can command the other's obedience and use force to get it, a person who happens not to own means of production enters into service in the capitalist mode of production, knowing that he can end this service by means of a similarly voluntary transaction. That ending it would leave him with no way of obtaining his livelihood does not seem like a condition imposed upon him by capitalists; it seems imposed by the fact that nature requires humans to work in order to live. That he must obey the commands of his boss is, then, in his experience, an episode bounded by the voluntary agreement to sell his labor entered into in the past and the voluntary agreement to stop selling his labor that he could enter into in the future, subject of course to the impersonal constraints of nature. That he takes these voluntary agreements as the boundaries by reference to which he comprehends the course of his service to the capitalist arises quite as ordinarily as taking the visible horizon as that by which one comprehends the course of the sun.

At this point, some Marxists will object that my argument places too much weight on exchange, and thus runs against Marx's own emphasis on the primacy of production relations.[30] But this objection is wrong-headed. By the primacy of production relations, Marx meant to indicate that the nature of capitalism was determined by the objective relation among people engaged in material production, specifically, the relation between workers who own no means of production and the capitalists for whom they work. Nothing I have said denies this. And, the claim that ideology arises from accurate perception of exchange supports rather than controverts the notion that taking exchange as primary is erroneous.

Exchange, then, accurately perceived, is what leads workers in capitalist societies to believe that they are free though they take orders most of their waking lives. It is what leads conventional economists to think that capitalism is no more than a series of mutually rational exchanges (rational because utility-maximizing, utility-maximizing because free). Thus, partisan ideological beliefs result from accurate perception of exchange, when its local nature is not seen and the rest of capitalism is, by default, assumed to be more of the same. And the law follows suit.

IDEOLOGY AND LAW

Law, wrote Marx, in *The Poverty of Philosophy*, "is only the official recognition of fact."[31] For capitalist law, the decisive fact is exchange. Law in capitalism is the official recognition of the fact of the economic relations in which exchangers stand to one another. This insight—which will guide the materialist explanation of criminal law that I shall develop in this section—must be credited to the work of the Soviet legal theorist Evgeny Pashukanis, whose *General Theory of Law and Marxism* was published in Russian in 1924.[32] Among the things for which Pashukanis argued was the notion that law was a product of capitalism and consequently had no legitimate place in socialism. As Stalin took firm control of the USSR and saw fit to use the law to shore up that control, Pashukanis came eventually into disfavor. He recanted his views to some extent, but it was too late. By 1937, he had been declared an enemy of the people and shortly thereafter "disappeared." Recently rediscovered by western Marxists, Pashukanis's work was first the object of lavish praise and subsequently the target of harsh criticism. I do not intend to endorse or defend the whole of Pashukanis's theory. He aimed at a general theory of law and made only a few observations about criminal law, which is my main concern here. In particular, he had little to say about the specific content of the criminal law, and even less about such related matters as the constitutional protections against overzealous criminal prosecution that characterize mature capitalist legal systems. In what follows, I shall start with his basic insight about the relation between law and exchange and try to show that it can be developed into an explanation of the content of the criminal law and of the constitutional protections. Along the way, I shall have occasion to indicate how the Marxian theory of law differs from both legal positivism and legal idealism. At the close of this section, I shall very briefly suggest how the account thus developed escapes the criticisms commonly leveled against Pashukanis's theory.

Marx writes that parties to an exchange

> must behave in such a way that each does not appropriate the commodity of the other, and part with his own, except by means of an act done by mutual consent. They must, therefore, mutually recognize in each other the rights of private proprietors. This juridical relation, which thus expresses itself in a contract, whether such contract be part of a developed legal system or not, is a relation between two wills, and is but the reflex of the real economic relation between the two.[33]

Exchangers must in fact refrain from forcing those with whom they would trade to part with their goods or services or money. Official recognition of this fact takes the form of according to exchangers "the rights of private proprietors." And since this recognition is of a piece with the ideological failure to perceive the coerciveness reproduced in exchanges between proprietors of capital and proprietors of labor, exchanges are understood legally as acts of the free will of the parties as long as no overt violence is used or threatened. Consequently, exchangers treat one another as *free subjects* whose freedom is expressed in their *right to dispose of their property without interference from others.*

It is the difference between what capitalists own and what workers own that, for Marx, makes it possible to reproduce a coercive relation through free exchange. If the law follows ideology in representing the relation between exchangers as noncoercive, then the law must abstract from this difference in what is owned and treat each party as having the same right to dispose of his property irrespective of what that property is. But this abstraction is not the law's doing. It has, as we saw above, already occurred in fact in the sphere of exchange. There, differences in social power between individuals are transformed into differences in the products owned by individuals equal in power. Each has the same power to dispose of whatever he happens to own, however different that is from what others happen to own. Accordingly, that power—the owner's right over his property and his freedom to exercise that right—is abstracted from the differences in what people own. The law reflects this in its formality. The legal right of property is an empty form to be filled in with different content, depending on what an individual owns. It just happens that what some people own is factories and what others own is their bodies, but their property rights in these things are the same. And their freedom to dispose of their property is the same.[34] Thus, exchangers must treat each other as *equal* free subjects with equal property rights—that is to say, as legal *persons*.[35]

We saw in the previous section that ideology is not to be understood as merely an illusion. Ideology reflects the real way in which capitalism appears to its participants. By the same token, the ideological nature of law reflects the real relations in which exchangers stand to one another. The written law, even the institutions of law (from lawmakers to law enforcers), are not the source of law. They reflect real, objective, "legal" relations between members of a capitalist society, relations that exist, so to speak, on the ground first, and only later on the page, or in the courts for that matter. But it is here that the "inversion" of which Engels wrote does its ideological work. Though the law is a reflection of the relations of exchangers "on the ground," it appears that the law is an expression of rationality itself, with the consequence that the relations among exchangers seem so as well. The theoretical formulation of this inverted view is called "legal idealism."

The legal idealist thinks that law exists first as idea, the idea of freedom or of the rights of autonomous subjects.[36] On this view, individuals endowed with such ideas about themselves and one another enter into relations appropriate to these conceptions. Cause and effect are precisely the reverse of their order for the materialist. The idealist sees social relations as products of legal ideas, and the latter sees legal ideas as products of social relations.[37] Marx gives the label "juridical illusion" to the failure to "regard the law as a product of the material relations of production, but conversely [as the perception of] the relations of production as products of the law."[38] And it should be clear that, in falling for this illusion, idealism hides the historical nature of law. Tracing the source of law to ideas suggests that, rather than reflecting a particular time-bound social arrangement, the law expresses timeless rational conceptions. With this, capitalist law looks like sweet reason itself, and capitalism like sweet reason in action. The effect of legal idealism is to legitimate the existing mode of production by making it appear as a manifestation of eternal rational essences.

The Marxist is no more a legal positivist than a legal idealist. The positivist defines law as the command of the sovereign backed by credible power.[39] This notion hides the socially determined nature of law. It makes it seem that the law can be anything that the sovereign wants it to be, whereas the Marxist holds that the nature of law is determined by existing social relations, and thus those relations limit the range of things that the sovereign can effectively command. Where idealism makes the content of the law appear to be an eternal essence, positivism makes the content of law appear to be a local accident. Neither grasps the way in which historically transitory forms of social organization shape the law.

Tied to legal positivism is the belief in the primacy of the political. If law is taken as the command of the sovereign, then legal rules are understood to flow from political institutions that have jurisdiction over the members of society. This view is rejected by Marxism along with legal positivism because, from the Marxian standpoint, political institutions, like legal ones, are products of economic relations. Indeed, Marxism rejects the Hobbesian notion that society is impossible without political sovereignty. On the Marxian view, without political-legal institutions, people naturally organize themselves into some set of functioning economic relations, which are sustained by their effectiveness in satisfying needs, and thus by the long-term interest that each party has in being able to count on the continued cooperation of others. As such arrangements persist, political-legal institutions with the special task of maintaining those relations in their standard and normal form arise. Such institutions (courts, police, and the like) serve no doubt to stabilize the already-existing social relations and thus make them more dependable and effective. But rather than these political-legal institutions making possible the social relations, it is only as supports to those social relations that institutions have power at all.[40]

On one issue, however, both the positivist and the idealist seem to be on safer ground than the materialist. If, as the materialist claims, the law is no more than the reflection of the actual practice of economic exchange, how does the law come to function as a norm? A simple reflection would represent whatever occurs and thus could not identify some actions as infractions. The positivist avoids this difficulty because he defines law as command, and thus its normative dimension is built in. And the idealist is even better equipped, since he derives law from rational essences, and thus the law partakes of the normative authority of reason itself. How can the materialist account for the normative dimension of law that arises as a reflection of economic relations?

The answer to this is that law is not a simple reflection of economic relations, but an *idealized* reflection. As exchanges occur over and over, people naturally tend to average out the peculiarities of individual cases and discern a kind of "essential core." In time, when individual cases diverge enough from this essential core, they are seen as deviant and thus as violations. The legal reflex of economic relations, then, is not an exact replica, but the result of a kind of natural sifting out of arbitrariness and idiosyncrasy such that what emerges is a kind of idealized "average" which stands in a normative relation to particular instances. Moreover, the tendency to go from what happens "on average" to what is normative is a common feature of human social existence. The tendency of the statistical norm (what people can generally be expected to do) to become the moral norm (what is expected of people) is visible in early civilization (where, for example, natural and moral law are not distinguished from one another) and in advanced civilization (where, for example, existing business practice is often taken by courts as creating legally enforceable obligations). It is important to note that the fact that the law represents economic relations in this idealized form is what makes the juridical illusion of legal idealism plausible. With the law appearing as an ideal to which real instances are imperfect approximations, the dependence of the ideal on the real is obscured.

This brings us to a second question. It would seem that law that reflects (even the idealized "average" core of) exchanges would include not only the criminal law but also what we currently understand as contract or civil law. How can the theory that traces law to exchange account for the nature of the criminal law per se, with its special content and its unique remedies?

To answer this, note first that there is considerable overlap in the content of criminal and civil law; criminal acts, such as theft or battery, can also be causes of civil action. But this overlay is largely asymmetrical: virtually any criminal act can be a cause of civil action, but only some civil causes are subject to criminal prosecution. What this suggests is that the criminal law is more distinctive in its remedies than in its content. In general, criminal prosecution seeks punishment of the guilty, and civil action seeks recovery of damages from the one responsible for a loss. Now, on the materialist theory, both sorts of law—criminal and civil—represent the "essential core" of normal exchange and aim to rectify violations of or deviations from that core. Thus, to explain the nature of the criminal law per se, we must show why some classes of deviations from normal exchange are singled out for the distinctive "criminal" remedy, namely punishment. Since punishment is generally a graver matter than recovery of damages, we should expect the criminal law to be addressed to the most serious violations of normal exchange, while the civil law can be addressed to all violations.

Violations of normal exchange can be distinguished in the following way: some threaten the very possibility of free exchange by depriving people of the ability to dispose of their property. Other violations threaten not the possibility of free exchange but its success in meeting the wishes of the exchangers. What threaten the very possibility of exchange are acts of violence that overtly block the capacity of individuals to exercise their wills, acts of theft that overtly bypass the capacity of individuals to choose how their property is to be disposed of, and acts of deception that have the same effect, so to speak, behind the backs of their victims. These are so serious that they must be prevented in advance. And that requires a standing threat of punishment. Accordingly, the criminal law is primarily aimed at acts of violence, theft, and fraud.[41]

Less serious violations are compatible with the existence of exchange but cause exchanges to fall short in some way of the wishes of the exchangers. These violations are mainly failures to live up to the terms of explicit or implied contracts. They can be remedied by requiring performance or payment from the one responsible. These are suitable targets for the civil law, though nothing is lost by allowing the civil law to apply to recovery of losses due to the more serious violations as well.

Actual exchanges will be characterized by the full range of violations and deviations, from failure to meet agreed-upon deadlines to gross expropriation with the threat or use of violence. All such violations undermine the likelihood of the same parties exchanging again. Since it is generally in people's long-term interest that stable trading relationships be maintained, it will generally be in people's interest to eliminate such violations. Accordingly, over time the vast majority of exchanges, particularly those between people in continuing exchange relationships, will tend to be free of violations. Thus, an average core of exchange, characterized by absence of violence and fraud as well as by dependable fulfillment of agreements, will emerge as the norm. The law in general will represent this norm. However, of the violations, there is a class which stands out in the extremity of the threat it poses to the possibility of exchange. This is the class of threats and acts of violence, theft, and fraud, since all of these directly attack the ability of people to dispose of what they own according to their own free will. Consequently, the maintenance of stable exchange relations will require establishing a secure peace, free of violence, theft, and fraud.[42] Since these violations are so serious as to threaten the very possibility of ongoing exchange relations, they must be prevented by the standing threat of punishment. They are appropriately the subject of the criminal law.

On the whole, then, while the entire law in capitalism reflects the conditions of normal exchange, the content of the criminal law—the acts it identifies as "crimes"—are those that threaten the very possibility of normal exchange. Moreover, since the normal relations of exchange are not only idealized but (as we saw in the previous section) generalized to the whole of capitalism they will shape people's normative expectations beyond exchange. Thus they determine the limits which will be imposed on officials taxed with the job of finding and

prosecuting criminals, the shape of court proceedings, the relation of
punishment to offense, and the emphasis on the free will of the offender.
Accordingly, tracing law to its source in exchange, we can account for
at least the general content of criminal law and the general shape of
the criminal justice system and of the constitutional limits within which
that system operates. Here, briefly sketched and numbered for ease of
identification, are the main ways in which this works:

1. Normal exchange presupposes that people are treated as having
property rights in whatever they are to trade, and that must mean not
only goods but their bodies as well, since this is what workers trade
with capitalists for their wage. Crime then is any violation by one individual of the property rights of another in whatever he owns, including his body. This explains why the criminal law is primarily directed
against acts of violence, theft, and fraud. Moreover, since criminal law
protects an individual's body because he owns it (and not, say, because it is the earthly vessel of his immortal soul), the law will be
primarily concerned with injuries done to people's bodies against their
will—since otherwise such injuries do not violate the individual's
ownership of his body. This accounts for the liberal principle *volenti
non fit injuria* and thus, via generalization, for the tendency in capitalism to decriminalize (or reduce in importance) "victimless crimes" or
"moral offenses."

2. This account also tells us what we are not likely to see as crime in
capitalist society, namely, exercises of the power inherent in the ownership of property itself. Thus we will not generally find that death
due to preventable dangers in the workplace will be taken as murder,
since that would assume that the worker was somehow forced into
the workplace by the power inherent in his boss's private ownership
of the means of production.[43] Since that is just the power that is invisible in capitalism, the worker is taken as freely consenting to his job,
and thus freely accepting its risks. Accordingly, when the criminal law
is used against employers to get them to eliminate occupational hazards, it is never with the understanding that employers who do not
eliminate such hazards are violent criminals. If the criminal law is used
in these cases at all, it is as a regulatory mechanism applied to employers because this is the most efficient way to reduce the social costs
of occupational injury and disease. The treatment of guilty employers
is generally light-handed, even though far more people lose their lives
due to preventable occupational hazards than as a result of what the
law currently treats as murder.[44] In capitalism, subjection to one person is seen as arbitrary and thus unlawful coercion, but subjection to
the capitalist class is not seen at all.

3. The other side of criminal law, the limits placed on legal officials

in their pursuit of suspected criminals (for example, in the Bill of Rights), likewise reflects the generalized conception of people as owners of their bodies and other property. Accordingly, we find protections against official invasions of suspects' property (for example, the Fourth Amendment protections against unreasonable search and seizure) and against penetration of suspects' bodies or minds (for example, the Fifth Amendment protection against self-incrimination). Moreover, I think this accounts for the fact that corporal punishment, which was the norm in feudalism and slavery, tends to be eliminated in capitalism. The bodies of slaves are literally owned by their masters, and lords have natural (that is, parentlike) authority over their serfs. In these cases corporal punishment fits the existing social relations. In capitalism, employer and employee meet as owners of their respective bodies, and thus corporal punishment looks increasingly out of place.

The existence of these various limitations on what can be done to enforce the law is evidence that the Marxian view of law includes recognition of the way law functions not only to control the working class but as a limit on the behavior of the ruling class. Indeed, the Marxian view can be taken as claiming that it is precisely as a system that protects everyone alike in his property (including his body) by limiting both what citizens and law enforcers can do to the bodies (and other property) of other citizens that the law most effectively serves the purpose of keeping the working class selling its labor-power to owners of means of protection—both classes safe in the knowledge that no one can interfere with their right to dispose of what they happen to own. This is not to deny that the actual enactment of constitutional limits on the exercise of state authority is often and in substantial measure the result of political action by the working class.[45] The materialist view of law does not imply that such action is unnecessary; what it does rather is explain why action directed toward establishing certain legal rules is more likely to succeed than action directed toward other possible rules. Those familiar with Marx's discussion, in *Capital*, of the struggle to limit the length of the working day should see a parallel here. Of chief importance is Marx's claim that limiting the working day was a step in the development of capitalism, very much in the long-term interests of capitalists, and yet brought about by successful struggles of the working class.[46]

4. As crime is a violation of normal exchange, so punishment is thought of on the same model of equivalence as exists in exchange. "Punishment emerges as an equivalent which compensates the damage sustained by the injured party."[47] And the commercial model doesn't end here. The adversary system reproduces it in court. "The public prosecutor demands . . . a 'high' price, that is to say a severe sentence. The offender pleads for leniency, a 'discount,' and the court passes sentence

in equity."[48] Crime deforms exchange, by taking with force rather than payment. Punishment restores exchange, by using force to pay the criminal back for his force. This is the tribute in retribution. And the court is the extraordinary market where this extraordinary exchange is negotiated. The scales in Justice's hands are the same as those used by the merchant.

5. Since exchange normally brings payment to an individual only when he freely chooses to offer up his goods or services for it, so then the payment of punishment comes due only when the offender has freely chosen to commit the offense for which the punishment is payment. Accordingly, liability for punishment is subject to conditions of the same sort as apply to liability to contractual obligations. One is not bound by a contract that he has not signed freely, or that he signed while insane, or in ignorance of its contents, and so on. Likewise, the offender is liable to punishment, and thus is truly a criminal, only if he has committed his violation freely, sanely, and with knowledge of what he was doing. And by the same logic, the law generally prohibits *ex post facto* attribution of criminal liability, since a person can hardly choose freely to violate a law before it has been passed.

Some readers will object that many of the features of capitalist law, thus explained, already existed before capitalism, say, in Roman law—and of course it is well known that capitalist law borrowed heavily from the Roman legal classics. In response, note first that Roman law was also that of a society in which commercial exchange played an important role. This shaped Roman law and, consequently, made it easily adapted to capitalist needs. Thus, the general hypothesis about the relationship between capitalist legal forms and exchange is not threatened. Second, and perhaps more important, is this: Marxism is not concerned with when ideas (legal ones, or technological ones for that matter, such as steam power) are invented. It is concerned with the social forces that are responsible for certain ideas taking root and becoming widespread. That legal forms in capitalism existed before capitalism no more shows that their current use is not caused by capitalism than the fact that steam power was known in ancient China shows that capitalism did not cause its use in modern times.

Here, then, we read, so to speak, off the face of exchange, albeit idealized and generalized, the main contours of criminal justice as it develops in capitalism. As I indicated at the outset, this is no more than a skeleton. It does not aim to account for the full rich detail of any particular criminal justice system. Actual criminal justice systems exist in societies with other modes of production present alongside dominant capitalism, and are affected by the complex interplay of human actions, and so on, so that each actual system—like each actual face—

will have a distinct physiognomy while sharing in the basic structure. Some criminal justice systems will be slower in eliminating "moral offenses," some will be stricter on occupational hazards, some will abolish the death penalty while others will retain it, and so on.[49] These specific outcomes will be a function of the strength that various social groupings (such as religious organizations, labor unions, academia, the press, and the like) come to have in the specific history of specific countries, and of all the largely unpredictable features that determine the outcome of particular battles over the content of the law and the funding of the legal apparatus. This notwithstanding, the Marxian claim is that criminal justice will tend toward the shape sketched out above. Forces that support that tendency will on the whole prevail, and forces that resist it will on the whole fight a rear-guard action.

Since many of the criticisms normally leveled at Pashukanis's theory of law may be thought applicable to the account just sketched, I want to consider briefly how those objections can be met. First, it is objected that Pashukanis, in arguing that the form of law is, so to speak, read off exchange, has violated Marx's strictures on the primacy of production.[50] But this is a version of the same mistaken objection treated in the previous section, and answerable in similar terms. Rather than endorsing the primacy of exchange, Pashukanis's theory explains one of the chief mechanisms by which exchange is mistakenly taken as primary. Second, it is objected that Pashukanis's theory cannot account for crimes that occur outside the context of exchange, such as assault or victimless crimes.[51] But I have shown that assault is also a violation of ownership rights in the very bodies that laborers must be able to sell for their wage. As for victimless crimes, these are properly understood as holdovers from other modes of production, which were characterized by the belief that the body was owned by God, not by the individual who happened to inhabit it. What Pashukanis's theory implies is that such laws will tend generally to decline in the face of capitalist development. And that seems largely—if haltingly—to be coming true. Pashukanis is criticized for failing to see that the law is not just a reflection of the economy but has impact on the economy.[52] But nothing in the theory denies that once law—with its basic structure derived from exchange—gets going, it could be used to shore up the economic system or alter it or for more far-flung purposes as well. This is really a matter of the "structure-versus-agency" problem which I discussed at the outset. Pashukanis's theory is of the legal structure, but it does not deny that within that structure, human actors can affect the details of the law. Finally, and along similar lines, Pashukanis is criticized for overlooking the role of the law as an instrument of class domination in the hands of the capitalist class.[53] Against this, two things should be noted. The main form of class domination in capitalism, according to Marx, is that which results from exclusive ownership of means of production by some while the rest effectively own nothing but their labor-power. Pashukanis's theory shows nicely how the law serves this form of domination all the while appearing to protect neutrally the property rights of worker and capitalist alike. As for the further uses or abuses of the law by the holders of power, Pashukanis aims to give us only the general structure the law will have. It does not deny that within that structure those with the power to do so will use the law to serve their ends.

LAW AND ETHICS

We reach now the question of the moral stance toward capitalist criminal justice that is appropriate if the foregoing account is correct. At the outset, I maintained that, to my way of thinking, Marxism has no moral theory of its own and thus no distinctive ethical concept of guilt or punishment or their kin. To be sure, Marxism describes capitalism as an exploitative system, meaning one in which workers are forced to work for capitalists at least in part without compensation. As unsavory as this may sound, in itself it is a descriptive claim. Nonetheless, Marxists characteristically regard exploitation, and consequently capitalism, as unjust or immoral. Broadly speaking, they reach this condemnation by one of three routes. One is to view capitalist exploitation as wrong because it promotes antagonistic or alienated relations between human beings.[54] The second way is to view the capitalist exploitation as wrong because it is a form of forced servitude or slavery.[55] The third way is to view capitalist exploitation as wrong because it is based on an unjust distribution of wealth, namely, the unjustifiable exclusive ownership by a few of the means of production.[56] I shall call these three views, respectively, "the alienation charge," "the slavery charge," and "the maldistribution charge." Each of these has moral implications for capitalist criminal justice. The task of identifying these implications is simplified by the fact that the second and third charges incorporate each other. The slavery charge accepts that private ownership of means of production is a case of unjust maldistribution (because it is a means of forcing servitude), and the maldistribution charge accepts that private ownership of means of production is a means of enslavement (because it is a power wrongly monopolized by a few). For our purposes, then, the charges against capitalism can be reduced to two: the alienation charge and the slavery-maldistribution charge. In this section, I shall briefly sketch out the implications of these two for the ethical evaluation of capitalist criminal justice—particularly with respect to guilt and punishment. I shall close with general observations that apply to both charges.

Those who raise the alienation charge point out that capitalism is a system in which each person's well-being is in conflict with that of others. Capitalism pits class against class (competing over the division of the economic product into wages versus profit), worker against worker (competing for jobs), and capitalist against capitalist (competing for market shares). Moreover, proponents of this charge hold that antagonism of interests is neither a necessary feature of human life nor a desirable condition. It is caused by capitalism and overcome only by socialism (at least largely, and then completely by communism). Criminal justice as it emerges in capitalism is understood as a means to regulate this antagonism of interests. But since it assumes that this antagonism is inevitable, criminal justice serves to confer permanent validity on capitalism. Moreover, criminal justice promotes this antagonism by teaching people that the rights of each are in conflict with the rights of others rather than mutually supportive, that freedom is *freedom from* invasion by others rather than freedom to develop with others, that what people owe each other is noninterference rather than a helping hand.

Also important is the fact that a society based on antagonism of interests is one in which people earn their daily bread only as long as someone else can profit as a result. When that changes, workers may find themselves in need and with little in the way of help from the rest of society. On this view, then, the large crime rates characteristic of capitalism are due to the fact that people in capitalism are taught to see their interests as in conflict with others' and thus trained to have limited altruism and fellow-feeling, and to the fact that a society based on antagonism of interests is one in which economic need and insecurity are endemic. When limited fellow-feeling meets economic need and insecurity, the result is crime.[57] The same system that calls criminals individually guilty, then, is responsible for the antagonism of interests that breeds crime in the first place. Thus, the upshot of this charge is that criminals are not—or at least not wholly—guilty of the crimes they commit. On this charge, then, criminals are in large measure unjustly punished for actions caused by the very system that punishes them.

On the slavery-maldistribution charge, the emphasis is on the wrongness and coerciveness of private ownership of means of production. Capitalism promotes a system of criminal justice based on protecting the freedom of individuals to dispose of what they rightly own; but the system itself is based on the wrongful appropriation of means of production, and with it the power to coerce others to labor without compensation. On this view, socialism cures capitalism not so much by replacing antagonism of interest with harmony but by replacing private ownership of means of production by a few with social ownership by everyone.

To understand the moral implications for criminal justice of this charge, imagine for a moment that we see someone take a sheep from the field owned by another. In response, suppose that we make the normal judgment that a theft, an unjust expropriation, has occurred. Now, suppose further that we learn that the field-owner had himself stolen (or unjustly expropriated) the sheep (or the field) from the sheep-taker (or his parents) some days (or some decades) before. Based on these new facts, we shall change our views about the moral status of the sheep-taking. Now we will be likely to say that the one we saw take the sheep was not, morally speaking, a criminal, but the opposite, a victim responding justifiably (or less unjustifiably than it seemed at first) to an earlier crime. Likewise, if we come to see ownership of means of production as itself a violation of justice (because unjustly maldistributive or unjustifiably coercive), we will see the things that people do in response to it as more just (or less unjust) than they appeared when we didn't question the justice of ownership of means of production.

On the slavery-maldistribution view, then, the individuals normally labeled "criminal" are seen as the victims of a prior "crime" to which they are responding. That criminals may not (and usually do not) see themselves as doing this only reflects the fact that they are taken in by capitalist ideology no less than law-abiding folks are. The "criminal" then is not a doer of injustice but the reverse. He is a victim of injustice trying to improve his situation by means that have been made necessary by the fact that capitalism leaves him few alternatives. Thus, the upshot of this charge is that criminals are not really morally guilty. They are in large measure unjustly punished for *re*acting against crimes perpetrated by the very system that punishes them.

In sum, the Marxian critique of criminal justice does lead to a moral condemnation of criminal justice under capitalism. This moral condemnation comes, so to speak, in two forms, both of which share the claim that capitalist criminal justice wrongly punishes people who do not deserve to be punished. In the first form, the alienation charge, they are thought not to deserve punishment because their acts are caused by socially conditioned antagonism to their fellows in conjunction with limited and unstable opportunities to satisfy their needs and desires. In the second form, the slavery-maldistribution charge, they are thought not to deserve punishment because their apparent crimes are themselves reactions against conditions which are themselves, morally speaking, criminal. Needless to say, it is possible for the same person to endorse both forms of condemnation.

Several things that apply to both charges are worth noting. First of all, in both cases, the features of capitalist criminal justice that come in for ethical condemnation reflect the very failure to see the dependence of reason's products on the mode of production about which I spoke at the outset. In the case of the alienation charge, the failure is that of not seeing that capitalist criminal justice emerges to regulate the antagonistic relations between human beings that capitalism produces. Seeing capitalist criminal justice as the product of independent reason, it seems that those antagonistic relations are a natural feature of human life which must always be so regulated. Then, capitalist criminal justice, rather than protecting capitalism against the crime it itself gives rise to, appears merely to be the necessary condition of any peaceful social coexistence. In the case of the slavery-maldistribution charge, the failure is of not seeing how property in capitalism is an expression of a particular and morally questionable constellation of social forces. Seeing capitalist criminal justice as the product of independent reason, it seems that the property criminal justice protects is a natural feature of human life which is always in need of such protection. Then, capitalist criminal justice, rather than protecting the interests of capitalists, appears merely to be protecting everyone's interest. What's more, it follows that the continued and heavily publicized activities of criminal justice serve to reinforce ideological blindness, on the first view, to capitalism's role in causing the attitudes and conditions that lead to crime, and, on the second view, to the moral dubiousness of capitalist property relations.

It must also be borne in mind that the ethical implications of both charges must be considered as general propositions which will fit actual criminal cases in varying degrees. For example, while the alienation charge suggests that criminals are not culpable because shaped by an antagonistic society, in actual cases, the degree to which individual lawbreakers have been so shaped will vary. There may be some who have largely escaped these deleterious influences and yet, out of selfishness or greed, commit crimes. Marxism naturally claims that the number of criminals of this sort is small compared to the number of criminals all told. But Marxism need not deny that there are some criminals like this, and thus that they deserve punishment. Likewise, on the slavery-maldistribution charge, while criminals are generally taken to be victims of the prior injustice of private ownership of means of production, actual criminals will differ in the degree to which they are so victimized and in the degree to which their actual crimes can be thought of as reactions thereto. Relatively privileged persons, or others whose crimes bear little relation to their class position (some rapists, for example), may well be more culpable than the general rule of criminals. It seems to me appropriate for Marxists to view responsibility—and thus guilt—as existing in varying degrees, relative to the actual impact of the social structure on a given individual's criminal act.

Finally, note that on neither of the two views we have discussed does the criminal emerge as any kind of "protorevolutionary," as is sometimes asserted of Marxism. On the alienation charge, the criminal is at best relieved of responsibility because he has been shaped by the social system to have antisocial attitudes and fated by that system to experience need and insecurity which, together with those attitudes, lead to crime. On the slavery-maldistribution charge, the criminal is at best a victim because he is the object of the unjust coercion or expropriation characteristic of private ownership of means of production. And his crime, rather than being a kind of rebellion against what victimizes him, is most often a narrowly self-interested striking out against whatever he can get his hands on. On both charges, Marxism does imply reduced or no blame for (most) criminals; but it does not imply any celebration of their acts. This is particularly so in light of the fact that most victims of crime are other exploited people, members or would-be members of the working class. Crime and criminality must on the whole be placed by Marxism among the costs of capitalism, lined up alongside poverty, unemployment, pollution, and the rest.

9

Legitimation Crisis in Contract Law: A Test Case for Critical Legal Studies and its Critics*

DAVID INGRAM

The Critical Legal Studies (CLS) movement has contributed enormously to our understanding of the deeper philosophical tensions animating liberal legal theory. Chief among them is an ambivalence with respect to distinctions (originally articulated in the social contract theories of Hobbes and Locke) between objective facts and subjective values, abstract rights and concrete goods, formal procedures and substantive outcomes, individual liberties and collective utilities, public domains and private interests. Classical liberalism and its formalist counterpart in nineteenth-century legal theory affirm these distinctions as fundamental to the legitimacy of the legal order; the neoliberalism associated with the defense of the modern welfare state does not.[1]

In the following essay I argue that this antinomy in liberal thought is symptomatic of contradictions inherent in the democratic institutions of the welfare state. These institutions manifest a profound ambivalence with respect to the priority of conflict over consensus. To the extent that capitalist society exhibits the strain of class conflict, its legal institutions remain compromised by opposed interests and values. From another perspective, however, compromise remains elusive in a system whose polarizing tendencies exacerbate conflict. Since opposed groups operating within the private sector cannot be counted on to resolve their differences, compromise must be manufactured in closed legislative chambers by leaders of the various parties or worked out by functionaries of the judicial establishment. Doubting the capacity of parliamentary politics to ensure compromise, neoliberals—in opposition to their liberal counterparts—support judicial, executive, and corporatist interventions in the private sphere that further remove the process of compromise formation from public oversight.

The legitimacy of these interventions ostensibly derives from their furtherance of public interests. However, it is my contention that such interests could not be determined rationally apart from democratic discussion aimed at reaching consensus. The substantive provisions for consensus on common goods would require the abolition of capitalist private property as well as the elimination of class stratification. The latter requirements are incompatible with those forms of bureaucracy that balance opposed interests—or adjudicate compromises—under contractualist assumptions.[2] This contradiction—that bureaucracy furthers a public interest whose very possibility it implicitly undermines—pervades social legislation. In the final analysis labor and welfare statutes assume the form of invasive constraints on the autonomy, equality, and democratic inclusion they ostensibly foster.

CONTRACTUALISM AND DEMOCRACY: AN HISTORICAL OVERVIEW

Only in the last two centuries has democracy found widespread acceptance as the preferred form of polity in the Western Hemisphere. Its popularity seems proportionate to its success in managing conflict and promoting peace. Yet, oddly enough, the intransigence of social conflict has determined the shape that this regime has taken. To the extent that social stratification and conflict prevail in capitalist societies, democratic conflict management remains limited to negotiating compromises between competing interest groups.

CLS advocates argue that this type of democracy does not *resolve* social conflict so much as *suppress* and *contain* it. They add that a system designed to facilitate compromises between competing classes privileges the most dominant interests and would tend to exacerbate conflict were it not for bureaucratic intervention undertaken in the name of a higher good. Many of them propose participatory models of democracy that are more amenable to fostering consensus on common interests than those prevailing in capitalist society. In response to this challenge, liberals in the classical tradition invoke what they take to be the inherent egoism of human nature and the fundamental incommensurability of particular interests. Conflicting needs, interests, values, and conceptions of the good are, they tell us, little more than expressions of personal preference and circumstantial caprice.

Consequently, achieving consensus on all but the most general principles of enlightened self-interest (contractualism) is thought to be futile
and not to be undertaken, for fear of inciting public intrusion into the
private affairs of the citizen.[3]

In contrast to the classical liberal's defense of the autonomy of the
private sector, the neoliberal advocates bureaucratic intervention for
the sake of furthering a public interest.[4] Despite their differences, both
share a disdain for participatory democracy. This disdain is founded
on a distinction between public reason, defined by economic theorems
of rational choice, and private morality. The distinction has its roots in
the social contractarian tradition of Hobbes and Locke. It was this tradition that first introduced a contractualist conception of public law
authorized by the confluence of private wills.[5] The public will embodying
this union was conceived as something abstract—instantiating the basic equality and freedom of human beings oriented solely toward self-
preservation. The moral domain—broadly speaking, that aspect of the
human condition encompassing desirable and felicitous ends—was henceforth consigned to the private sphere.

This privatization of moral ends would have been inconceivable within
the classical tradition of natural law dating back to Aristotle.[6] That
tradition had imbued self-preservation with a rational impulse toward
moral fulfillment. One's own happiness was thought to be organically
dependent on the happiness of all. Far from being a manifestation of
the merely private, desire, need, and interest ostensibly embodied—in
however imperfect a form—the governing precepts of a naturally and
divinely ordained hierarchy of being. Although Aristotle believed that
the precepts of morality were plain to rational persons, he assumed
that, due to circumstances of birth, education, or divine appointment,
some persons were better equipped than others to perceive the general good, and that they alone should be accorded the exclusive privilege of ruling. Thus his modest praise of restrictive forms of democracy
still echoes Plato's concern about the unstable, conflict-ridden mob rule
that occurs whenever the masses come to power.[7]

Thomas Hobbes took issue with the elitist implications of this concept of moral reason. Writing in the aftermath of the scientific revolution inaugurated by Galileo and Bacon in the seventeenth century and
constrained by the social realities of nascent capitalism, Hobbes repudiated teleological notions of reason and, in accordance with mechanistic
precepts, held that passions—above all, the fear of death—determined
behavior.[8] Self-preservation continues to be the natural end of human
endeavor in Hobbes's theory but is drained of any moral significance.
Hobbes reasoned that in a hypothetical state of nature each person
would have an *equal* and *unlimited* right to acquire whatever he deemed
necessary for survival, either singly or in combination with others. Driven

by their desire to assure themselves constant access to scarce resources, men embark upon an insatiable quest for power that cannot but terminate in a war of all against all. Here the voice of reason does not so much prescribe the ends of action as it does the means for maintaining action as such; it counsels us to seek peace whenever others are willing to do likewise. Reason is thus a slave to passion, calculating the shortest route to the long-term satisfaction of our most urgent desires. Hence, Hobbes's version of natural law does not articulate an ideally just order replete with virtues to be emulated. At most it specifies the minimum steps that any group of enlightened egoists with conflicting interests must take in setting up institutions of law and order conducive to their mutual self-preservation. Each realizes that he must lay down his natural right to all things, if others are willing to do so, and, by majority consent, transfer it to a person or group of persons authorized to issue and enforce legally binding commands.[9]

Despite Hobbes's defense of the natural equality of men and his appeal to democratic procedures in establishing government by consent, his contention that sovereign authority is above the law has not made him very popular with liberals. It is therefore not surprising that Locke has had a greater following among them. Locke stressed the importance of democratic procedures in the social contract, favored popular representation, and most importantly, implemented the private/public distinction in defending constitutionally limited government. Yet despite his inclusion of substantive considerations of equity in his formulation of natural right, his defense of private property and social inequality testifies to the continuing allure of Hobbes's contractualist conception of human nature. In Locke's account the state of nature is fast reduced to a state of war, once a market economy is established with its attendant social stratification.[10] Since Locke believed that women and laborers lacked the rationality and industry requisite for full citizenship, their inclusion in the social contract, he reasoned, should be marginal.[11] Thus, while Lockean principles may have justified majoritarian democracy, his assumptions about human nature and differential capacities implied a very limited franchise—one hardly conducive to public agreement on a common interest.[12]

Now Hobbes's contractualist assumptions anticipated a formalism that was only to emerge in practice by the end of the nineteenth century, long after social contractarian legal theories had lost their appeal. Rejecting Aristotle's conception of justice, he argued that one's desert (worth) amounted to what others were willing to pay for one's services—a clear anticipation of the *will* theory of contract that would emerge at the beginning of the nineteenth century.[13] Although natural law doctrines stressing equity (Rousseau, Paine, and Locke) were just as irrelevant to actual jurisprudence in the eighteenth century, they at least conformed to common law notions of equity in circulation at that time.[14] In truth the bourgeois public sphere of the eighteenth century mirrored contradictions inherent in both economic and moral conceptions of natural law. On the one hand the legitimacy of the legal order depended on the free consent of a public whose rational agreement on common interests was ostensibly guaranteed by the moral equality and autonomy of its members. On the other hand possession of these moral attributes was made contingent on ownership of private property.[15] In principle this public was inclusive and universal—ideally (as in Kant's *Rechtslehre*) rational, egalitarian, and democratic; in practice it was not. The contradiction between moral reason and economic reality intrinsic to the social contractarian legitimation of the capitalist state thus had its analogue in a common law that at once protected and limited contractual freedom in the name of equity.

As articulated in Blackstone's *Commentaries* and practically implemented in eighteenth-century common law, contracts primarily served to transfer title of property, enforcing performance in accordance with customary standards of equity. This requirement—that properties exchanged be of equal value—still resonated in the writings of political economists (Smith, Say, Ricardo) on whom Marx's own labor theory of value relied. However, with the expansion of capitalism this concept became untenable in practice. Contract law ceased to be subsumed under property law once the *market value* of goods became the standard for determining damages.

The will theory of contract that came into being in the early nineteenth century dispensed with equity considerations altogether. Under the title theory of exchange, law exhibited a substantive concern for equity that made it an imperfect vehicle for capital accumulation; not only were sellers not assured of the market value of their goods when payment was finally—and often belatedly—received, but the values exchanged had to be equivalent to one another according to predetermined standards. By interpreting contracts as "meetings of minds" or voluntary conjunctions of arbitrary wills, in which it was assumed that the contracting parties were seeking their own advantage, the will theory succeeded in detaching contract law from property law and whatever moral constraints it still contained. Civil courts now rewarded damages due to breach in accordance with the seller's or buyer's market-based expectations rather than on the terms originally negotiated. Once "consideration" was received even the most unfair bargain became irrevocable.

Whatever difficulties attended the will theory of contract resided in a residual reliance on local customs and merchant laws in determining the intent of the contracting parties. This, in turn, had a corrosive effect on the predictability of adjudication so necessary for efficient market calculations. Consequently, the will theory—with its focus on subjective intent—gave way to a formalist theory that defined the meeting of minds objectively, in terms of "the strict letter of contract" or other overt acts. As Morton Horwitz notes regarding the new wave of legal formalists:

> No longer finding it necessary to enter into battle against eighteenth-century just price doctrines, they could devote their energies to establishing in the second half of the nineteenth century a system of objective rules necessary to assure legal certainty and predictability. And having destroyed most substantive grounds for evaluating the justice of exchange, they could elaborate a legal ideology of formalism, of which Williston was a leading exemplar, that could not only disguise gross disparities of bargaining power under a facade of neutral and formal rules of contract law, but could also enforce commercial customs under the comforting technical rubric of "contract interpretation."[16]

As we shall see, legal formalism declined in the wake of the new social legislation of the 1930s. The doctrines of unconscionability, good faith, and reliance informing twentieth-century contract law reintroduce standards of equity, albeit under the guise of balancing private interests—hence the retention of contractualist assumptions.[17] Before examining the impact this transformation had on social law, I will briefly note the way in which the balancing of interests came to dominate the debate over democracy in postcolonial America. This is important, not only because it shows how contractualist assumptions about the ineradicable opposition between private interests continue to insinuate themselves into new standards of contractual equity emphasizing the balancing of interests (compromise), but because it anticipates the neocorporatist and neopluralist theories of democracy that accompany the rise of the welfare state.

It is hardly inconsequential that many of the debates prior to the ratification of the Constitution of 1787 centered around the conflict between premodern republican virtue—which, for the Jeffersonian faction, could only be exemplified in a yeoman democracy founded on an agrarian economy and solidified by *common* interests—and modern *egoism*, embodied in the commercial diversity and federalism (statism) defended by the Hamiltonian faction. The *Federalist Papers* can be seen as an extended debate over the possibility of reconciling the former and the latter. Can democracy, which presupposes an orientation toward the common good, be reconciled with the factionalism born of self-interest? Is federalism—the merging and balancing of national and regional interests—workable? The solution worked out by the Founding Fathers attempted to strike a balance between the classical virtue of substantive democratic justice (the public good) and formal liberty

(private interest). Democratic tendencies toward fragmentation or tyranny could be checked by bicameral legislature and an independent
executive (which later included an independent judiciary). For Madison, the separation of powers—no less than the multiplying of factions and commercial self-interest—could lead to a cancelling out of
particular interests, leaving the national interest intact and on top. [18]
Democracy was workable so long as the upper house of appointed
delegates could be counted on to defend the sanctity of private property and freedom of trade against the tyrannical leveling of the masses.
Contractualism thus trumped democracy.

By the time Tocqueville visited America in the 1830s the abstract,
"possessive" individualism inherent in the contractualist polity would
reveal the truth of this diagnosis in an altogether different phenomenon: the pressure toward conformity and increasing bureaucratization.[19]
The latter has become a major concern among contemporary theorists:
the leveling and "massifying" tendencies endemic to liberal democracy seem to nourish the kind of anomic disintegration and disorgani-
zation so favorable to "totalitarian" solutions.[20] Madison had no inkling
of this danger, despite his fear of majoritarian tyranny. Yet his thinking on the subject of tyranny is not radically dissimilar from one who
has been viewed variously as a critic of conformity and bureaucracy
and as a proponent of totalitarian democracy: Rousseau. Rousseau's
account of the social contract is also torn between classical virtue and
modern egoism, and his attempt to reconcile individual freedom and
collective governance likewise depends on the cancellation of private
wills. However, Rousseau was less enthusiastic about entrusting this
cancellation to a formal democratic process filtered through factions,
representatives, and distinct powers. The direct democracy he proposed
was to resolve the problem of tyranny by specifying certain conditions
under which a majority will would approximate a rational consensus.
These included homogeneity of life-styles and interests, general if not
absolute equality of circumstances, economic self-sufficiency and absolute autonomy of individual citizens, the absence of any political
culture in which corporate associations and particular interests might
form, and most importantly, a civic desire on the part of each to will
the common good.[21] Occasionally he suggests that the universal form
of the law might suffice to guarantee its expression of the General
Will.[22] Elsewhere, however, he acknowledges the fallibility of the masses
and recommends that laws be proposed by a wise Legislator. Coercing
minorities does not seem unreasonable to him since, under these conditions, it means forcing them to acknowledge their own best interest.[23]

Rousseau's organicism, which harks back to the earlier natural law
tradition of Aristotle, is fraught with many of the same contradictions
besetting earlier models of the social contract. He wants to ground the

autonomy and equality of rational subjects in the possession of private property but suspects that this conception of reason is too closely aligned with egoism and inequality. The universal moral reason he proposes to offset self-interest, however, is too abstract and formal to arouse esprit de corps in the people. Hence his appeal to natural sympathy, solidified by common mores and patriotism. Since he regards public discussion as an indicator of disagreement—and thus as evidence of the public's failure to perceive its true interest—he must ascribe rational insight to the superior wisdom of the legislator.[24]

This ascription anticipates later attempts to limit democratic participation in the name of a higher interest, whether that interest be identified with national security, the people, the laws of history, or the public welfare.[25] Despite talk of consensus, its underlying premise continues to be conflict. Consensus would be the outcome of private deliberation (or rational choice theory, to use contemporary language), conflict that of public debate, or *politics*. This dichotomy depends on substantializing reason and consensus and separating them from the procedures and conditions of public debate. On one hand modern societies *are* composed of persons living heterogeneous life-styles and possessing plural—and sometimes incompatible—interests. Liberalism acknowledges this fact but neglects the public nature of practical reason, which is oriented toward achieving a consensus that is not yet given. On the other hand the classical model of democratic self-governance shatters on the hard reality of complex organized political systems. It is administrators who govern, and it is they who, in collusion with the party system, shape public opinion. In conjunction with the debasement of political debate, the inevitability of bureaucracy—which, after all, satisfies the rational need for an efficient and impartial administration of law—seems to reinforce the impression that public reason must be vested in the private chambers of Congress, the Supreme Court, or the agencies of the executive. But the debasement of public debate, and with it the suppression of an egalitarian and universal political culture, are not inevitable side effects of bureaucratic administration. Indeed, if the people who elect the officials who appoint the administrators are irrational, the officials and administrators cannot be less so.

It was as if the failures of the revolutionary democratic tradition of Rousseau confirmed the worst fears of subsequent democratic reformers. Although the liberal movement for democratic reform that swept England in the nineteenth century was inspired less by the social contractarian tradition of Locke and Rousseau than by the utilitarian doctrine of Bentham and James Mill, it nonetheless evinced a recrudescence of contractualism at a decisive juncture in its argument. Utilitarianism supported deviations from common law practice, lent support to the will theory of contract, and so justified capitalism. But it also justified democracy—hence the problem: if the aim of legislation is the promotion of the greatest happiness for the greatest number, and if each person's happiness is to count as much as anyone else's, then the best system of legislation is elective representative government.

Although Bentham and Mill were both advocates of universal suffrage *in principle*, each eventually came out in support of a franchise limited to men possessing at least modest wealth and education.[26] They did so out of political expediency and the contractualist conviction that the primary justification for democracy was the *protection* of property against tyranny.[27] Both accepted the division between rich and poor as an unavoidable consequence of natural greed, and so had strong reservations about extending the franchise to the lower, uneducated classes. By the same token they accepted the justice of private property because it conformed to human nature as they understood it. Although the principle of diminishing utility favored a more equitable distribution of wealth, greed struck them as an all but irresistible incentive for optimizing aggregate utility. Given what they regarded as a *natural* propensity to acquire property—and thus a *natural* propensity to enter into contractual relations free from public constraint—it was natural to assume that the happiness of most if not all persons would be maximized by the production of more consumer goods, inequalities in distribution notwithstanding. And since such a system was clearly in the interest of the wealthy, the extension of the franchise to the poor became irrelevant.[28]

As a counterexample to the picture of utilitarian democracy depicted here one could, of course, mention the reform efforts of John Stuart Mill. Unlike his predecessors in the liberal tradition, he subscribed to Humboldt's view that "the end of man . . . is the highest and most harmonious development of his powers to a complete and consistent whole."[29] Consonant with this romantic conception of human nature, the proper function of democracy, he maintained, should not be limited to protection of property. It should also include the broadest expression of political opinion, conducive to the *development* of all persons as responsible citizens without regard to class or gender.[30] Although Mill was clearly concerned about the conformist tyranny of Rousseauian democracy, he nonetheless evinced a sympathy for the older republican—and egalitarian—virtues. Thus he hoped that obstacles to universal suffrage, especially disparities in wealth and education which retard the development of the working class and generate conflict, might be remedied by replacing the existing regime of wage exploitation with a competitive system composed of worker cooperatives.[31] Yet so captivated was he by the intransigence of conflict and the likelihood of class legislation that he could not but affirm a stronger role for an impartial and educated bureaucracy. Although the system of plural voting and appointed legislative commissioners that he proposed to offset the numerical advantage of the working class was incompatible with the participatory (and representative) democracy he so desired, it nonetheless anticipated the growing intervention of a bureaucracy conceived as proxy for a public interest (common good).[32] In this respect it manifested a scepticism with regard to the rationality of liberal democracy that was not different in principle from that articulated by neo-Hegelians at the turn of the century, who favored corporatist as well as bureaucratic solutions to social conflict.[33]

The rise of mass political parties in the twentieth century served to blunt the edge of class conflict and so disqualified Mill's worst fears. Yet it did so at the expense of abandoning his idealistic hope for a participatory democracy. To be sure, there were those like John Dewey, who continued to espouse the cause of participatory democracy. However, neo-Hegelian idealism and democratic pragmatism seemed ill-equipped to counteract the prevailing hierarchies of power. In endorsing the corporatist alliance between labor and capital that he saw emerging in the 1920s and 1930s, Dewey overestimated the functional organicism and egalitarianism of a scientific culture vis-à-vis the conflictual dynamics of capitalism.[34] On the contrary, it was mass plebiscitary democracy—not the broad dissemination of scientific intelligence—that initially provided the perfect vehicle for marshalling loyalty to the state. And, it was mass democracy that encouraged the deferential respect for elites (technocrats, bureaucrats, and party leaders) so conducive to the aims of corporatism and class compromise.[35] In England and America, where two major parties that nominally represented opposing class interests dominated the political arena, there was a tendency for each party to move toward a middle position in which alternatives were blurred and questions of economic justice suppressed. Even in the multiparty systems that prevailed on the Continent the various parties had to compromise their positions in order to form coalitions.

Not surprisingly, the conduct of elections in mass democracy lent credence to economic theories of partisan politics. Those by Joseph Schumpeter (1943) and Anthony Downs (1957) are particularly noteworthy. According to these theories, competing elites arrayed in opposing political parties offer various assortments of goods to the electorate in exchange for votes.[36] As Downs noted, when voters are evenly distributed along an ideological continuum, parties in a two-party system will move to the center; otherwise they will diverge from it. More disturbing for Downs was the implication, already well documented by Kenneth Arrow, that there is no decision procedure that can ensure a fair aggregation for certain distributions of preferences.[37] Arrow's "Impossibility Theorem" (1951), which proved the fundamental irrationality of collective choice procedures, is confirmed by the failure of political parties to link voter preferences with policy outcomes, to provide clear-cut options, and to rise above accommodation to secret compromises by elites. The democratization of mass parties in Britain and the United States during the 1970s only partially remedied these difficulties and was offset by countervailing tendencies strengthening the power of elites vis-à-vis the party rank and file.

Pluralists like Robert Dahl and Charles Lindblom defended the system in spite of its failure to satisfy principles of rational choice, arguing that mass parties generally permit vocal minorities to exercise some political influence in the form of voting blocs.[38] Given the irreducible plurality of opposing values and interests, the best that could be expected—so it was argued—would be a *polyarchical* rule by minorities that encouraged stable economic growth through compromise.[39] Indeed, the argument was made that the system actually produces an optimal equilibrium of supply and demand, despite the fact that, in such an oligopolistic system, *effective* demand (itself largely orchestrated by the parties themselves) is primarily skewed in favor of the wealthy and educated.[40] Despite their initial optimism, Dahl and Lindblom observed with increasing dismay the disequilibriating impact that economic corporations, government bureaucracies, and wealthy interest groups have on the democratic competition for power.[41] To offset the veto power of economic corporations on government policies, Dahl advocated the extension of democracy to the workplace and the limitation of privatized government bureaucracies.[42]

Recent trends in the evolution of mass parties during the last decade belie the optimism of pluralist theory. Mass parties have been weakened by their own internal dynamics, which compel them to ally with the mass media. The ubiquitous visibility of media-generated stars accounts for the capacity of incumbents and outsiders alike to generate campaign funds without relying on party support. Meanwhile the masses—having become increasingly disillusioned with the failure of parties to provide clear-cut alternatives—have redirected their loyalties toward the other beneficiaries of media attention: special interest groups.[43]

Although pluralist theory is bankrupt as a description of democratic politics, it continues to function as a powerful ideology preserving the contractualist notion of democracy as a form of power brokering among elites, whose market-simulating behavior ostensibly provides the checks and balances requisite for protecting minorities against hegemonic tyranny. Of course, political parties, plural interests, and compromise policies are not to blame for the rationality deficits and inegalitarianism of mass democracy. Under conditions of consensus-oriented participatory democracy—conditions that presuppose a noncontractualist ontology of

individuality and rationality and a noncapitalist market economy—
paradoxes of rational choice could be mitigated, if not dismissed as
irrelevant (see below).[44] Indeed, it may well be, as Jon Elster argues,
that the failure of rational choice theories to account for the peculiar
rationality of democratic political reform stems from their contractualist
neglect of *justice*.[45] That society can be made just appeals to a rationale
that is irreducible to the instrumental rationality governing the
maximization of individual or social utility.

It is the struggle for justice that at least partially undergirds the ideology of the welfare state. This ideology finds its penultimate justification in John Rawls' *The Theory of Justice* (1971). His version of the
social contract, which justifies substantive principles of justice by appeal to economic theorems of rational choice, still reflects contractualist
assumptions. But these are tempered by moral side constraints, so that
the principles chosen allow for paternalistic intervention by the state
in the name of distributive justice. Despite this concession, he continues to defend a rather sharp distinction between the public sphere,
consisting of such institutions as the constitution and legal system, and
the private sphere, consisting of the nuclear family and competitive
market. To the former he assigns political rights, to the latter economic
rights pertaining to distributive justice. Moreover, he defends the priority of political and civil liberties over distributive justice.[46] On this
reading, the fair value of political liberty comes to mean something
quite innocuous, namely, equal possession of voting rights and eligibility for office. Since formal political rights do not extend into the
private sphere, they have no regulative impact on socioeconomic inequalities and democratization of the workplace and society.[47] Hence
the fair value of associating with others in the consensual formation
and dissemination of public opinion is left largely unprotected.

Rawls admits that constitutional government ought to "insure the
fair value of political liberty for all persons" by securing the autonomy
of political parties "with respect to private demands . . . not expressed
in a public forum and argued for openly by reference to a conception
of the public good."[48] Since he concedes that inequities in wealth and
status undermine the fair value of political liberty by granting to some
a greater influence in the shaping of public opinion, it seems that he
should advocate greater economic equality than even his Difference
Principle will allow. Indeed, given his simplified indexing of primary
goods to wealth and income, he believes that the low esteem and political impotence of those at the bottom of the social ladder can be
offset by monetary compensations provided by the government. However, as I argue below, the paternalistic dependency fostered by the
client-provider relationship undermines the autonomy requisite for
political inclusion that redistribution ought to guarantee.

To sum up, contractualist assumptions have permeated liberal democratic theory from its very inception. But these assumptions are not without ambiguity. In the eighteenth and nineteenth centuries equity competed with contractual right. This tension was reflected in liberal democratic theory. Pluralist theory and the theory of checks and balances responded to the threat of majoritarian tyranny; thus they took for granted a conflict-oriented model of democracy that made no pretense about the fundamental irrationality of social choice. Developmentalist and corporatist theories defended the potential rationality of social choice, but only the former saw participatory democracy *in the broadest sense* as instrumental to social rationality. The rise of the welfare state reintroduced questions of equity that further tested classical liberal theories of law and democracy and lent credibility to consensus formation, democratic participation, and the politics of public interest. But it was the collapse of the distinction between state and civil society and the rise of bureaucracy and corporatism that disproved liberal theory's contractualist premises. Today these trends threaten to undermine both the legitimacy of a democracy that merely equilibriates the competing sources of effective demand and the efficiency of a social law that compensates for inequity through greater domination.

CRITICAL LEGAL STUDIES AND THE ANTINOMIES OF THE WELFARE STATE

The distinctions that emerged in the social contract theories of Hobbes and Locke eventually led Max Weber—perhaps the most influential legal theorist of the twentieth century—to privilege bureaucracy as the preferred mechanism for resolving social conflict. As is well known, Weber eventually made his peace with legal positivism, arguing that the legitimacy of modern formal law rests solely on its capacity to satisfy the demands of instrumental rationality, namely, freedom of choice functional for contractual obligation and predictability of enforcement functional for economic calculation. His ambivalent support of bureaucracy and his desire to rid law of any substantive consideration of equity are of momentous concern to us, since they echo the Hobbesian distinction between public (instrumental) reason and private (moral) interest that undercuts any support for participatory democracy.[49]

CLS advocates reject Weber's legal positivism, arguing that economic rationality is insufficient to generate, let alone sustain, even contractual obligations (Hobbes's dilemma), and that therefore moral considerations do underwrite the rule of law, rather than vice versa. Yet most accept the Hobbesian premise that any moral considerations of legal consequence lack rational (universal) validity. Among the few CLS critics who questioned this position was Roberto Unger. In *Knowledge and*

Politics (1976) he argued that the nominalist attack on philosophical essentialism inaugurated by Hobbes issues in fundamental antinomies that render liberalism—qua theory of knowledge, self, and society—incoherent. The most basic antinomy—between theories (concepts) and facts (particulars)—implies a use of reason that is strictly formal (procedural and abstract) and instrumental. If we accept this notion of reason then desires, values, ends—in short, substantive goods—will necessarily appear subjective, and public reason will oppose private autonomy.

Classical liberalism attempts to solve the problem of order and freedom by appealing to formal rights that apply equally and impartially to all, regardless of concrete differences in status and preference. Formal rules of legislation and adjudication are supposedly those that any disinterested rational agent would choose. Transcendent with respect to private aims, they warrant public sanction. This contractualist position thus sees the state as the sole guarantor of property rights. However, with the advent of the welfare state the scope of public interest expands; it now harbors a claim to *substantive* justice. In Unger's opinion the classical liberal justification of the state has long ceased to be valid since the formal bureaucratic neutrality presupposes an untenable distinction between public rules (procedures) and private values (goals). Basic rights, he contends, are not transcendent with respect to conflicting private aims and therefore are not inherently impartial (rational). This caveat applies equally to legislation and adjudication.

Legislative neutrality is impossible for reasons mentioned above: formal democracy encourages the aggregation of conflicting interests in ways that favor the most dominant and powerful interests. Adjudicative neutrality is impossible because any single rule will serve multiple purposes and so must be interpreted in light of subjective standards of good. However, without *shared* conceptions of good there will be no consensus regarding the meaning of laws. Once adjudication ceases to be formally limited by clear precedent, the distinction between an impartial judiciary and a partisan legislature collapses. A judiciary whose autonomy is regarded as integral to the containment of majoritarian attacks on fundamental rights now reveals itself as personal domination.[50]

Unger argues that the blurring of legislation and adjudication is propelled by the logic of law itself. The demands of legal impartiality require that formal equality give way to substantive equity. In contrast to the formal jurisprudence of the nineteenth century, the "procedural equality" enforced by the Realist School in the 1930s mandated equity in bargaining power, thereby preventing workers from "freely" assenting to formal agreements that were deemed coercive. Substantive justice would rectify bargaining inequities further, for equity lies "in the control of unjust enrichment, in the justification of a policy of income distribution, and in the definition of a criterion of public interest for the control of administrative agencies."[51]

Without procedural safeguards and equity considerations protecting against economic duress contract law would fail to *formally* distinguish a *voluntary* "meeting of minds" from coercive agreement. Thus courts are now responsible for interpreting indeterminate, open-ended standards and general clauses of legislation designed to police unconscionable contracts, to void unjust gain, to regulate economic concentration, and to ensure that government agencies act in the public interest. However, this responsibility can only be discharged by adopting policy-oriented forms of legal reasoning that undercut any formal appeal to abstract permissions and entitlements. Courts and administrative agencies must balance conflicting interests in light of changing circumstances, thereby making it increasingly difficult to sustain rigid categories of classification and criteria of analogy. In private law the determination of whether a contract was negotiated in good faith will require entering into the practices and belief systems of specific social groups. In public law the determination of criminal liability will require balancing the judgments of trained specialists against the background of the defendant's life history and the peculiar circumstances of his crime.[52] In both cases instrumental considerations—moral, political, and economic—involving the advancement of public good may override any formal appeal to "inalienable" rights.

Duncan Kennedy extends Unger's analysis of liberalism's antinomies by arguing that jurists are torn between two *antithetical* moral visions. The *"formalist"* jurisprudence espoused by classical liberalism is *individualistic*; freedom implies absence of restraint, favoring a market allocation of goods and limited liability in commercial law. The *substantive* vision is *altruistic*; freedom implies access to resources, favoring government redistribution and extended liability. The former is implicated in modes of reasoning that appeal to well-defined *rules*; it ensures maximum predictability (fair warning) and limited judicial discretion in ways that promote self-reliance. The latter is implicated in modes of reasoning that appeal to vague *standards*; it ensures inclusiveness and flexibility in ways that promote the spreading of burdens for the sake of the common good.[53]

Many CLS advocates contend that adjudication and legislation combine both moral visions. To begin with, it has been argued (by Dworkin and Unger) that in some cases (namely the hard ones) all laws require interpretation against the background of substantive moral principles not expressly stated in them.[54] Unless one argues (as Dworkin does against his CLS opponents) that interpretation need not be subjective and irrational, this view will entail the radical indeterminacy of law and, with it, a high potential for political conflict in the courts.[55] Although I am inclined to agree with Dworkin that interpretation need not be subjective, I agree with his CLS opponents that, within the contractualist parameters of capitalist democracy—especially the welfare state—indeterminacy with respect to the public good, and therewith *some* indeterminacy with respect to the meaning of the law, is inevitable.[56]

Kennedy, however, argues a stronger claim: not only do different moral views bear upon the same subcategory of law (a fact that entails neither contradictory nor indeterminate outcomes), but *any* legal doctrine (or case) will be equally susceptible to either an individualist or altruist moral interpretation, so that contradictory judgments are not only possible, but inevitable. With the spread of public interest law, the scope for conflict and irrationality has especially dire consequences, since it means that administrative interventions designed to alleviate the irrationality inherent in the politics of conflict-oriented democracy are equally irrational.

If the history of labor and welfare law is any indication of the contradictions informing public interest legislation generally, then a brief examination of the decisive precedents shaping it should confirm Kennedy's diagnosis. On the one hand the U.S. Supreme Court has interpreted the relationship between employers and employees, providers and clients, in accordance with contractual assumptions. Employees and recipients of aid do not have unqualified entitlements to work and welfare because the latter are still under the private control of business and government. On the other hand, the law tacitly recognizes entitlements to work and welfare based on equity—rights that, in principle at least, cannot be exchanged or contractually forfeited. Social law thus fosters substantive justice, autonomy, and democracy while functionally compensating for the weakness of the system within acceptable contractualist parameters.[57] But the price that must be paid for this intervention is a bureaucracy that frustrates democratic self-determination and provokes popular resistance, as can be seen in the fragmentation of the party system and the emergence of alternate channels of protest.

This crisis is exemplified in the case of labor law. During the Lochner era (named after a 1905 Supreme Court decision invalidating a New York law limiting bakery employees to 10-hour work days and 60-hour weeks), courts upheld property rights by striking down federal and state laws regulating wages, hours, and work conditions. This extreme deference to contractualism did not officially end until 1938, when Justice Harlan Fiske Stone ruled in footnote number 4 of *U.S. v. Carolene Products Co.* that courts would henceforth give a higher level of protection to personal rights like those contained in the First Amendment than to property rights. This change was already foreshadowed by the Wagner Act of 1935.

The explicit aim of the Wagner Act was to promote industrial democracy as well as industrial peace, bargaining equity, economic recovery, and freedom of choice. Yet, with the exception of industrial peace, the goals stated above were undercut by the Court's subsequent emphasis on contractualism and public interest doctrine. From 1937 to 1941 the courts refused to inquire into the substantive justice of labor contracts (*NLRB v. Jones and Laughlin Steel Co.*); allowed employers to offer permanent positions to workers hired to replace striking employees (*NLRB v. Mackey Radio & Telegraph*); and prohibited workers from threatening midterm work stoppages while permitting employers to unilaterally impose terms and conditions of employment upon concluding lawful negotiations to impasse (*NLRB v. Sands Manufacturing Co.*).[58] The former of these rulings also redefined employee rights as public rights, thereby condoning bureaucratic intervention by the NLRB. Having subsumed labor law under the doctrine of public interest, this decision removed labor disputes from *democratic* oversight by the public at large. It instituted a corporatist solution that transferred power from rank-and-file workers to union leaders, redefined the union as a trustee of public interest, and thus restricted union activity to negotiating wage and benefits. While workers were denied the right to engage in sitdown strikes—a tactic that underscored their right to the means of production—they were also deprived of an effective voice within the union.

Subsequent decisions continuing up to and beyond the Taft-Hartley Act of 1947 repeatedly testified to a contractualism that was as hostile toward employee collective action as it was friendly toward long-range economic planning.[59] If the enforcement of expectancy rights already belies the supposition of contractual freedom, business's right to withhold wages is even clearer proof of its right to compel submission.[60] Thus, although the history of labor law in the United States bears witness to a willingness to implement industrial democracy, it does so inconsistently and in a highly truncated form—one that is largely subordinated to contractual and bureaucratic restrictions. In the wake of the Reagan-Bush administration's insistence on using "cost-benefit" calculations to determine the scope of public interest doctrine, Justice Harry A. Blackmun's candid remarks about the function of labor law accurately gauge the extent to which contractualism has gained the upper hand:

> In establishing what issues must be submitted to the process of bargaining, Congress had no expectation that the elected union representative would become an equal partner in the running of the business enterprise in which the union's members were employed. . . . [I]n view of an employer's need for unencumbered decision making, bargaining over management decisions that have a substantial impact on the continued availability of employment should be required only if the benefit, for labor-management relations and the collective bargaining process, outweighs the burden placed on the conduct of the business.[61]

Social law finds itself in a similar conundrum; by processing "clients" through the contractual channels of bureaucratic administration it defeats its own purpose—to foster autonomy, self-respect, and democratic inclusion. Here the contradiction is spread over a two-tiered system of provisions skewed along gender lines.[62] Unlike social security, disability pay, and Medicare—social insurance schemes largely funded by the contributions of male wage earners and employers—AFDC, welfare, and Medicaid have been targeted toward domestic households mostly (60–81%) headed by women. Whereas the former have been regarded as entitlements, the latter—funded by general tax revenues—have not (at least not entirely). From the very beginning states and local municipalities were permitted broad discretion in establishing eligibility requirements, determining both quantity and quality of relief distributed, and overseeing the behavior of clients. In the 1960s welfare was finally recognized as a kind of entitlement; one no longer forfeited other constitutional rights in being an eligible recipient. However, during the 1970s and 1980s states were once again permitted to establish punitive ceilings in the dollar amount of stipends, to send caseworkers into homes, and to impose restrictive work requirements (workfare).

The fact that provisions drawn from public insurance schemes are regarded as full-fledged entitlements clearly indicates the contractualist assumptions embedded in this kind of aid. It thereby illuminates the peculiar kind of contradiction at the heart of unemployment and, to a lesser extent, disability compensation. Workers—mostly males—who have staked their identities as autonomous, dignified breadwinners—are now placed in the position of having to accept monetary compensation for something that has no market-based monetary equivalent: their own self-respect. Their entitlement to compensation is based on something they no longer possess; lacking bargaining power, they cannot force the settlement of compensation in a way that would fully match what they are entitled to: a safe, fulfilling job. The situation is different in the case of welfare provisions. Women who accept this aid know that their domestic labor is not legally protected and publicly recognized; they have therefore grown up with different expectations than men. However, if they feel the stigma of dependency less than men, they suffer worse for lack of legal status; they are truly clients, whose rights can be forfeited in return for aid. Because they have no clear right to the state's charity—and here the contractualist assumption of the state as a *private* agency controlling private capital is quite evident—they feel the contradiction of social legislation more directly.[63]

However, the greatest obstacles facing welfare recipients today are not simply political; they are legal. Recipients not only lack the knowledge and wherewithal to initiate appeals on their behalf; the random shifts in appellate policy could not be absorbed adequately by caseworkers. Deprived of normal due process, recipients have lost whatever autonomy and respect they had gained in the previous decade. Ultimately, this loss stems from the contractual relationship that is imposed on the provider and client; as provider the state possesses the same discretionary powers over its resources as do owners of private property.[64] Thus the entitlements of welfare recipients amount to as much—and as little—as the rights of workers to collective bargaining.

Beyond Rational Choice: Public Interest and Democracy

I have tried to show how a predominant strand of classical liberal thought—contractualism—has continued to thrive in the political and legal institutions of the welfare state. Contractualism is an accurate barometer of the social antagonism permeating capitalist society, since it presupposes the separation of public reason and private interest. To the former it ascribes neutral procedures for the impartial aggregation and adjudication of interests. To the latter it ascribes acquisitive and possessive behaviors oriented toward the maximization of personal utility.

To be sure, the separation of reason and interest was never more than partially instantiated in the theory and practice of classical liberal democracy and jurisprudence. Pluralists and economists agree that the competitive model of mass party politics does not provide a rational method for fairly aggregating interests and protecting minorities (or majorities) from domination. Liberals like Dworkin agree with legal realists and CLS advocates that legal decisions in hard cases are not the mechanical outcome of formal procedures, but reflect the moral interpretations of jurists—interpretations that are bound to be subjective, indeterminate, and conflicting relative to the antagonisms of the society they mirror.

The separation between public reason and private interest seems even less pertinent to the theory and practice of the welfare state. This state arose in response to new demands for social justice that accompanied the intensification of conflict endemic to a crisis-prone market economy. Its right to intervene in the private sphere was premised on the assumption that a common good, or public interest, could be determined rationally and implemented bureaucratically against the conflicting economic interests that asserted themselves in legislative chambers. In general, the trend toward corporatism and compromise went hand in hand with the rise of greater judicial intervention—the latter most evident in labor and welfare law. As we have seen, labor and welfare law exemplify an evolutionary development within law itself; formal rights securing negative freedom (civil, contractual, and political freedom from arbitrary constraint) can only provide equal protection when interpreted in light of the substantive requirements for their enforcement. But here too the realization of social justice (the elevation of all citizens to the rank of fully autonomous agents and their inclusion in the political community as equals) is undermined by residual contractualist assumptions—assumptions that substitute bureaucratic decision for democratic self-determination.

As I remarked in my discussion of Rousseau, the central weakness of contractualism and, therewith, the central weakness of conflict-oriented models of democracy, resides in the identification of political rationality with instrumental (economic) reason. Consensus on shared norms—indeed, collective choice in general—is seen as an abnormal, if not impossible, outcome of plebiscitary democracy. To the extent that consensus and rational choice are possible, they must be generated by technical and political elites who, ostensibly occupying a neutral position above the fray of competing interests, wield the power of publicity and law.

To counter this model one must appeal to an alternate conception of rationality, whose *modus operandi* is dialogical and democratic. This conception accepts the collapse of the public reason/private interest distinction but does not consign the discovery of a public interest to economists deploying rational choice theorems.[65] Recent research by Karl-Otto Apel and Jürgen Habermas has shown the importance of consensual communication—and thus participatory democracy—for developing an alternate model of practical reasoning that undercuts the public reason/private morality distinction underlying classical liberalism.[66] Hobbes based this distinction on a conception of reason limited to two sorts of operations: the *instrumental* capacity to infer cause and effect so as to most efficiently bring about some end; and the *logical* capacity to infer decisions from preferences, norms, and values by rules of deductive reasoning. Neither operation alone or in combination with the other is sufficient to determine the rationality of *ends*. Nor can one simply appeal to plebiscitary democracy in deciding this matter. The rational aggregation of preferences ignores the process of discussion by which these preferences are shaped; the quality of a preference—its rationality—is at least as important as its quantity. But the rationality in question transcends the instrumental and deductive capacities of the isolated individual; it presupposes a concerted effort of critical reflection, or dialogue. Stated differently, democracy consists of more than just the passive registration and representation of given interest positions; it also consists of the discursive formation of public opinion. The latter should not only shape the legislative agenda, it should also contribute to the critical articulation and revision of individual needs.

Social and political inequalities prevent persons from contributing
to the formation of public opinion by denying them the educational,
cultural, and material resources and opportunities necessary for equal
participation. Indeed, social and political domination colors the very
language we use to talk about our needs, thereby suppressing alternative vocabularies of self-understanding. By contrast, rational speakers
are committed to treating themselves and others as equals who are
capable of reaching consensus on common interests free from the distortions of ideology. Indeed, it is the good-faith effort in reaching accord
on mutually satisfactory arrangements—not the accord itself—that ultimately legitimates legal authority.

The concept of collective intelligence outlined above is compatible
with the liberal defense of pluralism and civil rights. The communitarian
ideal it embodies does not entail the priority of substantive goods over
abstract principles of justice. Such a priority would obtain only if thick
conceptions of the good adhered in a fixed nature (*pace* MacIntyre) or
common tradition (*pace* Sandel).[67] However, since the capacity to interpret our identities critically—in opposition to existing needs and roles—
reflects an irreversible accomplishment of rationalization that is conascent
with liberal pluralism, thick conceptions of the good can be expected
to materialize only under conditions of rational, consensus-oriented
democracy. Here, formal rights and procedures inherent in the (democratic) idea of reason mutually condition the public goods that inform
concrete institutions. Thus justice and solidarity, no less than rights
and goods, complement one another.[68]

If, true to its liberal heritage, democratic rationality does not require
the submission of all categories of private life to public scrutiny, it
nonetheless requires that the distinction between private and public
interest itself be drawn in the course of public debate rather than taken
for granted as naturally fixed in the manner of contractualism. By the
same token, it does not preclude the rationality of compromise legislation balancing opposed interests, or the necessity of administrative
interventions on behalf of specific interests.[69] It does, however, provide a collective forum by which opposed interests must be justified
publicly and, if possible, resolved in the form of a higher public interest. Although it does not circumvent the paradoxes of decision theory,
it mitigates the antagonisms that make them so palpable to administrators, who seek any excuse to override legislative deadlocks. Indeed,
it shows just how misplaced the economic criticism of democracy is,
for rationality in this context is less a matter of aggregating preferences than of shaping rational individuals.[70]

From an institutional standpoint it makes more sense to talk about
participatory democracy of this kind at the level of small-scale, local
organizations (I make no predictions regarding the feasibility of larger-

scale "teledemocracy").[71] Although a modest case can be made for in-stitutionalizing participatory democracy in the "public sphere," a stronger case can be made for extending it to economic organizations. Indeed, I have argued elsewhere that the very notion of free action entails a right to such participation.[72] Such rights, which include the right to safe, fulfilling work, would serve to mitigate the contradictions inher-ent in labor and welfare law—contradictions that evince the contractualist assumptions of a capitalist society. However it is conceived, workplace democracy—be it in or outside the home—must not insulate decisions about production and consumption from broader public oversight. Nor can it always presume to be the privileged political institution in a society in which political parties will continue to organize support for a broad range of national and international issues.

If it should further turn out that the kind of social interaction, socialization, and cultural transmission requisite for the reproduction of modern societies essentially implicates rational communication of this sort, then egalitarian and emancipatory predispositions are even more deeply entrenched in everyday cognitive and interactive compe-tencies than contractualists have hitherto assumed. Supposing this to be the case, we can explain why capitalism and its modern-day pre-suppositions—plebiscitary democracy and bureaucracy—exacerbate rather than ameliorate social disintegration. Bluntly stated, they fail to satisfy the subjective *and* intersubjective conditions of democratic le-gitimation and inclusion requisite for social stability. The proliferation of political interest groups that operate outside mainstream partisan politics is but one sign of this legitimation crisis.[73] The other is the inability of government bureaucracies to intervene in the private lives of citizens without arousing new demands for popular representation and participation.[74]

10

Constituting the Modern State: The Supreme Court, Labor Law, and the Contradictions of Legitimation

CARL SWIDORSKI

I was led by my studies to the conclusion that legal relations as well as forms of state could neither be understood by themselves, nor explained by the so-called general progress of the human mind, but that they are rooted in the material conditions of life.[1]

Law, legal institutions, and legal discourse are part of the process by which dominant elites and classes strive to maintain power and hegemony in a society and are resisted. The law, a product of group and class struggle, helps constitute a political system. It is part of a complex social process in which it is shaped by social forces, and in turn, helps shape those forces. Hence, the law is a force of both oppression and liberation—an arena of social conflict contested to promote or retard social change.

This article draws upon recent theoretical work of critical legal scholars to study the role the U.S. Supreme Court plays in constituting the modern state. The Court is the most visible manifestation of law in the United

States, and its role in maintaining and stabilizing the political system deserves attention. The Court has fulfilled two principal functions since the New Deal era: (1) legitimating the transformation of property that has occurred in the modern capitalist economy; and (2) managing social conflict by ensuring formal, but limited, representation for select groups, primarily before the administrative agencies of the modern state.

In the process of carrying out these two roles the Court has faced various contradictions that exemplify the dynamic process by which law constitutes (and, in turn, is constituted by) political, economic, and social forces. The Court's rulings in labor law, civil rights, and civil liberties since the New Deal reflect a democratic elitist theory of politics embedded in modern corporate liberalism. This theory assumes that conflict is interest group-based, not class based, and that the state has an important role to play in stabilizing and managing the political economic system. Growth, or the priority of the process of reproduction, is accepted as the shared societal goal. Permissible conflict by legitimate interests is to be channeled by state institutions and resolved if possible by administrative or judicial means. Finally, certain important societal decisions should remain off the visible public agenda and be determined in the private or quasi-public sphere if at all possible.

In this article I first present a critical theoretical position on the function of law and the role of the U.S. Supreme Court. I then illustrate how the Court has helped to develop a national labor policy that has limited the power of working people and channeled union behavior into "legitimate" channels. Finally, I suggest that this labor law model of the role of the Court can help us understand the Court's decisional behavior in other areas of law, using civil rights decisions in the area of race to illustrate my argument.

CRITICAL THEORIZING ABOUT THE LAW

Gramsci suggests that law, legal institutions, and legal discourse are part of the process by which dominant elites and classes strive to maintain power and hegemony in a society and are resisted. He contends that the modern bourgeoisie, unlike previous ruling classes, has constructed an ideology to justify its domination. Law is a part of the "educational" process through which this domination is maintained.[2]

The modern capitalist state needs to validate itself ethically, not just to the ruling elites but to society as a whole. To successfully maintain power, a dominant class must have its interests "conceived of and presented, as being the motor force of a universal expression, of a development of all 'national energies.'"[3] In order for this to happen, hegemony "must operate in a dualistic manner: as a 'general conception of life' for the masses, and as a 'scholastic programme' or a set of principles which is advanced by a sector of the intellectuals."[4] Law is an important element in this educative process. The ideological function of the law, and more particularly the Constitution as interpreted by the Supreme Court, is a way of knowing, of making sense of the world. The ideological role of the Constitution has been described as "a kind of bourgeois fairy tale." In this story, political and economic struggle are subsumed in a discourse about legality instead of morality, and politics becomes reduced to the maneuverings of lawyers and judges.[5]

The law is not epiphenomenal, nor does it develop simply as a direct response to the preferences and needs of the dominant political-economic class. The most innovative and creative work in the critical legal tradition begins with a rejection of simplistic notions of economic determinism.[6] This critical/revisionist research tradition attempts to develop a theoretical understanding of the way the law ultimately reflects and sustains the existing social order in any society, yet has its own relative autonomy and internal logic.

If legitimation and social conflict management are the key functions of the Supreme Court, then, as the work of the so-called Crits makes clear, legal discourse is one significant dimension of the legitimizing process. The process through which legal discourse is created and the legal profession is trained illustrates links between the academy and corporate and governmental institutions. The terms of legal discourse are taken for granted. Law is studied to strengthen, not challenge, it. Questions of coercion and control are seldom considered, while technical expertise in specialized areas of the law is pursued. The question of equality or equal protection of the laws does not get raised in class terms but in the language of individualism. In this fashion, legal discourse helps legitimate existing power relationships and discourages the kind of political action which empowers people and groups to do things collectively that they are incapable of doing alone.

Even more significant than legal discourse are the actual policies developed and implemented by legal institutions and the effects these policies have on shaping the tactics, strategies, and consciousness of groups and individuals.[7] Thus, critical legal theory suggests that it is best to approach a major legal institution as a political-economic one and explore its relationships with the broader society of which it is a part. The law, and in this case the Supreme Court, is a significant constitutive element of the social totality.

The contradictions evident in law demonstrate the problems with more inflexible structural and instrumental views of the law. A key contradiction is "the duality of bourgeois legal ideology."[8] On the one hand, U.S. law has promoted a contractarian vision of society and historically protected property rights. It has been flexible in doing this, adapting the meaning of property to the changing dynamics of capitalist development. On the other hand, the law has paid varying degrees of attention to principles such as the right of communities to regulate property in the public interest and freedom of speech, press, and association. It also has, at times, articulated a conception of human freedom from arbitrary state power. Some of these progressive commitments arose from the struggle of the bourgeoisie to gain political power, a struggle in which freedoms such as speech and worship were critical to the task of overcoming the power of Crown and Church. Others arose from the American experience. For example, the Revolutionary War and the struggle of the 1780s between small farmers and commercial aristocrats produced certain commitments to political liberty reflected in the Bill of Rights. The Thirteenth, Fourteenth, and Fifteenth Amendments promised a constitutional revolution in the relationship between individuals and the national government, even though the promise went largely unfulfilled until the 1950s. Because of these dualistic traditions, the general predominance of property rights has been tempered by social struggles in which other political, social, and economic interests were asserted by small farmers, workers, women, organized labor, African-Americans, and other disadvantaged groups. Therefore, an analysis of the role of the Supreme Court must recognize that the law does not just reflect the power of the ruling class. It sometimes helps restrain the exercise of that power.

Another contradiction arises from the fact that liberal-democratic law promotes a particular conception of freedom and equality. It fosters a formal, if primarily negative, definition of liberty and a limited commitment to equality of opportunity. The concrete experience of that freedom often results in gross maldistribution of societal resources or social isolation for many people. Yet, at the same time, it creates opportunities for the dominated to reject the formal definitions of the law and work to construct the kind of transformative freedom and equality paid lip service to by the law.

Finally, at any given historical juncture, gaps exist in the law. These gaps may be clarified and filled in to meet the interests of the powerful, or conversely, they may be exploited by forces seeking to promote change. One example of this phenomenon, although generally unsuccessful, has been the effort to redefine the nature of property rights. Certain legal scholars have been trying to reformulate the concepts of property and citizenship in order to legitimate "new property" rights that would benefit all citizens.[9] These "new property" rights would be based on conceptions of property as life, liberty, and human capacities as opposed to more traditional conceptualizations based on things and fungible assets.

My emphasis in this tradition is on the dialectical relationship between law and the political economy. However, examining the *relative* autonomy of the law and the Supreme Court does not require the conclusion that the law or the Supreme Court is in some sense fundamentally autonomous of the existing system of power and domination:

> Historically, state institutions have escaped political and ideological constraints arising from private capital's strategic influence over investment, output, and employment only in rather exceptional circumstances.
> Even then, the very form and structure of the state, and of the law which is the states' language, has continued to exhibit an "essential identity" with the essence of capitalism . . . sufficient to ensure that even those courses of action consciously chosen and pursued by state managers out of institutional self-interest, or out of idealistic concern for the public interest, courses of action demonstrably damaging to the interests of particular capitalists, will in the long run exhibit an overall bias toward reproduction of the political-economic status quo.[10]

Or to use the less academic language of the general counsel of the International Brotherhood of Teamsters: "The judicial result that promotes capitalism is the decision that can be predicated with regular certainty."[11]

CRITICAL LEGAL THEORY AND THE SUPREME COURT

The Supreme Court is best understood as a relatively autonomous institution that nevertheless reflects the class structure of U.S. capitalism while helping to shape, maintain, and reproduce it. The relative autonomy of the Court rests on its partial independence from the direct political process; its discretion in choosing what cases to hear and not to hear; its power of judicial review, both when used and not used; and the general acceptance of its decisions. In fulfilling its two major roles, however, the Court does not seriously challenge the political-economic elite. But it can't be so one-sided in its decisions as to undermine its legitimacy both as internalized by the justices and accepted by the larger political community. Therefore, the Court must sometimes respond to the demands of the relatively powerless.

The Court uses an ideology of neutrality and the "rule of law" to gain acceptance for its decisions and help legitimate and stabilize the existing political-economic system. Aiding this legitimation process is the ideological belief that the law is democratic and the Court, as the neutral interpreter of that law, is a democratic institution. However, since impartiality and objectivity are not possible in the law, the Supreme Court must respond as an institution to conflicts inherent in the capitalistic system while at the same time maintaining its image as a neutral yet democratic institution. Given this, particular cases, often the subject of intense scrutiny and debate by journalists and political scientists, are not that significant. What really counts is the process itself and how it helps contain the internal stresses of the system and maintain the existing power arrangements by legitimizing both incremental reforms and the political system as a whole.[12]

The conventional interpretation of the role of the Supreme Court after the New Deal "revolution" of 1937 is that it abandoned the field of economic policy-making to the executive and legislative branches and took up a new agenda—civil liberties and civil rights. Supposedly, the Court became the key institutional defender of individual rights. For much of the post–New Deal era, especially during the time when Earl Warren was Chief Justice, the Court was considered a liberal and progressive institution that served to redress some of the limited faults of a political system assumed to be benign, democratic, and even, for a time, nonideological. In fact conservative critics of the Court frequently charged it with being too activist on behalf of the less powerful in U.S. society.[13] Academics generally presented a sympathetic and palliative assessment of the role of the Court. At times these judgments took on the veneer of an age-old problem in U.S. academia—Constitution (and Court) worshipping.

A more realistic assessment of the role of the modern Court must place the changes in the Court's agenda and doctrine within the context of the changes in the nature of modern capitalist society, particularly the relationships between corporations, the government, and organized labor. The reigning paradigm for understanding the development of U.S. constitutional law shifted from contract to rational management (domination) and administration. This new paradigm recognized the changing nature of property relations from those of autonomy, contract, and independence to contingency, administration, and dependence.

> Because capitalism is a system which has been built on the juridical foundation of property rights, we assume that it requires and capitalists desire that property be sacrosanct and that private property rights extend into ever more realms of social intervention, whereas in reality the whole history of capitalism has been one of a steady decline, not an extension of property rights.[14]

At the doctrinal level, the post-1937 Court transformed legal principles to ratify the "new social contract" entered into by big business, big government, and big labor. The doctrinal symbol of the new judicial approach to economic matters was the famous footnote 4 of *U.S. v. Carolene Products* (1938), which established the principle of the "double standard" for due process review.[15] According to this standard, the

Court would apply different levels of judicial scrutiny and constitutional protection to civil liberties or civil rights issues as opposed to claims based on traditional property rights. Legislative and administrative regulation of property would be presumed constitutional and be subject only to minimal judicial scrutiny primarily based on whether there was a rational basis for the regulation. On the other hand, greater constitutional protection and stricter judicial scrutiny would apply to legislative and executive restrictions on individual rights in three areas: (1) where "specific prohibitions of the Constitution" such as found in the Bill of Rights were involved; (2) where legislation restricted the "political processes which can ordinarily be expected to bring about repeal of undesirable legislation"; and (3) where statutes were directed at "particular religious or national or racial minorities."

This "double standard" supposedly symbolized a new liberal, individual rights orientation by the Court. However, conventional analysts generally failed to recognize that the "result was nothing less than a significant qualitative transformation in the constitutional status of 'property' itself."[16] Property in a modern corporate society was no longer to be treated legally as a relatively unfettered domain of individual freedom and autonomy requiring special constitutional protection by the Court. In fact, it had not been for some time, even if a legal fiction that it had was maintained. The Court abandoned this legal fiction and explicitly enunciated a view of modern property rights as involving a series of relationships with the administrative state. The Court was recognizing that modern property was subsumed under the concept of "social capital."[17]

This doctrinal accommodation recognized the reality of a new social contract, albeit a continuously changing and contradictory one, among business, labor, and government. Organized labor initially became a junior partner in return for recognition and protection of its right to organize, promises of higher wages and better working conditions, and various social programs. Government assumed important responsibilities for rationalizing the market and managing the economy by using Keynesian fiscal policy to help regulate the business cycle. The principal purpose behind this new social contract was not to challenge capitalism or seriously undermine corporate prerogatives, but to use the expertise of the modern state to coordinate, guide, and supplement the functioning of the modern capitalistic economy.

As the new social contract evolved over time, important institutional changes took place. There has been a period of increased nationalization and bureaucratization of policy-making, from the 1930s through the 1970s, and a period of property rights rhetoric and selective deregulation under the Reagan/Bush administrations. The position of labor in the new social contract came under attack almost immediately after the passage of the National Labor Relations Act (NLRA). While a series of accommodations were reached in the 1950s and 1960s to maintain a junior partner status for labor, the decline of the labor movement has been precipitous since the late 1970s.

Other social groups besides organized labor gradually became incorporated into the social contract. Racial minorities, women, consumer groups, environmentalists, and other organized interests slowly gained varying degrees of formal representation before and in the administrative agencies of the state. The Supreme Court played an important role in this process of accommodation by helping ensure certain limited kinds of representation for interests that were strong enough and organized enough to be considered problematic.

Thus, judicial review in the modern administrative state means that "its dominant purpose is no longer the prevention of unauthorized intrusions on private autonomy, but the assurance of fair representation for all affected interests in the exercise of legislative powers delegated to agencies."[18] The Court proceeded to articulate an idealized vision of democratic elitism—a pluralistic, liberal society in which all "legitimate" social groups were guaranteed representation and the right to pursue their self-interest in a political system in which the Court played a significant role in ensuring that the rules of the game were "fairly" administered.

THE SUPREME COURT AND LABOR LAW

The development of labor law offers a striking example of the dual role of the modern Supreme Court. Even though primary responsibility for developing labor law rests with Congress and the National Labor Relations Board (NLRB), the Supreme Court nonetheless has played a key role in this area by reviewing decisions of the NLRB and interpreting key provisions of the major labor statutes. In the process, the Court has helped create a legal ideology and institutional structure to legitimate a corporation-dominated workplace characterized by hierarchy and class domination.

The NLRA, heralded by some as the most radical law ever passed by Congress, had from its inception the central purpose of stabilizing social conflict and promoting industrial peace.[19] It clearly provided workers with important legal benefits, principally the legal right to organize unions and have employers engage in collective bargaining. It also granted union organizers and members First Amendment freedoms they had systematically been denied by the courts.[20] But, in the process, it shaped and confined union activities. The NLRB was created to act in the "public interest" and promote national policy objectives, not the specific private interests of either labor or management.

The NLRA, therefore, was a key policy in reconstituting the state during the New Deal. It legitimated collective bargaining as a major element of economic policy yet at the same time reshaped the nature of collective bargaining. Employees' new rights to organize and bargain were to be exercised subject to state determination of how this process might best serve the public interest. J. Warren Madden, the first chair of the NLRB, and Charles Fahy, the General Counsel, envisioned the Act as transforming the natural economic struggle between labor and capital into a civilized legal-rational process that "removed the causes" of much of the industrial conflict in the United States.[21]

The government's willingness to provide certain forms of protection to labor was conditioned by two major considerations. First, the collective action of workers could not threaten the state's predominance. Second, the state had to accommodate the needs of leading sectors of U.S. corporate capitalism. This system of "industrial pluralism," while bringing positive benefits to workers, was conditioned upon its contribution to higher productivity and efficient capital accumulation.[22]

The Supreme Court has been instrumental in fostering the industrial pluralist ideology developed by professional labor relations specialists. This system of labor-management relations justified collective bargaining while denying class conflict. Its ideology tied collective bargaining to private determination of wages and working conditions. Voluntary arbitration was absolutely central to this ideology as a means of resolving industrial conflict without significant governmental (especially judicial) intervention in particular disputes. The NLRA was viewed as an institutional framework for self-governing labor-management relations.[23]

The industrial pluralist ideology envisioned a mini-democracy in the workplace mirroring the features of a liberal representative democracy. Consent of the governed, not power and domination, would prevail. However, this model was based on the flawed assumption that management and labor had equal power in the workplace. The Court, fundamentally accepting this industrial pluralist ideology, has interpreted the NLRA to confer "no substantive rights upon labor at all."[24] Instead, it has emphasized a procedural interpretation that has made the Act a bare legal framework to facilitate private ordering by business and labor. Under this interpretation, labor increasingly has become disadvantaged and bound by a legal structure initially portrayed as conferring radical substantive rights on it.

The Supreme Court has been instrumental in developing national labor policy since the passage of the NLRA. Several decisional trends have been especially important. The Court initially was particularly forceful in ruling that the "public interest" in industrial stability was to be given priority over workers' "rights" of self-organization.[25] Even during the initial years of vigorous policy initiative by the NLRB, the courts continued to apply common law contract doctrines developed prior to the NLRA which treated employees as more or less passive beneficiaries of contracts negotiated on their behalf by unions.[26] Furthermore, the Court asserted that the NLRA did not protect a wide variety of employee activities from restraint or prosecution under various federal, state, and local laws.

> The fundamental policy of the Act is to safeguard the rights of self-organization and collective bargaining and thus by the promotion of industrial peace to remove obstructions to the free flow of commerce. . . . [T]he purpose of the Act is to promote peaceful settlements of disputes by providing legal remedies for the invasion of the employees' right, to assure them self-organization and freedom in representation, not to license them to commit tortious acts or to protect them from the appropriate consequences of unlawful conduct.[27]

The federal courts' hostility to a wide variety of worker self-activity not compatible with the legal-rational processes of the Act was demonstrated in a series of subsequent decisions condemning "work-ins," improper striking and picketing, boycotting, and "violence."[28] The courts also made clear that the rights and prerogatives of employers were not abrogated by the NLRA.[29] Thus by the early 1940s, both the courts and the Board saw the fundamental purpose of the Act as stabilizing labor-management relations through promoting and enforcing contracts and disciplining spontaneous worker activity. By this time, much of the national union leadership had come around to this industrial pluralist vision also.[30]

After 1940, conservatives in Congress and business groups increased their attacks on unions and national labor policy, despite the increasingly constrictive nature of that policy on collective rank-and-file activity. After World War II and the postwar strike wave, this reactionary alliance was successful in passing the Taft-Hartley Act, an attempt to weaken the workplace and political power of labor. The anti-union attack was part of a broader effort to eviscerate New Deal social welfare programs and prevent the passage of price control legislation and a major national housing program. Yet Taft-Hartley did not bring about as fundamental a change in national labor policy as some think.

Many of the policies embodied in Taft-Hartley—confirming the authority of central union bureaucracies over the rank and file; preserving management's unrestricted power to control the workplace; and establishing rule-conscious grievance procedures to facilitate settlements and prevent strikes or other forms of direct action—had already been adopted by the Board prior to 1947. Only a few provisions, such as the explicit outlawing of the closed shop, introduced significant changes in national labor policy.[31]

Nonetheless, the Taft-Hartley law helped entrench the industrial pluralist model and significantly expanded the limiting and channeling features of national labor policy. By the early 1950s a few union leaders were saying that the labor movement would have been better off without the Wagner Act, but most had accepted the industrial pluralist model, which made unions quasi-public agencies—increasingly regulated by the state, limited in the use of their economic powers, yet responsible for performing important functions to facilitate the performance of the economy.

The Court created a federal substantive law of collective bargaining agreements. It saw a legislative intent, after the post–World War II strike wave, of promoting no-strike clauses in collective bargaining. The quid pro quo for the no-strike clauses was a system of private grievance arbitration that the Court quickly developed into the national labor policy. The Court legitimated the system of private arbitration in the famous *Steelworker's Trilogy* decisions of 1960.[32] It decided that almost all disputes that occurred while a contract was in effect were subject to arbitration by a "neutral" third party. Traditional forms of union pressure, such as strikes, were forbidden while the arbitration was in process. The *Trilogy* decisions "helped create this new man of labor, who is more or less a paralegal."[33] These decisions exemplify how the law confines labor and ultimately leaves it subordinate to capital, yet does so in a manner that is not overtly oppressive.

The doctrines enunciated in these cases and in other areas, such as the development of exceptions to the preemption doctrine, required courts to promote arbitration without scrutinizing the results of the disputes. These doctrines institutionally endorsed the industrial pluralist model of courts not interfering with the self-governing relations of management and labor. Neither the courts nor the NLRB were to be the primary agencies of adjudicating these social disputes.

The Court extended this restrictive interpretation of labor law in two key decisions of the 1960s. The doctrine that an agreement containing an arbitration clause implied a no-strike promise,[34] combined with the power of courts to use injunctions to force unions to stop striking pending arbitration,[35] provided the legally coercive element to enforce the arbitration system. The unions' principal economic source of power, the strike, could not only be discouraged but enjoined, increasingly making the industrial pluralist model one of compulsion, not voluntariness. Effectively, these decisions made strikes illegal in the United States for "the life of the contract," usually a three- to four-year period. The Court extended this doctrine to safety disputes so that, for example, miners who walked out of work because of life-threatening working conditions could be ordered back to work while their "grievance" was arbitrated, even when a union had deliberately removed its no-strike commitment from the contract.[36]

One major problem with this system of private arbitration, at least for those advocating more public participation and control over labor-management relations, involved the issue of remedies. Arbitrators can issue awards. They can use reason, logic, and argument. But they have no pre-hearing power to intervene in disputes, and the arbitration process is slow and time consuming. While time drags on, employers can take unilateral actions with irreparable consequences for employees such as subcontracting out work, closing parts of a plant, or operating a plant despite serious safety problems. The NLRB on the other hand can, in theory, intervene in such disputes. It is empowered to gain access to company records and premises, issue subpoenas, issue cease and desist orders, withhold certification for unlawful union conduct, and order bargaining. But the acceptance of this system of private arbitration has effectively limited the NLRB's potential role, ultimately to the disadvantage of workers.

A second major problem with this system concerns the supposed impartiality of the arbitrator. Arbitrators intervene in workplace disputes to defuse tensions, ensure order, and facilitate the continuity of operations.

> But, as with any form of social order, it is important to see who benefits from industrial orderliness, and at whose expense it is achieved. It is in disorder that workers experience and exercise their power in the production process. The entire history of the labor movement is a history of workers creating "disorder." . . . Only in the midst of "disorder" do workers have the leverage to press for their demands. Thus by intervening to preserve order, arbitrators are not only nonneutral, they are acting consistently on the side of management.[37]

Today, the NLRA obligates employers to bargain collectively once a union is certified and proscribes certain activities as unfair labor practices. But to obtain these legal protections, unions have been forced to give up many of their most effective economic weapons. The "right" to strike is restricted or implicitly waived, and secondary boycotts and sympathy strikes are prohibited. Meanwhile, employers' economic weapons are not similarly curtailed. They still can lock out employees, reduce wages, lay off workers, change production methods, and even discharge union leaders.

This summary of labor law leads to certain conclusions about the role of the Supreme Court in managing conflict and legitimating the social order.[38] First, labor law encourages workers to pursue their interests through self-organization yet at the same time channels that pursuit into narrow, institutionalized forms in which only "legitimate" conflict is allowed. In the attempt to institutionalize conflict, forms of worker activity that exhibit class solidarity come in for particularly harsh treatment by the law.

Second, labor law both permits and limits employee participation in governing the workplace. The legitimacy of worker participation is recognized but tends to be confined to market concerns, primarily compensation and working conditions. The attempts of workers to exert more influence over the organization of the work process or long-range planning is restricted. Generally, the more important the decision to employer control, such as decisions over investment, disinvestment, long-range planning, and the basic scope of operations, the fewer bargaining rights unions have concerning it.

Third, labor law encourages a distancing between the union as an institution and its members as individuals. Courts have enhanced the institutional interests of unions at the expense of their own members, while unions in turn have accepted a role in preserving industrial peace and performing managerial and disciplinary functions in the workplace.

This industrial pluralist model has come under increasing strain over the past fifteen years. The state increasingly has intervened more directly in the workplace over the past several decades through legislation such as Title VII of the Civil Rights Act of 1964, the Occupational Safety and Health Act (OSHA), and the Employee Retirement Income Security Act (ERISA). This creates a problem of doctrinal incompatibility between the procedural interpretation of the law, embodied in the industrial pluralist vision, and the new reality of direct state intervention. In the process, the courts have confronted substantive issues that do not easily fit into the procedural framework of the NLRA. Court decisions of the past fifteen years indicate an increasing tendency to uphold such direct government regulation of the workplace, restricting some of the items that can be negotiated through private voluntary agreements achieved through collective bargaining.[39] Even more significantly, the increased power of capital, exercised by not negotiating and exercising managerial prerogatives, combined with the takeover of the NLRB by Reagan-Bush appointees, encouraged more substantive actions by the courts and the NLRB.[40]

Court decisions of the past two decades, which reflect or are compatible with the corporate counterattack against labor, have resulted in more pro-corporate decisions and facilitated a less "benevolent" mediation by the NLRB, an agency originally created to help "equalize" bargaining power between labor and management. Recent decisions increasingly have favored management and suggest that corporate dominance over labor in the market is considerably less mediated by administrative structures of the state than it was twenty to thirty years ago. Of course, this reflects the fact that many of the administrative agencies of the state in the labor-management area have been taken over by "purer" corporate partisans than in the past. These developments illustrate the tension and partial breakdown in the"social contract" of the 1930s. Yet despite these developments and the changed political-economic environment, the overall effect of labor law remains basically the same—managing social conflict, promoting stability, channeling discontent, legalizing repression, and helping shape the consciousness of workers.

The Court has articulated a democratic elitist vision in which participation in the collective bargaining system is legitimate only if it occurs through proper administrative channels designed to moderate social conflict and prevent it from spilling over beyond acceptable boundaries. Justice Brennan's opinion in *Boys Market* makes this explicitly clear:

> As labor organizations grew in strength and developed toward maturity congressional emphasis shifted from protection of the nascent labor movement to the encouragement of collective bargaining and to administrative technique for the peaceful resolution of industrial disputes.[41]

However, it is not only the development of labor law which illustrates the dual role of the modern Supreme Court. This labor law model can be applied to other areas of constitutional law. Analyzing the development of constitutional doctrine in the area of civil rights from this perspective provides a more realistic assessment of the role of the modern Supreme Court than the idealized vision of it as a champion of equality or defender of fundamental constitutional values.

CIVIL RIGHTS: RACE

The Supreme Court had a very progressive image on the issue of race until the latter years of the Burger Court. Few people remember the Court's nineteenth-century record of upholding slavery and denying African-Americans citizenship prior to the Civil War; eviscerating the Thirteenth, Fourteenth, and Fifteenth Amendments in the 1870s and 1880s; and being indifferent to claims of equal protection of the law during the first half of the twentieth century. Instead, the Supreme Court is generally remembered for being in the forefront of efforts to promote racial equality during the 1950s and 1960s, with liberals in particular wishing for a liberal president who will appoint liberal justices and restore the Court to the glory days of the Warren era. But a broader context is required to understand the Court's decisions on race.

The Court's racial equality decisions can be best understood as part of the effort to incorporate blacks into the periphery, if not the mainstream, of American life. Blacks largely were excluded from the benefits of the New Deal and the social contract among business, government, and organized labor. By the 1950s, this exclusion was becoming a domestic problem and an international embarrassment for the United States. "The Supreme Court finally condemned Jim Crow practices only when establishment interests concluded that the laws were both an embarrassing liability to domestic tranquility and a heavy burden on post World War II foreign policy."[42] Institutionally, the Court was in the forefront of this effort. But very similar to the incorporation of organized labor into the post–New Deal social contract, the gains for African-Americans were made on terms acceptable to the dominant class.

In return for increased representational rights, legal rights, and social welfare programs, the modern state attempted to steer black participation into acceptable channels. Even then, the gains that were made were partly in response to the activities of African-Americans pursuing their collective interests. However, the Court still was an important institutional mechanism both for legitimating African-Americans' demands for equal protection of the laws and for attempting to manage the ensuing conflict on terms compatible with pluralist, liberal democracy. The legal gains of the period were important to African-Americans, enhancing their capacities to act in a variety of forums, thus making the law an arena of struggle for their advancement. But the contributions of the law should not be overstated. Judged by results, antidiscrimination law has served to rationalize racial discrimination more than to solve the problem:

> ... for as surely as the law has outlawed racial discrimination, it has affirmed that Black Americans can be without jobs, have their children in all black, poorly funded schools, have no opportunities for decent housing, and have very little political power, without any violation of antidiscrimination law.[43]

During the first era of the Court's antidiscrimination decisions, roughly 1954 to 1967, it primarily focused on declaring unconstitutional various forms of state-supported segregation and upholding recently passed civil rights legislation. The Court did not wrestle to any significant degree with more fundamental problems. However, beginning in the mid-1960s, it had to begin to confront the more problematic issues associated with institutional racism: de facto segregation; ostensibly neutral practices that had discriminatory effects; and remedies for discrimination. After a brief period in which the Court's decisions provided hope that it would address the substantive results of segregation and discrimination, the Court became complacent, refusing to address seriously the history or contemporary reality of institutional racism.

The Court insisted on using the de jure concept to assess segregation. It also established the standard that a record of deliberate or intentional discrimination had to be shown rather than a demonstration of the segregative or discriminatory effects of particular practices. This approach met the formal standard of abstract equality before the law, compatible with liberal democracy, but avoided facing the more fundamental economic, social, and cultural conditions facing African-Americans. To do so would have required the Court to challenge the promises of liberal democracy and raise issues of class, the issue that a legitimating institution will avoid if at all possible.

Since the early 1970s, decisions in the areas of education, employment, and voting illustrate a lukewarm attitude, at best, by the Court toward effective remedies for discrimination. In fact, six key decisions in 1989 were considered to be such setbacks for civil rights that Congress passed a new civil rights law in 1991 to counter the Supreme Court's decisions. The recent record in affirmative action cases further demonstrates that the legal system will not be that helpful for repairing the damage of past degradation. The Court apparently will support affirmative action programs only under three limited conditions: (1) if there is a congressional statute that recognizes the need for remedial action; (2) if individual claimants can prove they are direct victims of past discrimination; or (3) if the program is a voluntary, private, and limited agreement. Beyond this, the Court's affirmative action decisions do not offer much hope for those who seek group remedies for group wrongs.

The Court's record on race in the modern era is very mixed. As with organized labor, the Court has attempted to legitimate the presence of African-Americans in the post–New Deal social contract and has attempted to engineer black participation in the political system into appropriate channels. But by refusing to take the effects of discriminatory practices very seriously, and by limiting its vision of effective remedies, the Court has even failed to fulfill the liberal agenda of integrating blacks into the mainstream of the U.S. political and economic systems. The formal changes in the law have not been matched by significant substantive changes in the day-to-day existence of most black Americans.

CONCLUSIONS

The law, like religion, the media, and other social processes, is part of the constitutive process of a political system. But the law is unique in that it symbolically represents the "will of society"; it is the state's language and is the "benevolent" side of legitimate state force and violence. While the law is not merely a tool of the capitalist class or the inevitable result of a particular social-economic structure, it does help constitute a political process of domination and resistance.

To understand the role and function of the Supreme Court, the law's most visible manifestation in the United States, we must examine it in terms of its relationship to the changing dynamics of a capitalist economy and the modern administrative state. Generally, the development of constitutional law by the Court has been compatible with the needs of the ruling classes, but this development has occurred through a process of contradiction, conflict, and resistance. Since 1937, the Supreme Court has played a significant institutional role in the process of trying to defuse class conflict by attempting to accommodate different groups into the modern social contract on terms acceptable to the dominant corporate capital class. At times it has been receptive to the claims of groups with less access to other institutional alternatives. But it has not significantly challenged the policy preferences of the corporate-dominated state. For example, the Court played no significant role in promoting civil liberties or civil rights until the modern era. It has been most protective of rights when social movements and organized labor pushed aggressively for change, as during the 1930s and 1960s, and least protective during periods of retrenchment, as during the 1950s and 1980s.

By further exploring the labor law model of legitimation and conflict management developed in this article, scholars might find more fruitful ways of examining the role of the Court than through the stagnant, pluralist, "protector of individual rights" perspective that dominates analysis of the Court. This chapter attempts to contribute to the theoretical understanding of the way the law ultimately reflects and sustains the existing social order, yet has its own relative autonomy and internal logic. The law's mode of discourse, decisions, and institutional patterns of activity are unique and to some degree relatively autonomous of the dominant corporate capitalist class. Yet in another sense, the law is inherently instrumental:

> . . . Laws are necessarily the instruments of a particular social order. None can survive without them. But then what is at issue, in any conflict about particular law, is the underlying definition of the desired social order. . . . To challenge that order is to challenge those laws.[44]

Thus the law, and in this case the Supreme Court, must be understood as an important constitutive element of our corporate-capitalist, liberal democracy.

11

The Chaotic Indeterminacy of Tort Law: Between Formalism and Nihilism*

DENIS J. BRION

INTRODUCTION

Two legal academicians have recently offered general discussions of the law, discussions that, taken together, embrace the polar positions of a conceptual spectrum that extends from nihilistic indeterminacy to formalistic structure. In "Legal Formalism: On the Immanent Rationality of Law,"[1] Ernest Weinrib offers a detailed and passionate defense of the idea that the law can be accurately described in terms of an implicit and antecedent internal rational structure, its "inner coherence." He argues that the law is altogether distinct from politics and that it can only be understood from within itself. The function of judges is to "make transactions and distributions" in the social world conform to the "latent unity" of the law. The function of legal scholars is to make explicit the internal coherence and intelligibility of the law.

In *The Disorder of Law: A Critique of Legal Theory*,[2] Charles Sampford sets out to criticize the various theories of law that seek to describe it as systematic. His principal thesis is that society itself is without system—his term is the "social melee"—and that the law, as an integral part of society, is correspondingly disordered—the "legal melee." He concludes that, because of this disorder, the impact of legal doctrine on social and individual practices is strongly attenuated. Moreover, because the law is no more than "an important set of institutions in the melee," any attempt at change in the law is not likely to have

179

wide impact on society. Although Sampford does not draw the conclusion expressly, his analysis is consistent with a more general critical analysis of the law that proceeds from the premise that structures of power in society strongly determine what people do. As a consequence, social practices conform to the ad hoc needs of the power structure, and the law does no more than track, and provide a veneer of justification for, these practices.

The approaches of Weinrib and Sampford can be said to fall along a spectrum because they are both concerned with the problem of legal indeterminacy. Each seems to make the implicit assumption that the law does not function autonomously of structures of social, economic, and political power if it is indeterminate, if, that is, one cannot predict with a high degree of accuracy how the legal process will resolve particular disputes. One might describe Sampford as occupying the pessimistic pole of this spectrum, despairing of the possibility that the law can function autonomously. Weinrib, by contrast, is the optimist, urging on those concerned with the law in the task of perfecting its formalistic structure, and thereby as well enhancing its predictability and autonomous function.

The rather plain fact of the matter, of course, is that the law is indeed indeterminate, thereby posing the nihilist-formalist conundrum. By way of addressing this conundrum, I propose in this essay to analyze the law of tort through the lens of chaos, an emerging scientific theory of the nature of physical reality. My purposes are to engage in a critique of the views of Weinrib and Sampford, and to develop an alternative approach to the law that describes it as, simultaneously, doctrinally indeterminate, as Sampford would have it, and yet fully capable of constraining, as Weinrib would want it. My general thesis is that chaos, as a metaphor for the way that law functions, is a powerful tool for better describing and understanding the law. Viewing tort law as chaotic process makes it possible to reformulate the question of order implicit in the projects of both Weinrib and Sampford, thereby revealing both how each of these polar views carries a degree of plausibility and how each is incomplete in a way that ultimately disables it from functioning as a useful tool for description, explanation, and prescription.

In the discussion that follows, I first offer a brief explanation of chaos theory. I then analyze tort cases that would seem to be completely in conflict, offer an explanation that reconciles them, and draw the parallel between that explanation and chaos theory. Finally, I probe the capacity for the law, as described in chaotic terms, to achieve that constraint that the formalists seek and the anti-formalists despair of being possible.

CHAOS—AN EMERGING SCIENTIFIC PARADIGM

Chaos is as much a way of doing science as it is a theory about the nature of physical reality.[3] It exemplifies Thomas Kuhn's description of the course of scientific practice over time.[4] According to Kuhn, there is no single enduring way of engaging in science. Instead, there is a succession of particular paradigmatic scientific practices, one dominating the scientific community for a time as "normal science," eventually to be replaced by an alternative paradigm, which begins as "deviant science." Chaos theory appears to be a deviant science, with the potential to replace today's normal science, which is founded on the simple and elegant laws of motion that Isaac Newton set out in 1687 in his *Mathematical Principles of Natural Philosophy*. Newtonian science was, as well, a revolution in its day, positing as it did a spiritless clockwork universe inhabited by humans as initially bemused and increasingly manipulative observers. Newton's alternative world contrasted sharply with the traditional paradigm that had held sway through the preceding medieval period, which posited a reality in which humans were intimately bound up in and interconnected with visible and invisible spirits who worked their power, often capriciously, through the phenomena of everyday experience.

Perhaps the most crucial aspect of Newtonian science, in terms of the enterprise of this essay, is the matter of methodology. Newtonian science proceeded from a small set of simple and general laws that Newton deduced from the phenomena of physical reality. Subsequent scientific investigators, extending the reach of the world model consequent on Newton's laws, have sought to derive increasingly sophisticated mathematical formulations in order simultaneously to confirm Newton's laws and to embrace experimental data.

Consistently with the course of development of scientific paradigms generally, the focus of Newtonian science has been ever more narrow and particular. Newtonian science builds up a picture of the world from detailed pictures of each subsystem. It is reductive, seeking to achieve a precise conception of a world, external to the observer, the fundamental components of which proceed from a set of eternal, unchanging physical laws.

The practice of normal science after Newton, however, has had to accommodate itself with the measurable phenomena of an unruly and disordered world. The more comprehensively that Newtonian mathematical formulations have embraced experimental data, the more that they have tended to become too complex to be solved. Moreover, experimental data do not always conform, even in the simplest systems, to the predictions of Newton's laws. The law of the conservation of energy, for example, predicts that a pendulum, once set in motion, will swing indefinitely with a fixed amplitude and period. A real world pendulum, as we well know, will soon wind down to a state of motionlessness, the inevitable result of friction. Viewed through the lens of Newtonian science, friction is an imperfection in the physical world that causes it to deviate from the ideal of Newton's laws rather than a fundamental aspect of the physical world that Newton's laws fail fully to capture.

Newtonian science, then, has found it necessary to adopt particular practices that accommodate the deviation of real world phenomena from the elegant simplicity of theory embodied in mathematical expressions. One practice has been the use of simplifying assumptions in order to make otherwise insoluble problems of mathematical description tractable. A second has been to ignore aberrational data, on the ready explanation that it is generated either by friction or by measurement error. These practices, however, begun as interim steps to be rectified when theory developed sufficiently, ultimately have assumed a dominant role.

Fluid dynamics provides a ready example. We all can visualize the upward flow of smoke from a lighted cigarette resting on the lip of an ashtray. For a few moments, the rising smoke follows a smooth, vertical path. Soon enough, and inevitably enough, the pattern becomes turbulent, regardless of how carefully we attempt to isolate the system of cigarette, smoke, and air column from apparent outside disturbances. Newtonian science is capable of generating mathematical descriptions, faithful to Newton's laws, that describe the period of smooth flow for the cigarette smoke. The pattern of turbulence, however, is outside the reach of the descriptive powers of Newtonian science, at best explainable by an attribution to exogenous sources of disturbance but not amenable to description even with the most sophisticated mathematical formulations.

In practice, then, Newtonian science has increasingly bracketed data that is aberrational to the predictions of ever more sophisticated extensions of theory based on Newton's laws. This practice has not, of course, diminished the manipulative power of Newtonian science, as the continuously increasing level of technological sophistication of western culture convincingly demonstrates. This methodological choice, however, has led to the potential stagnation of theoretical development. Investigative sophistication has revealed increasingly large areas of natural phenomena that are aberrant from the predictions of Newton's laws.

Chaos, as deviant science, literally arose from the radical practice of pursuing the seemingly intractable and aberrant data that Newtonian science ignored. This practice is grounded in pragmatic theory, by which the meaning of a physical object is given by the complete specification of its behavior. Behavior is not determined by essence; rather, behavior is its essence. By its focus on process, chaos theory adopts the emerging principle of current particle theory that sees reality as background in unactualized potential.

The rise of chaos theory came at the happy conjunction of two circumstances. The animating cause arose with an initial small and scattered number of scientists in a variety of particular fields who became impatient with the practice of ignoring phenomena that may well be aberrant from the predictions of Newtonian theory but that are entirely typical of the behavior of the real world. The enabling cause was the availability of desktop computers. These machines gave ready and inexpensive access to a tool capable of performing quickly almost unimaginably long streams of iterative calculations, tasks that would take lifetimes of mathematicians to perform by hand. Because the beginning of chaos was the pursuit of disorder, it could not easily proceed without such a computational tool.

This pursuit of deviance has led to a revolutionary conception of reality. At first, these scattered investigators, working in a wide variety of fields and mutually unaware of their endeavors, found that physical processes which seemingly degenerated into states of non-Newtonian disorder eventually developed further into patterns recognizable as states of order. It is the nature of this order, however, that was revolutionary.

The significance of what these investigators were independently finding emerged when they began to interact and mutually to confirm their results. Order, they were finding, was, paradoxically, complex rather than simple. A process taken far enough inevitably emerges from disorder to order. This order, however, tends to be masked behind surface disorder. Moreover, the order that a process displays tends to be approximate—it follows a general pattern, but it does not replicate this pattern precisely.

For example, one could describe the motion of a simple pendulum by plotting momentum and position on a Cartesian graph. The plot of this data will trace out a circle. Now introduce another degree of freedom—say, by allowing some play in the bearing on which the pendulum is suspended—so that it also wobbles back and forth in a plane perpendicular to its usual motion. A trace of the momentum and position information about this more complex pendulum would yield the doughnut-shaped surface of a torus. Taking a cross-sectional slice anywhere on this torus again yields a circle, replicating the basic order of the plot of the pendulum's motion.

This recurring pattern of a circle is an example of a more general characteristic of chaotic order. Investigators find similarity not only in the patterns of order that particular processes follow, but also in the patterns found across diverse kinds of processes. All natural processes, whether smoke rising from a cigarette into undisturbed air, the population of a species in the presence of a natural predator, or the weather, follow similar patterns of development from order through disorder to order. Moreover, a process can reach any of a number of patterns of order. There is no single pattern; just as importantly, the number of patterns is not unlimited. Furthermore, looking backward in time from one of these states of order, there is a distinct path of development; looking forward, however, it is not possible to predict which of the alternative possible patterns will emerge. Finally, the clockwork Newtonian world posits that the size of the change in the final state of a system is proportional to the size of the change in initial conditions; in the emerging world of chaos, a small change in initial conditions can cause a large change in final conditions.

As chaos theory has developed, a new terminology has emerged with it. The possible alternative states of order toward which a process might move are its "strange attractors." The critical stage determining which strange attractor the process might move toward is the "bifurcation point." Small changes in initial conditions can become magnified at the bifurcation point, having the power to lead to large changes in the later process.[5] The consequences of this potential are called the Butterfly Effect—the beating of the wings of a butterfly in Hawaii being capable of ultimately generating a massive weather pattern in New England.

Chaos theory generates a conception of the world that is as revolutionary today as the picture that Newtonian science developed in the first blush of its emergence. Reality, according to chaos theory, is better described as a dynamic order of processes than as a static order of structures. Moreover, reality—the dynamic pattern of initial conditions, bifurcation points, and strange attractors—replicates throughout all processes. Weather patterns over North America, over a region such as the Midwest, and over a single state are strikingly similar; the same phenomenon occurs in depictions of a rugged landscape at various scales. The world, that is, can be found in a grain of sand.

Newtonian science poses a radical dichotomy between order and disorder. The physical universe can only be either one or the other. In the field of population theory, for instance, a Newtonian approach posits that steady populations are regulated by a deterministic mechanism; an erratic population, therefore, must be subject to some unpredictable exogenous factor:

Either deterministic mathematics produced steady behavior, or random external noise produced random behavior. That was the choice.
In the context of that debate, chaos brought an astonishing message:

simple deterministic models could produce what looked like random behavior. The behavior actually had an exquisite fine structure, yet any piece of it seemed indistinguishable from noise. The discovery cut through the heart of the controversy.[6]

Chaos thus represents a substantial step in the breakdown both of Cartesian logic and of the Cartesian dichotomy between the observer and the observed which generated the Newtonian revolution and the larger Enlightenment project. One radical difference between Newtonian science and chaos is exemplified by the contrast in logical method. Newtonian science epitomizes the logic of deduction and induction. Chaos, on the other hand, proceeds by incorporating the logical step of abduction—the continual reformulation of hypothesis as investigation generates data which deviates from complete confirmation of the starting hypothesis.[7]

A second aspect of this breakdown is the strong relativity of what we know of physical reality—what we see depends crucially on the vantage point from which we look at it. A billiard ball, for instance, looks, from a distance of, say, one hundred yards, like a point in space. From a distance of one foot, it looks like a globe. From a distance of one micron, it looks like the view that an observer would have hovering over the surface of an earth-like planet with dramatic landscape features. This description can extend indefinitely as the level of observation is extended to the atomic and subatomic levels. In the sense of finding the ultimate building blocks of the physical world, we may never get to the point where it is "turtles all the way down." In the sense of general patterns of order replicated at greatly different scales, however, chaos tells us that, paradoxically, there may be nothing but turtles.

Another example of this indefinite, and potentially infinite, scale of description is the problem of measurement—measuring, say, the coastline of England. The answer that we get depends crucially on the length of the measuring stick that we use—the longer the stick, the more it will bridge irregularities smaller than itself. That is, there simply is no single, definitive length of this coastline; the length that we find depends on our point of view. And, there is no possibility of a convergence of successive views—no possibility of reaching a single turtle. The measuring stick functions exactly like the paradigm that we select for our world view—there is no world out there to be captured by a single description; description instead is a function of the observer interacting with the observed. We can only hope to make a principled choice of the measuring stick.

According to the mechanistic Newtonian picture of the world, it is possible to trace the workings of the clockwork universe both backward and forward into time—"Give me the state of the system at any particular time, and I can tell you its state at any other past or future time." The radical limitation of Newtonian science, however, is that only closed systems can be clocklike. As chaos theory recognizes, the world is an open system. According to chaos, then, there is no certainty or predictability of the sort that Newtonian science offers. At bifurcation points, there is only predictive indeterminacy—we cannot know what order might emerge; we know only that, in the long term, one or another of a set of possible orders will emerge, and only in the sense of the larger, though more diffuse, dynamic order that clusters around strange attractors.

The Law of Tort

Chaos offers a complex description of the nature of dynamical systems, one that relegates the description offered by Newtonian dynamics to a special limiting case. This leads to the question of parallelism—if we can posit that distinct areas of human action, history, say, or perhaps law, are also dynamical systems, is their behavior similar to the behavior that chaos theory describes for physical systems? To explore this question, we will pursue the disorder that Charles Sampford finds in the law by describing what we find in terms of chaotic order. Assuming that this as well can be done credibly, we will be left to consider how such a description bears on the question that lies at the core of the approaches of Sampford and Weinrib—what role can law play in the arena of human action?

Charles Sampford's disorder is accurate enough as a surface description of the law as text. As a synchronic matter, as the Restatement project has demonstrated, there is extreme difficulty in deriving a rational structure of doctrine that comprehensively embraces the accumulation of relevant judicial decisions at any particular moment. Just as the Newtonian scientist must discard as aberrational some of the data that descriptive experimentation yields, the legal formalist must discard as aberrational some judicial decisions in order to construct a rational structure in any particular doctrinal area. Moreover, even when it is possible to derive a coherent doctrinal structure in this way, there is unruliness over time—the tendency for doctrine to shift away from any apparent momentary structure. In *The Transformation of American Law, 1780–1860*, Morton Horwitz describes these shifts in a variety of doctrinal areas, with these consequences for treatise writers who attempt to capture the common law in a comprehensive structured statement:

> The common law is especially cruel to those whom it casts aside. It either ignores them, soon forgetting that they ever existed, or,

more usually, uses them as authority for propositions that they did not accept.[8]

In order to illustrate the potential of chaos theory to provide a way out of the nihilist-formalist conundrum, let us look at two related cases that were separately decided by the Judicial Committee of the English Privy Council, sitting as the highest court of appeals for the Commonwealth countries. These cases—celebrated as the *Wagon Mound* cases—arose out of the same events. In late October 1951, the freighter *Wagon Mound* lay at the Caltex Wharf in the harbor of Sydney, Australia, taking on fuel. Due to the carelessness of the *Wagon Mound*'s engineering officer, a large quantity of the oil overflowed into the water. The oil spread across the surface of the water to Sheerlegs Wharf, located about six hundred feet from the freighter. Its owner, Morts Dock & Engineering Co., used Sheerlegs Wharf for ship building and ship repair work. At the time, two ships, owned by Miller Steamship Co., were tied up alongside for repairs.

When the manager at Sheerlegs Wharf noticed the oil, he suspended welding work in progress for fear of a fire. He then consulted with the manager of the Caltex Wharf, who assured him that it was safe to resume work. When welding resumed, Murphy's Law took over—molten metal from the welding work dropped onto cotton waste floating on the water surface and ignited it, which in turn ignited the oil. The resulting fire caused considerable damage to Sheerlegs Wharf and to the two ships tied up alongside.

Wagon Mound 1,[9] decided in 1961, was an action by Morts Dock against Overseas Tankship (U.K.), Ltd., the charterers of the freighter, for damage to the wharf. *Wagon Mound 2*,[10] decided in 1966, was an action by Miller Steamship against Overseas Tankship for the damage to its ships. One might expect, of course, that the outcomes would be similar—either Overseas Tankship is liable both to Morts Dock and to Miller Steamship for the harm resulting from the carelessly spilled fuel, or it is liable to neither.

In both cases, the Privy Council cast the issue in terms of causation, and expressly based its decisions on foreseeability. In *Wagon Mound 1*, the Court held that the discharge of the oil was negligent, and that any physical damage from the oil having come into contact with Sheerlegs Wharf was foreseeable and therefore actionable. The Court further held, however, that it was not foreseeable that the oil was capable of being set afire; thus, the fire damage to Sheerlegs Wharf was not actionable:

> For it does not seem consonant with current ideas of justice or morality that for an act of negligence, however slight or venial, which results in some trivial foreseeable damage the actor should be liable for all consequences however unforeseeable and however grave, so

long as they can be said to be "direct." It is a principle of civil liability, subject only to qualifications which have no present relevance, that a man must be considered to be responsible for the probable consequences of his act. To demand more of him is too harsh a rule, to demand less is to ignore that civilized order requires the observance of a minimum standard of behaviour.[11]

In *Wagon Mound 2*, by contrast, the Court held that it was unreasonable for the engineering officer of the *Wagon Mound* not to have considered the risk of fire when determining what steps ought to have been taken to avoid the spill. The Court came to this conclusion even though the trial court had found that fire was foreseeable only in "very exceptional circumstances." It was unreasonable, however, in the view of the Court to ignore even that small a risk because "it was so easy to prevent" the spill from happening.

It is clearly difficult to reconcile these cases as exemplars of the doctrine of foreseeability. The Court itself attempted to distinguish the two cases on the basis of the findings of the respective trial judges. In *Wagon Mound 1*, the trial judge had found that the "defendants 'did not know and could not reasonably be expected to have known' that the oil was capable of being set afire when spread on water." In *Wagon Mound 2*, a different trial judge had found that "the risk of fire from the spillage . . . could become an actuality only in very exceptional circumstances" and that "the chances of the required exceptional circumstances happening whilst the oil remained spread on the harbour waters . . . [were] remote."

To the Court in *Wagon Mound 2*, there was a crucial difference between the finding in the first case that the fire "was not foreseeable at all" and the finding in the second case—according to the Court, "not a primary finding of fact but an inference from the other findings"— that the fire "was not reasonably foreseeable." That is, "some risk of fire would have been present to the mind of a reasonable man in the shoes of the ship's chief engineer." It is this forced distinction that forms the basis of the outcome in *Wagon Mound 2*. That the distinction is forced is clear given the Court's assertion in *Wagon Mound 1* that it is "too harsh a rule" to demand that "the actor should be liable for consequences however unforeseeable and however grave so long as they can be said to be 'direct.'"

The *Wagon Mound 1* analysis turns solely on the issue of foreseeability—while there was a direct causal link between the oil spill and the fire damage, the causal chain was simply too long, and the damage was simply too remote. The *Wagon Mound 2* analysis clearly is as much about duty of care as it is about foreseeability. The damage to the plaintiff arose from "exceptional circumstances" whose foreseeability was "remote." As small as that risk was, however, the steps required to avoid that risk were even less burdensome. Defendant, that is, had violated its duty of care to plaintiff by unreasonably failing to avoid a risk. To the trial judge in *Wagon Mound 2*, the issue of foreseeability turned on the probability of harm; to the Court the issue of foreseeability turned on the ease or difficulty of avoiding the harm.

To recount the Court's analyses in the two cases, then, simply leaves us with the question of why the Court in *Wagon Mound 2* chose to manipulate its inquiry into the issue of causation by importing into that inquiry the issue of duty of care. For the effect of this manipulation is that, in the second case, the Court used the issue of causation as a determinant of liability. In the first case, by contrast, the Court used the causation issue as a device for *limiting* liability.

Indeed, to state the matter in this way suggests an alternative approach to the puzzling difference in outcomes. Posit that the reason why the *Wagon Mound 1* Court held that the causation requirement was not satisfied was because plaintiff lost. Posit that the reason why the *Wagon Mound 2* Court held that the causation requirement was satisfied was because plaintiff won.

In this view, "causation" functions only as a particular doctrinal label that describes as a formal matter what the case is "about." Appeal to causation doctrine, however, does not tell us, *ex ante*, how the *Wagon Mound 1* dispute ought to come out—it would require little effort for Charles Sampford to demonstrate that judicial precedent in the area of causation is so disordered (in his terms) that it would support either outcome of this dispute.

Look, however, beyond the surface of the *Wagon Mound 1* opinion and its formal characterization of the dispute. The Court in *Wagon Mound 1* made clear that it was consciously trying to limit liability in a case in which a direct though remote chain of causation was present— "it is too harsh a rule" to impose liability for *all* direct consequences. What is striking about this is its strong resonance with Oliver Wendell Holmes, Jr.'s seminal *The Common Law*. In his treatment of liability, Holmes asserted:

> A man need not, it is true, do this or that act,—the term *act* implies a choice,—but he must act somehow. Furthermore, the public generally profits by individual activity. As action cannot be avoided, and tends to the public good, there is obviously no policy in throwing the hazard of what is at once desirable and inevitable upon the actor.[12]

Indeed, we have here a core principle that must underlie any approach to the law of harms—our culture values political freedom, not least because society as a whole benefits from the unrestricted economic activity of self-interested individuals. Too strict a law of harms would inhibit this activity, to the detriment of all.

Now, look beyond the surface rhetoric of causation in the *Wagon Mound 2* opinion. Here, the Court emphasized the carelessness of the engineering officer instead of reaching an outcome *despite* this carelessness, as it had in *Wagon Mound 1*. The oil spilled because of carelessness. Although the possibility of harm was "remote," the spill could have been avoided with little effort, and it was blameworthy for this effort not to have been made. This analysis is equally striking—we have here another core principle of the law of harms, the idea of individual responsibility within a society that holds an ordered set of values. The cost to the engineering officer to exercise greater care was quite low; the benefit to society of avoiding harm, even though it was not highly probable, was considerable if it did occur. Such an analysis exemplifies currently strong normative positions that place heavy emphasis on the economic rationality of individual action.

Perhaps most striking of all is that the two principles that lay beneath the surface of the two opinions appear throughout the law of harms as major elements of a set of recurring themes. We can briefly recount these familiar themes:

1. *Calabresian*. Minimize the sum of the costs of accidents and of the costs of avoiding accidents.
2. *Holmesian*. Limit the liability of risk takers for accidents in order for society to gain the derivative benefits of risk taking without having to socialize the costs of entrepreneurship.
3. *Deep Pocket*. Decrease the enduring tendency toward a divergence in the distribution of wealth across society by concentrating the costs of accidents on the more affluent party.
4. *Puritan*. Assign liability for harm-causing events whenever possible as a correlative to the conception that we live in a moral universe.
5. *Cosmological*. Assign liability on the basis of physical causation as a correlative to the conception that we live in a universe that is not capricious.

By analyzing the *Wagon Mound* cases in terms of large themes that continually recur in the law of tort, we begin to see the emergence of a possible order underlying the chaotic disorder of the decisions. We have implicitly posited multiple layers of elements making up the legal process—the themes that underlie the formal outcome to the dispute (injunction granted, appeal denied), the outcome that generates the answer to the formal issue (did defendant proximately cause the harm?), and the formal issue itself around which the parties expressly litigate the case.

To say all this does not, of course, extricate us from our puzzle. Although most tort decisions can be seen as exemplifying one or another of these themes, there is no necessary order. The problem is that these themes mutually conflict—applied to the same facts, they yield different results, as seems to be apparent in the *Wagon Mound* cases. That is, whether one or another of these outcome-determinative themes is to apply to a particular dispute is a matter of judicial choice. Thus, identifying these themes that ultimately determine the answer to the formal issue does not explain why a court chooses those themes.

What prevents this choice from being a matter of mere caprice? In the two *Wagon Mound* cases, it is caprice if the two cases are factually and analytically the same. There is, of course, one considerable distinction between the two cases—the identity of the plaintiff. Can we argue that this is a distinction that does make a difference, that is, that the Court could, because of this distinction, plausibly give different weights to the various themes that it had available?

In *Wagon Mound 1*, the litigation involved two entrepreneurs engaged in their particular entrepreneurial activities. Moreover, although the Court gave little express attention in its opinion to this factor, these activities of the plaintiff were as much a part of the factual chain of causation as those of the defendant. As an entrepreneur, Morts Dock understands only too well that society does give legal recognition to the claim of the entrepreneur that society gains a substantial derivative benefit from its relatively unfettered activities. Society does so through such devices as the liability limitation function of incorporation acts and the widespread administrative practice of keying pollution control programs to the economic viability of the regulated entities. And Morts Dock thus understands that its claim for an entrepreneur's shield from liability is hollow if it demands too strenuously that the same claim by Overseas Tankship ought not be recognized in this particular case. Because of the identical entrepreneurial nature of the activities of the two parties, then, there is no basis for choosing between them, and the just outcome is to let the loss fall where it occurred.

By contrast, *Wagon Mound 2* involved a plaintiff, Miller Steamship, which was entrepreneurially passive in the chain of events that led to harm, a consumer of the entrepreneurial product of a third party. Here, the entrepreneur's Holmesian shield from private claims, in the all too typical circumstances in which no publicly funded compensation scheme operates, works to place the costs of advancing the general welfare onto particular, and randomly determined, entrepreneurially passive individuals. Because they are passive, these randomly determined individuals do not directly benefit from the liability shield. Moreover, the entrepreneur enjoys the benefit of its activity directly, and enjoys the lion's share of it. The passive individual shares only in the derivative benefit as one member of the large general public. Justice here demands that there be some minimum level of internalization of the costs of entrepreneurship. Cost internalization is especially appropriate if it can be required of an actor whose actions are in some sense blame-worthy and if carrying it out meets the criterion of efficiency, which the *Wagon Mound 2* opinion takes pains to demonstrate.

In both cases, moreover, it is difficult to construct an argument that the remaining themes can be appropriately chosen. There is no reason to believe that there are any wealth distributional disparities among the parties, or the possibility of creating such disparities by any par-ticular combination of outcomes, that would call into play the Deep Pocket theme. Nor are there any differences in the factual chains of causation that would require an appeal to the Cosmological theme on which to base differing outcomes in the two cases.

If this analysis is successful, then the identification of a set of themes and the description of their function in the adjudicative process have provided a principled explanation for the divergent results in the *Wagon Mound* cases. Or, to put the matter the other way around, having iden-tified a nontrivial difference between the two cases that is relevant to the themes that are latent in each, and having plausibly described the absent themes as not being immediately relevant, we have disorder, in the sense that an *ex ante* appeal to the doctrine of causation will yield indeterminacy, but we do not necessarily have caprice.

In addition, this analysis opens up the possibility of a more general explanation of the contours of common law adjudication. Consistent with the fundamental commitment in western democracies to a plu-ralism of values, there is no general hierarchal ordering of the values that underlie the implicit themes to which judges appeal, whether con-sciously or not, in deciding common law actions. Each theme sounds in values held by at least some members of society; there is, however, no consensus across society giving primacy to any particular value. What does occur is that a hierarchy of relevance among these values emerges only through the process of considering the circumstances of a particular case. This explains, for instance, why courts, in cases in which the formal issues generate a dichotomy of values presenting the court with a line-drawing problem, repeatedly assert that they cannot hope to fashion a general rule, but instead can only analyze and de-cide on a case-by-case basis.

CONSEQUENCES

It is the burden of this essay that the disorder as Sampford describes it is no more useful an account of the law than the ordered rational structure that Weinrib hopefully offers. And these accounts are inac-curate because of the proposition that it is of limited usefulness to try to understand the law as a structure of doctrine. Instead, it is better understood as a series of events—in Karl Llewellyn's phraseology, judges doing something about the disputes before them.[13]

When we look at the law in this way, we see that it exhibits an underlying regularity that, while I refrain from using the term *order*, with all its formalist connotations, can at least be called a *quasi-order*. This quasi-order appears not at the level of doctrine but instead at the deeper level of theme. Moreover, chaos provides a highly useful model for providing the descriptive terms of this quasi-order. The moments of judicial decision amount to the bifurcation points of chaos theory—the choice of outcome is not predetermined by an antecedent structure of legal rules. Corresponding to the strange attractors of chaos theory are the multiple, but nevertheless limited, themes of the law of tort—the paths from the bifurcation points lead to one or another of these themes. And, as we saw with the *Wagon Mound* cases, a seemingly small difference in the facts acted as a Butterfly Effect, reversing the resolution of the dispute.

PROCESS

This exercise in analogy necessarily raises the "So what?" question—what advantage do we gain by attempting to look at judicial decisions on tort disputes "through the eyes of" chaos theory? We can work toward an answer to this question by inquiring with more particularity into what it is that the formalists and antiformalists are doing. Weinrib and Sampford are both occupied with legal description. Moreover, they both proceed on the implicit assumption that law is best described in terms of structure. And underlying this assumption is the deeper assumption that the law cannot function autonomously of societal structures of power unless it is determinant, and that it cannot be determinant without exhibiting a rational doctrinal structure. Sampford and Weinrib differ only on the question of whether it is possible to find this rational structure within judicial doctrine. It is clear that Sampford has the stronger position—like Newtonian scientists, the legal formalist must discard significant amounts of data in order to demonstrate that what remains possesses a coherent structure.

Chaos theory, by contrast, provides a method of inquiry that takes as its starting point the formalist's aberrational data, the cases left over from Newtonian attempts at structural description, and pursues them by looking into the process by which these aberrations arose. It then asks in what directions that process might take us. Chaos theory thus suggests that law might be better described in terms of process rather than structure. Under such an approach, the law will appear as a process of dispute resolution driven by themes, with a dynamic body of doctrine generated through an abductive process by the outcomes to the disputes.

Our analysis of the *Wagon Mound* cases indeed proceeded on that implicit assumption. We took two cases as exemplars of data aberrational from the formalist's assumption of an underlying Newtonian order, inquired into the implicit thematic determinants of the outcomes, and arrived at the continual habit of common law judges to "decide on a case-by-case basis." Were our analysis to continue in the traditional way, it would follow the academician's habit. It would treat this judicial habit as something of an unfortunate cop-out; it would assume that, as the judges indulge their habit in a particular doctrinal area, a structure will sooner or later emerge; and it would take as the task at hand teasing out whatever inchoate structure might lurk in the data and nudging the judiciary along so that this structure will fully emerge sooner rather than later.

Let us instead look more closely at this "case-by-case" process itself. What is it that judges actually tend to do? Take as a starting point the proposition that judges are expected to reach, and tend to seek, a just resolution of the dispute at hand. There is, of course, no definition of the substantive content of justice that commands general consent. Our inquiry, however, is being made into the process by which courts resolve these disputes. Thus, we can proceed from this starting point by asking what sort of justice results from the nature of that process.

We can begin this inquiry with fundamental elements of the process— the public character of the proceedings and the embodiment of the result in a written opinion explanatory of that outcome. By explaining its decision, a court can engage in the particular, immediate, and outward-looking function of resolving the dispute in a way that appeals to the sense of justice of the parties, particularly to that of the losing party. Courts cannot lightly forego this opportunity. There will be a loser of each dispute that comes before the judicial process. The judicial process, which cannot command that disputants resort to it, will erode its relevance as it demoralizes the losers.

As an attempt to persuade its audience of the justness of the outcome, the opinion is, of course, an exercise in rhetoric. To be persuasive, however, the court must couch its opinion in terms that the audience can understand, that is, in terms of the audience's sense of justice. This sense of justice will be grounded in community values. Moreover, because the process is adversarial, the parties, through their counsel, have an opportunity to feed into it their individual, partisan, community value-based accounts of the justice of the particular case.

When we describe this outward-looking function, then, we find a process of mutual feedback that is strongly oriented to community values. In a pluralistic society, however, these values will necessarily be multifarious, mutually conflicting, and constantly shifting. This outward-looking function, then, will not be anchored in a foundation of principle that is either coherent or stable.

A second function of the decisional process proceeds in terms of the general and derivative. This is the inward-looking function of analogy—appealing to the accumulation of prior decisions for guidance in resolving the dispute at hand. Such an exercise necessarily risks committing the is-ought fallacy—giving normative weight to the fact that other judges have in the past reached particular outcomes in particular disputes. What saves the analogical function from committing this fallacy is that carrying it out serves the value of justice as regularity—the compelling need to treat like cases alike. Justice as regularity cannot be a sufficient condition of justice; it often is, however, a necessary condition.

In practice, of course, this seemingly straightforward function proceeds with considerable complexity. This is inevitable, given what it is to which judges appeal when they analogize—past decisions which themselves are based in part on the outward-looking function of particular justice. That is, because the values to which particular justice appeals are themselves in conflict, the outcome of precedent cannot be free of conflict, and the appeal to analogy will necessarily be complicated.

What we have, then, is a judicial process with strong outward-looking and inward-looking aspects. Because of their nature, however, these two aspects mutually conflict. Nor can the conflict be remedied by fully dispensing with one aspect or the other.

The inward-looking function generates one pole of the conflict. At any one moment, it is always possible, looking backward post hoc, to discern an apparent pattern, accompanied by inevitable aberrant data, in the accumulated decisions in any particular doctrinal area. Indeed, the formalist project is plausible because this apparent pattern is an entirely normal phenomenon. At the most practical level of real world affairs, the very existence of this pattern induces reliance. Moreover, this reliance is justifiable because the ordinary business of life cannot proceed with friction held to a tolerable level without some order and predictability. Call one pole of the conflict *heritage*—the apparent structure of rules and principles that we can derive at any one moment from the accumulation of decided cases.

The outward-looking function generates the other pole of the conflict. A society that is located in a stable physical environment, and that is closely attuned to its rhythms, will possess a relatively stable set of values. To the extent that maintaining this adaptation is itself a strong value, there will be little toleration for a debate over values. By contrast, a society that manifests a commitment to the autonomous individual through strong protection of such rights as free expression, and which develops and readily implements a continually expanding technological capacity that enables it to manipulate and recreate its physical environment, can keep its societal functions relevant and vital only through a flexible accommodation of a pluralism of values in its political processes. Call the other pole of the conflict *heresy*—the emerging values of society that point urgently toward an outcome to a particular dispute that is aberrant in terms of heritage, the current apparent pattern of outcomes in the decided cases.

What are we to make of a legal process with such a strong, built-in conflict? Were we working here with a conception of the law as structure, we surely would be at an impasse. Structure requires the resolution of conflict, and, however we might go about describing the law, we assuredly will find that the judiciary has not resolved this functional conflict. We have, however, taken our project to be the exploration of the possibility, and usefulness, of describing the law in process terms. And process requires only that conflict be accommodated, not necessarily resolved, for the reason that an ongoing process with a function of addressing emergent values that are not evolving toward an end state cannot have as its purpose the development of a substantive end state of values that a formalist project necessarily entails.

The question, then, is what do judges do about this endemic conflict? To start with, it is clear that this conflict, though endemic, is not incessant. In many (the great bulk of) legal disputes, there will be no conflict between the apparent structure of doctrine to be found in precedent and the matrix of emergent community values. In these disputes, justice as regularity will provide a sufficient basis for resolving the disputes. Thus, our focus is on those disputes that remain, cases in which the inward- and outward-looking functions lead to conflicting outcomes. Let's define these as the "hard" cases.

Perhaps to state the obvious, a court has, in a hard case, three general choices—to decide in accordance with particular justice, to decide in accordance with justice as regularity, or to decide on the basis of some compromise between the two. Each choice has its downside. As we have already seen, a decision that runs counter to, or compromises, particular justice risks demoralizing the loser. A decision that runs counter to, or compromises, justice as regularity risks political controversy— the ululation of editorial writers charging that a court has once again usurped the legislative function by making the law instead of applying it.

Of the two dangers, the former perhaps is ultimately the more threatening. This is because violation of the demands of particular justice tends to erode the relevance of the process of law to the ongoing pattern of disputes that manifest the friction of social and political intercourse. Violation of the demands of justice as regularity, by contrast, tends to place the judicial process squarely in the middle of political conflict, which is where a trenchant observer of the American system, Alexis de Tocqueville, concluded that we intend for it to be.

Indeed, the ritual of the opinion provides a useful tool for dealing with this paradox. In order to avoid the appearance of departing from justice as regularity, the court can attempt to mask the departure, either by making a forced distinction between the case at hand and precedent or by attempting to create a misleading veneer of analogy—discontinuity masked as continuity. Judges can use the process of drawing analogies, that is, both to engage in justice as regularity and to depart from justice as regularity. In this way, a court can limit the instances in which its audience will see it engaging in an overt choice between the demands of particular justice and the demands of justice as regularity.

The enduring flux of common law doctrine makes clear that there is a strong accommodation of particular justice in what judges do. Whether overtly or behind attempts at masking, courts have succeeded in engaging doctrine in a slow but continuing process of renewal, a clear example of abduction by which the doctrinal major premises never achieve stability. That this process is slow, and that a staple of academic legal writing is the jeremiad over "outdated rules that have outlived their usefulness," makes clear that courts are also not stinting the demands of justice as regularity. Rather than resolving the fundamental functional conflict of the dispute resolution process, the accumulation of judicial outcomes has maintained the conflict in tension. Because the common law seems always to be in the abductive process of renewal in response to dominant social values, it is clear that judges are maintaining this tension creatively as well.[14]

The consequence of the conflicting functions of the law as process and the accommodation of that conflict by maintaining the demands of those functions in tension is a surface texture of the law that exactly fits Sampford's description of disorder. If we accept either that we cannot or that we ought not resolve this conflict, then, at the surface level of the law, the accumulated outcomes of individual disputes, we have conceded disorder. And, the enduring failure of the formalist project suggests strongly that we must concede disorder at the underlying level of doctrine as well.

What lies below the level of doctrine? Our analysis of the *Wagon Mound* cases argued that, at the level of the individual dispute, the particular circumstances of the case tend to generate varying degrees of relevance among the themes that express the underlying matrix of community values. By looking at a case, and the opinion that explains it, *ex post*, we can read it as if the court had resolved the dispute by asking, "Given these facts, which theme(s) best capture this dispute?"

As an *ex ante* matter, however, is there any reason to believe that the selection of themes does not depend solely on the outcome, and that the court selects the outcome on the basis of considerations that lie outside of the law? After all, it is a common phenomenon for an opinion to read exactly as if the court started with the outcome and worked back to a rationale that represents the best way of supporting that outcome. A scrap of evidence that might well speak to this question is the recurring phenomenon of judges reporting, sometimes with reference to the rationale selected to support a particular outcome, more often with reference to the outcome itself, that "the opinion won't write." This suggests that the judge has encountered a conflict between theme and outcome. This further suggests that, when the opinion "won't write," there is a synergism within the confines of a particular case between the facts of the case and the emergent values that underlie the set of themes available to the court.

Nor is this surprising. No theme is fully generic; as we saw when we tried to relate them to the *Wagon Mound* cases, each is at least in part oriented to a particular kind of dispute context. Even if the set of themes is stable over the short term, reaching an outcome to a particular dispute on the basis of themes, then, would be a tractable problem with relatively determinant answers. It is only in the accumulation of decisions that disorder appears.

Before addressing the ultimate matter of legal autonomy, perhaps it would be well to recapitulate the complex picture of the dispute resolution process that is emerging. On the surface appears the disordered accumulation of outcomes of individual cases. At the next level down (the simile of an onion might not be inapt) one can derive at any particular time a Newtonian structure of doctrine that seems to capture the bulk of the cases, with a nagging, ever-present body of unruly data that cannot be fit into the structure—aberrant cases that would appear as "noise" in an exercise in Newtonian science. At a level further down is the opinion that rationalizes the outcome, a rhetorical exercise that both reveals and conceals the moment at which the court reaches its determination. However extended this moment might be in the real world, it does represent a bifurcation point, a point at which the outcome is yet to be determined. Next is the set of themes, at least in practice limited in number, to which these judicial opinions appeal. While in the abstract they come in no lexical order—comprising a potential game of Rock, Paper, and Scissors—one theme seems to dominate in any particular case, functioning as a strange attractor beyond the bifurcation point. Finally, there are the pluralistic, mutually conflicting, and continually evolving societal values that underlie these themes.

AUTONOMY

This brings us to the problem that is the ultimate focus of this essay—if the description of law as a process sensitive to societal values is accurate, a sensitivity that strongly generates predictive indeterminacy in the law, does the fact of this indeterminacy preclude the law from carrying out its presumed function of constraining what we do in ways that serve justice? Our culture has no telos, no enduring societal consensus on a single, overarching principle with which to establish a hierarchy of values that would render the dispute resolution process determinant. Moreover, we have described the heresy toward which the law seems always to tend only in terms of societal values. Furthermore, the pattern of societal values—at least those that dominate the loci of public discourse that include the law—tends to conform to the values of those who hold social, economic, and political power. If our description is accurate, then, are the worst fears of the formalists realized—that if law does not achieve coherence, structure, and *ex ante* determinacy it will be no more than a tool of justification for those who may hold power? How is it possible for the law as process to impose constraints on the powerful?

And the answer, it must be clear, is that precisely because there is no coherence in the pluralistic mix of societal values, the judicial opinion is an opportunity for the court to reach, and rationalize, whatever outcome that it deems proper. Values, perhaps paradoxically, impose no constraint on what a court can do, leaving the court free to do as it wishes—impose the particular values that it holds personally, ratify the existing distribution of power across society, or seek to achieve justice.

By analogizing to chaos theory as a means of description, we can see that structure is not the necessary condition of integrity; a disordered surface of legal doctrine does not thereby entail a law incapable of constraining what people do in seeking to achieve justice. We can also see that a law that does achieve justice cannot live up to the simplistic ideal of the Rule of Law—as some reified substance that exists apart from individuals. Rather, law is inevitably a consequence of what the principal actors in the legal process do. And it will be just only to the extent that these actors seek to do justice. Individuals ultimately are responsible for whether justice is achieved. We cannot leave that responsibility to some exogenous formalist's ideal of law; and we cannot abandon the possibility of responsibility through a nihilist's concept of subservient law.

Surely the law in fact is indeterminate in part because some judges do impose their own ideology or ratify existing unjust distributions of power. This indeterminacy, however, is the result of the imperfection of human action. It is not a symptom of the impossibility of autonomy in the law, as the nihilist-formalist conundrum would have it.

12

Perversions of Justice: Examining the Doctrine of U.S. Rights to Occupancy in North America

WARD CHURCHILL

For the nation, there is an unrequited account of sin and injustice that sooner or later will call for national retribution.
—George Catlin (1844)

Recognition of the legal and moral rights by which it occupies whatever land base it calls its own is perhaps the most fundamental issue confronting any nation. Typically, such claims to sovereign and proprietary interest in national territoralities devolve, at least in considerable part, upon supportable contentions that the citizenry is preponderantly composed of persons directly descended from peoples who have dwelt within the geographical area claimed since "time immemorial."[1] The matter becomes infinitely more complex in situations where the dominant—or dominating—population comprises either the representatives of a foreign power or immigrants ("settlers") who can offer no such assertion of "aboriginal" lineage to justify their presence or ownership of property in the usual sense.[2]

History is replete with instances in which various peoples have advanced philosophical, theological, and juridical arguments concerning their alleged entitlement to the homelands of others, only to have them rebuffed by the community of nations as lacking both moral force and sound legal principle. In such cases, the trend has been that international rejection of "imperial" pretensions has led to the inability of those nations extending such claims to sustain them.[3] Modern illustrations of this tendency include the dissolution of the classic European empires—those of France, Netherlands, Portugal, and Britain in particular—during the post–World War II period, as well as the resounding defeat of the Axis powers' territorial ambitions during the war itself. Even more recent examples may be found in the breakup of the Soviet (Great Russian) and Yugoslavian (Serbian) states, and in the extreme controversy attending maintenance of such settler states as Northern Ireland, Israel, and South Africa.

The purpose of this essay is to examine the basis upon which another contemporary settler state, the United States of America, contends that it possesses legitimate—indeed, inviolate—rights to approximately two and a quarter billion acres of territory in North America.[4] Through such scrutiny, the philosophical validity of U.S. legal claims to territorial integrity can be understood and tested against the standards of both logic and morality. This, in turn, is intended to provide a firm foundation from which readers may assess the substance of that image generated by the sweeping pronouncements so frequently offered by official America and its adherents over the years: that this is a country so essentially "peaceful," so uniquely enlightened in its commitments to the rule of law and concept of liberty, that it has inevitably emerged as the natural leader of a global drive to consolidate a "New World Order" in which the conquest and occupation of the territorality of any nation by another "cannot and will not stand."[5]

RIGHTS TO TERRITORIAL ACQUISITION IN INTERNATIONAL LAW

From the outset of the "Age of Discovery" precipitated by the Columbian voyages, the European powers, eager to obtain uncontested title to at least some portion of the lands their emissaries were encountering, quickly recognized the need to establish a formal code of juridical standards to legitimate what they acquired.[6] To some extent, this was meant to lend a patina of "civilized"—and therefore, it was imagined, inherently superior—legality to the actions of the European crowns in their relations with the peoples indigenous to the desired geography. More importantly, however, the system was envisioned as a necessary means of resolving disputes between the crowns themselves, each of which was vying with the others in a rapacious battle over the prerogative to benefit from wealth accruing through ownership of given regions in the "New World."[7] In order for any such regulatory code to be considered effectively binding by all Old World parties, it was vital that it be sanctioned by the Church.[8]

Hence, the mechanism deployed for this purpose was a theme embodied in a series of papal bulls begun by Pope Innocent IV during the crusades of the late thirteenth century.[9] The bulls were designed to define the proper ("lawful") relationship between Christians and "infidels" in all such worldly matters as property rights. Beginning in the early sixteenth century, Spanish jurists in particular did much to develop this theory into what have come to be known as the "Doctrine of Discovery" and an attendant dogma, the "Rights of Conquest."[10] Through the efforts of legal scholars such as Franciscus de Vitoria and Matías de Paz, Spanish articulations of Discovery Doctrine, endorsed by the Pope, rapidly evolved to hold the following as primary tenets of international law:[11]

1. Outright ownership of land accrued to the Crown represented by a given Christian (European) discoverer only when the land discovered proved to be uninhabited (*territorium res nullius*).[12]
2. Title to inhabited lands discovered by Crown representatives was recognized as belonging inherently to the indigenous people thereby encountered, but rights to acquire land from, and to trade with, the natives of the region accrued exclusively to the discovering Crown vis-à-vis other European powers. In exchange for this right, the discovering power committed itself to proselytizing the Christian gospel among the natives.[13]
3. Acquisition of land title from indigenous peoples could occur only by their consent—by an agreement usually involving purchase—rather than through force of arms, so long as the natives did not arbitrarily decline to trade with Crown representatives, refuse to admit missionaries among them, or inflict gratuitous violence upon citizens of the Crown.
4. Absent these last three conditions, utilization of armed force to acquire aboriginally held territory was considered unjust and claims to land title accruing therefrom to be correspondingly invalid.
5. Should one or more of the three conditions be present, then it was held that the Crown had a legal right to use whatever force was required to subdue resistance by natives and impound their property as compensation. Land title gained by prosecution of such "just wars" was considered valid.[14]

Although this legal perspective was hotly debated at the time (it still is, in certain quarters) and saw considerable violation by European colonists, it was generally acknowledged as the standard against which international conduct would be weighed.[15] By the early seventeenth century, the requirements of Discovery Doctrine had led the European states, England in particular, to adopt a policy of entering into formal treaties—full-fledged international instruments in which the sovereignty of the indigenous parties to such agreements were, by definition, officially recognized as equivalent to that of the respective crowns—as an expedient to obtaining legally valid land titles from American Indian peoples, first in what is now the state of Virginia, and then in areas further north. Treaties concerning trade, professions of peace and friendship, and the consummation of military alliances were also quite common.[16] Undeniably, there is a certain overweening arrogance embedded in the proposition that Europeans were somehow intrinsically imbued with an authority to restrict unilaterally the range of those to whom Native Americans might sell their property, assuming they wished to sell it at all. Nonetheless, in its recognition that indigenous peoples constituted bona fide nations holding essentially the same rights to land and sovereignty as any other, the legal posture of early European colonialism seems rather advanced and refined in retrospect. In these respects, the Doctrine of Discovery is widely viewed as one of the more important cornerstones of modern international law and diplomacy.[17]

With its adoption of Protestantism, however, Britain had already begun to mark its independence from papal regulation by adding an element of its own to the doctrine. Usually termed the "Norman Yoke," this concept asserted that land rights devolve in large part upon the extent to which the owners demonstrate a willingness and ability to "develop" their territories in accordance with a scriptural obligation to exercise "dominium" over nature. In other words, a person or a people is ultimately entitled to only that quantity of real estate which s/he/they convert from "wilderness" to a "domesticated" state.[18] By this criterion, English settlers were seen as possessing an inherent right to dispossess native people of all land other than that which the latter might be "reasonably expected" to put to such "proper" uses as cultivation.[19] By the same token, this doctrinal innovation automatically placed the British Crown on a legal footing from which it could contest the discovery rights of any European power not adhering to the requirement of "overcoming the wilderness" per se.

This last allowed England simultaneously to "abide by the law" and to directly confront Catholic France for ascendancy in the Atlantic regions of North America. After a series of "French and Indian Wars" beginning in the late 1600s and lasting nearly a century, the British were victorious, but at a cost more than negating the expected financial benefits to the Crown that had led it to launch its colonial venture in the first place. As one major consequence, King George II, in a move intended to preclude further warfare with indigenous nations, issued the Proclamation of 1763. This royal edict stipulated that all settlement or other forms of land acquisition by British subjects west of a line running along the Allegheny and Appalachian Mountains from

Canada to the Spanish colony of Florida would be suspended indefinitely, and perhaps permanently. English expansion on the North
American continent was thereby brought to an abrupt halt.[20]

ENTER THE U.S.

The new British policy conflicted sharply with the desires for personal
gain evident among a voracious elite that had been growing within
England's seaboard colonial population. Most of the colonies held some
pretense of title to "western" lands, much of it conveyed by earlier
Crown grant, and had planned to use it as a means of bolstering their
respective economic positions. Similarly, members of the landed gen-
try such as George Washington, Thomas Jefferson, John Adams, James
Madison, and Anthony Wayne all possessed considerable speculative
interests in land parcels on the far side of the 1763 demarcation line.
The only way in which these could be converted into profit was for
the parcels to be settled and developed. Vociferous contestation and
frequent violation of the proclamation, eventually enforced by George
III, became quite common.[21] All in all, this dynamic became a powerful precipitating factor in the American Revolution, during which many
rank-and-file rebels were convinced to fight against the Crown by promises of western land grants "for services rendered" in the event their
revolt was successful.[22]

There was, however, a catch. The United States emerged from its
decolonization struggle against Britain—perhaps the most grievous
offense that could be perpetrated by any subject people under then
prevailing law—as a pariah, an outlaw state that was shunned as an
utterly illegitimate entity by most other countries. Desperate to establish itself as a legitimate nation, and lacking any other viable alternatives with which to demonstrate its aptitude for complying with
international legality, the new government was virtually compelled to
observe the strictest of protocols in its dealings with Indians. Indeed,
what the Continental Congress needed more than anything at the time
was for indigenous nations, already recognized as respectable sovereignties via their treaties with the European states, to bestow a comparable recognition upon the fledgling United States by entering into
treaties with it.[23] The urgency of the matter was compounded by the
fact that the Indians maintained military parity with, and in some cases
superiority to, the U.S. Army all along the frontier.

As a result, both the Articles of Confederation and subsequent Constitution of the United States contained clauses explicitly and exclusively restricting relations with indigenous nations to the federal
government, insofar as the former were recognized as enjoying the
same politicolegal status as any other foreign power.[24] The United States

also officially renounced, in the 1789 Northwest Ordinance and elsewhere, any aggressive intent concerning indigenous nations, especially with regard to their respective land bases:

> The utmost good faith shall always be observed towards the Indians; their land and property shall never be taken from them without their consent; and in their property, rights, and liberty, they shall never be disturbed ... but laws founded in justice and humanity shall from time to time be made, for wrongs done to them, and for peace and friendship with them.[25]

This rhetorical stance, reflecting an impeccable observance of international legality, was also incorporated into such instruments of agreement with European states as the United States was able to obtain during its formative years. For instance, in the 1803 Louisiana Purchase of much of North America west of the Mississippi from France, the federal government solemnly pledged itself to protect "the inhabitants of the ceded territory ... in the free enjoyment of their liberty, property and the religion they profess."[26] Other phraseology in the purchase agreement makes it clear that federal authorities understood they were acquiring from the French not the land itself, but France's monopolistic trade rights and prerogative to buy any acreage within the area its indigenous owners wished to sell.

The same understanding certainly pertained to all unceded Indian country claimed by Britain under Discovery Doctrine east of the Mississippi, after it was quit-claimed by George III in the Treaty of Paris concluding the Revolution. Even if English discovery rights somehow "passed" to the new republic by virtue of this royal action, an extremely dubious premise in itself, there still remained the matter of obtaining native consent to literal U.S. ownership of any area beyond the 1763 proclamation line.[27] Hence, the securing of indigenous agreement to land cessions must be added to the impressive list of diplomatic and military reasons why treaty-making with Indians comprised the main currency of American diplomacy throughout the immediate postrevolutionary period. Moreover, the need to secure valid land title from native people through treaties far outlasted the motivations of diplomatic and military necessity, these having been greatly diminished in importance after U.S. victories over Tecumseh's alliance in 1794 and 1811, Britain in the War of 1812, and the Red Stick Confederacy during 1813–1814.[28] The treaties were and remain, in substance, the basic real estate documents anchoring U.S. claims to land title— and thus to rights of occupancy—in North America.

What was most problematic in this situation for early federal policymakers was the fact that in gaining diplomatic recognition and land cessions from indigenous nations through treaties, the United States was simultaneously admitting not only that Indians ultimately owned virtually all of the territory coveted by the United States, but that they were really under no obligation to part with it. As William Wirt, an early attorney general, put it in 1821: "[Legally speaking,] so long as a tribe exists and remains in possession of its lands, its title and possession are sovereign and exclusive. We treat with them as separate sovereignties, and while an Indian nation continues to exist within its acknowledged limits, we have no more right to enter upon their territory than we have to enter upon the territory of a foreign prince."[29] A few years later, Wirt amplified his point:

> The point, once conceded, that the Indians are independent to the purpose of treating, their independence is to that purpose as absolute as any other nation. Being competent to bind themselves by treaty, they are equally competent to bind the party that treats with them. Such party cannot take benefit of [a] treaty with the Indians, and then deny them the reciprocal benefits of the treaty on the grounds that they are not independent nations to all intents and purposes.... Nor can it be conceded that their independence as a nation is a limited independence. Like all other independent nations, they have the absolute power of war and peace. Like all other independent nations, their territories are inviolate by any other sovereignty.... They are entirely self-governed, self-directed. They treat, or refuse to treat, at their pleasure; and there is no human power that can rightly control them in the exercise of their discretion in this respect.[30]

Such enjoyment of genuine sovereign rights and status by indigenous nations served, during the twenty years following the revolution (roughly 1790–1810), to considerably retard the assumption of lawful possession of their land grants by revolutionary soldiers, as well as consummation of the plans of the elite caste of prerevolutionary land speculators. Over the next two decades (1810–1830), the issue assumed an ever-increasing policy importance as the matter of native sovereignty came to replace Crown policy in being construed as *the* preeminent barrier to U.S. territorial consolidation east of the Mississippi.[31] Worse, as Chief Justice of the Supreme Court John Marshall pointed out in 1822, any real adherence to the rule of law in regard to native rights might not only block U.S. expansion, but—since not all the territory therein had been secured through Crown treaties—cloud title to significant portions of the original thirteen states as well.[32] Perhaps predictably, it was perceived in juridical circles that the only means of circumventing this dilemma was through construction of a legal theory—a subterfuge, as it were—by which the more inconvenient implications of international law might be voided even while the republic maintained an appearance of holding to its doctrinal requirements.

EMERGENCE OF THE MARSHALL DOCTRINE

Not unnaturally, the task of forging the required "interpretation" of existing law fell to Marshall, widely considered one of the great legal minds of his time. Whatever his scholarly qualifications, the Chief Justice can hardly be said to have been a disinterested party, given not only his vociferous ideological advocacy of the rebel cause before and during the revolution, but the fact that both he and his father were consequent recipients of 10,000-acre grants west of the Appalachians, in what is now the state of West Virginia.[33] His first serious foray into land rights law thus centered in devising a conceptual basis to secure title for his own and similar grants. In the 1810 *Fletcher v. Peck* case, he invoked the Norman Yoke tradition in a manner that far exceeded previous British applications, advancing the patently absurd contention that the areas involved were effectively "vacant" even though very much occupied—and in many instances stoutly defended—by indigenous inhabitants. On this basis, he declared that individual Euroamerican deeds within recognized Indian territories might be considered valid whether or not native consent was obtained.[34]

While *Peck* was obviously useful from the U.S. point of view, resolving as it did a number of short-term difficulties in meeting obligations already incurred by the government vis-à-vis individual citizens, it was in itself a tactical opinion, falling far short of accommodating the country's overall territorial goals and objectives. In the 1823 *Johnson v. McIntosh* case, however, Marshall followed up with a more clearly strategic enunciation, reaching for something much closer to the core of what he had in mind. Here, he opined that because Discovery Rights purportedly constricted native discretion in disposing of property, the sovereignty of discoverers was to that extent inherently superior to that of indigenous nations. From this point of departure, he then proceeded to invert all conventional understandings of Discovery Doctrine, ultimately asserting that native people occupied land within discovered regions at the sufferance of their discoverers rather than the other way around. A preliminary rationalization was thus contrived by which to explain the fact that the United States had already begun depicting its borders as encompassing rather vast portions of unceded Indian country.[35]

Undoubtedly aware that neither *Peck* nor *McIntosh* was likely to withstand the gaze of even minimal international scrutiny, Marshall next moved to bolster the logic undergirding his position. In the two so-called Cherokee Cases of the early 1830s, he hammered out the thesis that native nations within North America were "nations like any other" in the sense that they possessed both territories they were capable of ceding and recognizable governmental bodies empowered to cede these areas through treaties.[36] On the other hand, he argued on the basis of the reasoning deployed in *McIntosh*, they were nations of a "peculiar type," both "domestic to" and "dependent upon" the United States, and therefore possessed of a degree of sovereignty intrinsically less than that enjoyed by the United States itself.[37] The essential idea boils down to a presumption that, while native peoples are entitled to exercise some range of autonomy in managing their affairs within their own territories, both the limits of that autonomy and the extent of the territories involved can be "naturally" and unilaterally established by the federal government. At base, this is little more than a judicial description of the classic relationship between colonizer and colonized,[38] but put forth in such a way as to seem at first glance to be the exact opposite.

While it might be contended (and has been, routinely enough) that Marshall's framing of the circumstances pertaining to the Cherokee Nation, already completely surrounded by the territorality of the United States by 1830, bore some genuine relationship to then prevailing reality,[39] it must be reiterated that he did not confine his observations of the situation to Cherokees, or even to native nations east of the Mississippi. Rather, he purported to articulate the legal status of *all* indigenous nations, including those west of the Mississippi—the Lakota, Cheyenne, Arapaho, Comanche, Kiowa, Navajo, and Chiricahua Apache, to name but a few—that had not yet encountered the United States in any appreciable way. Self-evidently, these nations could not have been described with the faintest accuracy as domestic to or dependent upon the United States. The clear intent belied by Marshall's formulation was that they be made so in the future. The doctrine completed with elaboration of the Cherokee Cases was thus the pivotal official attempt to rationalize and legitimate a vast campaign of conquest and colonization—absolutely contrary to the customary law of the period—upon which the United States was planning to embark in the years ahead.[40]

A final inversion of accepted international legal norms and definitions stems from this, that being an outright reversal of what was meant by "just" and "unjust" warfare.[41] Within Marshall's convoluted and falsely premised reasoning, it became arguable that indigenous nations acted unlawfully whenever and wherever they attempted physically to prevent exercise of the U.S. "right" to expropriate their property. Put another way, Indians could be construed as committing "aggression" against the United States at any point they attempted to resist the invasion of their homelands by American citizens. In this sense, the United States could declare itself to be waging a "just"—and therefore lawful—war against native people on virtually any occasion where force of arms was required to realize its territorial ambitions. *Ipso facto*, all efforts of native people to defend themselves against systematic dispossession and subordination could thereby be categorized as "unjust"—and thus unlawful—by the United States.[42]

In sum, the Marshall Doctrine shredded significant elements of the existing Laws of Nations. Given the understandings of these very same legal requirements placed on record by federal judicial officials such as Attorney General Wirt and Marshall himself, not to mention the embodiment of such understandings in the Constitution and formative federal statutes, this cannot be said to have been unintentional or inadvertent. Instead, the Chief Justice engaged in a calculated exercise in juridical cynicism, quite deliberately confusing and deforming accepted legal principles as an expedient to "justifying" his country's pursuit of a thoroughly illegitimate course of territorial acquisition. Insofar as federal courts and policy-makers elected to adopt his doctrine as the predicate to all subsequent relations with American Indians, it may be said that he not only replicated the initial posture of the United States as an outlaw state, but rendered it permanent.

EVOLUTION OF THE MARSHALL DOCTRINE

The Cherokee Cases were followed by a half-century hiatus in important judicial determinations regarding American Indians. On the foundation provided by the Marshall Doctrine, the government felt confident in entering into the great bulk of the at least 371 treaties with indigenous nations by which it professed to have gained the consent of Indians in ceding huge portions of the native land base, assured all the while that by its self-anointed position of superior sovereignty, it would be under "no legal obligation" to live up to its end of the various bargains struck.[43] Well before the end of the nineteenth century, the United States stood in default on virtually every treaty agreement it had made with native people, and there is considerable evidence in many instances that this was intended to be so from the outset.[44] Aside from the fraudulent nature of U.S. participation in the treaty process, there is an ample record that many of the instruments of cession were militarily coerced while the government implemented Marshall's version of just wars against Indians. As the U.S. Census Bureau put it in 1894:

> The Indian wars under the United States government have been about 40 in number [most of them occurring after 1835]. They have cost the lives of . . . about 30,000 Indians [at a minimum]. . . . The actual number of killed and wounded Indians must be very much greater than the number given, as they conceal, where possible, their actual loss in battle. . . . Fifty percent additional would be a safe number to add to the numbers given.[45]

The same report noted that some number "very much more" than

8500 Indians were known to have been killed by government-sanctioned private citizen action—dubbed "individual affairs"—during the course of U.S.-Indian warfare.[46] In reality, such citizen action is known to have been primarily responsible for the reduction of the native population of Texas from about 100,000 in 1828 to less than 10,000 in 1880.[47] Similarly, in California, an aggregate indigenous population that still numbers approximately 300,000 had been reduced to fewer than 35,000 by 1860, mainly because of "the cruelties and wholesale massacres perpetrated by [American] miners and early settlers."[48] Either of these illustrations offers a death toll several times the total number officially acknowledged having accrued through individual affairs within the whole of the forty-eight contiguous states.

Even while this slaughter was occurring, the government was conducting what it itself frequently described as a "policy of extermination" in its conduct of wars against those indigenous nations that proved "recalcitrant" about giving up their land and liberty.[49] This manifested itself in a lengthy series of massacres of native people—men, women, children, and old people alike—at the hands of U.S. troops. Among the worst were those at Blue River (Nebraska, 1854), Bear River (Idaho, 1863), Sand Creek (Colorado, 1864), Washita River (Oklahoma, 1868), Sappa Creek (Kansas, 1875), Camp Robinson (Nebraska, 1878), and Wounded Knee (South Dakota, 1890).[50] Somewhat different, but comparable, methods of destroying indigenous peoples were evidenced in the forced march of the entire Cherokee Nation along the "Trail of Tears" to Oklahoma during the 1830s (55 percent attrition),[51] and the internment of the bulk of the Navajo Nation under abysmal conditions at the Bosque Redondo from 1864 to 1868 (35 to 50 percent attrition).[52] Such atrocities against humans were coupled with an equally systematic extermination of an entire species, the buffalo or North American bison, as part of a military strategy to starve resistant Indians into submission by "destroying their commissary."[53]

All told, it is probable that more than a quarter-million Indians perished as a direct result of U.S. extermination campaigns directed against them.[54] By the turn of the century, only 237,196 native people were recorded by census as still being alive within the United States,[55] perhaps 2 percent of the total indigenous population of the U.S. portion of North America at the point of first contact with Europeans.[56] Correlating rather precisely with this genocidal reduction in the number of native inhabitants was an erosion of Indian land holdings to approximately 2.5 percent of the lower forty-eight states.[57] Small wonder that, barely fifty years later, Adolf Hitler would explicitly anchor his concept of *lebensraumpolitik* (politics of living space) directly upon U.S. practice against American Indians.[58] Meanwhile, even as the 1890 census figures were being tallied, the United States had already moved beyond the "Manifest Destiny" embodied in the conquest phase of its continental expansion and was emphasizing the development of colonial administration over residual indigenous land and lives through the Bureau of Indian Affairs (BIA), a subdivision of the War Department that had been reassigned for this purpose to the Department of Interior.

This was begun as early as 1871, when Congress—having determined that the military capacity of indigenous nations had finally been sufficiently reduced by incessant wars of attrition—elected to consecrate Marshall's description of their "domestic" status by suspending further treaty making with them.[59] In 1885, the United States moved for the first time to directly extend its internal jurisdiction over reserved Indian territories through passage of the Major Crimes Act.[60] When this was immediately challenged as a violation of international standards, Supreme Court Justice Samuel F. Miller rendered an opinion that consolidated and extended Marshall's earlier assertion of federal plenary power over native nations, contending that the government held an "incontrovertible right" to exercise authority over Indians as it saw fit and "for their own good."[61] Miller also concluded that Indians lacked any legal recourse in matters of federal interest, their sovereignty being defined as whatever Congress did not remove through specific legislation. This decision opened the door to enactment of more than 5000 U.S. statutes regulating affairs in Indian country by the present day.[62]

One of the first of these was the General Allotment Act of 1887, "which unilaterally negated Indian control over land tenure patterns within the reservations, forcibly replacing the traditional mode of collective use and occupancy with the Anglo-Saxon system of individual property ownership."[63] The Act also imposed for the first time a formal eugenics code—dubbed "blood quantum"—by which American Indian identity would be federally defined on racial grounds rather than by native nations themselves on the basis of group membership/citizenship.[64]

> The Allotment Act set forth that each American Indian recognized as such by the federal government would receive an allotment of land according to the following formula: 160 acres for family heads, eighty acres for single persons over eighteen years of age and orphans under eighteen, and forty acres for [non-orphan] children under eighteen. "Mixed blood" Indians received title by fee simple patent; "full bloods" were issued "trust patent," meaning they had no control over their property for a period of twenty-five years. Once each person recognized by the government as belonging to a given Indian nation had received his or her allotment, the "surplus" acreage was "opened" to non-Indian homesteading or conversion into the emerging system of national parks, forests, and grasslands.[65]

Needless to say, there proved to be far fewer Indians identifiable as

such under federal eugenics criteria than there were individual parcels available within the reserved land areas of the 1890s. Hence, "not
only was the cohesion of indigenous society dramatically disrupted by
allotment, and traditional government prerogatives preempted, but it
led to the loss of some two-thirds of all the acreage [about 100 million
of 150 million acres] still held by native people at the time it was
passed."[66] Moreover, the land assigned to individual Indians during
the allotment process fell overwhelmingly within arid and semi-arid
locales considered to be the least productive in North America; uni-
formly, the best watered and otherwise useful portions of the reservations were declared surplus and quickly stripped away.[67] This, of course,
greatly reinforced the "dependency" aspect of the Marshall thesis and
led U.S. Indian Commissioner Francis Leupp to conclude approvingly
that allotment should be considered as "a mighty pulverizing engine
for breaking up [the last vestiges of] the tribal mass" which stood as a
final barrier to complete Euroamerican hegemony on the continent.[68]

As with the Major Crimes Act, native people attempted to utilize
their treated standing in federal courts to block the allotment process
and corresponding erosion of the reservation land base. In the 1903
Lonewolf v. Hitchcock case, however, Justice Edward D. White extended
the concept of federal plenary power to hold that the government
possessed a right to unilaterally abrogate whatever portion of any treaty
with Indians it found inconvenient while continuing to consider the
remaining terms and provisions binding upon the Indians.[69] In essence,
this meant that the United States could point to the treaties as the
instruments that legally validated much of its North American land
title while simultaneously avoiding whatever reciprocal obligations it
had incurred by way of payment. White also opined that the government's plenary power over Indians lent it a "trust responsibility" over
residual native property such that it might opt to "change the form"
of this property—from land, say, to cash or "services"—whenever and
however it chose to do so. This final consolidation of the Marshall
Doctrine effectively left native people with *no* true national rights under U.S. law while voiding the remaining pittance of conformity to
international standards the United States had exhibited with regard to
its Indian treaties.[70]

THE OPEN VEINS OF NATIVE AMERICA

A little-discussed aspect of the Allotment Act is that it required each
Indian, as a condition of receiving the deed to his or her land parcel,
to accept U.S. citizenship. By the early 1920s, when most of the allotment the United States wished to accomplish had been completed, there
were still a significant number of native people who had not been

"naturalized," either because they'd been left out of the process for one reason or another, or because they'd refused to participate. Consequently, in 1924 the Congress passed a "clean-up bill" entitled the Indian Citizenship Act, which imposed citizenship upon all remaining indigenous people within U.S. borders whether they wished it or not.[71]

The Indian Citizenship Act greatly confused the circumstances even of many of the blooded and federally certified Indians insofar as it was held to bear legal force, and to carry legal obligations, whether or not any given Indian or group of Indians wished to be U.S. citizens. As for the host of non-certified, mixed-blood people residing in the U.S., their status was finally "clarified"; they had been definitively absorbed into the American mainstream at the stroke of the congressional pen. And, despite the fact that the act technically left certified Indians occupying the status of citizenship within their own indigenous nation as well as the U.S. (a "dual form" of citizenship so awkward as to be sublime), the juridical door had been opened by which the weight of Indian obligations would begin to accrue more to the U.S. than to themselves.[72]

All of this—suspension of treaty making, extension of federal jurisdiction, plenary power and "trust" prerogatives, blood quantum and allotment, and the imposition of citizenship—was bound up in a policy officially designated as the compulsory assimilation of American Indians into the dominant (Euroamerican) society.[73] Put another way, U.S. Indian policy was carefully (and openly) designed to bring about the disappearance of all recognizable Indian groups, as such.[74] The methods used included the general proscription of native languages[75] and spiritual practices,[76] the systematic and massive transfer of Indian children into non-Indian settings via mandatory attendance at boarding schools remote from their communities,[77] and the deliberate suppression of reservation economic structures.[78] As Indian Commissioner Charles Burke put it at the time, "It is not consistent with the general welfare to promote [American Indian national] characteristics and organization."[79]

The assimilationist policy trajectory culminated during the 1950s with the passage of House Concurrent Resolution 108, otherwise known as the "Termination Act of 1953," a measure through which the United States moved unilaterally to dissolve 109 indigenous nations within its borders.[80] Termination was coupled to the "Relocation Act," a statute passed in 1956 and designed to coerce reservation residents to disperse to various urban centers around the country.[81] The ensuing programmatic emphasis upon creating an American Indian diaspora has resulted, by 1990, in over half of all Indians inside the U.S. being severed from their respective land bases and generally acculturated to non-Indian mores.[82] Meanwhile, the enactment of Public Law 280, placing many reservations under the jurisdiction of individual states of the

Union, reduced the level of native sovereignty to that held by counties or municipalities.[83] This voided one of the last federal pretenses that the government maintained a degree of consideration that Indians retained "certain characteristics of sovereign nations."

The question, of course, arises as to why, given the contours of this aspect of federal policy, the final obliteration of the indigenous nations of North America has not long since occurred. The answer, apparently, resides within something of a supreme irony. This is that, unbeknownst to the policy-makers who implemented allotment policy against Indians during the late nineteenth century, much of the ostensibly useless land to which native people were consigned has turned out to be some of the most mineral rich on earth. It is presently estimated that as much as two-thirds of all known U.S. "domestic" uranium reserves lie beneath reservation lands, as well as perhaps a quarter of the readily accessible low-sulfur coal and about a fifth of the oil and natural gas. In addition, the reservations are now known to hold substantial deposits of copper, zinc, iron, nickel, molybdenum, bauxite, zeolites, and gold.[84]

Such matters were becoming known by the early 1920s.[85] Federal economic planners quickly discerned a distinct advantage in retaining these abundant resources within the framework of governmental trust control, an expedient to awarding extractive leases, mining licenses, and the like to preferred corporate entities in ways that might have proven impossible had the reservations been liquidated altogether. Hence, beginning in 1921, it was determined that selected indigenous nations should be maintained in some semblance of being, and Washington began to experiment with the creation of "tribal governments" intended to administer what was left of Indian country on behalf of an emerging complex of interlocking federal/corporate interests.[86] In 1934, this resulted in the passage of the Indian Reorganization Act (IRA), a bill that served to supplant virtually every remaining traditional indigenous government in the country, replacing them with federally designed "tribal councils" structured along the lines of corporate boards and empowered primarily to sign off on mineral leases and similar instruments.[87]

The arrangement led to a recapitulation of the Marshall Doctrine's principle of indigenous "quasi-sovereignty" in slightly revised form: now, native nations were cast as always being sovereign enough to legitimate Euroamerican mineral exploitation on their reservations, never sovereign enough to prevent it. Predictably, under such circumstances the BIA negotiated mining leases, duly endorsed by the puppet governments it had installed, "on behalf of" its "Indian wards." These leases have typically paid native people 15 percent or less of market royalty rates on minerals taken from their lands.[88] The "super profits" thus generated for major corporations have had a significant positive effect on U.S. economic growth since 1950, a matter amplified by the fact that the BIA also "neglected" to include land restoration and other environmental clean-up clauses in contracts pertaining to reservation land (currently, Indians are always construed as being sovereign enough to waive such things as environmental protection regulations, never sovereign enough to enforce them).[89] One consequence of this trend is that, on reservations where uranium mining has occurred, Indian country has become so contaminated by radioactive substances that the government has actively considered designating them as "national sacrifice areas" unfit for human habitation.[90] At this juncture, planning is also afoot to utilize several reservations as dump sites for high-level nuclear wastes and toxic chemical substances that cannot be otherwise conveniently disposed of.[91]

Further indication of the extent and virulence of the colonial system by which the United States has come to rule Native America is not difficult to find. For instance, dividing the 50 million-odd acres of land still nominally reserved for Indian use and occupancy in the United States by the approximately 1.6 million Indians the government recognized in its 1980 census, reveals that native people—on paper, at least—remain the largest landholders on a per capita basis of any population sector on the continent.[92] Given this, in combination with the resources known to lie within their land and the increasingly intensive "development" of these resources over the past forty years, simple arithmetic strongly suggests that they should also be the wealthiest of all aggregate groups.[93] Instead, according to the federal government's own data, Indians are far and away the poorest in terms of both annual and lifetime per capita income. Correspondingly, we suffer all the standard indices of dire poverty: North America's highest rates of infant mortality and teen suicide, death from malnutrition, exposure, and plague.[94] Overall, we consistently experience the highest rate of unemployment, lowest level of educational attainment, and one of the highest rates of incarceration of any group. The average life expectancy of a reservation-based American Indian male is currently less than forty-five years; that of a reservation-based female, barely over forty-seven.[95]

In Latin America, there is a core axiom that guides understanding of the interactive dynamics between the northern and southern continents of the Western Hemisphere. "Your wealth," Ladino analysts point out to their Yanqui counterparts, "is our poverty."[96] Plainly, the structure of the relationship forged by the United States vis-à-vis the indigenous nations of the northern continent itself follows exactly the same pattern of parasitic domination. The economic veins of the prostrate Native North American host have been carefully opened, their contents providing lifeblood to the predatory creature that applied the knife. Such are the fruits of John Marshall's doctrine after a century and a half of continuous application to the "real world" context.

<h2>INTERNATIONAL SLEIGHT OF HAND</h2>

It's not that the United States has failed to attempt to mask the face of this reality. Indeed, in the wake of World War II, even as the United States was engaged in setting a "moral example" to all of humanity by assuming a lead role in prosecuting former Nazi leaders for having ventured down much the same road of continental conquest that the United States itself had pioneered,[97] Congress passed what it called the Indian Claims Commission Act.[98] The premise of the bill was that all nonconsensual—and therefore illegal—takings of native property that had taken place during the course of American history had been "errors," sometimes "tragic" ones.[99] As a means, at least figuratively, of separating U.S. historical performance and expansionist philosophy from the more immediate manifestations of the Nazis, the new law established a commission empowered to review the basis of U.S. land title in every quarter of the country, and to award retroactive monetary compensation to indigenous nations shown to have been unlawfully deprived of their lands. Tellingly, the commission was authorized to set compensation amounts only on the basis of the estimated per acre value of illegally taken land *at the time it was taken* (often a century or more before) and was specifically disempowered from restoring land to Indian control, no matter *how* the land was taken or *what* the desires of the impacted native people might be.[100]

Although the life of the commission was originally envisioned as being only ten years, the magnitude of the issues it encountered, and the urgency with which its mission to "quiet title" to aboriginal land rights came to be viewed by the Euroamerican status quo, caused it to be repeatedly extended.[101] When it was ultimately suspended on September 30, 1978, it still had sixty-eight cases docketed for review, despite having heard and ostensibly "disposed of" several hundred others over a period of three decades.[102] In the end, while its intent had been the exact opposite, it had accomplished nothing so much as to establish with graphic clarity how little of North America the United States could be said to legally own.

> The fact is that about half the land area of the country was purchased by treaty or agreement at an average price of less than a dollar an acre; another third of a [billion] acres, mainly in the West, were confiscated without compensation: another two-thirds of a [billion] acres were claimed by the United States without pretense of a unilateral action extinguishing native title.[103]

This summary, of course, says nothing at all about the approximately 44 million acres of land currently being taken from the Indians, Aleuts, and Inuits of the Arctic north under provision of the 1971 Alaska Native Claims Settlement Act,[104] or the several million acres of Hawaii stripped away from the natives of those islands.[105] Similarly, it says nothing of the situation in such U.S. "possessions" as Guam, Puerto Rico, the "U.S." Virgin Islands, "American" Samoa, and the Marshall Islands.

Serious challenges to commission findings have been mounted in U.S. courts, based largely on the cumulative contradictions inherent to federal Indian law. As a consequence, the Supreme Court has been compelled to resort to ever more convoluted and logically untenable argumentation as a means of upholding certain government assertions of "legitimate" land title. In its 1980 opinion in the Black Hills Land Claim case, for example, the high court was forced to extend the Marshall Doctrine's indigenous domesticity thesis to a ludicrous extreme, holding that the United States had merely exercised its rightful internal power of "eminent domain" over the territory of the Lakota Nation when it expropriated 90 percent of the latter's land a century earlier, in direct violation of the 1868 Treaty of Fort Laramie.[106] Similarly, in the Western Shoshone Land Claim case, where the government could show no documentation that it had ever even pretended to assume title to the native land at issue, the Supreme Court let stand the Claims Commissions's assignment of an arbitrary date on which a transfer supposedly took place.[107]

During the 1970s, the American Indian Movement (AIM), an organization militantly devoted to the national liberation of native North America, emerged in the United States. In part, the group attempted the physical decolonization of the Pine Ridge Reservation in South Dakota (home of the Oglala Lakota people), but was met with a counterinsurgency war waged by federal agencies such as the FBI and U.S. Marshalls Service, and surrogates associated with the reservation's IRA Council.[108] Although unsuccessful in achieving a resumption of indigenous self-determination at Pine Ridge, the tenacity of AIM's struggle (and the ferocity of the government's repression of it) attracted considerable international attention. This led, in 1980, to the establishment of a United Nations Working Group on Indigenous Populations, under the auspices of the U.N. Educational, Scientific and Cultural Organization (UNESCO), an entity mandated to assess the situation of native peoples globally and produce a universal declaration of their rights as a binding element of international law.[109]

Within this arena, the United States, joined by Canada, has consistently sought to defend its relations with indigenous nations by trotting out the Marshall Doctrine's rationalization that the United States has assumed a trust responsibility over rather than outright colonial domination of native North America.[110] Native delegates have countered, correctly, that trust prerogatives, in order to be valid under international law, must be tied to some clearly articulated time interval, after which the trustee nations resume independent existence. This has been successfully contrasted to the federal (and Canadian) government's presumption that it enjoys a permanent trust authority over indigenous nations; assumption of permanent plenary authority over another nation's affairs and property is the essential definition of colonialism, it is argued, and is illegal under a number of international covenants.[111]

The United States and Canada have responded with prevarication, contending that their relationship to native North America cannot be one of colonialism insofar as United Nations Resolution 1541 (XV), the so-called Blue Water Thesis, specifies that in order to be defined as a colony a nation must be separated from its colonizer by at least thirty miles of open ocean.[112] The representatives of both countries have also done everything in their power to delay or prevent completion of the Universal Declaration of the Rights of Indigenous Peoples, arguing, among other things, that the term "peoples," when applied to native populations, should not carry the force of law implied by its use in such international legal instruments as the Universal Declaration of Human Rights (1948), Covenant on Civil and Political Rights (1978), and the International Convention on Elimination of All Forms of Racial Discrimination (1978).[113] The United States in particular has implied that it will not abide by any declaration of indigenous rights that runs counter to what it perceives as its own interests, a matter that would replicate its posture with regard to the authority of the International Court of Justice (the "World Court")[114] and elements of international law such as the 1948 Convention on Prevention and Punishment of the Crime of Genocide.[115]

Meanwhile, the United States has set out to "resolve things internally" through what may be intended as a capstone extrapolation of the Marshall Doctrine. This has assumed a drive to convince Indians to accept the premise that, rather than struggling to regain the self-determining rights to separate sovereign existence embodied in their national histories and treaty relationships, they should voluntarily merge themselves with the U.S. polity. In this scenario, the IRA administrative apparatus created during the 1930s would assume a position as a "third level of the federal government," finally making indigenous rights within the United States inseparable from those of the citizenry as a whole. This final assimilation of native people into the "American sociopolitical mainstream" would obviously void most (or perhaps all) potential utility for Indian rights that exists or might emerge from international law over the next few years. The option is therefore being seriously pursued at this juncture by a Senate Select Committee on

Indian Affairs, chaired by Hawaii Senator Daniel Inouye (who has already done much to undermine the last vestiges of rights held by the native people of his own state).[116]

U.S. OUT OF NORTH AMERICA

During the fall of 1990, President George Bush stepped onto the world stage beating the drums for what he termed a "just war" to roll back what he described as the "naked aggression" of Iraq's invasion and occupation of neighboring Kuwait. Claiming to articulate "universal principles of international relations and human decency," Bush stated that such aggression "cannot stand," that "occupied territory must be liberated, legitimate governments must be reinstated, the benefits of their aggression must be denied to aggressive powers."[117] Given the tone and tenor of this Bushian rhetoric—and the undeniable fact that Iraq had a far better claim to Kuwait (its nineteenth province, separated from the Iraqis by the British as an administrative measure following World War I) than the United States has to virtually any part of North America[118]—one could only wait with bated breath for the American president to call air strikes in upon his own capital as a means of forcing his own government to withdraw from Indian country. Insofar as he did not, the nature of the "New World Order" his war in the Persian Gulf harkened tends to speak for itself.

The United States does not now possess, nor has it ever had, a legitimate right to occupancy in at least half the territory it claims as its own on this continent. It began its existence as an outlaw state and, given the nature of its expansion to its present size, it has adamantly remained so through the present moment. In order to make things appear otherwise, its legal scholars and its legislators have persistently and often grotesquely manipulated and deformed accepted and sound legal principles, both internationally and domestically. They have done so in precisely the same fashion, and on the same basis, as the Nazi leaders they stood at the forefront in condemning for crimes against humanity at Nuremberg.

In no small part because of its success in consolidating its position on other peoples' land in North America, the United States may well continue to succeed where the Nazis failed. With the collapse of the Soviet Union, it has emerged as *the* ascendant military power on the planet during the late twentieth century. As the sheer margin of its victory over Iraq has revealed, it now possesses the capacity to extend essentially the same sort of relationships it has already imposed upon American Indians to the remainder of the world. And, given the experience it has acquired in Indian affairs over the years, it is undoubtedly capable of garbing this process of planetary subordination in a legalistic attire symbolizing its deep-seated concern with international freedom and dignity, the sovereignty of other nations, and the human rights of all peoples. At a number of levels, the Marshall Doctrine reckons to become truly globalized in the years ahead.

This is likely to remain the case, unless and until significant numbers of people within the United States as well as without come to recognize the danger, and the philosophical system that underpins it, for what they are. More importantly, any genuine alternative to a consummation of the Bushian vision of world order is predicated upon these same people acting upon their insights, opposing the order implicit to the U.S. status quo both at home and abroad. Ultimately, the dynamic represented by the Marshall Doctrine must be reversed, the structure it fostered dismantled, within the territorial corpus of the United States itself. In this, nothing can be more central than the restoration of indigenous land and indigenous national rights in the fullest sense of the term. The United States—at least as it has come to be known, and in the sense that it knows itself—must be driven from North America. In its stead then would reside the possibility, likely the *only* possibility, of a genuinely just and liberatory future for all humanity.

13

Marriage, Law, and Gender: A Feminist Inquiry*

NAN D. HUNTER

Reflecting on the problems and possibilities inherent in the concept of same-sex marriage is especially intriguing as we approach the turn of the century. That is not because the idea is new. A series of constitutional challenges to the exclusion of gay male and lesbian couples from the matrix of rights and responsibilities that comprise marriage were brought and failed twenty years ago.[1] Nor is it because there is a substantial body of newly developed constitutional doctrine that would undergird litigation to establish such a claim.[2] It is because there is a rapidly developing sense that the legalization of marriage for gay and lesbian Americans is politically possible at some unknown but not unreachable point in the future, that it shimmers or lurks—depending on one's point of view—on the horizon of the law.

The most dramatic development to date in the campaign to establish a right to gay marriage occurred in May 1993, when the Hawaii Supreme Court ruled that, under the state constitution, marriage could not be limited to opposite-sex couples unless the state could demonstrate a compelling interest in doing so.[3] The outcome of the case on remand is not yet known. If the statute falls, however, the stage will be set for a series of challenges in other states that would inevitably result from gay and lesbian couples legally married in Hawaii seeking recognition elsewhere. Whatever the result, it seems inevitable that lesbians and gay men will continue to press a second wave of litigation challenges to marriage laws, forcing courts to engage with the issue in a political context that has changed significantly since the 1970s.

A series of events prior to the 1993 Hawaii decision helped to propel the issue of legal recognition of gay relationships into widespread public consciousness. A number of municipalities have adopted domestic partnership laws granting recognition for limited purposes to unmarried couples (usually to both heterosexual and homosexual couples) who met certain functional criteria roughly comparable to marriage.[4] The most widely publicized of the campaigns associated with such laws occurred in San Francisco. In 1989, the San Francisco Board of Supervisors enacted a domestic partners ordinance.[5] The ordinance was repealed later that year by voters in a referendum election, but a revised version was adopted by voters in November 1990.[6] The "partnership" statute that comes the closest to marriage is that of Denmark, which amended its marriage law to permit lesbian and gay couples to join in "registered partnerships" carrying most of the rights of marriage, the primary exception being for eligibility to adopt children.[7]

This sense that legalization of gay marriage is a real possibility has in turn triggered multiple debates. The mainstream public debate centers on whether the current exclusionary laws promote a moral good in preserving "traditionalism" in family relationships, or perpetuate the moral evil of injustice.[8] Within the lesbian and gay community, an intense debate has also arisen, not about whether the exclusionary laws are good, but about whether seeking the right to marry should be a priority.[9] Proponents of a campaign for marriage rights have framed their arguments largely in terms of equality for lesbians and gay men[10] and have employed a body of rights discourse that has animated the major civil rights struggles of this century.[11] Opponents have relied on two primary arguments. First, they invoked a feminist critique of marriage as an oppressive institution[12] that lesbians and gay men should condemn, not join. Second, these activists have drawn on the politics of validating difference, both the difference of an asserted gay identity and culture that resist assimilation, and the differences between persons who would marry and those (homosexual or heterosexual) who would for go marriage and thereby, it is argued, become even more stigmatized.[13] Analogous tensions between equality-based and difference-based strategies have buffeted feminist theory for the last decade.[14]

The question of whether the law should recognize same-sex marriage has its own intrinsic importance, both as a matter of law and as a liberationist goal. This essay, however, seeks to position that issue in a different theoretical context by framing the question primarily as one of gender systems, rather than of minority rights. It then analyzes the major doctrinal debates in law concerning proposals to reform family regulatory schemes and suggests the need to synthesize those with proposals for the legal recognition of lesbian and gay relationships. Lastly, it analyzes efforts to secure legal protection for lesbian and gay relationships as an example of the problematics of rights discourse and proposes a political and rhetorical strategy distinct from a legal strategy as a means to minimize the intrinsic limitations of rights claims.

MARRIAGE AS NATURE

Decisional law on the issue of gay marriage is most striking for its brevity and tautological jurisprudence. In each of the pre-Hawaii cases, the justices of the respective courts (not one of whom dissented) seem somewhat astonished at even having to consider the question of whether the limitation of marriage to opposite-sex couples is constitutionally flawed.[15] These cases tell us nothing about equality or privacy doctrine. Instead, their holdings are grounded in statements about what the courts believe marriage *is*. Their significance lies in their thorough conflation of gender, nature, and law.

Marriage is, after all, a complete creation of the law, secular or ecclesiastical. Like the derivative concept of illegitimacy, for example, and unlike parenthood, it did not and does not exist without the power of the state (or some comparable social authority) to establish, define, regulate, and restrict it. Beyond such social constructs, individuals may couple, but they do not "marry." Moreover, although marriage may have ancient roots, its form has not been unchanging. It is a historically contingent institution, having existed with widely differing indicia and serving shifting social functions in various cultures.[16] Marriage can be defined empirically as "a socially approved union between unrelated parties that gives rise to new families and, by implication, to socially approved sexual relations. But beyond that minimal definition, there is no linguistically valid explanation of what marriage entails."[17] Yet in each of the rulings in a lesbian or gay marriage challenge, the courts have essentialized as "nature" the gendered definitional boundaries of marriage.[18]

It was the assumption that gender is an essential aspect of marriage that enabled these courts to so easily rebuff the analogy to *Loving v. Virginia*,[19] which held that the equal protection clause forbade the criminalization of marriage between persons of different races. The Minnesota Supreme Court drew "a clear distinction between a marital restriction based *merely* upon race and one based upon the *fundamental* difference in sex."[20] The Washington court in *Singer* similarly dismissed *Loving* as inapposite because irrelevant to the definition of marriage.[21] Having done so, it was then free, in its analysis of the plaintiff's sex discrimination claim, to reason that because neither men nor women could marry a person of the same sex, there was no sex discrimination, thus repeating the identical separate-but-equal logic rejected by the Supreme Court in *Loving*.[22] By so casually distinguishing *Loving*, both courts simultaneously essentialized gender and ignored the history of the essentialization of race in marriage law.

The constructed basis of this essentialized definition is illustrated by the fact that, for most of American history, race also defined who could marry. Under the slave codes, African-American slaves could not law-fully marry, either other slaves or any other person, of any race.[23] After slavery was abolished, laws establishing race as a defining element of marriage did not disappear, nor were they limited to a handful of states. Not until 1948 did the California Supreme Court declare that state's antimiscegenation law unconstitutional, the first such ruling in the nation.[24] Statutes prohibiting miscegenation, carrying penalties of up to ten years in prison, were in effect in twenty-nine states in 1953.[25] The Motion Picture Production Code, a voluntary but effective self-regulator of the content of Hollywood films, forbade depiction of inter-racial sex or marriage until 1956.[26] *Loving* was not decided until 1967.

Race, as a biological characteristic, is a fact of nature. Race also exists, however, as a social category, onto which multiple meanings and power relationships are inscribed. What changed between the time of the slave codes and the decision in *Loving* was not the biological but the social aspects of race. Today, the state formally defines eligibility for marriage on the basis of sex, a biological category. In reality, how-ever, the definition of marriage is grounded on gender, the social cat-egory. The key to this distinction lies in how gender-determined *roles* were once invoked, with equal assurance, as the "nature" of marriage.

For many decades, courts proclaimed and enforced the precept that marriage necessitated not only an authority and dependence relation-ship, but one that was gendered. One's status as either husband or wife determined all duties and obligations, as well as one's right to name, domicile, physical integrity, property, and other attributes of personhood.[27] When faced with nonconforming individuals, courts struck down their attempts to alter these gender-determined aspects of marriage in terms that underscored the perceived fixedness of the male authority/female dependence "nature" of marriage.[28]

The legal landscape on which the possibility of lesbian and gay marriage is being debated may not differ greatly from that of twenty years ago in its treatment of homosexuality,[29] but it is a different world as to the regulation of the terms and conditions of marriage. Two de-cades of feminist litigation efforts have established virtual equality in formal legal doctrine.[30] The Supreme Court has repeatedly stricken sex-based classifications in family law, whether of the male as the eco-nomic provider for women and children[31] or of the female as solely the wife and mother.[32]

What feminist litigation has not been able to do is achieve social and economic equality. In such areas as no-fault divorce, alimony, and child support, the enforcement by law of a presumed equality that usually does not exist has, in fact, operated to the detriment of many women.[33] The terms of marriage as a legal institution (as in, for example, the right to a separate name or domicile) have changed dramatically. But the social power relations between men and women inside or outside of marriage have changed much less significantly.

The legalization of lesbian and gay marriage would not, of course, directly shift the balance of power in heterosexual relations. Gay marriage is not a panacea. It could, however, alter the fundamental concept of the particular institution of marriage. Its potential is to disrupt both the gendered definition of marriage and the assumption that marriage is a form of naturally, if not legally, prescribed hierarchy.[34]

With the erosion of legally enforceable authority and dependence statuses as a central defining element of marriage, all that remains of gender as the formal structural element of marriage are the foundational constructs of "husband" and "wife." The once elaborate *de jure* assignations of gender status in marriage have now been reduced to only their most minimal physical manifestation, the gendered pair of spouses. Claims for the legalization of lesbian and gay marriage raise the question of what, without gendered content, could the social categories of "husband" and "wife" mean.

Seizing on the same definitional concerns as those expressed by the courts, conservatives have ridiculed the challenge to husband and wife constructs posed by the idea of lesbian and gay marriage in order to mobilize the social anxiety that that possibility precipitates. Taunts such as "Who would be the husband?" have a double edge, however, if one's project is the subversion of gender. Who, indeed, would be the "husband" and who the "wife" in a marriage of two men or of two women? Marriage enforces and reinforces the linkage of gender with power by husband/wife categories, which are synonymous with the social power imbalance between men and women. Whatever the impact that legalization of lesbian and gay marriage would have on the lives of lesbians and gay men, it has fascinating potential for denaturalizing the gender structure of marriage law for heterosexual couples.

Marriage between men or between women could also destabilize the cultural meaning of marriage, creating for the first time the possibility of marriage as a relationship between members of the same social status categories. However valiantly individuals try to base marriages on genuine equality, no one can erase his or her status in the world as male or female, or create a home life apart from culture. Same-sex marriage could create a model in law for an egalitarian kind of interpersonal relation, outside the gendered terms of power, for many marriages.[35] At the least, it would radically strengthen and dramatically illuminate the claim that marriage partners are presumptively equal.

Beyond "nature," the other most likely argument in defense of exclusionary marriage laws is also, at bottom, gender-based. The *Singer* court found that, even if the denial of same-sex marriage did constitute sex discrimination, it fell within the exception to Washington state's Equal Rights Amendment, which permits differential treatment based on the unique physical characteristics of the sexes. The court reasoned that "marriage exists as a protected legal institution primarily because of societal values associated with the propagation of the human race," and that "it is apparent that no same-sex couple offers the possibility of the birth of children by their union."[36] Inability to bear children, however, has never been a bar to marriage, nor is it a ground for divorce.[37] Persons who lack the ability or the intent to procreate are nonetheless allowed to marry. The real interest behind the procreation argument probably lies in discouraging child*rearing* by homosexual couples. That concern stems from the fear that the children will be exposed, not to negligent or inept parenting, but to the wrong models of gender, implicitly marked as legitimate.[38]

To date, the marriage law debate concerning lesbian and gay couples has been framed, both in the larger public and within the lesbian and gay community, as revolving around a claim of rights for particular persons now excluded from marriage. The implicit corollary is that this issue affects only lesbians and gay men. That is much too restricted a focus. The extent of the opposition to the legalization of lesbian and gay marriage indicates not mere silliness or stupidity, as it would if the change were of little consequence to the larger world, nor is it solely a manifestation of irrational prejudice.[39] Legalization of lesbian and gay marriage poses a threat to gender systems, not simply to antilesbian and antigay bigotry.[40]

What is most unsettling to the status quo about the legalization of lesbian and gay marriage is its potential to expose and denaturalize the historical construction of gender at the heart of marriage. Those who argue that marriage has always been patriarchal and thus always will be make the same historical mistake, in mirror image, as courts that have essentialized the "nature" of marriage.[41] There is no "always has been and ever shall be" truth of marriage. Nor is the experience of marriage and family life problematic to women in identical ways.[42] Certainly marriage is a powerful institution, and the inertial force of tradition should not be underestimated. But it is also a social construct. Powerful social forces have reshaped it and will continue to do so.[43]

Although the theory used in future litigation to secure legalization of lesbian and gay marriage will likely be grounded on an equality or a due process privacy or associational claim for lesbians and gay men, the impact, if such a challenge prevails, will be to dismantle the legal structure of gender in every marriage.

MARRIAGE AS FUNCTION AND CONTRACT

During the same period of the last twenty years, when legalization of lesbian and gay marriage has been attempted and so far has failed, a variety of other proposals for pluralizing the law of intimate relationships have been advanced. Contemporary family law now includes an enormous body of law and commentary addressing the range of issues posed by the formation and dissolution of cohabiting, unmarried heterosexual unions. Yet despite the obvious similarities between those issues and the efforts to secure benefits for lesbian and gay couples, there have been virtually no linkages between the family law theorists (mostly feminists) and the lesbian and gay rights advocates.

New family law models for heterosexuals have emerged in response to profound demographic changes that have reshaped the social experience of marriage. Marriage is still central to the adult life experience of a large majority of Americans, but there has been a dramatic alteration in its role and timing. A majority of Americans will spend more of their lifetimes outside, rather than as part of, married-couple households.[44] Cohabitation, often for a significant period of time, frequently precedes marriage and/or remarriage.[45] The number of unmarried cohabiting heterosexual couples increased by more than 500 percent from 1970 to 1989.[46] The average American marriage does not last a lifetime, but a much more modest 9.6 years.[47] The American divorce rate doubled between 1966 and 1976, peaked in 1981, and has dropped somewhat since, but remains much higher than it was twenty years ago.[48] Concomitant with that shift, there has been an enormous growth in the remarriage rate, so much so that one-third of all marriages are remarriages.[49] As of 1989, the number of Americans who had never married, by the age of forty-five, remained low: 6 percent for women and 8 percent for men.[50] The rate of nonmarriage differed significantly by race. Of all Americans at age forty-five, 7.3 percent had never married; for African-Americans, the comparable figure was 14.4 percent.[51]

For many Americans, then, the formation of couples and coupled households will, over the course of a lifetime, include both nonmarital cohabitant unions as well as marriages, often multiple times. The response of the law has been contradictory. The law still penalizes cohabiting couples, both directly[52] and indirectly.[53] The courts also, however, have undertaken the adjudication of increasing numbers of civil disputes initiated by persons in relationships comparable to marriage. In that context, two distinct lines of doctrine have emerged.[54]

In situations involving the dissolution of the relationship and disputes between the two partners, many courts have adopted contract law principles to decide the allocation of economic assets and responsibilities based on the terms of the agreement expressed or implied between the parties.[55] The focus of such an analysis is on the intent of the parties. In opting for a contract measure, virtually all of these courts have explicitly rejected the possibility of declaring a constructive marriage and applying a jurisdiction's divorce law.[56] To do so, they have reasoned, would be to frustrate a presumed desire of the parties not to marry and to subvert the interest of the state in preserving a clear boundary between marriage and nonmarriage.

In situations involving the eligibility of the nonmarital family unit or its members for benefits from the state or from third parties, courts have developed a different approach, a jurisprudence of functionalism. In the functionalist approach, courts seek to identify by objective criteria those relationships that are the "functional and factual equivalent"[57] of marriage. A functionalist approach to family law underlay the recognition of common-law marriage, which was widespread in the nineteenth century,[58] and was used to mitigate the effects of a race-bound definition of marriage in cases involving slaves.[59] The leading functionalist case to have reached the U.S. Supreme Court involved an extended multigenerational household, which the Court ruled had to be considered as one family to determine eligibility to live in a neighborhood zoned for single-family units.[60] Functionalism can also operate to the detriment of nonmarital couples, as when governmental benefits are denied on the grounds that the couple should be treated as married, even when they are not, because they are presumed to be enjoying the same economies of shared expenses.[61]

The high-water mark of functionalism to date with regard to homosexual couples was the ruling of the New York Court of Appeals in *Braschi v. Stahl Associates*[62] that a gay couple must be treated as a family for purposes of the provision in New York's rent control law that protected surviving "members of the family" from eviction in the event of the death of the named tenant. In interpreting the rent control law, the court reasoned that

> [it] should not be rigidly restricted to those people who have formalized their relationship by obtaining, for instance, a marriage certificate or an adoption order. The intended protection against sudden eviction should not rest on fictitious legal distinctions or genetic history, but instead should find its foundation in the reality of family life.[63]

The court went on to articulate a set of criteria for a "family":

> [T]he exclusivity and longevity of the relationship, the level of emotional and financial commitment, the manner in which the parties have conducted their everyday lives and held themselves out to society, and the reliance placed upon one another for daily family services. . . . [I]t is the totality of the relationship as evidenced by the dedication, caring and self-sacrifice of the parties [that] should, in the final analysis, control.[64]

Domestic partnership laws represent the most successful attempt to date to merge the two lines of doctrine into codified rights and benefits laws.[65] The status of domestic partner is not limited by sexual orientation; both lesbian and gay as well as straight couples may register.[66] Politically, domestic partnerships serve as a mechanism for achieving legal protection for lesbian and gay couples without seeking legalization of lesbian and gay marriage.[67] Such provisions have been adopted in ten municipalities.[68] Domestic partnership laws present a way of solving, by legislation, two problems that arose in the case-by-case development of functionalist and contract principles: the uncertainty of definitional boundaries for a nonmarital relationship and the risk of fraudulent claims.[69] The statutes set out objective definitions of relationships that can qualify for domestic partner status and establish a mechanism, usually a registration system, for verifying whether a particular couple has self-declared as a partnership.[70] The procedure for terminating a partnership involves filing a notice with the registry.[71]

The domestic partnership laws enacted to date have established benefits primarily in the areas of bereavement and sick leave for municipal employees based on the illness or death of a partner; tenancy succession and other housing-related benefits; and health insurance benefits for partners of municipal employees.[72] All have been enacted by municipal, rather than state or federal jurisdictions, and so cannot alter provisions of the state or federal laws that accord benefits based on marriage in areas such as tax, inheritance, or most public benefits.

Moreover, most domestic partnership laws emphasize their functionalist, rather than their contractual, aspects. Their focus, and the bulk of the political support for them, concerns the creation of a claim for entitlement by the nonmarried couple to rights or benefits offered by a third party to married couples. Most also, however, contain language that at least arguably establishes a contract between the two persons themselves.[73] The most recent of the laws, adopted by San Francisco voters, is the most explicit in this regard.[74]

The terms of the implied contract provisions of domestic partnership laws are far more libertarian than the state-imposed terms of marriage, however, and more limited than the scope of implied contracts potentially recognizable under *Marvin* and its progeny. Domestic partnerships cover only reciprocal obligations for basic support while the two individuals remain in the partnership. There is no implied agreement as to the ownership or division of property acquired during the term of the partnership, nor is there any basis for compelling one partner to support the other for any length of time, however short, after the partnership is dissolved.

These laws thus go the farthest toward removing the state from regulation of intimate relationships. The issue of whether the state should

be expelled raises an old and continuing debate. Feminists have exposed the law's long-professed tradition of noninterference in certain
aspects of family life as a mask for the ceding of control to those who
wield greater power in the domestic sphere.[75] Some feminists have
attacked the contract doctrine embodied in *Marvin*[76] for applying a market
ideology that will inevitably disfavor those with less power in the market.
These writers favor the imposition of constructive marriage as to certain terms, especially regarding support and property, when unmarried couples end a relationship. They argue that permitting judges to
infer that a marriage exists, rather than simply attempting to discern
the intent of the parties, operates as a necessary guarantor of balance
between socially unequal parties.[77]

The feminist debates on regulation by the state have assumed, however, that only heterosexual unions were at issue.[78] Conversely, the
debates about domestic partnerships have generally been based on the
model of a lesbian or gay couple.[79] It is true that the terms of a domestic partnership would serve as a floor, rather than a ceiling, for
establishing the mutual obligations between partners. Nothing in these
statutes would preclude a partner from also asserting an implied contract for an equitable division of property, for example, when the partnership dissolves. But that possibility does not address—much less
solve—the underlying problem of whether an imbalance in power led
to which terms, if any, were agreed to between the couple. On the
other hand, imposing marriage or marriage-like terms on all long-term
relationships either ignores the ways that same-sex couples cannot be
assumed to pose the same issues of imbalance of power, or it lends
the imprimatur of the state once again to a classification that renders
lesbian and gay Americans invisible.

These two conversations about reformulating the law of relationships—one among feminists critical of neutral forms that ignore power
differentials and the other among lesbian and gay rights advocates
critical of *de jure* exclusions of a minority—need to be joined. And
each needs to be reconstituted to incorporate the concerns and experiences of marriage and family, which are shaped by race as powerfully
as by gender or sexual orientation.[80] Careful analysis of who will be
affected in precisely what ways by any given option, with a critical
examination of both marriage reform and of partnership proposals,
has only begun.[81]

As between legalizing lesbian and gay marriage and seeking domestic partnership laws, neither strategy is complete without the other.
Reforming marriage, alone, diversifies only by eliminating gender from
the definition of marriage; creates no mechanism by which to reject,
rather than to seek to refashion, the customs of marriage; and offers
no choice except marriage for any couple seeking any of the benefits

of legal recognition. Domestic partnership laws, without the degendering of marriage, create a second-class status rather than an alternative,
leaving lesbian and gay couples still excluded from marriage by force
of state law; in no sense, without a marriage option available, could
they be assumed to be "choosing" partnership. What these and most
other proposals for reform share is the goal of pluralizing marriage
and family law. As the discussion in this section illustrates, however, strategies for pluralization cannot avoid questions of equality and
power.

<h2 style="text-align:center">RIGHTS AND BEYOND: LAW AS DISCOURSE</h2>

A campaign by lesbian and gay Americans to assert a "right" either to
marry or to secure certain benefits through domestic partnership laws
can be situated not only in a matrix of legal doctrine relating to the
family, but also within an ongoing dialogue about the politics of rights.
The invocation of rights claims is one of the most powerful weapons
available to a movement seeking justice for the excluded and
disempowered. The very framing of one's assertions in terms of rights
highlights one's membership in, and thus the justifiable reciprocity of
one's claim on, the larger *polis*. It evokes American cultural understandings of rights, a culture in which "the sense of legal rights as
claims whose realization has intrinsic value can fairly be called
rampant."[82] And it signals connection with a specific historical tradition of rights-based movements, thereby invoking a universalized call
for equality, as well as group-specific demands for elimination of in-
vidious social rules.

Rights claims are hardly unambiguous strategic choices, however.
Many writers, especially those associated with Critical Legal Studies
(CLS), have argued at length about the inherent limitations of rights
frameworks.[83] They point out that the American political system has
enormous capacity to absorb and co-opt seemingly radical demands
for change;[84] to truncate the range of political discourse to fit the boundaries of arguments for individualized, atomized entitlements;[85] and, ultimately, to legitimate hierarchies of power, which rights claims can
amend but never overturn.[86] The political viability of rights-based
movements depends on an acceptance—and thus strengthening—of the
existing system, which in turn preserves patterns of dominance by some
social groups over others. Thus, the reduction of radical demands to
claims of "rights under the law" perpetuates belief systems that teach
that other, more transformative modes of change are impossible, unnecessary, or both.[87] Rights claims thereby become self-crippling, these
writers argue, if not self-defeating, to the very people who make them.

The body of scholarship critical of rights claims has provoked a series of responses that, in part, defend the role of rights claims in bringing about fundamental change. This more recent scholarship, recalling the history of movements for racial and gender equality, has accused the CLS critique itself of hyper-abstraction and has sought to contextualize rights discourse as part of a radical, effective political strategy.[88] Writers have argued that the process of organizing and litigating empowers and emboldens those who make such claims. Indeed, the very act of asserting rights both signals and strengthens a refusal to continue to accept previously unchallenged systems of subordination. That refusal itself constitutes a major disruption in hegemonic discourses of power.[89] Organized movements to assert rights function as incubators, modifiers, and regenerators of demands for far-reaching change.[90]

The political debate over whether to seek legalization of lesbian and gay marriage or legal protection through domestic partnership statutes, or both, constitutes another venue for this larger debate over the strategic uses of rights claims. Advocates for some form of legal recognition of lesbian and gay relationships face the dilemma posed by Kimberlé Williams Crenshaw:

> Although it is the [system's] need to maintain legitimacy [by incorporating principles of nondiscrimination] that presents powerless groups with the opportunity to wrest concessions from the dominant order, it is the very accomplishment of legitimacy that forecloses greater possibilities. In sum, the potential for change is both created and limited by legitimation. The central issue that the [Critical Legal Studies writers] fail to address . . . is how to avoid the "legitimating" effects of reform if engaging in reformist discourse is the only effective way to challenge the legitimacy of the social order.[91]

Solving that conundrum is beyond the reach of this chapter. But at least some part of a practical response to it may lie in seeking to more deliberately develop strategies that incorporate but do not necessarily privilege law, campaigns that seek legal reform as one ultimate goal, but which also, simultaneously and intentionally, deploy arguments not limited so severely by the bounds of "rights talk."

The impact of law often lies as much in the discourse created in the process of its adoption as in the final legal rule itself. What a new legal rule is popularly understood to signify may determine more of its potential for social change than the particulars of the change in the law. The social meaning of the legalization of lesbian and gay marriage, for example, would be very different if legalization resulted from political efforts framed as ending gendered roles between spouses rather than if it were the outcome of a campaign valorizing the institution of marriage, even if the ultimate "holding" is the same. Similarly, the meaning of securing for lesbians and gay men the right to adopt or to raise children is vastly different if understood as reflecting the equal worth of lesbian, gay, and heterosexual role models, rather than as justified by the view that a parent's sexual orientation has no impact on, and thus poses no danger to, the sexual orientation of a child.

For feminists both inside and outside the lesbian and gay rights movement, the current focus on the possibility of legalization for lesbian and gay marriage provides an opportunity to develop ways to address the issues of hierarchy and power that underlie this debate. The politics of both gender and sexuality are implicated. The social stigma that attaches to sexuality outside of marriage produces another hierarchy, parallel to the hierarchy of gender. Simply democratizing or degendering marriage, without also dislodging that stigma, would be at best a partial reform.

Faced with such difficult issues, advocates for change should consider formulating specifically rhetorical strategies that can be utilized in long-term political efforts, in addition to the rights claims that ground litigation. A concept of "gender dissent" might form one such theme. In contrast to much of the equality rhetoric used in the lesbian and gay marriage debate, "gender dissent" does not imply a desire merely to become accepted on the same terms within an unchallenged structure of marriage. Nor does it connote identity based on sexual orientation; anyone can dissent from a hierarchy of power. Rather, it conveys an active intent to disconnect power from gender and an adversary relationship to dominance. Its specific expression could take a variety of forms, appropriate to differing contexts and communities. The goal of such a strategy would be enhancement of an openness to change and maximization of the potential for future and ever broader efforts to transform both the law and the reality of personal relationships.

CONCLUSION

The most widely felt impact of legalization of lesbian and gay marriage would derive from its potential to remove gender from the definition of marriage. Much of the ongoing debate about a lesbian and gay marriage strategy, which has been framed as a claim for equality against a critique of marriage as an inherently sexist institution, fails to address that possibility. Proposals for reforming family law outside the lesbian and gay rights arena, however, also have ignored the potential for degendering the law of marriage. Pragmatic advocates will frame litigation in this area in terms of rights claims such as equality, privacy, and freedom of association. In addressing the culturally complex issues that underlay marriage law, however, "rights talk" alone is an incomplete path to transformative change. Additional and creative initiatives, such as the concept of "gender dissent," are necessary.

14

Disembodiment:
Abortion and Gay Rights*

RUTH COLKER

In this chapter, I will argue that the abortion debate and the gay rights debate reflect disembodied discussions. This disembodiment creates a false duality between the body and our moral beliefs that detracts from the "good faith" of these debates. (As I have argued elsewhere, in order for a debate to proceed in good faith, each of the speakers must make comments that are embedded in respect for the people affected by the issue under discussion as well as the arguments made on each side of the issue.)[1] Moreover, it causes fundamental disrespect for the well-being of pregnant women, gay men, lesbians, and bisexual people. Finally, it contributes to a racially exclusive debate that fails to consider the insights of members of nonwhite ethnic communities, like the African-American community. I believe that a feminist and theological conception of embodiment could move us toward a more "good faith" discussion of abortion and gay rights in a way that could also help us work toward racial inclusiveness.

EMBODIMENT

Radical, feminist theologians conceptualize our understanding of the body in a holistic way that unites the body and morality. A key proponent of such a perspective is James B. Nelson, Professor of Christian Ethics at United Theological Seminary of the Twin Cities.[2] As Beverly Harrison has noted, his work attends "to the best feminist insights."[3] Nelson suggests that a "sexual theology" must "move beyond the

234

traditional confines of 'sexual ethics' into sexual theology which takes seriously the human sexual experience in our time and place as an arena for God's continuing self-disclosure at the same time that it takes seriously the implications of Christian faith for our sexual lives."[4]

Another way to conceptualize Nelson's sexual theology is to consider it a social justice framework. For example, Carter Heyward, a religious feminist, uses a social justice framework to "[beckon] us into solidarity with all women and other marginalized people."[5] Heyward concludes that in order to achieve social justice, women need to be able to develop "self-respect." She argues that the Church should take on the role of creating the holistic conditions for self-respect.[6]

As I will discuss below, this kind of social justice perspective, which Nelson and Heyward base in a sexual theology, is very consistent with the writings of many women of color, irrespective of whether the women of color explicitly ground their work in a sexual theology. If we would ground feminist issues, such as abortion and gay rights, in such a sexual theology then I believe that we might be able to begin to overcome some of the racial divisiveness in our society and in feminism. As many of my students have taught me, we cannot expect to have a progressive politics which is inclusive of African-American, Hispanic, Asian, Native, and white communities if we are not willing or able to discuss our politics in religious terms.[7]

I will argue that the absence of a genuine holistic religious dialogue about abortion and gay rights has harmed these movements in two quite different ways. First, it has caused the public debates about these issues to be highly polarized and divisive, with no seeming possibility for common ground. Second, it has caused the public debates largely to be debates among the members of the white community. Proponents of both of these causes have made little headway in creating bridges to women and men of color. These are substantial problems that I believe can be solved through the use of a fully embodied framework.

Thus, a holistic framework would not be limited by bipolar understandings of human sexuality and would allow us to understand and respect each other across differences. Such an understanding of human sexuality has been absent from discussions of abortion and gay rights by both sides of these issues. Opponents of abortion rights and gay rights have often tried to couch their arguments in religious views that are deeply bipolar and disrespectful of the lives of pregnant women, lesbians, gay men, and bisexual people. Nevertheless, proponents of abortion and gay rights have often seemed scared to make theological arguments, on the assumption that religion is always equated with conservative viewpoints.

RACIAL CRITIQUE OF FEMINISM

One way I believe that we can begin to add theological insights to our discussions of abortion and gay rights is to pay closer attention to the writings of African-American, Hispanic, Asian-American, and Native feminists (or "womanists"[8] as they sometimes prefer to be called). These writings often reflect the limited nature of feminist discourse and can help us learn how to discuss important issues in ways that build bridges. They are also often based on religious values.

Women of color have often felt excluded from American feminism because of its exclusion of racial concerns. For example, African-American women were asked to forgo their interest in voting as "blacks" for the sake of the "woman's vote."[9] In the "second wave" of feminism, women of color were again excluded through work such as that of Betty Friedan's *The Feminine Mystique* (1963). As vividly described by bell hooks, this work was unconsciously reflective only of the lives of middle- and upper-class, married white women:

> Betty Friedan's *The Feminine Mystique* is still heralded as having paved the way for the contemporary feminist movement—it was written as if these women did not exist. Friedan's famous phrase, "the problem that has no name," often quoted to describe the condition of women in this society, actually referred to the plight of a select group of college-educated, middle and upper class, married white women— housewives bored with leisure, with the home, with children, with buying products, who wanted more out of life. Friedan concludes her first chapter by stating: "We can no longer ignore that voice within women that says: 'I want some more than my husband and my children and my house.'" That "more" she defined as careers. She did not discuss who would be called in to take care of the children and maintain the home if more women like herself were freed from their house labor and given equal access with white men to the professions. She did not speak of the needs of women without men, without children, without homes. She ignored the existence of all non-white women and poor white women. She did not tell readers whether it was more fulfilling to be a maid, a babysitter, a factory worker, a clerk, or a prostitute, than to be a leisure class housewife.[10]

These feelings of exclusion continued to exist in the 1970s as the women's liberation movement became a larger force in American society. For example, Paula Giddings describes one incident that was reflective of how and why many black women felt alienated from the women's liberation movement. A group of third world women were carrying signs about Angela Davis at a Women's Liberation Day march in 1970. "[O]ne of the leaders of NOW ran up to us and said angrily, 'Angela Davis has nothing to do with women's liberation.' 'It has nothing to do with the kind of liberation you're talking about,' retorted Beal, 'but it has everything to do with the kind of liberation we're talking about.'"[11]

Nevertheless, religion has often been a source for drawing white and black women together. In 1920, a Methodist minister, Will Alexander, formed the Council for Interracial Cooperation in Atlanta.[12] The common ground of religion was an important aspect of this organization.[13]

A more explicit discussion of the importance of an inclusive religious dialogue can be found in the pathbreaking anthology, *This Bridge Called My Back: Writings by Radical Women of Color.*[14] This anthology is filled with writings that utilize religious imagery; the contribution that most strongly challenges white feminists to consider the religious heritage of women of color is that of Audre Lorde.

Lorde wrote an open letter to Mary Daly (a white feminist and theologian), criticizing her for ignoring the contributions of those who Lorde calls "our black foremothers"[15] in her work. Lorde criticized Daly for failing to discuss any examples from African myth, legend, or religion in her discussion of the nature of female power in her book, *Gyn/Ecology.* "What you excluded from *Gyn/Ecology* dismissed my heritage and the heritage of all other non-European women, and denied the real connections that exist between all of us."[16] Lorde observes that this kind of exclusion serves the forces of racial division in our society.[17]

Unfortunately, this cross-racial interdenominational work has not been a key feature of the "second wave" of feminism. As noted by Caroline Ramazanoglu,[18] recent "feminist texts often pay little attention to religion except to identify particular religions as sources of patriarchal ideology and practice."[19] This exclusion is problematic because "religion can be the dominant factor in the personal identity and cultural location of millions of women around the world. If religion is one of the most important and immediate factors which enables a woman to know who she is, and to give meaning to her life, an international feminist movement cannot afford to ignore religion."[20]

By saying that more attention to spirituality within feminism might make women of color feel more included, I do not mean to romanticize mainstream religion. The Black Church, for example, has itself been a tool for perpetuating sexism within the African-American community by existing within a male hierarchical structure.[21] Giddings provides many examples of the Black Church's exclusion of women from the nineteenth century to the 1970s. The following example ties this exclusion to the dominant role of the Black Church in the Civil Rights movement:

> One would think that Ella Baker, by virtue of her role in the creation of SCLC, would have had a decision-making role. Although she says she did not seek such a position, her observations of the organization are revealing:

There never would be any role for me in a leadership capacity with SCLC. Why? First, I'm a woman. Also, I'm not a minister. And second . . . I knew that my penchant for speaking honestly . . . would not be tolerated. The combination of the basic attitude of men, and especially ministers, as to what the role of women in their church setups is—that of taking orders, not providing leadership—and the . . . ego problems involved in having to feel that here is someone who . . . had more information about a lot of things than they possessed at that time . . . This would never have lent itself to my being a leader in the movement there.[22]

It is not, of course, only the Black Church that has been a tool to perpetuate sexism. Both the Catholic Church and various fundamentalist sects have also perpetuated sexism within American society. For example, the Catholic Church has frequently opposed all family planning and abortion services as well as encouraged parents to disown their lesbian or gay children. Similarly, the fundamentalist sects that support Operation Rescue have failed to criticize the murder of the Florida man, Dr. Gunn, who performed abortions.

The fact that religion has been used to exacerbate the oppression of pregnant women, gay men, lesbians, and bisexual people, however, does not mean that religion must be dismissed as an inherently negative dimension in people's lives. As I have argued above, a complete dismissal of religion as irrelevant to feminism may contribute to the alienation of people of color from feminism. The challenge then is to find ways to incorporate progressive religious views into feminism in order to help build cross-cultural bridges rather than to dismiss religion entirely.

ABORTION

A holistic view of sexuality would allow us to discuss sexuality in a way that could be connected to social justice issues. For example, Nelson argues that there is something obscene about a world that has an "order of priorities that starts off with bigger and better orgasms."[23] That observation, however, does not lead Nelson to be anti-sex. Instead, he says, "If there is danger of trivializing sex into superficial pleasure, there is also the danger of so trivializing sexuality that we fail to see the intricate, subtle, and far-reaching ways in which it permeates current social issues—issues which demand attention to those very sexual dimensions if significant alleviation of their injustice is to come."[24] Nelson therefore encourages us to discuss reproductive health issues from a social justice perspective in which we consider "women's rights to bodily control: the availability of therapeutic abortion services without regard to income or race; the elimination of coercive medical interference (particularly reflected in the alarming increase in sterilization of low-income women and in medical experimentation on the poor and institutionalized)."[25]

Such a holistic framework has unfortunately not always been present in public discussions of abortion and contraception. In addition, and I believe relatedly, the relationship of the pro-choice movement to the black Civil Rights movement has sometimes been a difficult one. One problem, I would suggest, is that the pro-choice movement has often single-mindedly focused on exactly one choice—that of abortion—without doing enough work to make that choice less necessary. Moreover, the pro-choice movement has, as its name suggests, been operating in an environment in which it believes that choices are genuinely possible if abortion is legal. For a young, poor woman, however, the legalization of abortion may be irrelevant to her ability to obtain an abortion if an affordable and accessible abortion provider does not exist in her community. These criticisms of the pro-choice movement have been consistently made by members of the African-American community for several decades; however, little has changed in the rhetoric or perspective of the pro-choice movement.

The birth control movement in the United States was created in the early twentieth century at a time of increasing racism. In 1906, for example, President Theodore Roosevelt described the falling birth rate among native-born whites as "race suicide" and admonished white women for failing to bear more children.[26] These kinds of arguments began to "popularize the idea that poor people had a moral obligation to restrict the size of their families, because large families create a drain on the taxes and charity expenditures of the wealthy and because poor children were less likely to be 'superior.'"[27]

This "race suicide" theme became a part of the pioneering birth control work of Margaret Sanger.[28] This history of racism was not overcome as the pro-choice movement developed in the late 1960s. Many African-Americans expressed discomfort with the pro-choice movement as it became a recognized political force in the United States.[29]

The racist suspicions that some African-Americans expressed in the late 1960s were again expressed in the 1970s. As described by Angela Davis, the abortion rights movement of the 1970s "reflected the tendency to blur the distinction between *abortion rights* and the general advocacy of *abortions*. The campaign often failed to provide a voice for women who wanted the *right* to legal abortions while deploring the social conditions that prohibited them from bearing more children."[30]

As I have argued elsewhere,[31] a reproductive health perspective that is part of a larger strategy to create class- and race-based equality in our society would be more appealing to poor women and women of color who are as concerned about the social conditions that make abortion necessary as in their desire to have access to safe and legal abortion services. A narrow pro-choice perspective will not draw these women into the feminist movement.

By a "narrow pro-choice" perspective, I mean a perspective that looks at abortion rights in isolation from reproductive health and women's lives. This view is reflected in two popular, recent books on abortion rights: Laurence Tribe's *Abortion: The Clash of Absolutes*[32] and Ronald Dworkin's *Life's Dominion*.[33]

The purpose of Tribe's book is to examine the highly rhetorical abortion rights debate to see if there is any common ground on abortion. He examines proposed areas for compromise such as waiting period rules, parental consent, etc., and concludes that these purported areas of compromise are not really compromises at all, because they would take away the right to have an abortion for certain groups of women.[34] In searching for common ground, Tribe starts from a very narrow premise regarding the concerns of the pro-choice movement—that they simply want to make abortion more accessible to women who face unwanted pregnancies. His discussion is almost entirely focused on the choices available to women *after* they have already experienced an unwanted pregnancy. By starting at that point, and relying very heavily on the possibilities of medical technology,[35] he entirely misses a discussion of the social conditions that make some women have to conclude that they cannot afford to carry the fetus to term, or some women experience an unintended pregnancy through rape or sexual abuse. The existence of unwanted pregnancies is a given for Tribe, and not a problem that he considers linked to the abortion issue. This narrow focus is especially disappointing because of the ways that it limits his search for common ground. Could we, for example, find common ground on social justice issues such as food, housing, education, and safety for women and their children? Aren't these issues that can be endorsed by both pro-life and pro-choice advocates?

An even more disappointing pro-choice analysis is offered by Ronald Dworkin.[36] Dworkin attempts to present a novel discussion of the abortion issue that will supposedly help us attain common ground. His central purpose is to help create a good faith dialogue; therefore, I would have expected him to use a holistic approach to achieve such dialogue.

At times, Dworkin does seem to be moving toward a good faith dialogue on abortion. He quite carefully argues, for example, that both pro-choice and pro-life advocates agree that the fetus is a life so that the real moral question is what significance we choose to attach to that life. He tries to show that few people consider that life to actually be a *person* with all of the rights that personhood entails. By pointing out this source of common ground, he could help us take a step toward agreement on important issues like prenatal care, contraception, day care, etc.

Unfortunately, the argument that Dworkin develops from his observation about our valuation of life does not, in my view, move toward a good faith dialogue. There are two key reasons why his argument fails. First, he rarely discusses the significance of *women's* lives. For much of the book, one gets the sense that the only life implicated in the abortion debate is that of the fetus. A discussion of the fetus is entirely disembodied from women's lives—physically, emotionally, and socially. I believe that one reason that the anti-choice movement has been so successful is that it has created a disembodied discourse about abortion—a discussion in which fetuses are blown up on posters to exaggerated dimensions and are not found in women's bodies.[37] Dworkin contributes to this disembodied discussion by having chapter after chapter discuss fetal life while, at best, making passing references to women's lives. As I said at the outset of this essay, a good faith dialogue must be premised on a respect for the values held by each side of a debate as well as respect for the personhood of the participants in the debate. Dworkin's discussion fails this test because he does not show sufficient respect for the pro-choice position about the importance of valuing the lives of pregnant women.

For example, rather than describe in graphic detail how women's bodies, lives, and emotions are vastly affected if they cannot choose whether to have an abortion, Dworkin assumes a pregnant woman has the right to control the use of her body for reproduction.[38] This assumption makes it unnecessary for him to present evidence about the impact of abortion on women's lives. The sole question under his framework is whether the state has a compelling reason for interfering with that right.[39] Assuming a crucial part of the argument means that he fails to convince people that limitations on abortions do dramatically affect women's lives. By giving women's lives only fleeting reference, he therefore does not accord sufficient respect to pregnant women under his framework. Dworkin may do a good job in pushing pro-choice advocates to understand the values articulated by pro-life advocates but, by failing to discuss women's lives, he does not do a good job in pushing pro-life advocates to understand the values articulated by pro-choice advocates.

In addition, Dworkin relies on a somewhat disembodied conception of religion to argue that the state cannot constitutionally infringe on a woman's right to choose to have an abortion. Dworkin argues that the central disagreement that divides people on the abortion issue is how best to respect the fundamental idea that human life is sacred.[40] From that premise, he argues that "freedom of choice about abortion is a necessary implication of the religious freedom guaranteed by the First Amendment, and that women therefore have a right to that freedom for that reason, though for others as well."[41] In other words, by outlawing abortion, a state is impermissibly establishing a religious point of view on an issue about which women should be entitled to make intrinsic value choices.

This is a disembodied argument, because it is premised on the assumption that we should not tolerate political views having a religious, moral basis. In Dworkin's words:

> So the popular sense that the abortion issue is fundamentally a religious one, and some lawyers' sense that it therefore lies outside the proper limits of state action, are at bottom sound, though for reasons somewhat more complex than is often supposed. They rest on a natural—indeed, irresistible—understanding of the First Amendment: that a state has no business prescribing what people should think about the ultimate point and value of human life, about why life has intrinsic importance, and about how that value is respected or dishonored in different circumstances.[42]

I call Dworkin's discussion "somewhat disembodied," because he does not dismiss religious arguments entirely. Instead, he only dismisses them when the issue is "fundamentally a religious one." Nonetheless, I do not find his distinction between fundamentally religious and nonfundamentally religious to be very useful. It is not the extent of religiosity underlying a view that creates problems; it is the substantive policy choices that the religious view entails that are problematic. What is problematic about the state adopting an anti-abortion perspective—out of its religious valuation of fetal life—is that that valuation is tremendously disrespectful of the lives of women. Because Dworkin completely fails to place the abortion discussion in the context of women's lives, he must make an argument that is premised on the notion that political ideas should always be disembodied from fundamentally religious ideas. Dworkin's argument would force us to disembody law from certain religious-moral beliefs without examining the content of those beliefs—something that I have argued in this essay would be very destructive to our ability to live in a holistic way in society.

Instead, I would suggest, we need to find arguments for why the *particular* moral perspective that is taken by the anti-abortion community is unconstitutional. The problem is not that it is a religious perspective. The problem is that the particular substance of this religious perspective results in tremendous disrespect for the lives and well-being of pregnant women. Fetal lives, which have not reached the state of personhood, are valued over the lives of adult pregnant women when abortion is regulated. That is an unconstitutional valuation because it conflicts with the Fourteenth Amendment's guarantee of equal protection on the basis of gender. Dworkin needs to look to the Fourteenth Amendment rather than the First Amendment to understand why this substantive perspective is unconstitutional.

Although Dworkin's and Tribe's perspectives are too narrow, Dworkin is correct to emphasize the importance of talking about our affirmation of life in the pro-choice movement. Such a perspective could do a better job in speaking to the concerns of poor women and women of color, because it would be more clear about its affirmation of *life*. Women of color often emphasize that we must view reproductive decisions in the context of trying to value the lives of men, women, and children. Dorothy Roberts, an African-American woman, does an excellent job in contrasting a narrow pro-choice perspective with one that more fully embraces the needs of poor women and women of color:

> What are the limitations on poor women's reproductive freedom? To answer that question we must first come to an understanding of what reproductive choice means. Supreme Court jurisprudence has definitely recognized only a minimal piece of reproductive rights— the freedom to decide, without active government interference, whether to use contraceptives and whether to terminate a pregnancy. Some commentators have suggested that that is the full extent of a woman's right to control her reproductive health.
>
> Let me suggest a different definition. It involves a broader concept of both the words "reproductive" and "choice." A woman's reproductive life is clearly implicated in more than just the decision to use contraceptives and to have an abortion. Reproduction encompasses a range of events and conditions from the ability to bear children, to conception, to carrying a fetus, to abortion, to delivering a baby, to caring for a child. Each stage in turn involves myriad decisions that the woman must make; her decisions at each stage may be affected by numerous factors—economic, environmental, legal, political, emotional, ethical. Reproductive freedom then must extend, for example, to decisions about sterilization and medical treatment during pregnancy; it must include access to fertilization technologies and to prenatal and perinatal care.[43]

Although this holistic perspective has not been embraced by the U.S. Supreme Court, as reflected by the abortion funding cases,[44] it is inaccurate to say that no branch of the "white" feminist movement has embraced it. For example, Dorothy Roberts concludes her description of a wide-ranging reproductive choice perspective by quoting Kathryn Kolbert's definition: "Reproductive freedom means the ability to choose whether, when, how, and with whom one will have children."[45] Kathryn Kolbert is a white woman who used to be a staff attorney for the ACLU's Reproductive Freedom project and is currently vice president of the Center for Reproductive Law and Policy, a nonprofit organization devoted to enhancing reproductive freedom.

When my African-American students criticize the white women's movement for its insensitivity to racial concerns, I often point to examples such as the work of Kolbert to show how mainstream organizations, like the ACLU, often do place a major priority on working on behalf of poor women and women of color. I often ask whether the problem is the actual work and perspective of the mainstream women's movement or the media's willingness to exaggerate any problems within the women's movement. In exasperation, one of my male, African-American students finally answered my question. He said (as best as I can remember):

> Professor, you don't seem to understand. We don't *expect* the white women's movement not to be racist, because it is a part of the society in which we live. We're not saying that the women's movement is more racist than the rest of society; in fact, it's probably less racist. But, as African-Americans we simply have very little expectations from the white women's movement. That's why we don't trust it and prefer often to work within our own African-American organizations. Sure, there are a lot of white women like yourself who do good work but don't expect us to feel comfortable working in your movement given the larger society in which we all live.[46]

Because of this fundamental distrust of whites by many African-Americans (which is quite understandable), white feminists must do much more than simply fail to be explicitly racist if they want to make people of color feel comfortable working with them. There is no way that we can eliminate the racism of our larger society overnight so that this distrust will not exist, but we can be extremely vigilant within our movement not to condone the kinds of racist statements that I have described above. More fundamentally, we need to base our priorities within the women's movement on issues that deeply touch the lives of poor people and people of color in ways that will make them feel welcome and valued.

Unfortunately, white feminists who purport to use a holistic pro-choice framework do not always sufficiently validate life in their work. For example, Rosalind Petchesky appears to embrace a holistic perspective in the preface to her book, *Abortion and Woman's Choice*:

> *Abortion and Woman's Choice* aims to provide a holistic understanding of abortion from a feminist perspective, including the history of its practice and state policies to contain it; the social, economic, and cultural conditions under which women utilize it; and the legal, moral, and political battles that surround it.[47]

Despite this purportedly holistic framework, Petchesky does not seem comfortable in affirming fetuses as part of the chain of life, including human life. This problem becomes evident in Petchesky's work in her chapter titled "Morality and Personhood." Petchesky devotes this chapter to attacking the notion that the abortion issue can be resolved by simply viewing the fetus as a person, with all of the rights available to all persons. Not once in this strong attack on fetuses as persons does Petchesky contend with or discuss the idea that fetuses may be a form of life that is deserving of our respect (while we also make abortions permissible). To the extent that she raises the life argument, she does so in a way that simply equates it with the personhood argument. For example, she says "Any serious discussion of the moral and ethical issues of abortion must be prefaced by a clear understanding that the status of the fetus and whether it shall be regarded as a 'person' or a 'human life' do not exhaust the bases for moral inquiry about abortion. Whether anyone can be compelled to carry and nourish a fetus she does not want is also a moral issue."[48]

I agree with Petchesky that the situation of women in our society is a fundamental moral issue that is basic to social justice in our society. But, as Dworkin powerfully argues, the value of the fetus as a member of the entity called "human life" is also a moral issue. Petchesky discusses morality in a bipolar framework—if women's condition is a moral issue then the fetus's life is not. Moreover, if the fetus is not an entity deserving of protection of *persons* then, according to Petchesky, it is not an entity deserving of protection as *life*.

That kind of highly bipolarized discussion, which tries to minimize the significance of the fetus as being part of the chain of life, is highly disembodied. Petchesky rightly accuses the anti-abortion movement of disembodying fetuses from women's bodies in their imagery of fetuses. Petchesky, however, also disembodies fetuses by disconnecting them from the chain of life. A fetus need not be a *person* in order to be a life. A dog is not a person, but we cringe when someone is cruel to a dog. Why do we cringe? Because we value the life of the dog and see our valuation of a dog's life as connected to how we treat all lives, including human life.

Petchesky's refusal to acknowledge the value of a fetus's life to some women who have abortions makes her unable to discuss negative feelings that some women may have about their abortion decision. For example, this is what Petchesky says about some women, particularly African-American women feeling "guilty" about having abortions:

> The first thing that must be said about guilt is that it does not exist in a vacuum but in a context shaped by history, politics, and religious and moral codes. . . . The strong moral antagonism toward abortion of many women in black communities may be inseparable from the long experience of dangerous, unhygienic, "quack" methods to which black women were disproportionately exposed; their sense of "wrongness" is imprinted with the reality and the fearful tales of danger and death.[49]

This kind of statement is entirely dismissive of the legitimacy of religious views, particularly those within the African-American community. How can Petchesky "tell" African-American women that they are "wrong" to have a moral antagonism toward abortion? Those kinds of statements, in my view, are not the way to build bridges between white women and African-American women. It would make more sense to start with basic, accepted moral premises, like the valuation of life, and then to see where a dispute about abortion rights may occur. Statements like Petchesky's are not likely to enhance interracial dialogue.

Because we live in a world that is fundamentally disrespectful of the lives of poor people and racial minorities, it takes tremendous energy and courage for poor people and racial minorities to value their own lives. A narrow, pro-choice perspective does not value the lives of the fetuses whose lives are regretfully terminated when an abortion occurs. In my own work on abortion and theology, I have found that many pro-choice activists are extremely uncomfortable when I talk about the potential sadness that may result from the termination of a fetus's life. They often do not even want me to talk about fetuses as being a "life." (They seem to presume that as soon as I call a fetus a "life" that I have called it a "person"—which I deliberately have not done.) Not being able to talk about fetuses as part of the spectrum of life, however, contributes to our not being able to talk about the social conditions that make abortion a necessity rather than a choice. Abortion as necessity rather than choice is what women like Angela Davis would like to eliminate. But if we cannot talk about unfortunate abortions or painful abortions or abortions that regretfully terminate life then we are unlikely to be able to talk about the social conditions that make abortion a necessity rather than a choice.

Thus, Tribe's, Dworkin's, and Petchesky's arguments concerning abortion are not holistic. They each are willing to discuss the value of fetal life or the value of women's lives but none of them fully discusses the value of all of human life, including both fetuses and women. It is only when we can begin to have such a fully embodied discussion that we will truly move toward a good faith dialogue on abortion.

LESBIANS, GAY MEN, AND BISEXUAL PEOPLE

INTRODUCTION

A holistic understanding of sexuality would make two major contributions to the area of gay rights. First, it would no longer permit liberals to try to counter an anti-gay rights perspective by simply saying that it is a "religious" point of view. Instead of trying to separate law and morality, we would strive to find respectful ways to discuss morality. (This contribution will be similar to the contribution that I identified in the abortion context.) Second, it would no longer permit liberals or conservatives to talk in rigid gay/straight dichotomies. Instead, the category of bisexuality would have to be recognized and respected. Moreover, separatism as a political tactic would have to be rejected. These insights would also help us move to a more racially inclusive dialogue because, as we will see below, the gay rights movement within the African-American community tends to be more tolerant of bisexuality and less separatist than the white gay rights movement.

BOWERS V. HARDWICK

Proponents of gay rights have not typically considered religious arguments to be on their side. As I will discuss below, they are correct to criticize the way religious arguments have helped to justify anti-gay decisions such as *Bowers v. Hardwick*,[50] in which the Supreme Court upheld a sodomy statute that was only enforced against gay men and lesbians. Nevertheless, they are wrong to rely on the disembodied argument that religious arguments have no place in deciding issues like the constitutionality of the Georgia statute at issue in *Bowers*.

An embodied discussion of the *Bowers* decision would show us that the proponents of state sodomy statutes do support their views with religious arguments. Their religious arguments, however, are not the only religious arguments available on the sodomy issue. Opponents of state sodomy statutes often hide behind the argument that a state cannot codify a religious point of view on the sodomy issue. By using this anti-religion argument (which is inherently a disembodied argument), they avoid discussing the lives of the individuals who are affected by state sodomy statutes. Their arguments are therefore disembodied in two senses: they try to avoid making any religious arguments and they do not discuss the wholeness of the lives of gay, lesbian, and bisexual people. Rather than give up the moral high ground on sodomy statutes to religious fundamentalists, I therefore suggest that proponents of gay rights argue that they, in fact, have a religious perspective that is constitutionally permissible because it offers respect for the lives of all people.

In *Bowers v. Hardwick*[51] the Supreme Court relied on a religious perspective to uphold the criminalization of homosexual sexual activity. Justice Burger, in his concurring opinion, for example, provided support for the Supreme Court's position through reference to the fact that "condemnation of those practices is firmly rooted in Judeo-Christian moral and ethical standards." He summarized this history by stating that "to hold that the act of homosexual sodomy is somehow protected as a fundamental right would be to cast aside millennia of moral teaching."[52]

The dissent in *Bowers* does not question whether a religious perspective could help invalidate the sodomy statute. Instead, using a line
of reasoning similar to Dworkin's in the abortion context, the dissent
argues that the religious nature of the majority's perspective demonstrates its constitutional invalidity.

The dissent therefore argued that it was constitutionally impermissible
for the state of Georgia to codify a point of view that had theological
roots. It described this theological perspective as unconstitutional because
it was religiously intolerant. In fact, the state was codifying a particular religious perspective rather than being intolerant of a religious point
of view. Its intolerance extended to gay and lesbian people, not to
members of any religious organization.

The problem with the dissent's argument is that whatever position
the state of Georgia takes with respect to sodomy will conflict with
some religious viewpoint on sodomy. The current statute codifies a
religious fundamentalist perspective (among others). Repeal of the statute
would codify a more liberal religious perspective, like that held by
James Nelson and others, quoted earlier. The dissent seems to assume
that there is only one religious perspective on sodomy—an anti-sodomy perspective. Thus, according to the dissent, the only way that the
state would be codifying a religious perspective would be by endorsing an anti-sodomy perspective. In fact, religious views on sodomy
are much more complex than acknowledged by the dissent. It is much
too simplistic to say that the state should not criminalize sodomy because it should not establish a religious point of view.

Instead, I believe that the proponents of gay rights should argue
that the state has a religious perspective that is constitutionally
impermissible. Such an argument does not seem to be cognizable under the framework proposed by the dissent. The dissent says:

> The assertion that "traditional Judeo-Christian values proscribe" the
> conduct involved cannot provide an adequate justification for the
> statute. That certain, by no means all, religious groups condemn
> the behavior at issue gives the States no license to impose their judg-
> ments on the entire citizenry. The legitimacy of secular legislation
> depends instead on whether the State can advance some justifica-
> tion for its law beyond its conformity to religious doctrine.[53]

That statement reflects the law/morality distinction at its worst. It
suggests that proponents of gay rights must find secular ways to argue why a state cannot codify an anti-sodomy perspective. An author
like James Nelson who embeds his support for gay rights in a holistic
understanding of the beauty of human sexuality would have to find a
secular translation for his viewpoint. Censoring religious-moral arguments, in my view, makes us a less loving and compassionate society.

What if Martin Luther King could not have argued for civil rights within a religious framework? What if Dr. King could not be quoted by the courts, because he represented a religious perspective? Such censoring of speech would dull our senses and humanity.

Again, I would suggest that we should not ask whether a viewpoint fits into the secular or religious camp. (In fact, don't most arguments about human sexuality fit into a religious camp?) Instead, we should look closely at whatever viewpoint is being offered—secular and religious—and decide whether it is a viewpoint that provides sufficient respect for the lives of people in our society. It is the disrespectful aspect of a perspective that we should find intolerable, not its religious content.

As with the abortion issue, I believe that the only way that we can successfully argue that the Georgia statute is unconstitutional is to make reference to an equal protection argument—to show that the state has unconstitutionally failed to respect the very integrity of the lives of gay, lesbian, and bisexual people. The Court has consistently avoided that line of reasoning because it does not want to acknowledge that homosexuals constitute a "suspect class" and thereby have to recognize the long history of discrimination against homosexuals.

The failure to use an equal protection analysis, however, in my view results in a failure to discuss the lives of gay, lesbian, and bisexual people in a meaningful way. The particular individual who was arrested for violating the Georgia sodomy statute, for example, is entirely absent from both the dissent's and majority's disembodied discussion. What did it mean for Michael Hardwick to know that his life style was condemned by the state of Georgia and even subject to prosecution? How is the act of sex, itself, transformed, degraded, and manipulated when it is made illegal? How is the basic self-respect of gay, lesbian, and bisexual people affected by such state statutes? The dissent's anti-religion argument is not only unpersuasive but avoids those difficult and tragic questions. As anti-miscegenation statutes harmed the self-respect of African-Americans, anti-sodomy statutes harm the self-respect of gay men, lesbians, and bisexual people. This human experience, however, is absent from our constitutional discourse.

REJECTING DUALITIES: AFFIRMING BISEXUALITY AND REJECTING SEPARATISM

Affirming Bisexuality

A holistic understanding of human sexuality would also force us to reject dualities. In this section, I will argue that a holistic understanding of sexuality could move us beyond the gay/straight dichotomy and see all of us at different points of experiencing our bisexuality. Nelson takes an important step in that direction when he writes:

The problem of patriarchal or sexist dualism may be even more basic to anti-gay feeling. This might be experienced in several related ways. One is the heterosexual's possible anxiety about homosexual feelings within the self. While for the sake of economy I have been using "gay" and "heterosexual" in ways that might suggest two sharply distinct and mutually exclusive groups, current research indicates that people commonly tend toward some degree of bisexuality. Most, for reasons not yet fully understood, develop a *dominant* orientation toward one side or the other.[54]

Similarly, Marvin Ellison offers some insights about sexuality and embodiment that are useful for this discussion. Ellison argues that the dominant sexual categories of heterosexual and homosexual do not do justice to the "realities and complexities of our lives."[55] Ellison challenges us to live comfortably with change and ambiguity rather than to rely on fixed categories of sexuality. Another way of understanding Ellison's commentary would be to suggest that we embrace bisexuality as part of a continuum of sexuality rather than rely entirely on gay and straight labels to explain our lives.

Embracing bisexuality can be very threatening to a society that orders itself on neat bipolar concepts. What does it mean to be bisexual? The common stereotype is that one always has two sexual partners of the "opposite" sex. That stereotype arises out of the assumption that gay men, lesbians, and bisexual people are purely sexual creatures—at all moments being involved with all eligible sexual partners. (Society has trouble imagining a celibate or monogamous gay, lesbian, or bisexual person.)

For example, in *Ben-Shalom v. Marsh*,[56] the court of appeals affirmed the discharge of a lesbian from the military despite the fact that there was no evidence in the record of her ever having engaged in any lesbian sexual activity. The court justified her discharge by assuming that lesbians are inherently always engaged in sexual activity. In the court's words:

> It is true that actual lesbian conduct has not been admitted by plaintiff on any particular occasion and the Army has offered no evidence of such conduct. Judge Gordon found no reason to believe that the lesbian admission meant that plaintiff was likely to commit homosexual acts. We see it differently. Plaintiff's lesbian acknowledgement if not an admission of its practice, at least can rationally and reasonably be viewed as reliable evidence of a desire and propensity to engage in homosexual conduct. . . . To this extent, therefore the regulation does not classify plaintiff based merely upon her status as a lesbian but upon reasonable inferences about her probable conduct in the past and in the future.[57]

Gay and lesbian people have no identity beyond their sexual identity within mainstream culture (i.e., they are gay and lesbian rather than people). Bisexual people can also be defined in that way—as irresistibly sexual creatures who always have at least two partners. It would be wonderful to see the day when people would refuse to identify with the labels of straight or gay. Instead, they might say, "I am a bisexual woman who, at present, has no intimate partner," or ". . . at present, has a partner who is a woman," or ". . . at present, has several partners who are men," or whatever. But it would deeply challenge sexual dualities and the defining of gay, lesbian, and bisexual people as purely sexual to define one's sexual orientation in a nonstatic, fluid way.

An example may illustrate this point. I recently spoke at a feminist jurisprudence symposium in Chicago and ran into a "noted feminist" who I talk to maybe once every two or three years (and who I will call Giddy). We also have a mutual acquaintance who is well known in the feminist community (who I will call Sally). Giddy remarked that she knew that I had recently married a man (I made no secret of this fact by writing about it in an article for the *Yale Journal on Law and Feminism*).[58] She also remarked that Sally was engaged to be married to a man. She said that she was very interested in this phenomenon, wanted to write her next book on "hasbians," and hoped that I would let her interview me.

Unfortunately, my bisexual identity was not sufficiently developed to understand why I felt so deeply insulted by her comments so I just smiled, changed the subject to my daughter who I was holding in my arms, and did not adequately respond to her insult. She had used the fact of my current relationship with a man to erase my fifteen-year history of being involved predominantly with women. (Sally, too, had had a long history of being involved with women before her current engagement.) Those histories constitute who we are at the present time and who we will be tomorrow. Speaking for myself, and I suspect Sally, as well, I did not leave behind my love and attraction for women when I got involved with a man. The obsession with categorization that Giddy represented, however, insisted upon pigeonholing me as "straight" and my lesbian past as irrelevant to who I am. Thus, Giddy had to use the negative label "hasbian" to describe me. This is especially disappointing given Giddy's reputation in the feminist and lesbian communities for writing insightful work on sexuality and sexual abuse.

What I did not know at the time was that the phrase "hasbian" was not original to Giddy. It is a term coined by the lesbian community to "describe" women like me. Stacey Young has offered this critique of the term:

I object to the expression because it defines a person *only* in terms of what she once was. To refer to a woman as a "hasbian" implies that all one need know about her is her relationship to that exalted state, lesbianism. The term "hasbian" also, of course, evokes the word "has-been" which *Webster's* defines as "a person or thing which was formerly popular or effective, but is no longer so." What interests, then, does this term serve? Who has the power to define here, and at whose expense?[59]

I certainly do not mean to suggest that all lesbians have such a spiteful view of bisexuals. I, in fact, have found that some lesbians have been more supportive of my bisexuality than I have been myself. Bisexuality, however, challenges lesbians' (and other people's) feelings and actions concerning inclusiveness. When bisexuals can exist within the community of women in their wholeness rather than as stereotypes then we will have created a more genuine feminist and lesbian politics.

So far, I have talked about the importance of moving beyond dualisms to embrace the existence of bisexuality, but I have not tied that step to a religious discourse. Other authors have made that link. In a recently published anthology, *Bi Any Other Name: Bisexual People Speak Out,*[60] the authors devote an entire chapter to "Spirituality: Healing the Splits." They argue that a fully embodied and holistic perspective would embrace bisexuality.[61]

A nondualistic spirituality could also be more inclusive of the way bisexuality is often experienced in the African-American and Hispanic communities. As Brenda Marie Blasingame argues, the highly bipolar gay rights debate, with its classification of "gay" and "straight," may make many people within the African-American and Hispanic communities feel unwelcome.[62]

Blasingame's discussion provides excellent insight into the bridges that must be crossed if people of color are to feel more welcome in the "gay" movement. When we can start talking about people who have sex with people of the same sex without making any assumptions about whether they also have sex with people of the opposite sex then we may have a more racially inclusive politics. Our bipolar orientation about sexuality therefore contributes to a misleading understanding of how people actually experience sexuality in their lives while also making people in various ethnic communities not feel a part of the gay rights movement.

In sum, the disembodied nature of our gay rights discourse is a problem both within society as a whole and within the gay rights community. In society at large, there is the assumption that the only religious perspective on gay rights is opposed to gay rights. Proponents of gay rights have ceded the moral high ground and tried to make arguments that insist we keep morality separate from politics. A more holistic perspective would argue for gay rights from the perspective that gay people deserve protection from persecution as persons not because we should abstractly separate law and politics. Within the gay community, a holistic perspective would also help us see across our differences—to recognize the full range of human sexuality that can be expressed. It would help us move beyond the rigid dichotomies of gay and straight to recognize the bisexuality in many of us. Moreover, such a holistic dialogue might be more inclusive of us across racial differences by not requiring us to identify with rigid categories that are in conflict with our cultural experiences.

Rejecting Separatism

Another important consequence of a holistic perspective is a rejection of separatism. Separatism requires people to identify with one aspect of themselves—woman, black, gay, handicapped, etc. For an African-American lesbian, for example, separatism would require her to separate herself into three distinct categories, none of which would accord sufficient respect to her humanness. In addition, separatism in the women's movement has often meant that the movement was an all-white movement, paying little attention to racial and class issues.

Bell hooks does an excellent job in describing the alienation that occurs with a woman's-only feminist movement:

> Anti-male sentiments alienated many poor and working class women, particularly non-white women, from the feminist movement. Their life experiences had shown them that they have more in common with men of their race and/or class group than bourgeois white women. They know the sufferings and hardships women face in their communities; they also know the sufferings and hardships men face and they have compassion for them.[63]

A separatist perspective reflects a nonholistic political perspective. In a wonderful dialogue, Barbara Smith and Beverly Smith reflect on the inadequacies of a separatist perspective:

> Bar: So seldom is separatism involved in making real political change, affecting the institutions in the society in any direct way. If you define certain movement issues as straight women's issues, for example reproductive rights and sterilization abuse, then these identifiable sexual/political issues are ones you are not going to bother with. We have noticed how separatists in our area, instead of doing political organizing, often do zap acts. For example they might come to a meeting or series of meetings then move on their way. It is not clear what they're actually trying to change. We sometimes think of separatism as the politics without a practice.
> Bev: One of the problems of separatism is that I can't see it as a philosophy that explains and analyzes the roots of all oppression and is going to go toward solving it.[64]

This anti-separatism perspective is related to the role of African-

American women in the church. Bell hooks, for example, describes the
role of African-American and white women within the cultural groups
in their community. African-American women, she suggests, have always played a prominent role in the church; white women have had a
more submissive role within cultural organizations. Summarizing from
this cultural difference, hooks says: "Without the material input of black
women, as participants and leaders, many male-dominated institutions
in black communities would cease to exist; this is not the case in all
white communities."[65] Asking African-American women to be separatists
is therefore asking them to break their important ties to the Black Church.
That makes no political sense and would contribute to the law/moral-
ity dichotomy that I have criticized above.[66]

CONCLUSION

In this essay, I have attempted to discuss two highly divisive issues—
abortion and gay rights. I doubt that I have changed anyone's views
on these issues, but I do hope that I have succeeded in suggesting
how we could discuss these issues in a more holistic way that would
be more respectful across our differences. It is only when we engage
in a more respectful discussion that I believe we can hope to find some
common ground that is also more racially inclusive.

15

Hate Speech, Freedom, and Discourse Ethics in the Academy

PATRICIA S. MANN

The issue of hate speech on college campuses is a vexed one today. As academic communities have begun to better reflect the cultural diversity of American society, incidents of hostility and violence between students have increased. In response, many colleges and universities have enacted codes of conduct that include specific sanctions against "hate speech," hoping thereby to discourage a ubiquitous form of racist, sexist, and homophobic behavior.[1] Yet many people believe that restrictions against hate speech are inconsistent with a commitment to First Amendment rights of free expression. Indeed, a constitutional cloud has hovered over campus hate speech restrictions ever since a federal court voided a much publicized University of Michigan speech code in 1989, declaring it unconstitutionally vague and overbroad (a ruling to which the Supreme Court subsequently refused to hear challenges).[2]

The hate speech controversy cannot be satisfactorily resolved, however, until two fundamental questions are more fully explored: (1) Should sanctions against hate speech be deemed an important instrument for combating racism, sexism, and homophobia on college campuses? (2) Can hate speech restrictions be formulated and theoretically justified in such a way as to forestall either capricious or repressive applications? I believe both questions can be answered affirmatively, and in this article I will attempt to demonstrate that restrictions on campus hate speech are socially and politically warranted at this time.

255

I

I will begin by outlining two theoretical cum methodological foundations of my analysis. In the first place, I take it as historically self-evident in the late twentieth century that interpretations and applications of our most basic legal and political principles are likely to change over time, sometimes quite radically. Despite plentiful evidence for the mutability of liberal doctrines, however, legal and political philosophers tend toward disciplinary conservatism, inasmuch as they are loath to relinquish economic or political paradigms that have served them well in the past. The current hate speech controversy has been provoked, I contend, by a radical disjuncture between previous paradigms of contested political speech and the contemporary phenomenon of hate speech.

It is relevant to point out that we continue to be governed by the same overarching principles of liberalism that were previously interpreted as denying the rights of citizenship to women and minorities. John Adams, one of the Founding Fathers of our democracy, laughingly dismissed the entreaties of his wife, Abigail Adams, when she pleaded in 1776 that women be granted explicit political rights in the new American constitution. And in Article I, Section 2 of the U.S. Constitution, Adams, along with Thomas Jefferson and others, decreed that a (male) Negro counted as only 3/5 of a citizen for purposes of representational apportionment and taxes. The infamous Dred Scott decision of 1857 reaffirmed the racist original intentions of the Founding Fathers.[3] Certainly few would contend that these are any longer defensible political positions. Yet it is wrong to regard these particular policies of racial and sexual exclusion as simply doctrinal mistakes that have now been corrected. Racial and sexual exclusions remain part of the political fabric of our society after more than a century of struggle by women and minorities, and the process of altering anti-democratic doctrinal meanings and applications has been a slow and painstaking one. Only gradually, with the Fourteenth and Fifteenth Amendments after the Civil War, with the Nineteenth Amendment in 1920, with *Brown v. Board of Education* in 1954, and finally with the 1964 Civil Rights Act have women and racial and sexual minorities acquired the legal tools to begin to assert their full citizenship. The hate speech controversy is arguably another chapter in this long struggle.

The historical record of an evolving liberalism should make us hopeful with respect to further doctrinal developments and wary of rigid interpretations of particular political principles. Notice that substantive alterations of political meaning have not been confined to issues of women's or minorities' rights, but have occurred across the whole spectrum of democratic theory. For example, hardly anyone in the nineteenth century would have predicted the degree to which laissez-faire notions of economic agency would be deemed to be subject to restriction in the context of countervailing social concerns in the twentieth century. Environmental and affirmative action goals are only the most recent grounds for imposing government limitations upon the contractual freedoms of individuals. In light of this phenomenon, J. M. Balkin points out that while arguments for an unrestricted freedom of contract were initially part of a progressive agenda they have now become identified with conservative policies, and he suggests that doctrines of free speech may be undergoing a similar political realignment.[4] Indeed, one of the most confusing features of the current hate speech controversy is the fact that progressive legal thinkers such as Nadine Strossen, a general counsel to the ACLU, are vehemently opposed to hate speech restrictions. While many of Strossen's arguments are both reasonable and persuasive, she relies upon what I will show to be dubious analogies between the now standard First Amendment paradigm of political dissent and the recent problem of hate speech.[5]

The second assumption shaping this article is at once theoretical and strategic. While past arguments for restricting hate speech have focused primarily upon the harms of racist speech, I maintain that the case for hate speech restrictions becomes much more compelling when we broaden the analysis to take account of sexist and homophobic speech acts as well. In his seminal 1982 article advocating a common law tort analysis of racist speech, Richard Delgado dismisses possible comparisons between sexist and racist slurs and epithets. He asserts that insults to women are "qualitatively different" and therefore not of concern to those formulating legal strategies for opposing hate speech.[6] While recent articles show more formal sympathy toward the concerns of women and homosexuals, hate speech theorists continue to emphasize the harms associated with racist speech acts. Mari Matsuda, for example, agrees that sexist and homophobic hate speech may also warrant public restriction, yet she believes that sex and gender forms of oppression operate so differently from racism that they require a separate critique. Accordingly, she directs her arguments toward the criminalization of "a narrow, explicitly defined class of racist hate speech."[7] One of the most respected proponents of hate speech restrictions, Stanford University law professor Charles Lawrence, does include sexist and homophobic speech acts within the rubric of campus hate speech that should be subject to regulation (as does the highly controversial Stanford speech code written by his colleague, Thomas Grey). But despite his welcome gestures of multicultural inclusiveness, his attention is also concentrated on the harms of racist speech on college campuses.[8]

By contrast, I think the case for the legal significance of a category of hate speech is much enhanced by the fact that the slurs and epithets of hate speech function in a like manner in relation to diverse social groups. It is true that women, racial, ethnic and religious minorities, and homosexuals typically confront different modes of domination and subordination. Despite the fact that all of these groups experience employment discrimination, for example, workplace practices of racism, misogyny, and homophobia are often quite distinct, as is the subject's experience of them. This has made for serious difficulties in planning joint political actions against the capitalist, patriarchal, racist, homophobic institutions that oppress us, one and all. Unfortunately, while we readily admit to the political wisdom of coalition politics, our diverse and sometimes conflicting group interests constrain coalitional commitments.

In this political context, one of the most significant features of hate speech is that it operates similarly in relation to various oppressed groups: in each case the verbal aggressor wields conventional phrases or epithets of opprobrium and contempt with the reasonable expectation of embarrassing, diminishing, subordinating, or silencing the racially or sexually vulnerable subject. In each case, the verbal aggressor taps into historically embedded structures of social oppression through the use of particular phrases and relies upon these deep structures to effect the damages of hate speech. It is possible to identify the systemic wrongfulness of the hate speech act in each case in terms of the aggressor's willful invocation of these deeply rooted social and psychological structures of domination and subordination. Whether or not the victim psychologically reacts to the hate speech, the existence of these structures of social oppression means that her social position relative to the speaker and others within range of the speech act will be diminished in that moment and place.[9]

One of the most persuasive political arguments for hate speech restrictions is that we can thereby target a form of behavior that operates with similar destructiveness in relation to the otherwise diverse problems of racism, sexism, and heterosexism. Considering the seriousness of these problems in contemporary society, there would seem to be stronger political grounds for a hate speech exception to the First Amendment than were advanced for the "fighting words," obscenity, or defamation exceptions that are now considered standard.[10] The overwhelmingly negative tone of current judicial responses to hate speech restrictions perhaps reflects the fact that a majority of presiding justices were raised in an era in which these forms of hierarchy were taken for granted; such justices may simply have difficulty in imagining a society in which racism, sexism, and homophobia no longer have a legitimate place in everyday speech. By the same token, hate speech restrictions may be an effective means of compelling those who unself-

consciously retain elements of a racist, sexist, and homophobic cultural imagination to confront the existence of these biases in their current patterns of thought and behavior.[11]

II

In the *Republic*, Plato convincingly demonstrates that despite our ability
to experience injustice as individuals, we can only formulate a notion
of justice by first considering the good of the community as a whole,
then determining our conception of fairness to individuals in relation
to the harmonious workings of the larger community.[12] The problem
of hate speech suggests an interesting implication of Plato's analysis
for a nonidealist, historicist worldview. If we assume an evolving conception of social justice and injustice, it is plausible to suppose that
conceptions of social injustice may develop that are not readily addressed within the dominant vision of a just society. Efforts to respond
directly to newly identified problems of injustice may even seem to
create greater injustices when viewed from the dominant political perspective. It may be that only by interrogating and rearticulating our
overarching notions of social justice can we achieve the ability to respond to the new experiences of injustice in ways that do not simply
create more social conflict.

I think that current problems of racism, sexism, and homophobia
need to be understood in terms of such a lag between evolving local
perceptions of injustice and more inflexible, overarching conceptions
of justice. These latter are readily disrupted but only slowly altered in
response to new notions of injustice. The bitter social and theoretical
disputes currently arising in discussions of racism, sexism, and
homophobia will be adequately dealt with only if we are willing to
reformulate some of our larger visions of individual and community
relationships. Indeed, given the systemic cultural embeddedness of racial
and sexual hierarchies at this point in time, it seems likely that social
values and practices that many of us continue to take for granted will
have to be altered in order to advance beyond a merely superficial
opposition to these forms of domination. Of course, basic changes are
already being proposed, and duly contested, in various social contexts.
In the economic realm, for example, affirmative action policies remain
a highly controversial response to racist and sexist forms of workplace
discrimination because they necessarily challenge deep-seated notions
of market competition and fairness.

Within educational institutions, within the workplace, and on public
streets, it is a rare woman or minority who does not experience racism, sexism, or homophobia in the context of hate speech. Yet when it
is suggested that hate speech be prohibited in order to put a stop to

this injustice, large numbers of apparently reasonable and sympathetic people insist that such a cure would create even greater injustices. Even many women and minorities oppose hate speech restrictions. "How can this be", ask those who see such restrictions as a plausible means of diminishing the palpable harms of acts of hate speech. If as a nation we are opposed to racism, sexism, and homophobia, how can it be unjust to prohibit speech actions that enact and perpetuate these relationships? Because they are speech acts, say their civil libertarian respondents, and the protection of individual speech acts, particularly those with political content, are part of the fundamental fabric of our constitutionally guaranteed freedom. However strenuously we decide to oppose racism or sexism, we must choose a method that does not target people's political ideas or beliefs, no matter how much we may disapprove of them, conclude those who presume that First Amendment liberties are a cornerstone of a just society.

Our national vision of a just society has been defined in terms of a conception of the freedom of speech that appears to preclude hate speech restrictions. The question at hand is whether in attempting to act upon our quite recent and in many ways still superficial national commitment to eradicate racism, sexism, and homophobia we may be led to modify either the extent of our commitment to free speech or, perhaps, simply our notion of how best to encourage free speech. Note that a belief in what are technically referred to as "viewpoint-neutral" speech rights is much more than an esoteric ideological position in American society. Unlike laissez-faire economic doctrines that have been eroded by the harsh criticisms of Marxists and other progressives for a century and more, a commitment to free speech has a relatively populist and nonpartisan history in this country. The First Amendment is called into service by progressive and conservative causes, and by eccentric individuals of all political hues. Thus whenever I have raised the issue of campus speech codes in my introductory philosophy classes at the Borough of Manhattan Community College (CUNY), the preponderance of my racially, ethnically, and sexually diverse students have remained unswayed by my arguments for speech restrictions.[13]

Many advocates of hate speech restrictions explain the harmful consequences of hate speech acts and then seek to show, as Kent Greenawalt has put it, that restrictions prohibiting them involve only "a modest, warranted exception to content neutrality."[14] That is, they attempt to minimize the degree to which hate speech codes will really restrict speech. In my experience, this sort of strategy is not very effective in persuading people to support speech codes. The problem is that in making clear the need for hate speech restrictions, it also becomes apparent that common, everyday forms of speech will be prohibited.

I think we will only create broad acceptance of sanctions against hate speech by explicitly confronting and criticizing the political vision of earlier thinkers who conceived of unrestricted speech as a basic, "natural" element of individual freedom. Given the recent and still partial entrance of women and cultural minorities into the social and political mainstream, I believe it has become possible and necessary to develop a more subtle analysis of intellectual freedom, according to which the ability to speak is only one of several normative dimensions of intellectual and political agency.[15] As women and minorities have begun to participate in cultural and political venues still dominated by "straight white men," we have noticed that it is not merely the right to speak, but the corresponding right to be listened to and recognized for one's ideas, that constitutes the basis for democratic participation. Without the right to be heard and recognized as a political agent, one may speak and one's words will be without any political significance. A meaningful standard of free speech today must include both a right to speak and a right to have one's words respectfully received. Insofar as hate speech taps into racist and sexist cultural subtexts that radically devalue the personhood of women and minorities, it interferes with this broader notion of their speech rights. The right to engage in hate speech is thus in direct conflict with the speech rights of women and minorities.

Having shown the multiple dimensions of intellectual freedom, we may then argue that a conception of social justice is no longer satisfied by an abstract right to speak one's mind, but rather demands conditions under which each person may fully exercise her or his intellectual and political agency. Insofar as hate speech characteristically operates to inhibit the ability of particular citizens to speak and/or to be given a respectful hearing, it may cease to be judged a form of speech deserving constitutional protection. Yale law professor Owen Fiss explains this shifting locus of a democratic concern with speech rights: "The state might also have the right to interfere with the general advocacy of an idea when that advocacy has the effect of interfering with the speech of others. In that instance, the state ban on speech does not restrict or impoverish public debate, but paradoxically enough, broadens it, for it allows all voices to be heard. The state acts not as a censor, but rather as a parliamentarian, requiring some to shut up so others can be heard."[16]

III

It may be wise, at this point, to retrace our steps in order to show how such an analysis both builds upon and modifies earlier conceptions of the freedom of speech. In his classic essay *On Liberty*, J. S. Mill provides one of the most powerful accounts of how principles of free speech intersect with the democratic privilege to think and act as we wish. In the first place, he emphasizes the danger of a tyrannical, vulgar majority imposing its customary opinions upon everyone within a democracy. Against all such despotic populist impulses, he asserts the right of individuals to hold unorthodox views, as well as to indulge unconventional tastes and pursuits so long as they do not "harm others." He maintains that the political values of liberty and autonomy, whereby individuals are expected to formulate their own conceptions of the good life, demand the protection of eccentric beliefs and behavior. He also argues that nonconforming individuals are a primary source for socially progressive ideas and advances in knowledge. If "the despotism of custom" is allowed free rein it will stand in the way of human progress and the pursuit of truth; false ideas must be fully heard and responded to if true ideas are not "to abide as prejudices," he asserts.[17]

In the United States today, commitment to free speech is firmly grounded in this nineteenth-century Millian tradition, the pursuit of truth and individual autonomy always cited as basic values protected by the First Amendment. A third normative strand, emphasizing the role of free expression within a self-governing society, is also woven into the political fabric of First Amendment defenses. Alexander Meiklejohn, echoing earlier arguments of James Madison in the *Federalist Papers*, eloquently articulates this political role of free speech, particularly explaining the place of political dissent within the democratic process. His guiding premise is that the First Amendment was meant to guarantee a robust and full process of discussion within a democracy, such that citizens would become aware of all possible political options, as the basis for fulfilling their responsibility of self-government. "To deny citizens who are to decide an issue acquaintance with information or opinions . . . is for the result to be ill-considered. . . . It is that mutilation of the thinking process of the community against which the First Amendment is directed," he proclaims.[18] All points of view must be available to citizens deciding upon the policies by which their community should be governed.

Indeed, the exemplary twentieth-century judicial defenses of free speech have been arguments for allowing politically or artistically radical or unpopular views to be expressed. As Oliver Wendell Holmes said (in a dissenting opinion) in 1929, it is "the speech that we hate" that we must make sure to protect.[19] Not that our system has always achieved this ideal. The now infamous era of the McCarthy trials in the 1950s is a common touchstone for civil libertarian arguments against all content-based restrictions upon speech. Current norms of free speech appear to have been graven into the judicial conscience at those historical moments when our system failed to fully respect the right of individuals to express political dissent.

Of course, racist, sexist, and homophobic speech may readily be seen as the newest example of political "speech that we hate." For many legal thinkers it is a straightforward inference to conclude that we must protect hate speech as we protect other forms of political speech. Thus we find Isabelle Katz Pinzler, director of the women's project at the American Civil Liberties Union, responding to proposals to restrict sexist hate speech with a breezy refutation: "I think it [sexual comments, catcalls from strangers on the street] is a political statement, that women are sex objects and that they belong in the home. . . . Let me hasten to say that it is a political message I hate; still, we have to defend political speech that we hate."[20]

But do we? Hate speech is, in fact, the common, everyday expression of racial and sexual hierarchies that have prevailed unquestioned for centuries. Today, when these relations of domination have been questioned, it is the speech of those who would continue to enforce the old hierarchies. It is the coercive voice of what unfortunately remains a very powerful viewpoint on subliminal political and psychological levels within our society. In the context of a formal societal repudiation of sexism, racism, and homophobia, why should we defend speech that taps into these traditional structures of oppression? Indeed, is it not hypocritical to claim that we are opposed to the racial and sexual hierarchies that persist within our culture while defending speech acts that enact and perpetuate these relationships?[21]

First Amendment doctrine, like all constitutional doctrine, is necessarily formulated in the context of a historically developing set of political issues. For many of us today it is difficult to imagine a society in which hierarchies based upon race, gender, religion, ethnicity, and sexual preference were presumed to be natural or necessary. We cannot conceive of being the unprotesting objects of a racial or sexual contempt deemed legitimate by the society in which we live. Yet what we now label hate speech is an ugly and still powerful social trace of racial and sexual hierarchies that have been taken for granted for centuries. What many of us call hate speech is still part of the everyday, unremarkable linguistic fabric of various communities. People in these communities may see little or no contradiction between their use of conventional racist, homophobic, or misogynistic phrases and their participation in a just society. Should they have any doubts, the powerful ideological fabric of our "free speech" tradition, guaranteeing each of us the right to say and think whatever we wish, may all too readily allay these doubts.

Only during the last forty years or so has our society come to have even a formal ethical and political commitment to ending racism, sexism, and homophobia, but the quality of that commitment remains at issue. If we continue to conceive of hate speech according to earlier paradigms of libertarian social justice, opposition to hate speech acts will be trumped by a commitment to the freedom of speech. If instead we comprehend hate speech as enacting societywide racial and sexual hierarchies that our society is now committed to eradicating, it becomes apparent that our previous conceptions of the role of speech in a just society must be rethought. We need to decide what to do when the speech that we hate is neither eccentric nor unpopular, but rather habitual and oppressive. Without questioning the validity of the political commitment to protecting eccentric, unpopular, or dissenting speech, it is necessary to be highly skeptical of assumptions that social justice can be achieved through characterizing hate speech in terms of these paradigms of speech behavior.

Indeed, had a theorist such as J. S. Mill lived in our times, it is possible that even he would have seen grounds for hate speech restrictions. David Dyzenhaus reminds us that Mill's concern in *On Liberty* was not merely with political forms of tyranny, but with the various forms of social tyranny exercised by the majority. In fact, Mill judged private forms of moral coercion as "more formidable than many kinds of political oppression, since . . . it leaves fewer means of escape, penetrating much more deeply into the details of life, and enslaving the soul itself."[22] Mill formulated his famous harm's principle to limit the ability of the majority to act coercively by means of the state, but he was quite clear in expressing concern for private forms of social coercion as well, particularly those relating to the tyranny men wielded over women in the family.[23] Given the strength of Mill's concern with protecting each person's interest in autonomously exploring and pursuing their own individual conception of the good life, Dyzenhaus argues that it does not make sense to read the harm's principle narrowly or infer its protection of forms of speech that keep people from exercising autonomy.[24] Mill's actual analysis of the social harms that could be regulated by government was limited by his historical milieu; hate speech had not even been identified as a social phenomenon in the nineteenth century. Insofar as it can now be characterized as a tyrannical mode of speech that interferes with the Millian autonomy of women and minority students and faculty, it seems likely that were he alive today, Mill would support legislation regulating hate speech.[25]

Those who traditionally emphasized the role of free speech within the democratic process might also have supported restrictions upon hate speech. Fifty years ago, Alexander Meiklejohn was careful to distinguish between what he deemed a person's "unalienable right to speak" and a wrongful presumption that this implied that a person had an "unqualified right" to speak.[26] He used a traditional town meeting as his model for explaining the limits on speech which "any reasonable society" would set given democratic political goals. While "no speaker may be declared out of order because we disagree with what he intends to say," Meiklejohn maintains that "abusive or threatening speech" is always "out of order."

Emphasizing the relevance of the social framework within which a speech act occurs, as well as its circumstantial meaning, Meiklejohn expands upon his analysis of the town meeting to explain the reasonable limitations on speech in other social venues. He states that anyone who "interrupts irresponsibly the activities of a lecture, a hospital, a concert hall, a church, a machine shop, a classroom, a football field, or a home, does not thereby exhibit his freedom of speech. Rather he shows himself a boor, a public nuisance."[27] A person who becomes verbally abusive or who irresponsibly interrupts the activities of others may be "thrown out" or otherwise "abated, by force if necessary," Meiklejohn declares. He is very clear in specifying that it is indeed a speech act that is being restricted in such a case, and he maintains that the First Amendment does not forbid *these sorts* of abridgements of speech.[28] While hate speech was not an issue in his day, it is plausible to think that Meiklejohn would judge many contemporary acts of racist and sexist speech to be forms of verbal abuse warranting forceful abatement rather than First Amendment protection.

IV

There are thus clear legal precedents for adjudging campus hate speech as either a boorish form of verbal interruption having no place in a scholarly community, or worse, as a form of social tyranny compromising the developing autonomy of women and minority students newly invited to participate in academic life. Despite these strong grounds for concluding that hate speech does not deserve constitutional protection, a public furor has arisen in various cases in which a prominent university has decided to discipline a student for engaging in hate speech. For example, when Brown University chose to expel student Douglas Hann after he had engaged in abusive, bigoted speech (covering the spectrum of racism, anti-semitism, and homophobia) late one night in a dormitory courtyard, civil libertarians insisted that his constitutional rights to free speech were trampled upon.[29] Regardless of one's judgment of the severity of Hann's punishment (he had previously been warned and instructed to change his behavior after similar offenses), it is troubling that so many commentators dogmatically assumed that physical "rowdiness" could have warranted such punishment but that his hateful speech could not be legitimately penalized. After all, it was Hann's words, not his physical behavior that assaulted sleeping and studying students in their dormitory rooms; it was his bigoted words that echoed threateningly within those walls of their shared domestic space, penetrating their dreams and intimate conversations that night. Is it not obvious that such words, in such a social setting, contribute to an atmosphere in which cultural minorities may have difficulty in maintaining self-respect, as well as in developing relationships of trust and friendship with those students who represent the still dominant culture?[30] Campus hate speech taps into deeply embedded structures of racial and sexual domination and is capable of undermining the best efforts of all those seeking to encourage the participation of women and minorities within academic communities.

How can we explain the fact that despite the existence of legal and political principles capable of justifying campus speech codes, judicial and public opinions remain, for the most part, opposed? The best explanation may be discovered, perhaps, simply through reviewing popular conceptions of the academy. Whether ideally conceived as an elite community of scholars seeking abstract knowledge and truth, or more prosaically understood in terms of its role in responding to society's mandate for increasing scientific and technical knowledge production and training, the academy is considered the sort of place properly organized solely in terms of intellectual excellence. Thus ethical and political issues seem mere distractions from the serious intellectual business of universities. When Allan Bloom charged, in *The Closing of the American Mind*, that a foolish and inappropriate concern with political matters like feminism is destroying the integrity of education and the university today, his book became a best-seller.[31] For a great many people, apparently, the academy remains one place in our society in which abstract standards of transcendent or scientific truth yet prevail, a place where human relationships exist to facilitate intellectual achievements.

Despite the seductive quality of conservative rhetoric, however, we may confidently assert that the apolitical appearance of colleges and universities in the past was simply due to the fact that they were very homogeneous communities, made up of boys and men from similarly privileged cultural and intellectual backgrounds. While they were organized according to rigidly hierarchical social and intellectual schema, everyone knew the terms for participating and achieving recognition within his academy; daily scholarly practices as well as long-term intellectual goals were a matter of shared norms within the community.[32] Insofar as each student and instructor knew his rightful place within the academy, he could feel himself a member of a very exclusive, very harmonious society that fulfilled the ideal Platonic standards for both justice and the pursuit of knowledge.

The academy is no longer such an exclusive community, and not incidentally, knowledge production now reflects and participates in the normative conflicts and confusions within the academy, just as it previously partook of academic harmony. The multicultural academy is a site of social as well as intellectual turmoil. Women and men from culturally diverse backgrounds have recently been admitted to colleges and universities, but their rightful place within the academy remains a point of uncertainty and contention. No longer are the daily practices or intellectual goals of students or teachers a matter of shared norms. A diversity of creative and scholastic values and ways of life must now be acknowledged, as many different cultures enter the academy, and indeed as the walls between the academy and the larger society begin to break down. Unfortunately, potent forms of social injustice and conflict have also been introduced into the academy, as long-standing but no longer morally or politically legitimate hierarchies based upon gender, race, and ethnicity have entered the academy along with new female and minority recruits. Thus disorientation and discord mount. Intellectual hierarchies are called into question by alternative notions of achievement that often seem incommensurable with each other, while at the same time unjust racial and sexual patterns of domination and subordination distort reasonable efforts to negotiate across cultural differences. Campus hate speech is just one sign of the unsettling times that have come to academic life. There can be no justice and little harmony within the contemporary academy until there is once again some sort of structure enabling everyone to begin to determine their rightful place and to recognize the rightful place of others.

Insofar as hate speech is an egregious sign of deep-seated cultural conflicts on college campuses today, it is reasonable to hope that by grappling with hate speech we may gain insight into how to deal with the broader array of intellectual and cultural frictions in the academy. Those who dismiss the significance of hate speech (falsely) attempt to assimilate it with notions of legitimate political dissent. By contrast, I will call upon Jürgen Habermas's and Karl-Otto Apel's theory of communicative ethics (alternatively referred to as discourse ethics) in order to explain the significance of hate speech, as well as to explore ways of dissipating it.

The academy provides an ideal institutional setting for illustrating Habermas's belief that in order to understand many of our relationships to each other we need to think of ourselves as "communicative actors."[33] Habermas has been particularly concerned with specifying the conditions for achieving legitimate forms of political consensus within liberal democracies such as exist in Germany or the United States, and his theory of communicative ethics accordingly confines itself to analyzing the normative conditions for achieving political consensus. Many other contemporary theorists, however, extend the reach of communicative ethics much further. Jean Cohen and Andrew Arato, for example, maintain that it is a political ethic appropriate for articulating relationships within all those institutions in civil society, including the academy, within which rights of communication are primary.[34]

Most importantly, Seyla Benhabib suggests a variation on Habermas's theory of communicative ethics, in which it ceases to be a theory aimed at achieving a legitimate consensus, becoming instead a theory of how to maintain a just, ongoing process of rational discussion. "When we shift the burden for the moral test in communicative ethics from consensus to the idea of an ongoing moral conversation," states Benhabib, "we begin to ask . . . what would be allowed and perhaps even necessary from the standpoint of continuing and sustaining the practice of the moral conversation among us. The emphasis is now less on *rational agreement*, but more on sustaining those normative practices and moral relationships within which reasoned agreement *as a way of life* can flourish and continue."[35]

The multicultural academy seems in need of just such a moral communicative structure; and, happily, the basic principles for enacting such a discourse ethics are not overly complicated. According to Benhabib, only two fundamental moral norms are required: first, what she terms "the principle of universal moral respect," which requires "that we recognize the right of all beings capable of speech and action to be participants in the moral conversation"; second, what she calls "the principle of egalitarian reciprocity," according to which each person within moral conversations "has the same symmetrical rights to various speech acts, to initiate new topics, to ask for reflection about the presuppositions of the conversation, etc."[36] Clearly these are abstract ethical mandates, with differential applications in various institutional circumstances. Yet racial or sexual slurs or epithets would appear contrary to the spirit of any discourse community ruled by a norm of universal moral respect, regardless of how broadly or narrowly we decided to interpret that principle.

CONCLUSION

Incidents of campus hate speech thus provide an unambiguous occasion for academic communities to concern themselves with issues of discourse ethics. Moreover, restrictions on hate speech have a vital role to play within institutional efforts to build procedural norms of universal respect and egalitarian reciprocity into the academic structure.[37] We have seen that racist and sexist hate speech operate to deny the personhood of minorities and women, undermining the basic conditions for universal respect, and specifically for verbal reciprocity. For women and minorities an abstract ideal of free speech is worth little insofar as social structures that deny them recognition as persons are

operative. In imposing sanctions against hate speech we seek to empower all members of a multicultural academy both to speak and to
be received with respect.[38]

Hate speech, of course, will not be the only obstacle facing colleges
and universities attempting to institutionalize conditions for communicative ethics. There are a great many nonverbal forms of sexist and
racist behavior that are likely to be very difficult to eradicate. Katharine
T. Bartlett and Jean O'Barr warn about a whole spectrum of subtle
and practically invisible modes of discrimination that are nevertheless
capable of maintaining racial and sexual hierarchies within academic
life. Citing the results of two recent studies on everyday forms of campus
sexism, they discuss some of the forms of differential behavior within
the classroom as well as outside it through which faculty typically convey
greater respect for male students than for female students. These studies find that numerous behavioral signals by teachers, from tone of
voice, physical posture, or eye contact when asking a question, to fre-
quency of calling on a student by name, the time allowed for a student's answer, as well as the quality of response to student questions,
all operate to distribute greater amounts of respect and esteem to male
students than to female students. (More than thirty-five such modes
of subtle sexist subordination were noted in the two studies of sexism
on campus. Presumably, comparable patterns of behavioral prejudice
function to distribute greater amounts of respect and esteem to white
students than to students of color.)[39]

Racism and sexism are anchored in these behaviors, and until the
nonverbal ways in which dominant men assert their authority over
women and cultural minorities are confronted and transformed the
goals of communicative ethics will be fundamentally undermined. The
problem is that many of these implicitly sexist and racist patterns of
eye contact, voice tones, etc. still appear to be natural and acceptable
modes of behavior, defended as matters of personal, subjective interactive style. Bartlett and O'Barr worry that insofar as speech codes
focus attention on blatant, discursive forms of sexist, heterosexist, and
racist campus interaction, these less tangible forms of oppression will
continue unchecked, perhaps even intensifying in response to the regulation of overt behaviors like hate speech.

On the contrary, I think that insofar as the academic community is
working toward a communicative ethics standard for all interactions
between faculty, students, and administrators, hate speech restrictions
can play a pivotal role in enabling links to be forged between overtly
discriminatory discursive behavior and the less visible forms of discrimination identified by Bartlett and O'Barr. If members of the academic community acknowledge the mechanisms by which hate speech
denies the speech rights of women and minorities, they are more likely

to comprehend the analogous ways in which various "natural-seeming" nonverbal behaviors discriminate against women and minorities by denying them the recognition necessary for full participation in formal and informal discussions. Beginning with overt acts of hate speech, students and faculty can learn to recognize and repudiate more subtle patterns of domination and subordination engaged in by many individuals who would not want to think of themselves as racists, sexists, or heterosexists.

With careful planning hate speech restrictions can be integrated within a broader plan for achieving relationships of universal respect and egalitarian reciprocity within campus life. Hate speech codes will serve as political buoys, floating brightly above the murky depths of multicultural tensions, marking out the general existence and location of various less visible modes of racist and sexist behavior. In analyzing the speech acts, and more importantly, the speech relationships involved in hate speech as well as in nondiscursive patterns of domination, in frankly grappling with current problems of racism and sexism, we will necessarily commit ourselves to a more complex ideal of free speech than that of our forefathers. The incantatory equation of "speech" with "freedom" inevitably loses its power for us, and we may formulate instead a conception of freedom that pairs the right to speak with the right to be heard and recognized. Speech rights within a multicultural university must be premised upon the goal of guaranteeing these basic conditions of intellectual agency to all students and faculty alike.

In a very different radical moment twenty-five years ago, in the context of the Civil Rights and antiwar movements of the 1960s, Herbert Marcuse coined the term "repressive tolerance" to describe what he saw as hypocritical defenses of tolerance and the right of political dissent by those seeking to maintain a repressive status quo.[40] Insofar as hate speech currently operates as a verbal enforcement mechanism of oppressive racial and sexual power structures that our society has formally repudiated, its repressive functions are obvious, as are the costs of tolerating it. Marcuse expressed some faint hopes that a "subversive majority" could emerge that would attempt to reinstate freedom of thought. But he believed that the process of restoring freedom to a repressive society would itself require a certain amount of intolerance, for example, "restrictions on teachings and practices in the educational institutions which, by their very methods and concepts, serve to enclose the mind within the established universe of discourse and behavior— thereby precluding a priori a rational evaluation of the alternatives."[41]

Twenty-five years later, our categories of analysis are less utopian and our political rhetoric is much more restrained. Even so, we are faced with transformative possibilities Marcuse might have relished, although he could hardly have predicted or imagined them. Women and minorities constitute a potentially subversive multicultural majority within major social institutions such as the academy. Perhaps we should become accustomed to enunciating policies rather than dissenting. Let hate speech restrictions be a beginning.

NOTES

INTRODUCTION

1. See D. Caudill, *Disclosing Tilt: Law, Belief and Criticism* (Amsterdam: Free University Press, 1989), 37–69 for a description of the CLS movement.
2. See, e.g., *The Politics of Law*, ed. D. Kairys (New York: Pantheon Books, 1990); *Critical Legal Studies*, ed. A. Hutchinson (Totowa, NJ: Rowman & Littlefield, 1989).

CHAPTER 1

*This chapter is an expanded version of an article that appeared in *Canadian Journal of Law and Jurisprudence* 4 (1991): 145–64, under the title "Marxist Jurisprudence: Historical Necessity and Radical Contingency"; portions of this article previously published are reprinted here with permission. A modified version of that original article also appears in Belliotti's *Justifying Law* (Philadelphia: Temple University Press, 1992).

1. See K. Marx, "Economic and Philosophical Manuscripts" (1844) and "Excerpts from James Mill's Elements of a Political Economy" (1844), in *Early Writings*, trans. R. Livingstone and G. Benton (Harmondsworth: Penguin Books, 1975); R. Schmitt, *Introduction to Marx and Engels: A Critical Reconstruction* (Boulder: Westview Press, 1987), 151–59.
2. See Marx, "Economic and Philosophical Manuscripts"; D. Conway, *A Farewell to Marx: An Outline and Appraisal of His Theories* (Harmondsworth: Penguin Books, 1987), 34–41.
3. See K. Marx, *The Grundrisse: Foundations of the Critique of Political Economy (1857–58)*, trans. M. Nicolaus (Harmondsworth: Penguin Books, 1973); J. Elster, *An Introduction to Karl Marx* (Cambridge: Cambridge University Press, 1986), 41–56.
4. See K. Marx and F. Engels, "The German Ideology," in *Collected Works* (London: International Publishers, 1976), vol. 1; K. Marx, *Capital*, trans. D. Fernbach, 3 vols. (Harmondsworth: Penguin Books, 1976), vol. 1; P. Singer, *Marx* (Oxford: Oxford University Press, 1980), 25–34.
5. See Marx and Engels, "The German Ideology"; Marx, *Capital*, vol. 1; Singer, *Marx*, 25–34.
6. Marx, *Capital*, vol. 1; Schmitt, *Introduction to Marx and Engels*, 74–85; Conway, *Farewell to Marx*, 98–106; Elster, *Introduction to Karl Marx*, 81–101; Singer, *Marx*, 23–25, 50–54.
7. Marx, *Capital*, vol. 1; Schmitt, *Introduction to Marx and Engels*, 74–85; Conway, *A Farewell to Marx*, 98–106; Elster, *An Introduction to Karl Marx*, 81–101; Singer, *Marx*, 23–25, 50–54.
8. See Conway, *A Farewell to Marx*, 98–106; A. Buchanan, *Marx and Justice:*

The Radical Critique of Liberalism (London: Methuen, 1982), c. 5; A. Wood, "The Marxian Critique of Justice," in *Marx, Justice, and History*, ed. M. Cohen, T. Nagel, and T. Scanlon (Princeton: Princeton University Press, 1980), 3–41.

9. Schmitt, *Introduction to Marx and Engels*, 30.
10. Ibid.
11. Ibid., 36–38.
12. H. Collins, *Marxism and Law* (Oxford: Oxford University Press, 1984), 78.
13. Schmitt, *Introduction to Marx and Engels*, 36; J. Larrain, "Base and Superstructure," in *A Dictionary of Marxist Thought*, ed. T. Bottomore (Cambridge: Harvard University Press, 1983), 44.
14. T. M. Hyden, "A Critique of Marxist Legal Theoretical Constructs," *Studies of Soviet Thought* 28 (1984): 351.
15. Larrain, "Base and Superstructure," 43.
16. Schmitt, *Introduction to Marx and Engels*, 35.
17. Ibid., 36.
18. Ibid., 36–38.
19. Ibid., 36.
20. Ibid., 37.
21. Ibid.
22. Ibid., 38.
23. Ibid.
24. Marx and Engels, "The German Ideology"; Schmitt, *Introduction to Marx and Engels*, 54–56; Conway, *Farewell to Marx*, 170–77; Elster, *Introduction to Karl Marx*, 168–73.
    Engels explicitly used the term "false consciousness" in his letter to Franz Mehring, July 14, 1893, in K. Marx and F. Engels, *Selected Works* (Moscow: Progress Publishers, 1968), 690. ("Ideology is a process accomplished by the so-called thinker consciously, it is true, but with a false consciousness. The real motive forces impelling him remain unknown to him; otherwise it simply would not be an ideological process. Hence he imagines false or seeming motive forces.")
    Some theorists claim that Marx never explicitly used the term "false consciousness," but they admit that no substantive implications follow if they are correct. Thus, M. Seliger, in *The Marxist Conception of Ideology* (Cambridge: Cambridge University Press, 1977), 30–31, asserts, "It seems that Marx himself did not use the phrase 'false consciousness.' This makes no difference as far as his conception of ideological thought is concerned since instead of 'false,' Marx used 'incorrect,' 'twisted,' and 'abstract' besides nouns like 'illusion,' 'block,' etc. We may thus take 'false consciousness' to denote Marx's view as well."
25. See Larrain, "Ideology," in *A Dictionary of Marxist Thought*, 218–20; Collins, *Marxism and Law*, 40; R. G. Peffer, "Morality and the Marxist Concept of Ideology," in *Marx and Morality*, ed. K. Nielsen and S. C. Patten (Guelph, ON: Canadian Association for Publishing in Philosophy, 1981), 67–91.
26. Schmitt, *Introduction to Marx and Engels*, 58.
27. Ibid., 45.
28. Ibid., 47.
29. Collins, *Marxism and Law*, 95.
30. Ibid., 11–12.
31. Ibid., 11.
32. Ibid.

33. Ibid., 13.
34. Ibid., 136.
35. Ibid., 14.
36. Ibid., 48–49.
37. Ibid., 67–68.
38. Ibid., 72–73.
39. Ibid., 105.
40. Ibid., 106.
41. R. A. Belliotti, "The Rule of Law and the Critical Legal Studies Movement," *University of Western Ontario L. Rev.* 24 (1986): 67.
42. That is, Marxism cannot deny automatically the veracity of a perception or experience that does not support the conclusions of Marxism. On the other hand, critics of Marxism cannot accept automatically the veracity of such perceptions and experiences as evidence refuting Marxist conclusions.
43. Schmitt, *Introduction to Marx and Engels*, 37–38.
44. Ibid., 37.
45. Collins, *Marxism and Law*, 137.
46. Ibid., 31.
47. Ibid., 43.
48. Ibid.
49. Ibid., 106.
50. Ibid.
51. Ibid., 107.
52. E. Kamenka, "Law," in *Dictionary of Marxist Thought*, 276.
53. S. P. Sinha, *What Is Law?: The Differing Theories of Jurisprudence* (New York: Paragon House, 1989), 218.
54. Belliotti, "The Rule of Law"; "Is Law a Sham?" *Philosophy and Phenomenological Research* 48 (1987): 25; "Critical Legal Studies: The Paradoxes of Indeterminacy and Nihilism," *Philosophy and Social Criticism* 12 (1987): 145; "Radical Politics and Nonfoundational Morality," *International Philosophical Quarterly* 29 (1989): 33; "Beyond Capitalism and Communism: Roberto Unger's Superliberal Political Theory," *Praxis International* 9 (1989): 321.
55. M. V. Tushnet, "Marxism as Metaphor," *Cornell L. Rev.* 68 (1983): 290.
56. J. Frank, *Law and the Modern Mind* (New York: Brentano's, 1930).
57. C. MacKinnon, *Feminism Unmodified* (Cambridge: Harvard University Press, 1987).
58. R. Unger, *Passion: An Essay on Personality* (New York: Free Press, 1984).
59. M. Matsuda et al., *Words That Wound* (Boulder: Westview Press, 1993).
60. Ibid., 6.
61. Ibid., 7.
62. Ibid., 5.
63. See, e.g., Belliotti, *Justifying Law*, 211–54.

CHAPTER 2

1. G. A. Cohen, *Karl Marx's Theory of History: A Defence* (Princeton: Princeton University Press, 1963), 260.
2. A. Levine and E. O. Wright, "Rationality and Class Struggle," *New Left Review* 123 (September–October 1980): 55.
3. M. Fisk, *The State and Justice* (Cambridge: Cambridge University Press, 1989), 145.
4. A. Levine, E. Sober, and E. O. Wright, "Marxism and Methodological Individualism," *New Left Review* 162 (March–April 1987): 62–84.

5. J. Reiman, *The Rich Get Richer and the Poor Get Prison* (New York: Macmillan Publishing, 1990).
6. S. Gold, "Foucault's Critique of Functional Marxism," *Rethinking Marxism* 3 (Fall–Winter 1990): 297.
7. J. Elster, "Marxism, Functionalism, and Game Theory: The Case for Methodological Individualism," *Theory and Society* 6 (1982): 453–82; *Explaining Technical Change* (Cambridge: Cambridge University Press, 1983); "Further Thoughts on Marxism, Functionalism, and Game Theory," in *Analytical Marxism*, ed. John Roemer (Cambridge: Cambridge University Press, 1986), 202–20.
8. R. Miller, *Fact and Method* (Princeton: Princeton University Press, 1987), 122.
9. See generally G. A. Cohen, *Karl Marx's Theory of History*; "Reply to Elster on 'Marxism, Functionalism and Game Theory,'" *Theory and Society* 6 (1982): 483–95.
10. M. Foucault, *Power/Knowledge*, ed. C. Gordon (New York: Pantheon, 1977), 101.

CHAPTER 3

1. See D. Milovanovic, *A Primer in the Sociology of Law* (New York: Harrow and Heston, 1988); *Weberian and Marxian Perspectives on Law: Development and Functions of Law in Capitalist Mode of Production* (Aldershot, England: Gower Publishing, 1989).
2. S. Henry and D. Milovanovic, "Constitutive Criminology," *Criminology* 29 (1992): 293.
3. P. Beirne, "Empiricism and the Critique of Marxism on Law and Crime," *Social Problems* 26 (1979): 373; I. Balbus, "Commodity Form and Legal Form: An Essay on the Relative Autonomy of the Law," *Law and Society Review* 11 (1977): 571; A. Fraser, "The Legal Theory We Need Now," *Socialist Review* 40 (1978): 147; D. Milovanovic, "The Commodity Exchange Theory of Law: In Search of a Perspective," *Crime and Social Justice* 16 (1981): 41.
4. L. Althusser, *Lenin and Philosophy* (New York: Monthly Review Press, 1971).
5. D. Milovanovic, "The Political Economy of 'Liberty' and 'Property' Interests," *Legal Studies Forum* 11, no. 3 (1987): 147; *Weberian and Marxian Perspectives on Law.* A newly emerging perspective referred to as constitutive criminology/law is assimilable to the structural interpellation perspective. Postmodernist analysis that pays disproportionate attention to the ideological sphere can be better balanced and grounded, materialistically, by integrating the structural interpellation perspective as well as the constitutive view in law.
6. J. Habermas, *The Theory of Communicative Action* (Boston: Beacon Press, 1984).
7. See Milovanovic, "The Political Economy."
8. See K. Silverman, *The Subject of Semiotics* (New York: Oxford University Press, 1983).
9. See J. Lacan, *Encore* (Paris: Editions du Seuil, 1975); *Ecrits: A Selection*, trans. A. Sheridan (New York: Norton, 1977); *L'Envers de la Psychanalyse* (Paris: Editions du Seuil, 1991); see also *Feminine Sexuality: Jacques Lacan and the École Freudienne*, ed. J. Mitchell and J. Rose, trans. J. Rose (New York: W. W. Norton and Pantheon Books, 1985).
10. See Lacan, *Ecrits*, 292–325; D. Milovanovic, *Postmodern Law and Disorder: Psychoanalytic Semiotic, Chaos and Juridic Exegeses* (Merseyside, England:

Deborah Charles Publications, 1992); Lacan was also to conceptualize the structure and functioning of the desiring subject by the use of topology theory; see, e.g., D. Milovanovic, "The Decentered Subject in Law: Contributions of Topology, Psychoanalytic Semiotics and Chaos Theory" (paper presented at the 1993 Annual Meeting of Law and Society, Chicago, May 27, 1993); in Lacan's late thinking he was to develop an alternative conceptualization of the structure and functioning of the psychic apparatus based on borromean knots; see D. Milovanovic, "Borromean Knots and the Constitution of Sense in Juridico-Discursive Production, *Legal Studies Forum* 17, no. 2 (1993): 171.

11. On the idea of a discursive subject-position, see, e.g., M. Pecheux, *Language, Semantics, and Ideology* (New York: St. Martin's Press, 1982); Lacan was also to indicate how four fundamental forms of discourse exist: the discourses of the master, university, hysteric, and analyst. See D. Milovanovic, "Lacan's Four Discourses," *Studies in Psychoanalytic Theory* 2, no. 1 (1993): 3; for a psychoanalytic semiotic account of the construction of the legal text, see also D. Caudill, "Lacan and Legal Language: Meanings in the Gaps, Gaps in the Meanings," *Law and Critique* 8, no. 2 (1992): 169.

12. See J. J. Lecercle, *Philosophy Through the Looking Glass* (London: Hutchinson, 1985); G. Deleuze, *Nietzsche and Philosophy* (New York: Columbia University Press, 1983).

13. Lecercle, *Philosophy*, 196.

14. See, e.g., B. Jackson, *Law, Fact, and Narrative Coherence* (Merseyside, England: Deborah Charles Publications, 1991); Caudill, "Lacan and Legal Language," 183–89, 194–208; D. Milovanovic, "Re-Thinking Subjectivity in Law and Ideology: A Semiotic Perspective," *Journal of Human Justice* 4, no. 1 (1992): 31.

15. Lacan, *Feminine Sexuality*.

16. See, e.g., S. Sellers, *Language and Sexual Difference* (New York: St. Martin's Press, 1991); E. Grosz, *Jacques Lacan: A Feminist Introduction* (New York: Routledge, 1990).

17. See D. Caudill, "Lacan and Law: Networking with the Big O[ther]," *Studies in Psychoanalytic Theory* 1, no. 1 (1992): 25; "'Name-of-the-Father' and the Logic of Psychosis: Lacan's Law and Ours," *Legal Studies Forum* 16, no. 4 (1992): 421; "Jacques Lacan and Our State of Affairs: Preliminary Remarks on Law as Other," in *Law and the Human Sciences*, ed. R. Kevelson (New York: Peter Lang, 1992), 95; "Lacan and Legal Language."

18. D. Cornell, *Beyond Accommodation: Ethical Feminism, Deconstruction and the Law* (New York: Routledge, 1991); *Transformations: Recollective Imagination and Sexual Difference* (New York: Routledge, 1993).

19. P. Goodrich, *Languages of Law: From Logics of Memory to Nomadic Masks* (London: Weidenfeld and Nicolson, 1990).

20. B. Arrigo, "An Experientially-Informed Feminist Jurisprudence," *Humanity and Society* 17, no. 1 (1993): 28; "Deconstructing Jurisprudence: An Experiential Feminist Critique," *Journal of Human Justice* 4, no. 1 (1992): 13.

21. Milovanovic, *Postmodern Law*.

22. See Cornell, *Beyond Accommodation* and *Transformations*; Arrigo, "An Experientially-Informed Feminist Jurisprudence;" Milovanovic, *Postmodern Law*.

23. See, e.g., Cornell, *Beyond Accommodation* and *Transformations*; Milovanovic, *Postmodern Law*, 221–58; Milovanovic, "Lacan's Four Discourses."

24. See Caudill, "Name-of-the-Father."

25. Caudill, "Lacan and Legal Language."

26. Goodrich, *Languages of Law*; Cornell, *Beyond Accommodation* and *Transformations*.
27. See, e.g., K. Bartlett and R. Kennedy, eds., *Feminist Legal Theory: Readings in Law and Gender* (Boulder: Westview Press, 1991).
28. D. Milovanovic and J. Thomas, "Overcoming the Absurd: Legal Struggle as Primitive Rebellion," *Social Problems* 36, no. 1 (1989): 48; Henry and Milovanovic, "Constitutive Criminology."
29. Henry and Milovanovic, "Constitutive Criminology."
30. S. Bannister and D. Milovanovic, "The Necessity Defense, Substantive Justice and Oppositional Linguistic Praxis," *International Journal of the Sociology of Law* 18, no. 2 (1990): 179.
31. See, e.g., C. Groves, "Us and Them: Reflections on the Dialectics of Moral Hate," in *New Directions in Critical Criminology*, ed. B. MacLean and D. Milovanovic (Vancouver: The Collective Press, 1991), 111; D. Milovanovic, "Schmarxism, Exorcism and Transpraxis," *The Critical Criminologist* 3, no. 4 (1991): 5.

CHAPTER 4

* An expanded version of this essay appears under the title "Freud and Critical Legal Studies: Contours of a Radical Socio-Legal Psychoanalysis," in Ind. L. J. 66 (1991): 651–97, reprinted in *Legal Studies as Cultural Studies*, ed. J. Leonard (forthcoming, 1994).

1. R. Geuss, *The Idea of a Critical Theory: Habermas & the Frankfurt School* (Cambridge: Cambridge University Press, 1981), 918.
2. L. Kornhauser, "The Great Image of Authority," *Stan. L. Rev.* 36 (1984): 349.
3. D. McLellan, *Ideology* (Minneapolis: University of Minnesota Press, 1986), 73.
4. J. Thompson, *Studies in the Theory of Ideology* (Berkeley: University of California Press, 1984), 35, 61, 131.
5. A. Hunt, "The Theory of Critical Legal Studies," *Oxford J. Leg. Stud.* 6 (1986): 1, 12.
6. S. Frosh, *The Politics of Psychoanalysis: An Introduction to Freudian and Post-Freudian Theory* (London: MacMillan Education Ltd., 1987), 11.
7. S. Freud, *Civilization and Its Discontents*, ed. and trans. J. Strachey (New York: W. W. Norton, 1961), 44.
8. Frosh, *Politics of Psychoanalysis*, 46.
9. Ibid., 46–47.
10. Ibid., 60.
11. M. Jay, *The Dialectical Imagination: A History of the Frankfurt School and the Institute of Social Research, 1923–1950* (Boston: Little, Brown, 1973), 91.
12. H. Marcuse, *Eros and Civilization: A Philosophical Inquiry into Freud* (Boston: Beacon Press, 1955), 4, 16–20.
13. Ibid., xxvii.
14. S. Freud, *The Ego and the Id*, trans. J. Riviere, ed. J. Strachey (New York: W. W. Norton, 1960), 75.
15. Frosh, *Politics of Psychoanalysis*, 160.
16. E. Kurzweil, *The Age of Structuralism: Levi-Strauss to Foucault* (New York: Columbia University Press, 1980), 19.
17. See J. Lacan, *Ecrits: A Selection*, trans. A. Sherdan (New York: W. W. Norton, 1977).
18. Ibid., 1–7.
19. T. Eagleton, *Literary Theory: An Introduction* (Oxford: Basil Blackwell, 1983), 165–67.

20. Lacan, *Ecrits*, 147.
21. Eagleton, *Literary Theory*, 168–69.
22. S. Schneiderman, *Jacques Lacan: The Death of an Intellectual Hero* (Cambridge: Harvard University Press, 1983), 57, 118, 134, 151.
23. P. Gabel, "Dukakis's Defeat and the Transformative Possibilities of Legal Culture," *Tikkun*, March/April 1989, 15–16.
24. Ibid., 107–109.
25. J. Brenkman, *Culture and Domination* (Ithaca: Cornell University Press, 1987), 149–55, 174.
26. E. Ragland-Sullivan, *Jacques Lacan and the Philosophy of Psychoanalysis* (Chicago: University of Illinois Press, 1987), 272–73.
27. P. Smith, *Discerning the Subject* (Minneapolis: University of Minnesota Press, 1988), 20–23.
28. Gabel, "Dukakis's Defeat," 16, 106–109.
29. Brenkman, *Culture and Domination*, 166–68.
30. Ibid., 150.
31. Ibid., 167–68.
32. Ibid., 160–61.

CHAPTER 5

1. L. Goodstein, *Washington Post*, January 14, 1992, A3.
2. E. Cahn, *The Sense of Injustice: An Anthropocentric View of Law* (New York: New York University Press, 1949). Interestingly, Cahn does not include these types of injustices in his own list of types of injustices.
3. Ibid., 102.
4. For a vivid account of this horrid event, largely unknown in the United States, see N. Chomsky and E. Herman, *The Washington Connection and Third World Fascism*, vol. 1 (Boston: South End Press, 1979), 205–18.
5. J. Shklar, *The Faces of Injustice* (New Haven: Yale University Press, 1990).
6. E. Wolgast, *The Grammar of Justice* (Ithaca: Cornell University Press, 1987).
7. See *Justice: Alternative Political Perspectives*, ed. J. Sterba (Belmont: Wadsworth, 1992).
8. "[M]ost worked-out views as to what constitutes injustice involve at least an outline image of justice in a positive sense which goes beyond putting right the wrongs that have been done and include an impression of just human relationships." T. Campbell, *Justice* (Atlantic Highlands: Humanities Press International, 1988), 1.
9. This holds a lesson for communitarians, who advocate constructing a theory of the good. A theory of the bad creates far fewer difficulties than a theory of the good. Violations of liberty seem less likely to occur in avoiding harm than in promoting the good. When restraints on liberty do occur in the avoidance of harm, they are generally easier to justify than those restraints resulting from promoting the good. For example, countering the harm of racism may or may not result in promoting the good of integration.
10. J. Rawls, *A Theory of Justice* (Cambridge: Belknap Press, 1971), 8.
11. Ibid., 9.
12. Cunningham adopts the phrase "philosophy in the middle range" to describe this type of approach. F. Cunningham, *Democratic Theory and Socialism* (New York: Cambridge University Press, 1987), 19.
13. Campbell, *Justice*, 1–2.
14. "Where justice is thought of in the customary manner as an ideal mode or condition, the human response will be merely contemplative, and

contemplation bakes no loaves. But the response to a real or imagined instance of injustice is something quite different; it is alive with the movement and warmth in the human organism." Cahn, *Sense of Injustice*, 13. Wolgast objects to construing justice as an ideal, for "if justice were an ideal, it would not be subject to compromise." Wolgast, *Grammar of Injustice*, 135, fn. 19.

15. "The disillusionments men experience come from looking for justice in mansions, where it is not to be found, instead of at the street corners where it makes its appearance." Cahn, *Sense of Injustice*, 176.

16. "Philosophers rarely talk about cruelty. They have left it to the dramatists and historians, who have not neglected it." J. Shklar, *Ordinary Vices* (Cambridge: Harvard University Press, 1984), 7.

17. Wolgast, *Grammar of Justice*, 146.

18. "First and foremost it is the special kind of anger we feel when we are denied promised benefits and when we do not get what we believe to be our due." Shklar, *Faces of Injustice*, 83. I think that anger resulting from injustice operates on an even more primal level than a disappointed expectation. The feeling arises from harm done to ourselves or to another, irrespective of our expectations.

19. Ibid., 103.

20. Ibid., 87.

21. Rawls, *Theory of Justice*, Sec. 24.

22. Ibid., 137.

23. Gabriel Marcel notes, "We flee the suffering of others, avoiding those whose disease seems incurable. Thus a gulf widens between those who are happy and those who are not, and we end up feeling hatred and contempt for those who suffer." G. Marcel, "Creative Fidelity," in *Creative Fidelity*, trans. R. Rosthal (New York: Crossroad Publishing, 1982), 245.

24. B. Moore, *Reflections on the Causes of Human Misery and Upon Certain Proposals to Eliminate Them* (Boston: Beacon Press, 1972), 11.

25. H. K. Beecher, *Disease and the Advancement of Science* (Cambridge: Harvard University Press, 1960), 228.

26. D. Bakan, "Pain—The Existential Symptom," in *Philosophical Dimensions of the Neuro-Medical Sciences*, vol. 2, ed. S. Spicker and H. Engelhardt, Jr. (Dordrecht, the Netherlands: D. Reidel Publishing, 1976), 205.

27. S. Brownmiller, *Against Our Will: Men, Women and Rape* (New York: Bantam, 1975).

28. Shklar, *Faces of Injustice*, 116.

29. Wasserstrom has provided an in-depth argument for the elimination of group difference. See R. Wasserstrom, "On Racism and Sexism," in R. Wasserstrom, *Philosophy and Social Issues* (Notre Dame: University of Notre Dame Press, 1980).

30. For an excellent analysis of the positive aspects of group identity see I. Young, *Justice and the Politics of Difference* (Princeton: Princeton University Press, 1990), chapter 5.

31. Ibid., 167.

32. Ibid., 163.

33. S. Estrich, *Real Rape* (Cambridge: Harvard University Press, 1987).

34. Ibid., 36.

35. There is some evidence to link identity with an ethnic group and tolerance for pain. Italian women showed lower pain tolerance levels than Jewish or Irish women. See the works cited in B. Tursky, "The Evalua-

tion of Pain Responses: A Need for Improved Measures," in *Philosophical Dimensions*, 212.

36. S. Lukes, *Power* (New York: Macmillan, 1974).

37. Lukes has in mind R. Dahl's intuitive idea of power, "A has power over B to the extent that he can get B to do something that B would not otherwise do." R. Dahl, "The Concept of Power," *Behavioral Science* 2 (1957): 201–15.

38. Holden and Schumpeter, to take just two examples, formulate their definitions of democracy in terms of decision making.

39. Here Lukes addresses the works of P. Bachrach and M. Baratz, "The Two Faces of Power," *American Political Science Review* 56 (1962): 947–52; "Decisions and Nondecisions: An Analytic Framework," *American Political Science Review* 57 (1963): 641–51; *Power and Poverty: Theory and Practice* (New York: Oxford University Press, 1970).

40. Lukes, *Power*, 21.

41. Ibid., 24.

42. T. Wartenberg, *The Forms of Power: From Domination to Transformation* (Philadelphia: Temple University Press, 1990).

43. Ibid., 74.

44. M. Foucault, *Power/Knowledge*, ed. C. Gordon (New York: Pantheon, 1980).

45. F. Fanon, *Wretched of the Earth* (New York: Grove Press, 1963), 53.

46. Shklar, *Faces of Injustice*, 35.

47. Proponents of a proceduralist conception of democracy include C. Cohen, *Democracy* (Athens: University of Georgia Press, 1971); P. Singer, *Democracy and Disobedience* (Oxford: Oxford University Press, 1973); C. Beitz, *Political Equality: An Essay in Democratic Theory* (Princeton: Princeton University Press, 1989).

48. Some democratic theorists remain nonplussed even by the formal exclusion of otherwise qualified groups from the *demos*. See J. Schumpeter, *Capitalism, Socialism, and Democracy* (New York: Harper and Brothers, 1947), 243–45.

49. R. Dahl, *Democracy and Its Critics* (New Haven: Yale University Press, 1989), 129.

50. M. Minow, *Making All the Difference: Inclusion, Exclusion, and American Law* (Ithaca: Cornell University Press, 1990), 127.

51. "The scope of citizenship itself becomes a subject for ongoing democratic discussion and review." B. Barber, *Strong Democracy: Participatory Politics for a New Age* (Berkeley: University of California Press, 1984), 227.

52. J. Williams, "Race and Japan: A Cross-Cultural Journey," *Washington Post Magazine*, January 5, 1992, 25.

53. Open and fluid competition between interest groups characterizes a classical pluralist version of democracy. See R. Dahl, *A Preface to Democratic Theory* (Chicago: University of Chicago Press, 1956), 133, where he defines *polyarchy* (a realist's version of democracy) as "government by minorities."

54. Cahn, *Sense of Injustice*, 102.

CHAPTER 6

1. "Radical" and "liberal" are terms of multiple definition and use. I consider a radical critique to be one that calls for revolutionary or fundamental change of some sort, but not necessarily military overthrow, or political upheaval, or even immediate social change. That is, on my view,

a radical critique can call for incremental or evolutionary change, so long as the ultimate goal is monumental or profound. "Liberal" is harder to define because it standardly encompasses a broad swath of views ranging from communitarian to libertarian. But usually liberals are thought to fall somewhere between those two poles. I believe that all liberals are committed to freedom, justice, and the significance of individuals, although they may interpret these values in very different ways. Thus, on my view, it is possible for a radical critique to rest on liberal values. The two positions are not categorically antagonistic. However, whether a particular radical critique is compatible with a particular liberal view depends on the particulars of both. I will use the term "liberal" to stand for a commitment to freedom, justice in the form of equal treatment, and the significance of individuals.

2. *Reed v. Reed*, 404 U.S. 71 (1971).
3. 411 U.S. 677 (1973).
4. 410 U.S. 113 (1973).
5. 414 U.S. 632 (1974).
6. 417 U.S. 484 (1974).
7. See *Newport News Ship. and Dry Dock v. E.E.O.C.*, 103 S. Ct. 2622 (1983). The general rationale is that individuals cannot be treated differently on the basis of sex unless there is some clearly specifiable difference that justifies different treatment. Thus, so long as the sexes are similar they must be treated the same.
8. C. Littleton, "Reconstructing Equality," *Calif. L. Rev.* 75 (1987): 1279.
9. C. MacKinnon, *Toward a Feminist Theory of the State* (Cambridge: Harvard University Press, 1989).
10. Ibid., 237–38.
11. D. Rhode, *Justice and Gender* (Cambridge: Harvard University Press, 1989).
12. Littleton, "Reconstructing Equality."
13. N. Taub and W. Williams, "Will Equality Require More . . .?" *Rutgers L. Rev./ Civ. Rts. Dev.* 37 (1985): 825.
14. See *Griggs v. Duke Power*, 401 U.S. 424 (1971).
15. M. Minow, "Foreword: Justice Engendered," *Harvard L. Rev.* 101 (1987): 10.
16. The common formulation of the early debate over women's rights illustrates the problem. It was asked whether women, being different, should argue for equal rights or for special rights. Equal rights (i.e., identical rights) seemed to disadvantage women sometimes (e.g., as to pregnancy benefits), and so some argued that special rights were needed to accommodate women's special needs and circumstances. Others argued that only equal (i.e., identical) rights should be claimed because any special needs or differences acknowledged by women are always used to limit women in the long run, and special rights will be viewed as special favors that accommodate women's deficiencies. The problem is that if that is the way the issue is formulated, then women lose either way because the (unstated) norm is male. After all, who is it that women are different from? Whose rights (if equality is the standard) should women's rights be equal to? And if women's rights should sometimes be different from men's, why is it women's rights that are characterized as special? Why not formulate rights in terms of women's needs and characterize men's rights as special? One way makes as much sense as the other. The question is, who is the norm?
17. Minow, "Justice Engendered."

18. Some feminists consider all these principles to be patriarchal, but most feminists either do not specify their position on this point or hold a more contextually based view rather like that expressed here.

19. MacKinnon, *Toward a Feminist Theory*.

20. In *Reed v. Reed*, for example, it was held that a woman could not be barred from being the executrix of an estate on the basis of her sex, since there was no demonstrable difference between men and women in regard to administering an estate. The (patriarchal) state law that excluded all women as a class from that activity was clearly contradicted by our supposedly universal commitment to freedom and equal treatment and by our constitutional commitment to equal protection of the law.

21. See, e.g., D. Rhode, "The 'No Problem' Problem: Feminist Challenges and Cultural Change," *Yale L. J.* 100 (1991): 1731.

22. 628 F. Supp. 1264 (N.D. Ill. 1986).

23. It is worth noting that in *Castro v. Beecher*, 334 F. Supp. 930, 936 (D. Mass. 1976), an almost identical argument, that the underrepresentation of blacks in law enforcement was simply due to their lack of interest, was rejected by the court as racist. And in *Glover v. Johnson*, 478 F. Supp. 1075, 1086–88 (E. D. Mich. 1979), the argument that women did not need vocational training since women preferred unskilled jobs anyway was also rejected as prejudice. Thus, in the past courts have rejected justifications of disparities based on supposed lack of interest.

24. The court also ignored expert testimony from a historian who argued that history shows that women accept more competitive jobs whenever they become available. See J. Williams, "Deconstructing Gender," *Mich. L. Rev.* 87 (1989): 797.

25. Ibid.

26. The Sears managers, the statistical analyst, and the guidebook for hiring all systematically discounted applications of women for traditionally male positions (such as commission sales). The statistical analyst explained on the witness stand exactly how she went about discounting all applications of women for "male" jobs. Yet the court accepted this approach as appropriately reflecting the (supposed) interests of women, despite conflicting testimony by women that they had in fact wanted commission sales positions. This demonstrates the power of stereotypes, once accepted. See ibid., 813–20.

27. For example, in *Plessy v. Ferguson*, 163 U.S. 537, the case that established the legitimacy of racial segregation under the equal protection clause, the Court said (among other things): "The object of the amendment was undoubtedly to enforce the absolute equality of the two races before the law, but, in the nature of things, it could not have been intended to abolish distinctions based upon color, or to enforce social, as distinguished from political, equality, or a commingling of the two races upon terms unsatisfactory to either." Segregation was the norm. A mere constitutional amendment requiring racial equality could not rebut the presumption of the legitimacy of the status quo, hence the Court's interpretation of "equal protection" allowed the norm to stand. It appears clearly unjust to us today, but at the time it seemed perfectly reasonable, which attests to the strength of the status quo. How many reasonable and defensible sexist judgments of the 1980s and 1990s will seem similarly outrageous fifty years from now? We haven't the distance to tell.

28. During the Vietnam War 59,000 soldiers were killed, causing a storm of

public outrage. During the same period 54,000 women were killed by their male partners, without so much as a whisper of public protest. We can say we didn't know. (That's what the Germans said about the Jews.) But why didn't we know? It was public record. We didn't want to know. And we still don't. Women's voices are louder now, but we still mostly ignored the recent Senate report (Senate Report no. 197, 102nd Cong., 1st Sess. (1991)) noting that both rape and domestic violence have sharply increased in the past decade. Four million women are severely battered every year, the leading cause of injury for U.S. women (much greater than assault by strangers). From 2000 to 4000 women are now murdered by their male partners yearly. In 1990 more women were beaten by their male partners than were married. Nor can the increase of rape and battery be fully explained by better reporting, because the government systematically underestimates the numbers of such victims. See Senate Report no. 197.

29. Again using domestic violence as my example, women cannot escape this harm without legal intervention. Three-fourths of all reported domestic violence assaults occur after a woman has left her partner, and the majority of murdered battered women are killed after they leave. Between 1983 and 1987 battered women shelters reported over a 100 percent increase in women seeking refuge, and 1 million per year were turned away for lack of space. Yet funding in the past five years has been decreased. Half of all homeless women in the United States in the past decade were refugees of domestic violence. But legal response has been slow. Only fifteen states have laws that prosecute batterers and protect victims. See *gen.* K. Culliton, "Domestic Violence Legislation in Chile and the U.S." (unpublished manuscript).

CHAPTER 7

1. C. Gilligan, *In a Different Voice* (London: Harvard University Press, 1982); K. Silverman, *The Acoustic Mirror: The Female Voice in Psychoanalysis and Feminism* (Indianapolis and Bloomington: Indiana University Press, 1988); C. Gilligan, N. P. Lyons, and T. J. Hanmer, *Making Connections* (Cambridge: Harvard University Press, 1990).

2. L. Irigaray, *This Sex Which Is Not One*, trans. C. Porter (Ithaca: Cornell University Press, 1985), and *Speculum and the Other Woman*, trans. G. C. Gill (Ithaca: Cornell University Press, 1985); J. Kristeva, *Revolution in Poetic Language* (New York: Columbia University Press, 1984).

3. E. H. Barauck and L. Serrano, *Women Analyze Women in France, England, and the United States* (New York and London: Wheatsheaf, 1988); L. Brown and C. Gilligan, *Meeting at the Crossroads* (Cambridge: Harvard University Press, 1993); M. F. Belenky et al., *Women's Ways of Knowing: The Development of Self, Voice, and Mind* (New York: Basic Books, 1986).

4. J. Sayers, *Biological Politics: Feminist and Anti-Feminist Perspectives* (London: Tavistock, 1982); P. J. Mills, *Women, Nature and Psyche* (New Haven and London: Yale University Press, 1987); C. Pateman, *The Sexual Contract* (Cambridge: Polity Press, 1988).

5. J. Kristeva, *Desire in Language* (New York: Columbia University Press, 1980); *The Kristeva Reader*, ed. T. Moi (New York: Columbia University Press, 1986).

6. See, e.g., J. Sayers, *Sexual Contradictions: Psychology and Feminism* (London: Tavistock, 1986); *Coming to Terms: Feminism, Theory, Politics*, ed. E. Weed (New York and London: Routledge, 1989); T. Moi, *Sexual/Textual Politics:*

Feminist Literary Theory (London: Methuen, 1985); M. Whitford, *Luce Irigaray: Philosophy in the Feminine* (New York and London: Routledge, 1991).

7. C. Smart, *Feminism and the Power of the Law* (New York and London: Routledge, 1989); C. MacKinnon, *Toward a Feminist Theory of the State* (Cambridge: Harvard University Press, 1989).

8. C. MacKinnon, *Feminism Unmodified: Discourses on Life and Law* (London: Harvard University Press, 1987); "Feminism, Marxism, Method, and the State: Agenda for Theory," *Signs* 7 (1982): 515–44; "Feminism, Marxism, Method, and the State: Toward Feminist Jurisprudence," *Signs* 8 (1983): 635–58.

9. B. Arrigo, "Deconstructing Jurisprudence: An Experiential Feminist Critique," *Journal of Human Justice* 4, no. 1 (1992): 13–30; C. Littleton, "In Search of a Feminist Jurisprudence," *Harvard Women's L. J.* 10 (1987): 1.

10. B. Arrigo, "An Experientially-Informed Feminist Jurisprudence: Rape and the Move Toward Praxis," *Humanity and Society* 17 (1993): 28–47; C. Weedon, *Feminist Practice and Poststructuralist Theory* (Oxford: Basil Blackwell, 1987).

11. B. Arrigo, "Feminist Jurisprudence and Imaginative Discourse: Toward Praxis and Critique," in *Legality and Illegality*, ed. R. Janikowski and D. Milovanovic (New York: Peter Lang (forthcoming)); *Feminist Criticism: Theory and Practice*, ed. S. Sellers (New York: Wheatsheaf, 1991).

12. *Feminine Sexuality: Jacques Lacan and the École Freudienne*, ed. J. Mitchell and J. Rose, trans. J. Rose (New York: W. W. Norton, 1982).

13. Arrigo, "Deconstructing Jurisprudence."

14. D. Milovanovic, "Juridico-Linguistic Communicative Markets: Toward a Semiotic Analysis," *Contemporary Crises* 10 (1986): 281–304.

15. B. Arrigo, "Rooms for the Misbegotten: On SRO Social Designing and Social Deviance," *Journal of Sociology and Social Welfare* 21, no. 4 (forthcoming, 1994); "Deconstructing Jurisprudence"; "Rape and the Move Toward Praxis"; "Toward Praxis and Critique."

16. M. Foucault, *Madness and Civilization: A History of Insanity in the Age of Reason*, trans. R. Howard (New York: Vintage/Random House, 1965); *The Order of Things: An Archeology of the Human Sciences* (New York: Pantheon, 1970); *The Archeology of Knowledge* (New York: Pantheon, 1972); *Power/Knowledge: Selected Interviews and Other Writings 1972–1977* (London: Harvester, 1980).

17. Smart, *Feminism and the Power of the Law.*

18. Irigaray, *This Sex.*

19. E. Husserl, *Ideas Pertaining to a Pure Phenomenology and to a Phenomenological Philosophy*, trans. F. Kersten (The Hague: Martinus Nijhoff Publishers, 1983).

20. Gilligan, *Different Voice*; Gilligan, Lyons, and Hanmer, *Making Connections*; MacKinnon, "Agenda for Theory"; "Toward Feminist Jurisprudence"; *Feminism Unmodified*; *Toward a Feminist Theory.*

21. Foucault, *Madness and Civilization.*

22. E. Murray, *Imaginative Thinking and Human Existence* (Pittsburgh: Duquesne University Press, 1986).

23. Smart, *Feminism and the Power of the Law.*

24. Ibid., 9.

25. A. Bottomley, "Feminism in Law Schools," in *Women and the Law*, ed. S. McLaughlin (London: College of London Press, 1987).

26. Smart, *Feminism and the Power of the Law*, 21.

27. S. Dahl, "Taking Women as a Starting Point: Building Women's Law," *International Journal of the Sociology of Law* 14 (1986): 239–47.
28. Ibid., 32.
29. Smart, *Feminism and the Power of the Law*, 25.
30. Irigaray, *This Sex*, 86.
31. J. Lacan, *Ecrits: A Selection*, trans. A. Sheridan (New York: W. W. Norton, 1977); *The Four Fundamental Concepts of Psycho-Analysis*, trans. A. Sheridan (New York: W. W. Norton, 1978).
32. Irigaray, *This Sex*, 70.
33. Ibid., 72.
34. Ibid., 24.
35. Ibid., 25.
36. Ibid., 28.
37. Ibid., 75.
38. Ibid., 80.
39. Husserl, *Ideas Pertaining to a Pure Phenomenology*.
40. See, e.g., J. Baudrillard, *Selected Writings*, ed. M. Poster (Stanford: Stanford University Press, 1988); J. Habermas, *Reason and Rationalization of Society*, vol. 1 of *Communicative Action*, trans. T. McCarthy (Boston: Beacon Press, 1984); J. Derrida, *Of Grammatology* (Baltimore: Johns Hopkins University Press, 1976); G. Deleuze and F. Guattari, *Anti-Oedipus: Capitalism and Schizophrenia*, trans. R. Hurley, M. Seem, and H. R. Lane (New York: Viking, 1977); I. M. Young, *Justice and the Politics of Difference* (Princeton: Princeton University Press, 1990).
41. Gilligan, *Different Voice*; Gilligan, Lyons, and Hanmer, *Making Connections*; MacKinnon, "Agenda for Theory"; "Toward Feminist Jurisprudence"; *Feminism Unmodified*.
42. Gilligan, Lyons, and Hanmer, *Making Connections*, 3.
43. Ibid., 4.
44. MacKinnon, *Feminism Unmodified*, 38–39.
45. Gilligan, Lyons, and Hanmer, *Making Connections*, 3.
46. Foucault, *Power/Knowledge*.
47. Murray, *Imaginative Thinking*, 68.
48. M. Heidegger, *Being and Time*, trans. J. MacQuarrie and E. Robinson (New York: Harper and Row, 1964).
49. Murray, *Imaginative Thinking*, 69.
50. Ibid.
51. P. Ricoeur, "Creativity of Language," *Philosophy Today* 17 (1973): 111.
52. I. A. Richards, *The Philosophy of Rhetoric* (Oxford: Oxford University Press, 1936).
53. J. Swift, *Polite Conversation* (Oxford: Oxford University Press, 1738/1963), 53.
54. Murray, "The Phenomenon of Metaphor," *Phenomenological Psychology* 2 (1975): 281.
55. S. Langer, *Philosophy in a New Key* (New York: New American Library, 1951).
56. P. Wheelright, *Metaphor and Reality* (Bloomington: Indiana University Press, 1968).
57. Ibid., 129.
58. Irigaray, *This Sex*, 68–85.
59. Murray, *Imaginative Thinking*, 159–63.
60. Ibid., 169.

61. MacKinnon, *Feminism Unmodified.*

62. G. Morgan, *Imagination* (Beverly Hills: Sage Publications, 1993) and *Images of Organization* (Beverly Hills: Sage Publications, 1986); J. L. McKnight, "Regenerating Community," *Social Policy* 17 (1987): 54–58.

63. J. S. Ott, *The Organization Culture Perspective* (Belmont, CA: Dorsey Press, 1988).

64. Arrigo, "Rooms for the Misbegotten."

65. R. Unger, *False Necessity* (New York: Cambridge University Press, 1987).

66. Foucault, *Power/Knowledge.*

67. Ibid., 93.

68. W. Woodhull, "Sexuality and the Question of Rape," in *Feminism and Foucault,* ed. I. Diamond and L. Quinby (Boston: Northeastern University Press, 1988), 161.

69. Ibid., 168.

70. Ibid., 169.

71. Ibid., 171.

CHAPTER 8

* Reprinted from *Criminal Justice Ethics* 1989 (Winter/Spring): 30–50, by permission of The Institute for Criminal Justice Ethics, 899 Tenth Avenue, New York, NY 10019.

1. F. Engels, "Letter to Conrad Schmidt, October 1890," in K. Marx, *Selected Works,* ed. V. Adoratsky (Moscow and Leningrad: Co-operative Publishing Society of Foreign Workers in the U.S.S.R., 1935), 386.

2. On the difference between radicalism and Marxism, and for a general discussion of Marxism and criminology, see J. Reiman and S. Headlee, "Marxism and Criminal Justice Policy," *Crime and Delinquency* 27, no. 1 (1981): 24–47; J. Reiman, "Marxist Explanations and Radical Misinterpretations: A Reply to Greenberg and Humphries," *Crime and Delinquency* 28, no. 4 (1982): 610–17; see also A. Hunt, "The Radical Critique of Law: An Assessment," *International Journal of the Sociology of Law* 8 (1980): 33–46.

3. "In the course of our investigations we shall find, in general, that the characters who appear on the economic stage are but the personifications of the economic relations that exist between them." K. Marx, *Capital,* 3 vols. (New York: International Publishers, 1967), 1:85.

4. "The history of all hitherto existing society is the history of class struggles." K. Marx and F. Engels, *The Communist Manifesto* (New York: Penguin Books, 1967), 79.

5. Marx, *Capital,* 1:819.

6. Note here that Marx does not hold that the value of a commodity is equivalent to the actual amount of labor-time that goes into producing it. On that view, commodities would increase in value the more inefficiently they were produced. Instead, Marx, recognizing that a commodity will command a price no higher than that for which commodities like it are selling, takes the commodity's value to be determined by the average or socially necessary labor-time it takes to produce commodities of its kind. See *Capital,* 189. Furthermore, while Marx claims that value is equivalent to average labor-time, he assumes that values and market prices coincide only for the purposes of the argument of volume 1 of *Capital,* about the fundamental nature of capitalism. In the subsequent volumes, Marx shows at length the mechanisms in capitalism that lead prices to diverge from values. Even after these common misinterpretations of the theory

are eliminated, it must be admitted that Marx's labor theory of value has come in for so much criticism in recent years that many, even many Marxists, have given it up for dead. While I think that obituaries are premature, I also think that a trimmed-down version of the theory (one that doesn't claim to account for price formation, but simply insists that labor-time is what matters about economic products) avoids the criticisms and suffices to support Marx's account of capitalist exploitation. For a sketch and defense of this trimmed-down version of the labor theory, as well as an analysis of the "structural force" in capitalism, see J. Reiman, "Exploitation, Force, and the Moral Assessment of Capitalism: Thoughts on Roemer and Cohen," *Philosophy & Public Affairs* 16, no. 1 (1987): 3–41.

7. Marx, *Capital*, 1:171.
8. Ibid., 1:193–94.
9. Ibid., 1:184–86.
10. Ibid., 1:534.
11. Ibid., 1:309.
12. Ibid., 1:766.
13. Ibid., 1:737.
14. See, e.g., G. W. Domhoff, *Who Rules America?* (Englewood Cliffs: Prentice-Hall, 1967); M. Green, J. Fallows, and D. Zwick, *The Ralph Nader Congress Project: Who Runs Congress?* (Toronto and New York: Bantam Books, 1972); E. Greenberg, *Serving the Few: Corporate Capitalism and the Bias of Government Policy* (New York: Wiley, 1974); R. Miliband, *The State in Capitalist Society* (New York: Basic Books, 1969).
15. K. Marx, "Preface" in *A Contribution to a Critique of Political Economy*, in *The Marx-Engels Reader*, ed. P. Tucker (Guilford: Norton Publishing, 1978), 5.
16. Scholars generally agree that the term *ideology* was coined by Antoine Destutt de Tracy, who was among the intellectuals named in 1795 to direct the researches of the newly founded Institut de France. The *idéologues* of the Institut generally believed that existing ideas were prejudices rooted in individual psychology or in political conditions and that the path to liberation from these prejudices and thus toward a rational society lay in a science of the causes of ideas (literally, an *idea-ology*). Thomas Jefferson tried, unsuccessfully, to have Destutt de Tracy's theory made part of the original curriculum of the University of Virginia. See G. Lichtheim, "The Concept of Ideology," *History and Theory* 4, no. 2 (1965): 64–95.
17. K. Marx and F. Engels, *The German Ideology* (New York: International Publishers, 1947), 14.
18. Ibid., 19.
19. Marx, "Preface," 4.
20. Marx and Engels, *The German Ideology*, 14.
21. Marx, "Preface," 4.
22. "It is not the subject who deceives himself, but *reality* which deceives him." See Godelier, "Structure and Contradiction in Capital," in *Ideology in Social Science*, ed. R. Blackburn (New York: Vintage Books, 1973), 337.
23. For examples of theories of ideology that, in my view, do not adequately distinguish the falsity of ideology from the truth of science, see B. Fine, *Economic Theory and Ideology* (New York: Holmes and Meier, 1980), 1–2; see also G. Therborn, *The Ideology of Power and the Power of Ideology* (London: NLB, 1980), 4–5.
24. Examples of theories of ideology that trace its distortions to subjective illusions are the attempt by some members of the Frankfurt School to explain the affection of German laborers for fascism by means of a Freudian

account of the persistence of irrational authoritarian attitudes and the attempt of some sociologists to trace ideology to an existential need to reify a mythic worldview as protection against the terrors of meaninglessness. For the former, see M. Jay, *The Dialectical Imagination: A History of the Frankfurt School and the Institute for Social Research, 1923–1950* (Boston: Little, Brown, 1973). For the latter, see P. Berger and T. Luckmann, *The Social Construction of Reality: A Treatise in the Sociology of Knowledge* (Garden City: Doubleday, 1966).

25. Note that I am speaking of the general ideology of capitalism, rather than, say, the ideology of groups within capitalism, such as small shopowners or Catholics. For examples of Marxian analyses directed primarily to the study of the specific ideologies of particular groups within society, see C. Sumner, *Reading Ideologies: An Introduction into the Marxist Theory of Ideology and Law* (New York: Academic Press, 1979); see also Therborn, *The Ideology of Power*.

26. Marx, *Capital*, 1:176.

27. Ibid., 1:169.

28. Ibid., 1:72.

29. Ibid., 1:73.

30. See, e.g., ibid., 1:337.

31. K. Marx, *The Poverty of Philosophy* (Moscow: Foreign Languages Publishing House, 1955), 75.

32. E. Pashukanis, *Law and Marxism: A General Theory*, trans. B. Einhorn, ed. C. Arthur (London: Ink Links, 1978).

33. Marx, *Capital*, 1:88–89.

34. "The labor contract is to be freely entered into by both parties. But it is considered to have been freely entered into as soon as the law makes both parties equal *on paper*. The power conferred on the one party by the difference of class position, the pressure thereby brought to bear on the other party—the real economic position of both—that is not the law's business." F. Engels, *The Origin of the Family, Private Property, and the State* (New York: International Publishers, 1942), 64.

35. Pashukanis, *Law and Marxism*, 86–87, inter alia.

36. The classic case is G. Hegel, *The Philosophy of Right*, trans. T. Knox (New York: Oxford University Press, 1942).

37. Pashukanis, *Law and Marxism*, 86–87.

38. Marx, *Capital*, 1:615.

39. The classic case is J. Austin, *The Province of Jurisprudence Determined and the Uses of the Study of Jurisprudence* (New York: Noonday Press, 1954).

40. Pashukanis writes that "state authority introduces clarity and stability into the structure of law, but does not create the premises for it, which are rooted in the material conditions of production." Pashukanis, *Law and Marxism*, 94, 123. For a lucid account of law as stabilizing already-existing social practices and of the theoretical puzzles surrounding that notion, see H. Collins, *Marxism and Law* (New York: Oxford University Press, 1982), 77–90.

41. Pashukanis approvingly attributes to Aristotle "the definition of crime as an involuntarily concluded contract." Pashukanis, *Law and Marxism*, 169.

42. Pashukanis observes that the exchange contract, or *pactum*, derives from *pax* or peace. *Law and Marxism*, 167.

43. See J. Reiman, *The Rich Get Richer and the Poor Get Prison: Ideology, Class, and Criminal Justice* (New York: Pantheon, 1975), 141–42.

44. Ibid., 52–60.

45. One Marxist historian who has emphasized this aspect of the law is
    E. P. Thompson, *Whigs and Hunters: The Origins of the Black Act* (New
    York: Pantheon, 1975).
46. Marx, *Capital*, 1:231–97, 312–21.
47. Pashukanis, *Law and Marxism*, 169. See also A. Norrie, "Pashukanis and
    'the Commodity Form Theory': A Reply to Warrington," *International Journal
    of the Sociology of Law* 10 (1982): 431–34.
48. Pashukanis, *Law and Marxism*, 177.
49. See G. Rusche and O. Kirchheimer, *Punishment and Social Structure* (New
    York: Russell & Russell, 1968) for a classic Marxian-inspired historical
    study of the relationship between penal policy and the supply of and
    demand for labor.
50. B. Fine, *Democracy and the Rule of Law* (London: Pluto Press, 1984);
    R. Warrington, "Pashukanis and the Commodity Form Theory," *Inter-
    national Journal of the Sociology of Law* 9 (1984): 10–11; see also Norrie,
    "Pashukanis and 'the Commodity Form Theory,'" 425–27.
51. Collins, *Marxism and Law*, 109.
52. D. Milovanovic, "The Commodity-Exchange Theory of Law: In Search
    of a Perspective," *Crime and Social Justice* 16 (Winter 1981): 42.
53. Warrington, "Pashukanis and the Commodity Form Theory," 12; see also
    Norrie, "Pashukanis and 'the Commodity Form Theory,'" 424–25.
54. This is the view of, for example, A. Buchanan in *Marx and Justice* (Totowa:
    Rowman and Littlefield, 1982).
55. This is essentially the view argued for by, for example, A. Wood in "The
    Marxian Critique of Justice," *Philosophy and Public Affairs* 1, no. 3 (Spring
    1972): 244–82.
56. This is the view of, for example, M. Cohen in "Freedom, Justice, and
    Capitalism," *New Left Review* 126 (1981): 3–16. There is, by the way, a
    substantial literature on the question of whether Marxism holds that capi-
    talism is wrong because unjust or that justice is part of what is wrong
    with capitalism. See articles in *Marx, Justice, and History*, ed. M. Cohen, T.
    Nagel, and T. Scanlon (Princeton: Princeton University Press, 1980); *Marx
    and Morality*, ed. K. Nielsen and S. Patten, *Canadian Journal of Philosophy* 7
    (Suppl., 1981); *Nomos XXVI: Marxism*, ed. J. Pennock and J. Chapman (New
    York: New York University Press, 1983). See also N. Geras's review of the
    whole discussion in "The Controversy About Marx and Justice," *New Left
    Review* 150 (1985): 47–85. My own views are presented in "The Possibility of
    a Marxian Theory of Justice," in *Marx and Morality*, 307–22.
57. See, e.g., W. Bonger, *Criminality and Economic Conditions*, trans. H. Horton
    (Bloomington: Indiana University Press, 1969), 7–12, 40–47; D. Gordon,
    "Capitalism, Class, and Crime in America," *Crime and Delinquency* 19,
    no. 2 (1973): 174; and I. Taylor, "Against Crime and for Socialism," *Crime
    and Social Justice: Issues on Criminology* 18 (Winter 1982): 10.

CHAPTER 9

* Reprinted with permission from *Philosophy and Social Criticism*, where the
article appeared in Vol. 17, No. 4, p. 265, under the title "Contractualism,
Democracy, and Social Law: Basic Antinomies in Liberal Thought."

1. *Neoliberalism*, as it is used here, must be distinguished from the American neoliberalism of the 1980s, which advocated less government regulation
   of the economy.

2. Marx already perceived this contradiction in Hegel's political philosophy. See K. Marx, *Critique of Hegel's Philosophy of Right* (Cambridge: Cambridge University Press, 1970), 41 ff., and D. Ingram, "Rights and Privileges: Marx and the Jewish Question," *Studies in Soviet Thought* 35 (1988): 125–45.

3. Cf. F. Hayek, *The Road to Serfdom* (Chicago: University of Chicago Press, 1944), 52: *Law, Legislation and Liberty*, vol. 2 (Chicago: University of Chicago Press, 1976), 69.

4. Cf. S. P. Huntington et al., *The Crisis of Democracy: Report on the Governability of Democracies to the Trilateral Commission* (New York: New York University Press, 1975).

5. Any theory is contractualist that grounds public authority on an agreement between individuals conceived exclusively as private utility maximizers. So construed, social contract theories that acknowledge common moral ends (such as those inspired by Kant) are not purely contractualist.

6. Cf. L. Strauss, *Natural Right and History* (Chicago: University of Chicago Press, 1953).

7. Cf. Plato's scathing caricature of democracy in Book 8 of the *Republic*, trans. G. M. A. Grube (Indianapolis: Hackett Publishing, 1974), and Aristotle's preference for restricting participation to "husbandmen and those of modest fortune" (*Politics*, trans. B. Jowett (Oxford: Clarendon Press, 1905), 4.6.1292b, 6.4.1318b).

8. The following account of market assumptions in liberalism owes much to C. B. Macpherson's *The Political Theory of Possessive Individualism: Hobbes to Locke* (Oxford: Clarendon Press, 1962); *The Life and Times of Liberal Democracy* (Oxford: Oxford University Press, 1977); and *Democratic Theory: Essays in Retrieval* (Oxford: Clarendon Press, 1973).

9. As Hobbes puts it, "because the major part hath by consenting voices declared a Soveraigne; he that dissented must now consent with the rest; that is, be contented to avow all the actions he shall do, or else be justly destroyed by all the rest." Cf. T. Hobbes, *Leviathan*, ed. W. G. Pogson Smith (Oxford: Clarendon Press, 1929), chapters 14 and 18.

10. In 3.19 of J. Locke, *Second Treatise of Government*, ed. J. W. Gough (Oxford: Basil Blackwell, 1946), the state of nature is contrasted with the state of war, but in 3.21 and 9.123 it is not. At 8.111 Locke claims that it was only after the introduction of a money economy and its attendant social inequalities that ambition and luxury entered people's minds.

11. Cf. J. Locke, *Some Considerations of the Consequences of the Lowering of Interest and Raising the Value of Money* (London, n.p., 1691).

12. Cf. Locke, *Second Treatise*, chapter 8, para. 98.

13. Hobbes, *Leviathan*, 67.

14. E. Mensch, "The History of Mainstream Legal Thought," in *The Politics of Law*, ed. D. Kairys (New York: Pantheon, 1982), 18–39.

15. Cf. J. Habermas, *The Structural Transformation of the Public Sphere*, trans. T. Burger (Cambridge: MIT Press, 1989), 89–117.

16. M. Horwitz, "The Triumph of Contract," in *Critical Legal Studies*, ed. A. C. Hutchinson (Totowa: Rowman and Littlefield, 1989), 118–19.

17. P. Gabel and J. Feinman, "Contract Law as Ideology," in *Politics of Law*, 172–84.

18. Madison's use of the concept of checks and balances primarily applied to a bicameral legislature, not to a whole constitutional system. The constitutional use originally derived from the classical notion of "mixed gov-

ernment" designed to guarantee each class of persons—the monarch, the aristocracy, and the people—a special institutional power or office. Madison's use, by contrast, appears to be partially motivated by a concern for efficiency with regard to the application of distinct democratic values. Yet, in keeping with the older theory (qualified by his belief in legislative supremacy), he also defended the principle as a check on both the institutional concentration of power and majoritarian tyranny (*The Federalist Papers*, ed. R. P. Fairfield (Garden City: Anchor Books, 1966; Baltimore: Johns Hopkins University Press, 1981), bks. 10, 51). As Dahl notes (see below), the constitutional separation of powers has been less successful in checking majoritarian tyranny than the conflictual dynamics of pluralistic democracy (polyarchy). Unfortunately, these dynamics have also encouraged bureaucratic interventions that increasingly undermine democracy.

19. For Tocqueville's discussion of the "immense and tutelary power" of the democratic state, see A. Tocqueville, *Democracy in America*, vol. 2 (New York: Alfred A. Knopf, 1945), 318–19.
20. Cf. H. Arendt, *The Origins of Totalitarianism* (New York: Harcourt, Brace, 1951), chapter 10; and C. Lefort, *Democracy and Political Theory* (Minneapolis: University of Minnesota Press, 1988), pt. 1.
21. Most of these conditions are laid out in chapters 1, 3, and 4 of book 2 of J. Rousseau, *On the Social Contract*, ed. R. D. Masters, trans. J. R. Masters (New York: St. Martin's Press, 1978).
22. See ibid., chapter 6, book 2.
23. Cf. ibid., chapter 7, book 1, and chapter 7, book 2.
24. For an excellent discussion of the tensions animating Rousseau's social theory as these bear upon the residual contractualist assumptions of *le contrat social*, see J. Simon-Ingram, "Alienation, Individuation, and Enlightenment in Rousseau's Social Theory," *Eighteenth-Century Studies* 24, no. 3 (Spring 1991): 315–35.
25. Cf. I. Berlin, "Two Concepts of Liberty," in *Four Political Essays* (Oxford: Oxford University Press, 1970).
26. Bentham began by advocating a franchise limited to educated men of independent means (*Principles of Legislation* (New York: G. & C & H Carvill, 1830), chapter 13, sec. 9). As early as 1809 he advocated a householder franchise limited to those paying taxes on property (*Plan of Parliamentary Reform*, 1818 edn., in *The Theory of Legislation*, ed. C. K. Ogden (London: Paul, Trench, Trubner & Co., 1931), note 40, 127). By 1817 he had come around to accepting universal suffrage for all except those who were under age and illiterate and possibly women, but conceded that "for the sake of *union* and *concord*, many exclusions might be made" (ibid., 35–37, note 41). In 1820 he declared that he could support a more limited householder franchise but doubted that this would satisfy the "majority of adult males" who would be excluded (*Radicalism Not Dangerous*, in Bentham, *Works*, ed. Bowring, 11 vols. (London: Simpkin & Marshall, 1843), 3:199). Although Bentham acknowledged that women were entitled to the vote, he feared that the "confusion" generated by proposing this reform would "engross the public mind, and throw improvement, in all other shapes, to a distance" (*Constitutional Code*, in *Works*, ed. Bowring, 9:109). James Mill's defense of "one person, one vote" as a safeguard against tyranny in *An Essay on Government* (London: J. Innes, 1820) likewise vacillates between endorsing universal suffrage and supporting (on practical grounds) a franchise limited to the wealthiest two-thirds of all

males over forty years of age (roughly a sixth of the adult population). His reasoning seems to have been that the interest of women "is involved in either that of their fathers or that of their husbands"; the "great majority of old men have sons, whose interest they regard as their own"; and "the benefits of good government accruing to all, might be expected to overbalance . . . the benefits of misrule" which would accrue to the wealthiest two-thirds. Cf. J. Mill, *An Essay on Government*, ed. E. Barker (Cambridge: Cambridge University Press, 1937), 45–47, 49–50.

27. Arguing that "every body of men . . . is governed altogether by its conception of what is its interest, in the narrowest and most selfish sense of the word interest: never by any regard for the interest of others," Bentham concluded that "with the single exception of an aptly organized democracy, the ruling and influential few are enemies of the subject many: . . . and by the very nature of man . . . perpetual and unchangeable enemies" (*Constitutional Code*, in *Works*, ed. Bowring, 9:102–43).

28. As Mill put it, "the business of government is properly the business of the rich, and that they will always obtain it, either by bad means or good" ("On the Ballot," *Westminster Review*, July 1830).

29. J. S. Mill, *On Liberty*, in *The Utilitarians* (Garden City: Anchor Press/ Doubleday, 1973), 533.

30. J. S. Mill, *Principles of Political Economy*, book 4, chapter 7, secs. 1, 2, in *Collected Works*, ed. J. M. Robson, vol. 3 (Toronto and London: University of Toronto Press, 1965), 761–63.

31. Mill did not think that social inequality was a necessary consequence of capitalism and attributed existing disparities to past oppression (Mill, *Principles of Political Economy*, book 2, chapter 1, sec. 3, 207). Indeed, he believed that the rise of cooperatives in which workers are their own capitalists would bring a "moral revolution to society" promoting "the healing of the standing feud between capital and labour" and "the transformation of human life, from a conflict of classes struggling for opposite interests, to a friendly rivalry in the pursuit of a good common to all" (ibid., book 4, chapter 7, sec. 6, 792).

32. Since Mill, unlike Bentham, believed that pleasures associated with the intellect were superior to those of the body, he could not accept the view that the aim of government was to optimize production and consumption. However, he was afraid to extend the franchise to the working class prior to their having developed their collective intelligence, for this would lead to a class legislation every bit as debilitating as the one existing. In *Thoughts on Parliamentary Reform* (London: J. W. Parker and Son, 1859), Mill believed that the numerical advantage of the working class could be offset by a system of plural voting without having recourse to a limited franchise. So construed, an unskilled worker would receive one vote; a skilled worker two; a foreman three; a farmer, manufacturer, or trader three or four; a professional, artist, writer, public functionary, or university graduate five or six. However, in his *Considerations on Representative Government* (New York: Harper, 1962) he thought it wise (in addition to a plural voting provision) to exclude those on poor relief, those who had experienced bankruptcy, those who could not pay a direct head tax, and those who could not read, write, and reckon. See Mill, *Thoughts on Parliamentary Reform*, in *Collected Works* 19:324–25; and Mill, *Considerations on Representative Government*, in *Collected Works* 19:445–46, 470–76.

33. Hegel himself criticized majoritarian democracy based on "free unrestricted election" for its failure to respect the principle of constitutional republican

government (i.e., its failure to respect the higher rationality and universality of bureaucratically administered law) and its lack of political order. Although he saw public opinion as a potentially rational medium for expressing and shaping the subjective will of the citizen (whose consent is necessary for the legitimacy of the state) he also identified it with the conflictual and contractual politics of civil society, which, he noted, tends toward particularism. To counteract the irrational, disintegrative effects of uninformed public opinion, Hegel invoked the importance of public education and corporate representation based on occupational membership (the old system of estates)—institutions that integrate democratic input from the top down. Cf. G. W. F. Hegel, *Hegel's Philosophy of Right*, trans. T. M. Knox (Oxford: Clarendon Press, 1952), paras. 116–17, 288–90, 301–302, 308–309, 311, 315–18.

34. Cf. J. Dewey, *Liberalism and Social Action* (New York: G. P. Putnam, 1963) and *Individualism: Old and New* (New York: Capricorn Books, 1962). As Dewey's most influential advocate today, Richard Rorty has strongly endorsed the developmental democratic agenda. His defense, however, of a strong separation between public and private spheres (the pragmatic discourse of democratic solidarity versus the romantic discourse of aesthetic irony) undermines the developmentalist idea that the private and public critically inform one another. Cf. R. Rorty, *Contingency, Irony, and Solidarity* (Cambridge: Cambridge University Press, 1988).

35. The theory of democratic elites was originally worked out by Robert Michels and developed by Mosca and Pareto. Cf. R. Michels, *Political Parties* (New York: Collier Books, 1962).

36. Cf. J. Schumpeter, *Capitalism, Socialism, and Democracy* (London: Allen and Unwin, 1947); and A. Downs, *An Economic Theory of Democracy* (New York: Harper, 1957).

37. Arrow proved that if there are more than two alternatives, any democratic decision procedure preserving transitivity in reasoning will, under certain circumstances, require the imposition of decision from outside. The theorem holds for individual and group decision. Given three individuals (A,B,C), three alternatives (x,y,z), and the following distribution:

A prefers x to y, y to z, and x to z.
B prefers y to z, z to x, and y to x.
C prefers z to x, x to y, and z to y.

Each alternative is preferred by a combination of two individuals, hence no solution to the problem of sovereignty is possible. Translated into group choice involving 101 individuals, the following distribution

1 individual prefers x to y, and y to z,
50 individuals prefer z to x, and x to y,
50 individuals prefer y to z, and z to x,

yields the paradoxical result that 51 prefer x to y, 51 prefer y to z, and *assuming transitivity of choice*, 51 prefer x to z; while 100 individuals prefer the opposite. In this case, the rational principle of transitivity requires that a decision be imposed by one person against the preferences of all others. Only if we abandon the requirement of transitivity (or assume that the possible orderings of individual choices be "single-peaked") can the paradox be avoided. Cf. K. Arrow, *Social Choice and Individual Values* (New York: John Wiley and Sons, 1951), 51–59, 75–80.

38. Cf. C. Lindblom, *Politics and Markets: The World's Economic and Political Systems* (New York: Basic Books, 1977); B. Berelson, P. Lazarsfeld, and

W. McPhee, *Voting* (Chicago: University of Chicago Press, 1954); R. Dahl, *A Preface to Democratic Theory* (Chicago: University of Chicago Press, 1956), *Who Governs?* (New Haven: Yale University Press, 1961), and *Modern Political Analysis* (Englewood Cliffs: Prentice Hall, 1963); G. Almond and S. Verba, *The Civic Culture* (Princeton: Princeton University Press, 1963).

39. In the words of Dahl,

> With all its defects [the American political system] does nonetheless provide a high probability that any active and legitimate group will make itself heard effectively at some stage in the process of decision. . . . [So] long as the social prerequisites of democracy are substantially intact in this country, it appears to be a relatively efficient system for reinforcing agreement, encouraging moderation, and maintaining social peace in a restless and immoderate people operating a gigantic, powerful, diversified, and incredibly complex society.

Dahl, *A Preface to Democratic Theory*, 150–51.

40. Schumpeter observes that the assumption of perfect competition underlying the neoclassical economic theory of equilibrium does not obtain and he adds that "what we are confronted with in the analysis of political processes is largely not a genuine but a manufactured will." Schumpeter, *Capitalism, Socialism, and Democracy*, 263. For a defense of voter apathy in maintaining stability see Berelson et al., *Voting*, chapter 14. For recent discussions of class differential in political participation see S. Verba and N. Nie, *Participation in America, Political Democracy, and Social Equality* (New York: Harper and Row, 1972); and R. Cloward and F. Piven, *Why Americans Don't Vote* (New York: Pantheon Press, 1987).

41. R. Dahl, *Dilemmas of Pluralist Democracy: Autonomy vs. Control* (New Haven: Yale University Press, 1982).

42. R. Dahl, *A Preface to Economic Democracy* (Berkeley: University of California Press, 1985).

43. A. Ware, "Political Parties," in *New Forms of Democracy*, ed. D. Held and C. Pollitt (Beverly Hills: Sage, 1986), 110–34.

44. Pluralism deviates from classical liberal assumptions in its postulation of the primacy of groups over individuals as the agents of political action. However, it continues to embrace contractualist assumptions about human beings, viewing them as possessing fixed, subrational preferences. In general, it ignores individual differences within groups, and it neglects the internal, communicative relations between individuals and groups by which they constitute their own identities in the form of shared (consensual) understanding. Hence pluralism affirms conflict-oriented democracy as the norm, in spite of its irrationality as a mechanism for aggregating preferences. For a good critique of pluralist ontology, see C. Gould, *Rethinking Democracy* (Cambridge: Cambridge University Press, 1988), 97–100.

45. Rational choice theorists disagree on this point. David Gauthier argues that theorems of economic choice suffice to justify impartial (moral) constraints on utility maximizing behavior (cooperation being more maximizing than noncooperation). But his contractualist approach appears to exclude those who for whatever reason lack sufficient bargaining strength, and it nowhere speaks to the virtues of democracy as a vehicle of political rationality. Jon Elster, by contrast, has defended the rationality of participatory democracy on the grounds that it is reasonable, when faced with uncertain consequences, to forgo maximizing utility in favor of pursuing justice. Cf. D. Gauthier, *Morals by Agreement* (Oxford: Clarendon

Press, 1986), and J. Elster, *Solomonic Judgments* (Cambridge: Cambridge University Press, 1989).

46. Rawls' first principle of justice (the Principle of Equal Liberty) asserts that "each person has an equal right to a fully adequate scheme of basic liberties which is compatible with a similar scheme of liberties for all." These basic liberties consist of "political liberty (the right to vote and be eligible for public office) together with freedom of thought; freedom of speech and assembly; liberty of conscience and freedom of thought; freedom of the person along with the right to hold (personal) property; and freedom from arbitrary arrest and seizure as defined by the concept of the rule of law." J. Rawls, *A Theory of Justice* (Cambridge: Belknap Press, 1971), 62. The second principle of justice (the Difference Principle) provides a framework for evaluating the distribution of those goods whose possession, from a moral point of view, need not be strictly equal. It asserts, first, that "social and economic inequalities must be attached to offices and positions open to all under conditions of fair equality of opportunity"; and second, that such inequalities "must be to the greatest benefit of the least advantaged members of society." As Rawls puts it, "all social primary goods are to be distributed equally unless an unequal distribution of any or all of these goods is to the advantage of the least favored." Ibid., 303.

47. Cf. N. Daniels, "Equal Liberty and the Unequal Worth of Liberty," in *Reading Rawls*, ed. N. Daniels (New York: Basic Books, 1975).

48. Rawls, *Theory of Justice*, 266, 356.

49. I discuss Weber's ambivalence toward democracy and bureaucracy in "Dworkin, Habermas, and the CLS Movement on Moral Criticism in Law," *Philosophy and Social Criticism* 16, no. 4 (Fall 1990): 237–68.

50. R. Unger, *Law in Modern Society* (New York: Free Press, 1976), 180; *Knowledge and Politics* (New York: Free Press, 1975), 83–100.

51. Unger, *Knowledge and Politics*, 187.

52. Cf. M. Foucault, *Discipline and Punish: The Birth of the Prison* (New York: Pantheon, 1979).

53. D. Kennedy, "Form and Substance in Private Law Adjudication" in *Critical Legal Studies*, ed. Hutchinson, 36–55; "The Political Significance of the Structure of the Law School Curriculum," *Seton Hall Law Review* 14 (1983): 1.

54. Cf. R. Dworkin, *Law's Empire* (Cambridge: Belknap Press, 1986).

55. For a vivid account of the politics of conflict and compromise governing the Supreme Court from 1968 to 1975 see B. Woodward, *The Brethren* (New York: Simon and Schuster, 1979).

56. Cf. Ingram, "Dworkin, Habermas, and the CLS Movement on Moral Criticism in Law."

57. In the words of Claus Offe, "this strategy of maintaining the commodity form presupposes the growth of state-organized forms of production that are exempt from the commodity form." *Contradictions of the Welfare State* (Cambridge: MIT Press, 1984), 127.

58. K. Klare, "Judicial Deradicalization of the Wagner Act and the Origins of Modern Legal Consciousness, 1937–41," in *Critical Legal Studies*, ed. Hutchinson, 229–55.

59. K. Klare, "Critical Theory and Labor Relations Law," in *Politics of Law*, 65–88.

60. E. Mensch, "Contract as Ideology," in *Critical Legal Studies*, ed. Hutchinson, 148–55.

61. *First National Maintenance Corp. v. NLRB*, 101 S. Ct. 2579–81 (1981).
62. Cf. D. Pearce, "Women, Work, and Welfare: The Feminization of Poverty," in *Working Women and Families*, ed. K. Feinstein (Beverly Hills: Sage, 1979).
63. Cf. B. Nelson, "Women's Poverty and Women's Citizenship: Some Political Consequences of Economic Marginalization," *Signs* 10, no. 2 (Winter 1984): 209–31; and N. Fraser, *Unruly Practices: Power, Discourse, and Gender in Contemporary Social Theory* (Minneapolis: University of Minnesota, 1989), chapter 7.
64. R. Rosenblatt, "Legal Entitlements and Welfare Benefits," in *Politics of Law*, 262–75.
65. Democratic models of policy planning based on communicative rationality are discussed in J. Forester, *Critical Theory and Public life* (Cambridge: MIT Press, 1985).
66. Cf. K-O. Apel, "The Problem of Philosophical Fundamental Grounding in Light of a Transcendental Pragmatics of Language," in *After Philosophy*, ed. K. Baynes, J. Bohman, and T. McCarthy (Cambridge: MIT Press, 1987); and J. Habermas, *Theory of Communicative Action*, trans. T. McCarthy, 2 vols. (Boston: Beacon Press, 1984/87).
67. Ironically, when Sandel and MacIntyre oppose liberal justice to communitarian solidarity they endorse the dualisms endemic to contractualist political theory. However, their claim that true individuality and sociality complement one another is not incompatible with liberalism as such, but only with its contractualist variant. Cf. M. Sandel, *Liberalism and the Limits of Justice* (New York: Cambridge University Press, 1982), 40, 150, 180; and A. MacIntyre, *After Virtue* (Notre Dame: Notre Dame University Press, 1981), 205–206, 212–13. For a critique of the communitarian position see A. Gutmann, "Communitarian Critics of Liberalism," *Philosophy and Public Affairs* 14 (Summer 1985): 308–22; G. Doppelt, "Beyond Liberalism and Communitarianism: Towards a Critical Theory of Social Justice," *Philosophy and Social Criticism* 14 (1988): 271–92; and R. Ellis, "Toward a Reconciliation of Liberalism and Communitarianism," *Journal of Value Inquiry* 1991 (January): 55–64.
68. If the ideal of justice has conditional priority at all, it is because it instantiates a thin conception of the good (as Rawls puts it) that rational persons must share, simply in order to regulate disagreements about thicker conceptions of the good. For the purposes of this argument, it does not matter whether rationality as it is here conceived is truly universal or (to cite Rawls' more recent clarification of his method of justification) merely the best "charter for our social world" given "our history and the traditions embedded in our public life." Cf. J. Rawls, "Kantian Constructivism in Moral Theory: The Dewey Lectures 1980," *The Journal of Philosophy* 77, no. 9 (September 1980): 519.
69. For further discussion of the conditions of legitimate compromise see Ingram, "Dworkin, Habermas, and the CLS Movement," and D. Ingram, "The Limits and Possibilities of Communicative Ethics for Democratic Reform," *Political Theory* 21, no. 2 (1993): 294.
70. For a good critique of the kind of argument advanced by William Riker and other economic theorists (to the effect that democracy is subrational because it provides no rule for coherently aggregating preferences) see J. Bohman, "Communication, Ideology, and Democratic Theory," *American Political Science Review* 84, no. 1 (March 1990): 107. Also see W. Riker, *Liberalism Against Populism: A Confrontation Between the Theory of Democ-*

racy and the Theory of Social Choice (San Francisco: W. H. Freeman, 1982).
71. Cf. F. C. Arterton, *Teledemocracy: Can Technology Protect Democracy?* (Beverly Hills: Sage, 1987).
72. Cf. Ingram, "The Limits and Possibilities of Communicative Ethics."
73. Cf. J. Habermas, *Legitimation Crisis*, trans. T. McCarthy (Boston: Beacon Press, 1975).
74. Cf. Habermas, *Theory of Communicative Action* 2:361–73.

CHAPTER 10

1. K. Marx, *A Contribution to the Critique of Political Economy* (New York: Progress Publishers, 1970).
2. A. Gramsci, *Selections from the Prison Notebooks*, ed. Q. Hoare and G. Smith (New York: International Publishers, 1971). See also E. Greer, "Antonio Gramsci and 'Legal Hegemony,'" in *The Politics of Law: A Progressive Critique*, ed. D. Kairys (New York: Pantheon, 1982), 304–309, and C. Boggs, *Gramsci's Marxism* (London: Pluto Press, 1976).
3. Gramsci, *Prison Notebooks*, 182.
4. Boggs, *Gramsci's Marxism*, 39–40.
5. B. Ollman, Introduction to *The United States Constitution: 200 Years of Anti-Federalist, Abolitionist, Feminist, Muckraking, Progressive, and Especially Socialist Criticism*, ed. B. Ollman and J. Birnbaum (New York: New York University Press, 1990), 6.
6. For a sampling see M. Tushnet, "A Marxist Analysis of American Law," *Marxist Perspectives* 1 (1978): 96–116; I. Balbus, "Commodity Form and Legal Form: An Essay on the Relative Autonomy of the Law," *Law and Society Review* 11 (1977): 571–89; T. Kleven, "The Relative Autonomy of the United States Supreme Court," *The Yale Journal of Law and Liberation* 1 (1989): 43–66; M. McCann, "Resurrection and Reform: Perspectives on Property in the American Constitutional Tradition," *Politics and Society* 13, no. 2 (1984): 143–76; M. McCann and G. Houseman, *Judging the Constitution: Critical Essays on Judicial Lawmaking* (Glenview: Scott, Foresman, 1989); K. Klare, "Judicial Deradicalization of the Wagner Act and the Origins of Modern Legal Consciousness, 1937–1941," *Minnesota L. Rev.* 62 (1978): 265; and J. Brigham, "The Economy and the Court: 'Double Standard' as Institutional Practice," *Research in Law and Policy Studies* 1 (1987): 121–41.
7. See W. Forbath, *Law and the Shaping of the American Labor Movement* (Cambridge: Harvard University Press, 1991).
8. M. Tigar and M. Levy, *Law and the Rise of Capitalism* (New York: Monthly Review Press, 1977).
9. F. Michelman, "Property as a Constitutional Right," *Washington and Lee L. Rev.* 38 (1981): 1097; C. Reich, "The New Property," *Yale L. J.* 73 (1964): 733. For a critique of this approach see McCann, "Resurrection and Reform."
10. C. Tomlins, *The State and the Unions: Labor Relations, Law, and the Organized Labor Movement in America, 1880–1960* (Cambridge: Cambridge University Press, 1985), xxiii–xxiv.
11. J. Grady, "Broken Promises: The Failure of American Labor Law," *Labor L. J.* 41 (1990): 153.
12. Kleven, "Relative Autonomy of the United States Supreme Court."
13. See A. Bickel, *The Supreme Court and the Idea of Progress* (New York: Harper and Row, 1970), and R. Berger, *Government by Judiciary: The Transformation of the Fourteenth Amendment* (Cambridge: Harvard University Press, 1977).

14. I. Wallerstein, "The Bourgeois(ie) as Concept and Reality," *New Left Review* 167 (1988): 100.
15. 304 U.S. 144 (1938).
16. J. Brigham, "Constitutional Property: The Double Standard and Beyond," in McCann and Houseman, *Judging the Constitution*, 187–204. Brigham, "The Economy and the Court," 121–41; and McCann, "Resurrection and Reform," 143–76.
17. A. Fraser, "The Legal Theory We Need Now," *Socialist Review*, 1978: 40–41.
18. R. Stewart, "The Reformation of American Administrative Law," *Harvard L. Rev.* 88 (1975): 1712.
19. I. Bernstein, *The New Deal Collective Bargaining Policy* (Berkeley: University of California Press, 1950); J. Gross, *The Making of the National Labor Relations Board: A Study in Economics, Politics, and the Law* (Albany: SUNY Press, 1974); *The Reshaping of the National Labor Relations Board: National Labor Policy in Transition* (Albany: SUNY Press, 1981); and P. Irons, *The New Deal Lawyers* (Princeton: Princeton University Press, 1982).
20. Forbath, *Law and the Shaping of the American Labor Movement*.
21. Quoted in Tomlins, *The State and the Unions*, 159.
22. Tomlins, *The State and the Unions*.
23. K. Van Wezel Stone, "The Post-War Paradigm in American Labor Law," *Yale L. J.* 90 (1981): 1509; A. Cox, "Rights Under a Labor Agreement," *Harvard L. Rev.* 69 (1956): 601, "Reflections Upon Labor Arbitration," *Harvard L. Rev.* 72 (1959): 1482; and H. Shulman, "Reason, Contract, and Law in Labor Relations," *Harvard L. Rev.* 68 (1955): 999.
24. Van Wezel Stone, "Post-War Paradigm," 1513.
25. K. Klare, "Judicial Deradicalization of the Wagner Act."
26. Tomlins, *The State and the Unions*.
27. *NLRB v. Fansteel Metallurgical Corporation*, 306 U.S. 240, 257–58 (1939).
28. See *NLRB v. Sands Manufacturing Company*, 306 U.S. 332 (1939) (union's breach of contract arising over an honest difference of opinion about its terms entitled the employer to abrogate the contract and hire new employees); *NLRB v. MacKay Radio and Telegraph Company*, 304 U.S. 333 (1938) (striking employees not on strike over a dispute arising from an employer's unfair labor practice were not entitled to automatic reinstatement after the strike); *Southern Steamship Company v. NLRB*, 316 U.S. 31 (1942) (reminding the Board to consider other congressional national policy objectives and reconcile its administration of labor policy with those objectives); *C. G. Conn, Limited v. NLRB*, 108 F.2d 390 (7th Cir. 1939) (proscribing "work-in" tactics in a collective bargaining dispute); and *NLRB v. Condensor Corporation of America*, 128 F.2d 67 (3rd Cir. 1942) and *NLRB v. Draper Corporation*, 145 F.2d 199 (4th Cir. 1944) (finding the dismissal of wildcat strikers not to be an unfair labor practice).
29. For example, see *Associated Press v. NLRB*, 301 U.S. 103 (1937) (affirming employer's managerial prerogatives), and *Republic Aviation Corporation v. NLRB*, 324 U.S. 793 (1945) (emphasizing the need to balance the rights of workers against the "undisputed" right of employers to maintain discipline in the workplace).
30. N. Lichtenstein, *Labor's War at Home: The CIO in World War II* (Cambridge: Cambridge University Press, 1982).
31. Tomlins, *The State and the Unions*.
32. *United Steelworkers of America v. Warrior & Gulf Navigation Company*, 363 U.S. 574 (1960); *United Steelworkers of America v. American Manufacturing Company*, 363 U.S. 564 (1960); and *United Steelworkers of America v. Enterprise Wheel and Car Corporation*, 363 U.S. 593 (1960).

33. T. Geoghegan, *Which Side Are You On? Trying to Be for Labor When It's Flat on Its Back* (New York: Plume Books, 1992), 164.
34. *Local 174, International Brotherhood of Teamsters v. Lucas Flour Company*, 369 U.S. 95 (1962).
35. *Boys Market, Inc. v. Retail Clerks Local 770*, 398 U.S. 235 (1970).
36. *Gateway Coal Company v. United Mine Workers*, 414 U.S. 368 (1974).
37. Van Wezel Stone, "The Post-War Paradigm," 1565.
38. K. Klare, "Critical Theory and Labor Relations Law," in *The Politics of Law*, 65–88.
39. T. St. Antoine, "Major Labor and Employment Decisions of the Supreme Court, 1988–89 Term," in *Labor Law Developments, 1990*, ed. C. Holgren (New York: Matthew Bender, 1990), chapter 1.
40. For recent cases suggesting that the courts may be departing from the industrial pluralist model and playing a larger role in enforcing the terms of contracts and not automatically deferring to the private arbitration process see *W. R. Grace and Company v. Rubber Workers*, 461 U.S. 757 (1983), and *Lingle v. Norge*, 108 S.Ct. 1877 (1988). For a case indicative that the Board may be interested in taking a more active role see *General American Transportation Corporation*, 228 NLRB 808 (1977). Yet for the more traditional deference approach see *United Paperworkers v. Misco*, 108 S.Ct. 364 (1989), and *Consolidated Rail Corporation v. Railway Labor Executives Association*, 109 S.Ct. 2477 (1989).
41. 398 U.S. 235 (1970).
42. D. Bell, Jr., "Bakke, Minority Admissions and the Usual Price of Racial Remedies," *California L. Rev.* 67 (1979): 13.
43. A. Freeman, "Legitimizing Racial Discrimination Through Antidiscrimination Law: A Critical Review of Supreme Court Doctrine," *Minnesota L. Rev.* 62 (1978): 1050.
44. R. Williams, "Mining the Meaning: Key Words in the Miners' Strike," in R. Williams, *Resources of Hope* (London: Verso, 1989), 125–26.

CHAPTER 11

* This chapter is a substantially revised version of an essay titled "The Chaotic Law of Tort: Legal Formalism and the Problem of Indeterminacy," in Roberta Kevelson, ed., *Peirce and Law: Issues in Pragmatism, Legal Realism, and Semiotics* (New York: Peter Lang, 1991).

1. *Yale L. J.* 97 (1988): 949. Weinrib elaborates on this theme in "Understanding Tort Law," *Valparaiso U. L. Rev.* 23 (1989); 485, in which he applies his formalist approach to a particular category of the law.
2. C. Sampford, *The Disorder of Law: A Critique of Legal Theory* (New York: Basil Blackwell, 1989).
3. The discussion of chaos throughout this chapter is based on J. Briggs, *Fractals: The Patterns of Chaos* (New York: Simon and Schuster, 1992); J. Briggs and F. Peat, *Turbulent Mirror* (New York: Harper and Row, 1989); J. Gleick, *Chaos: Making a New Science* (New York: Viking, 1987); I. Prigogine and I. Stengers, *Order Out of Chaos: Man's New Dialogue with Nature* (Boulder: New Science Library, 1984; distributed by Random House); I. Stewart, *Does God Play Dice? The Mathematics of Chaos* (New York: Basil Blackwell, 1989).
4. T. Kuhn, *The Structure of Scientific Revolutions* (Chicago: University of Chicago Press, 1970).
5. The ready example is the auditorium sound system, when a small amount

of sound from the loudspeakers feeds back to the microphone, setting off a process that causes the amplifier to cascade out of control, creating a horrendous screech.

6. Gleick, *Chaos*, 78–79.
7. See "Abduction and Induction," in *Philosophical Writings of Peirce*, ed. J. Buchler (New York: Dover Publications, 1955), 150.
8. M. Horwitz, *The Transformation of American Law, 1780–1860* (Cambridge: Harvard University Press, 1977), 38.
9. *Overseas Tankship (U. K.), Ltd. v. Morts Dock & Engg. Co.*, [1961] A. C. 388.
10. *Overseas Tankship (U. K.), Ltd. v. The Miller Steamship Co.*, [1967] 1 A. C. 617.
11. [1961] A. C., at 422–23.
12. O. W. Holmes, Jr., *The Common Law* (Boston: Little, Brown, 1963), 77.
13. K. Llewellyn, *The Bramble Bush: On Our Law and Its Study* (Dobbs Ferry: Oceana, 1960), 12.
14. Alpheus Mason espoused the idea that American political processes ought not to establish a hierarchy among values but instead ought to compromise among them, maintaining them in a creative tension. See, e.g., A. Mason, "To Be More Safe: America's Continuing Dilemma," *Virginia Q. Rev.* 45 (1969): 545.

CHAPTER 12

1. This, in essence, is the legal concept of "aboriginal" land rights. One of the strongest and clearest articulations of the doctrine may be found in G. Jeze, *Etude Theoretique et Pratique sur l'Occupation comme Mode d'Acquerir les Territoires en Droit International* (Paris, 1896).
2. For a very solid analysis of the various problems at issue in this regard, see R. Taylor, *International Public Law* (London: Methuen Publishers, 1901). See also M. F. Lindley, *The Acquisition and Government of Backward Country in International Law: A Treatise on the Law and Practice Relating to Colonial Expansion* (London: Longmans, Green Publishers, 1926).
3. This principle is of course most plainly embodied in the United Nations Declaration on the Granting of Independence to Colonial Countries and Peoples (December 14, 1960). The complete text of the declaration is found in I. Brownlie, *Basic Documents on Human Rights* (Oxford: Clarendon Press, 1981), 28–30.
4. The comprehensive elaboration of the U.S. position may be found in F. S. Cohen, *Handbook on Federal Indian Law* (Washington, DC: Government Printing Office, 1942; Albuquerque: University of New Mexico Press, n.d.).
5. Broad analysis of such rhetoric by President George Bush during the 1990–91 Gulf War may be found in *Mobilizing for Democracy*, ed. G. Bates (Monroe, ME: Common Courage Press, 1991). See also *Collateral Damage*, ed. C. Peters (Boston: South End Press, 1992).
6. See A. Truyol y Serra, "The Discovery of the New World and International Law," *Toledo L. Rev.* 171 (1971): 305.
7. Probably the best delineation of these issues may be found in R. Williams, Jr., *The American Indian in Western Legal Thought: The Discourses of Conquest* (London: Oxford University Press, 1990).
8. The first solid evidence that the Church had become engaged in this process comes on May 3 and May 5, 1493, with the signing of two bulls by Pope Alexander VI which endorsed the rights of the sovereigns of Castille and Aragon to acquire the lands of newly discovered portions

of America while spreading Christianity among the natives thereof. See P. Gottshalk, *The Earliest Diplomatic Documents of America* (New York: n.p., 1978), 21.

9. On the bulls of Innocent IV (Sinibaldo Fiesco), see E. Nys, *Les Origins de Troit International* (Brussels and Paris, 1984), especially chapter 7. It is worth noting that Innocent himself was heavily influenced by the treatise of Thomas Aquinas in *Summa Theologica Secunda Secundae*, written around 1250; see H. A. Deane, *The Political and Social Ideals of St. Augustine* (New York: Columbia University Press, 1963).

10. See A. Nussbaum, *A Concise History of the Laws of Nations* (New York: Macmillan Publishers, 1954). See also L. Hanke, *The Spanish Struggle for Justice in the Conquest of America* (Philadelphia: University of Pennsylvania Press, 1949).

11. Vitoria's formulation of the doctrine is available under the title *De Indis et De Jure Belli Reflectiones*, published by the Carnegie Institution in 1917. The pivotal international legal theorist Emer Vattel drew heavily on Vitoria's discourse when drafting his *Laws of Nations* (Philadelphia: T. & J. W. Johnson Publishers, 1855). Overall, see J. H. Parry, *The Spanish Theory of Empire in the Sixteenth Century* (Cambridge: Cambridge University Press, 1940).

12. This principle derives directly from Roman law promulgated at least a century before Christ: see *Ancient Law*, ed. H. Maine (New York: H. Holt and Co., 1888).

13. This thinking is embodied in the bull *Inter Caetera* of May 4, 1493; Gottshalk, *Earliest Diplomatic Documents*, 21. The matter is also taken up about thirty years later by the renowned jurist John Mair, in his *Commentary on the Sentences of Peter Lombard* (n.p.); see Truyol y Serra, "The Discovery of the New World," 313.

14. Matías de Paz took the lead, in his *Concerning the Rule of the Kings of Spain Over the Indians*, in rejecting Aristotelian logic and formulating the concepts of just and unjust wars as applied to the Americas; see J. Diaz, "Los Doctrinas de Palacios Rubios y Matías de Paz ante la Conquista America," in *Memoria de El Colegio Nacional* (Burgos, 1950), 71–94. Matías' arguments led to promulgation of the Laws of Burgos, theoretically regulating all aspects of Spanish colonial practice. For an overview of where the discussion led, see L. Hanke, *Aristotle and the American Indians: A Study in Race Prejudice in the Modern World* (Bloomington and Indianapolis: Indiana University Press, 1959). For more on the relevant laws, see J. Taylor, *Spanish Law Concerning Discoveries, Pacifications, and Settlements among the Indians* (Salt Lake City: University of Utah Press, 1980).

15. For a sample of the sort of debates involved, see L. Hanke, *All Mankind Is One: A Study of the Disputation Between Bartlomé de Las Casas and Juan Ginés de Sepulvéda in 1550 on the Intellectual and Religious Capacity of American Indians* (DeKalb: Northern Illinois University, 1950). On general acceptance of the doctrine, see *Attitudes of the Colonial Powers Towards American Indians*, ed. H. Peckman and C. Gibson (Salt Lake City: University of Utah Press, 1969). An excellent textual source in the latter regard is *European Treaties Bearing on the History of the United States and Its Depedencies*, ed. F. G. Davenport, 2 vols. (Washington, DC: Carnegie Institution of Washington, 1917).

16. See D. B. Quinn, *England and the Discovery of America, 1481–1620* (New York: Alfred A. Knopf Publishers, 1974). See also H. C. Porter, *The Inconstant Savage: England and the American Indian, 1500–1600* (London:

Duckworth Publishers, 1979). A more general view may be found in J. H. Parry, *The Establishment of European Hegemony, 1415–1713* (New York: Harper and Row Publishers, 1966). For a selection of relevant texts with regard to England, see A. T. Vaughn, *Early American Indian Documents: Treaties and Laws, 1607–1789* (Washington, DC: University Publications of America, 1979).

17. See J. B. Scott, *The Spanish Origin of International Law* (Oxford: Clarendon Press, 1934). See also L. Oppenheim, *International Law*, vol. 1 (London: Longmans, Green Publishers, 1955). That these principles were not unknown to or misunderstood by early U.S. jurists is conclusively demonstrated by Felix S. Cohen in his essay, "The Spanish Origin of Indian Rights in the Law of the United States," *Georgetown L. Rev.* 31 (1942): 1.

18. The concept of the Norman Yoke emerged from the idea of "Natural Law": see F. von Gierke, *Natural Law and the Theory of Society, 1500–1800* (Cambridge: Cambridge University Press, 1934). For the concept's application in the New World setting, see K. Knorr, *British Colonial Theories, 1570–1850* (Toronto: University of Toronto Press, 1944). See also W. R. Jacobs, *Dispossessing the American Indian: Indians and Whites on the Colonial Frontier* (New York: Charles Scribner, 1972); A. T. Vaughn, *The New England Frontier: Puritans and Indians 1620–1675* (New York: Little, Brown, 1965); and Williams, *The American Indian*.

19. The seeds of the subsequent "reservation" systems developed by the United States and Canada may be seen to be embedded in this construction. The motivations underlying nearly three centuries of endemic falsification of indigenous American demographic and agricultural realities by Angloamerican "scholars" may also be discerned as residing within the theory of the Norman Yoke. In order to justify, or at least rationalize, the sorts of territorial acquisition undertaken by the British and their U.S. descendants, it was necessary that North America be very sparsely populated by peoples subsisting primarily on the basis of hunting and gathering. A good job of debunking such patent nonsense is found in F. Jennings' *The Invasion of America: Indians, Colonialism, and the Cant of Conquest* (New York: W. W. Norton, 1976). See also L. A. Stiffarm and P. Lane, Jr., "The Demography of Native North America: A Question of American Indian Survival," in *The State of Native America: Genocide, Colonization and Resistance*, ed. M. A. Jaimes (Boston: South End Press, 1992), 23–54.

20. For a good overview and contextualization of the French and Indian Wars, as well as the 1763 Proclamation, see D. E. Leach, *The Northern Colonial Frontier, 1607–1763*, Histories of the American Frontier Series (New York: Holt, Reinhart, and Winston, 1966). A focus on the last, and decisive, of these wars will be found in W. R. Jacobs, *Diplomacy and Indian Gifts: Anglo-French Rivalry Along the Ohio and Northwest Frontiers, 1748–1763* (Stanford: Stanford University Press, 1950). See also R. C. Downes, *Council Fires on the Upper Ohio* (Pittsburgh: University of Pittsburgh Press, 1940).

21. See M. Jensen, *Founding of a Nation: A History of the American Revolution, 1763–1776* (London and New York: Oxford University Press, 1979).

22. See T. P. Abernathy, *Western Lands and the American Revolution* (New York: Russell and Russell Publishers, 1959). See also G. Wood, *Creation of the American Republic, 1776–1787* (Chapel Hill: University of North Carolina Press, 1969).

23. V. Deloria, Jr., "Sovereignty," in *Economic Development in American In-*

dian Reservations, ed. R. D. Ortiz and L. Emerson (Albuquerque: Native American Studies Center, University of New Mexico, 1979). See also W. Mohr, *Federal Indian Relations, 1774–1788* (Philadelphia: University of Pennsylvania Press, 1933).

24. For an assessment of the centrality of Indian relations in congressional deliberations concerning the treaty-making provisions found in Article IX of the Articles of Confederation, and Articles I and VI of the Constitution (as well as its so-called Commerce Clause), see M. Jensen, *The Articles of Confederation: An Interpretation of the Socio-Constitutional History of the American Revolution, 1774–1788* (Madison: University of Wisconsin Press, 1940), 154–62, 190–232. Another useful reading is G. Schaaf, *Wampum Belts and Peace Trees: George Morgan, Native Americans and Revolutionary Diplomacy* (Golden: Fulcrum Publishers, 1990).
25. 1 Stat. 50 (1789).
26. Quoted in E. Lazarus, *Black Hills, White Justice: The Sioux Nation versus the United States, 1775 to the Present* (New York: Harper Collins Publishers, 1991), 158.
27. U.S. contentions that it gained "discovery rights" by virtue of the British capitulation are strained at best. Such rights, under both English and Spanish legal understandings, attached themselves solely to monarchs under the doctrine of "divine right." In other words, it is dubious that George III could have conveyed such rights upon the rebels, even had he desired to do so (and there is no language in the treaty suggesting that he did). At most, then, the United States could lay bona fide claim to only that territory—all of it east of the 1763 demarcation line—that the British Crown could be said to have acquired by prior treaties with indigenous nations. On the relationship between divine rights and discovery rights, see W. Ullman, *The Church and Laws in the Early Middle Ages* (London: Methuen Publishers, 1975).
28. On Tecumseh, see R. D. Edmunds, *Tecumseh and the Quest for American Indian Leadership* (Boston: Little, Brown, 1984). On the Red Sticks, see J. W. Martin, *Sacred Revolt: The Muskogees' Struggle for a New World* (Boston: Beacon Press, 1991).
29. Opinion rendered by the Attorney General (Op. Atty. Gen.), April 26, 1821, 345.
30. Op. Atty. Gen., 1828, 623–3. For further background, see H. Berman, "The Concept of Aboriginal Rights in the Early Legal History of the United States, *Buffalo L. Rev.* 27 (1978): 637. See also F. Cohen, "Original Indian Land Title," *Minnesota L. Rev.* 32 (1947): 28.
31. For context, see R. Horsman, *Expansion and American Policy, 1783–1812* (East Lansing: Michigan State University Press, 1967).
32. *Johnson v. McIntosh*, 21 U.S. (98 Wheat.) 543 (1823).
33. L. Baker, *John Marshall: A Life in Law* (New York: Macmillan Publishers, 1974), 80.
34. *Fletcher v. Peck*, 10 U.S. 87 (1810).
35. *Johnson v. McIntosh*, 21 U.S. (98 Wheat.) 543 (1823).
36. The cases are *Cherokee Nation v. Georgia*, 30 U.S. (5 Pet.) 1 (1831), and *Worcester v. Georgia*, 31 U.S. (6 Pet.) 551 (1832). In effect, Marshall held that indigenous nations should always be considered sovereign enough to transfer legal title to their lands to the United States, but never sovereign enough to possess a right to prevent U.S. assumption of ownership of those lands. Simultaneously, he denied comparable rights over Indian property to the various states, reserving them exclusively to the

federal government. Oddly, this last has led to Marshall being generally considered a "champion" of native rights.

37. This is a constitutional absurdity. The sort of limited sovereignty implied in Marshall's "domestic dependent nation" theory places indigenous nations in essentially the same "quasi-sovereign" status of subordination to the federal government as is possessed by the states of the union or Canadian provinces. Article 1, Section 10, of the U.S. Constitution specifically prohibits the states from entering into treaty relationships. Conversely, the federal government is prohibited from entering into a treaty relationship with states or provinces (or any entity other than another *fully* sovereign nation). The unprecedented (and untenable) politicolegal status invented by Marshall to describe the "partial sovereignty" he needed native nations to fulfill has been compared to "the biological impossibility of a woman's being part-pregnant."

38. For penetrating insights into the power relations involved, see A. Memmi, *Colonizer and Colonized* (Boston: Beacon Press, 1965).

39. For example, this is the basic argument advanced in C. F. Wilkinson, *Indians, Time and Law* (New Haven: Yale University Press, 1987).

40. It is interesting to note that the United States, without renouncing its own doctrine, took a leading role in defining the creation of an exactly similar juridical rationalization of expansionist intent by Nazi Germany to be a criminal endeavor. See F. Parrella, *Lebensraum and Manifest Destiny: A Comparative Study in the Justification of Expansionism* (unpublished M.A. thesis from Georgetown University).

41. For a comprehensive survey of the meanings of these terms in the international legal vernacular, see M. Walzer, *Just and Unjust Wars: A Moral Argument with Historical Illustrations* (New York: Basic Books, 1977).

42. One indicator of the pervasiveness with which this outlook has been implanted is that armed conflicts between the United States and indigenous nations are inevitably described as "Indian Wars" despite the fact that each one was demonstrably initiated by the invasion by American citizens of territory belonging to one or more native peoples. The so-called Indian Wars would thus be accurately depicted as "Settlers' Wars" (or, more appropriately yet, "Wars of Aggression by the United States").

43. The texts of 371 ratified treaties are reproduced verbatim in *Indian Treaties, 1778–1883*, ed. C. J. Cappler (New York: Interland Publishing, 1973). The Lakota scholar Vine Deloria, Jr., has collected more than thirty additional ratified treaty texts, raising the total to approximately 400. Furthermore, Deloria has compiled several hundred treaty texts never ratified by the Senate, but upon which basis the United States nonetheless contends it acquired legal title to specific portions of its current geography (California is a prominent example).

44. There are a number of indicators of this. One of the more salient was a tendency of the Senate to alter the terms and conditions of treaties negotiated with indigenous nations after the native leadership had signed. The modified treaty instruments were then passed into U.S. law and said to be binding upon the Indians involved, even though they'd never agreed to—or in some cases even been notified of—the new terms (the 1861 treaty with the Cheyennes and Arapahos, otherwise known as the Treaty of Fort Wise, is a good example). For details, see *Indian Laws and Treaties*, ed. C. J. Kappler, 5 vols. (Washington, DC: Government Printing Office, 1904).

45. U.S. Bureau of the Census, *Report on Indians Taxed and Indians Not Taxed*

in the United States (except Alaska) at the Eleventh U.S. Census: 1890 (Washington, DC: Government Printing Office, 1894), 637–68.

46. Ibid.

47. See Stiffarm and Lane, "The Demography of North America," 35–36. The government of first the Republic, and then the State of Texas maintained a bounty on Indian—any Indian—scalps until well into the 1870s; see W. W. Newcome, Jr., *The Indians of Texas* (Austin: University of Texas Press, 1961).

48. J. Mooney, "Population," in *Handbook of the Indians North of Mexico*, vol. 2, ed. F. W. Dodge, Bureau of American Ethnology Bulletin no. 30, Smithsonian Institution (Washington, DC: Government Printing Office, 1910), 286–87. See also S. F. Cook, *The Conflict Between the California Indian and White Civilization* (Berkeley: University of California Press, 1976).

49. For details and analysis, see D. Svaldi, *Sand Creek and the Rhetoric of Extermination: A Case-Study in Indian-White Relations* (Washington, DC: University Press of America, 1989).

50. Stiffarm and Lane, "The Demography of North America," 34.

51. See R. Thornton, "Cherokee Population Losses During the Trail of Tears: A New Perspective and Estimate," *Ethnohistory* 31, no. 31 (1984): 289–300.

52. See S. R. Johansson and S. H. Preston, "Tribal Demography: The Navajo and Hopi Populations as Seen Through Manuscripts from the 1900 Census," *Social Science History* 2, no. 3 (1878): 26. See also R. M. Salmon, "The Disease Complaint at Bosque Redondo (1864–1868)," *The Indian Historian* 10, no. 9 (1976): 2–7.

53. See T. McHugh, *The Time of the Buffalo* (Lincoln: University of Nebraska Press, 1972), 285. See also P. A. Hutton, *Phil Sheridan and His Army* (Lincoln: University of Nebraska Press, 1985), 246.

54. Scholarly sources suggest the actual total may have been as high as a half-million. See R. Thornton, *American Indian Holocaust and Survival: A Population History Since 1492* (Norman: University of Oklahoma Press, 1987), 49.

55. This nadir figure is reported in U.S. Bureau of the Census, *Fifteenth Census of the United States, 1930: The Indian Population of the United States and Alaska* (Washington, DC: Government Printing Office, 1937). Barely 101,000 Canadian Indians were estimated as surviving in the same year.

56. Estimating native population figures at the point of first contact is, at best, a slippery business. Recent demographic work has, however, produced a broad consensus that the standard anthropological estimates of "about one million north of the Río Grande" fashioned by James Mooney and Alfred Kroeber, as well as Harold Driver's subsequent upward revision of their calculations to "approximately two million," are far too low. The late Henry Dobyns, using more appropriate methodologies than his predecessors, computed a probable aggregate precontact North American Indian population of 18.5 million, about 15 million of them within present U.S. borders. H. Dobyns, *Their Numbers Become Thinned: Native American Population Dynamics in Eastern North America* (Knoxville: University of Tennessee Press, 1983). A somewhat more conservative successor, the Cherokee demographer Russell Thornton, counters that the figure was more likely about 12.5 million, perhaps 9.5 million of them within the United States. Thornton, *American Indian Holocaust and Survival*. Splitting the difference between Dobyns and Thornton leaves one with a total North American population of approximately 15 million,

about 12.5 million in the U.S. Interestingly, no matter which set of the newer estimates one uses, the overall attrition by 1900 is in the upper 90th percentile range.

57. The figure is arrived at by relying upon C. C. Royce, *Indian Land Cessions in the United States,* 2 vols., Smithsonian Institution, Bureau of American Ethnography, 18th Annual Report, 1896–97 (Washington, DC, 1899).

58. The idea was to destroy the *untermensch* ("subhuman") populations— Slavs, Poles, Jews, and Gypsies among them—of eastern Europe, replacing them on the lands thus vacated with "superior" Germanic "settlers," and thereby establishing Germany as a first-class world power. Hitler expressed this rather consistently during his career, beginning with the seminal *Mein Kampf* (New York: Houghlin, 1962). For instance, after outlining the necessity of a large continental land base for any country seeking a "world historical" role, he observed:

> Today many European states are like pyramids stood on their heads. Their European area is absurdly small in comparison to their weight of colonies, foreign trade, etc. We may say: summit in Europe, base in the whole world; contrasting with the American Union which possesses its base in its own continent and touches the rest of the earth only with its summit. And from this comes the immense inner strength of this state and the weakness of most European colonial powers. . . . Nor is England any proof to the contrary, since in consideration of the British empire we forget too easily the Anglo-Saxon world as such. The position of England, if only because of her linguistic and cultural bond with the American Union, can be compared to no other state in Europe. . . . For Germany, consequently, the only possibility for carrying out a healthy territorial policy [lies] in the acquisition of new land in Europe itself . . . suited for settlement by [Germans]. . . . [S]uch a colonial policy [must be] carried out by means of a hard struggle . . . not for territories outside of Europe, but for land on the home continent itself. . . . If land [is] desired in Europe, it [can] be obtained by and large only at the expense of Russia, and this [means] that the new Reich must again set itself on the march along the road of the Teutonic Knights of old, to obtain by the German sword sod for the German plow and daily bread for the nation. (*Mein Kampf,* 139–40)

In *Hitler's Secret Book* (New York: Grove Press, 1961), 44–48, he goes even further: "Neither Spain nor Britain should be models of German expansion, but the Nordics of North America, who had ruthlessly pushed aside an inferior race to win for themselves sail and territory for the future"; see N. Rich, *Hitler's War Aims: Ideology, the Nazi State, and the Course of Expansion* (New York: W. W. Norton Publishers, 1973), 8. Also see Parrella, *Lebensraum,* and Parrella, *Hitler's Secret Conversations, 1941– 1944* (New York: Octagon Books, 1953). Perhaps the very clearest articulation of the conceptual and practical linkages between Nazi performance in eastern Europe and nineteenth-century U.S. Indian policy may be found in a lengthy memorandum prepared by Freidrich Hossbach to record the content of a Führer Conference conducted on November 5, 1937; the relevant portion is contained in *Trial of the Major War Criminals before the International Military Tribunal,* 42 vols. (Nuremberg, 1947– 1949), 386-PS, 25:402ff.

59. Ch. 120, 16 Stat. 544, 566, now codified at 25 U.S.C. 71. According to its authors, the suspension did nothing to impair the standing of existing treaties between the United States and native nations.

60. Ch. 341, 24 Stat. 362, 385, now codified at 18 U.S.C. 1153; on context

and implementation of the act, see V. Deloria, Jr., and C. M. Lytle, *American Indians, American Justice* (Austin: University of Texas Press, 1983).
61. *United States v. Kagama*, 118 U.S. 375 (1886).
62. Deloria and Lytle, *American Indians.*
63. Ch. 119, 24 Stat. 388, now codified as amended at 25 U.S.C. 331 et seq., better known as the "Dawes Act," after its sponsor, Massachusetts Senator Henry Dawes.
       The quote is from R. L. Robbins, "Self-Determination and Subordination: The Past, Present and Future of American Indian Governance," in Jaimes, *State of Native America*, 93.
64. See M. A. Jaimes, "Federal Indian Identification Policy: A Usurpation of Indigenous Sovereignty in North America," in Jaimes, *State of Native America*, 123–38. It is noteworthy that official eugenics codes have been employed by very few states, mostly such unsavory examples as Nazi Germany (against the Jews), South Africa (against "coloreds"), and Israel (against Palestinian Arabs).
65. Robbins, "Self-Determination." Also see J. A. McDonnell, *The Dispossession of the American Indian, 1887–1934* (Bloomington and Indianapolis: Indiana University Press, 1991).
66. Robbins, "Self-Determination." Also see K. Kicking Bird and K. Dicjemeaix, *One Hundred Million Acres* (New York: Macmillan Publishers, 1973).
67. See D. S. Otis, *The Dawes Act and the Allotment of Indian Land* (Norman: University of Oklahoma Press, 1973).
68. F. E. Leupp, *The Indian and His Problem* (New York: Charles Scribner's Sons, 1910), 93.
69. 187 U.S. 553 (1903).
70. Customary international law (*jus cogens*) with regard to treaty relations was not formally codified until the Vienna Convention on the Law of Treaties was produced in 1969. However, all parties—including the United States, which has yet to ratify it—concur that its major provisions have been in practical effect for two centuries or more. Article 27 of the Convention states categorically that no state can invoke its own internal laws (including its constitution) as a basis to avoid meeting its treaty obligations. *Lonewolf* plainly defies this principle. On the Vienna Convention, see Sir I. Sinclair, *The Vienna Convention on the Law of Treaties* (Manchester: Manchester University Press, 1984). On the U.S. acknowledgment that its terms are valid and legally binding, see Senate Committee on the Judiciary, Subcommittee on the Constitution, *Hearing on Constitutional Issues Relating to the Proposed Genocide Convention Before the Subcommittee on the Constitution of the Senate Committee on the Judiciary*, 99th Cong., 1st Sess. (Washington, DC: Government Printing Office, 1985).
71. Ch. 233, 43 Stat. 25.
72. Jaimes, "Federal Indian Identification Policy," 127–28.
73. For the origins of this policy, see H. E. Fritz, *The Movement for Indian Assimilation, 1860–1890* (Philadelphia: University of Pennsylvania Press, 1963).
74. This is a clinically genocidal posture within the meaning of the term offered by Raphael Lemkin, the man who coined it:

> Generally speaking, genocide does not necessarily mean the immediate destruction of a nation, *except when* accomplished by mass killing of all the members of a nation. It is intended rather to signify a coordinated plan of different actions aimed at destruction of the essential foundations

of the life of national groups, with the aim of annihilating the groups themselves. The objective of such a plan would be disintegration of the political and social institutions, of culture, language, national feelings, religion, and the economic existence of national groups, and the destruction of personal security, liberty, health, dignity, and the lives of individuals belonging to such groups. Genocide is the destruction of the national group as an entity, and the actions involved are directed against individuals, not in their individual capacity but as members of the national group.

See R. Lemkin, *Axis Rule in Occupied Europe* (Washington, DC: Carnegie Endowment for International Peace, 1944), 79 (emphasis added).

75. As the Commissioner of Indian Affairs put it in his 1886 *Annual Report* (pp. xxiii–iv):

I [have] expressed very decidedly the idea that Indians should be taught the English language *only*. . . . There is not an Indian pupil whose tuition is paid for by the United States Government who is permitted to study *any* other language than our own vernacular—the language of the greatest, most powerful, and enterprising nationalities under the sun. The English language as taught in America is good enough for all her people of all races. (Emphasis added.)

76. Central Indian spiritual practices such as the potlatch of the nations of the Pacific Northwest and the sundance of the Lakota were prohibited under pain of criminal law. See D. Cole and I. Chaikan, *An Iron Hand Upon the People: The Law Against Potlatch on the Northwest Coast* (Seattle: University of Washington Press, 1990), and C. E. Jackson and M. J. Galli, *A History of the Bureau of Indian Affairs and Its Activities Among Indians* (San Francisco: R&E Research Associates, 1977).

77. On the boarding school system and its effects, see J. Noriega, "American Indian Education in the United States: Indoctrination for Subordination to Colonialism," in Jaimes, *State of Native America*, 371–402. It should be noted that such systematic transfer of the children of a targeted racial or ethnic group to the targeting group is defined as a genocidal act under Article II(e) of the 1948 Convention on the Prevention and Punishment of the Crime of Genocide.

78. The Lakota, for example, rapidly developed a basis for reservation self-sufficiency predicated in livestock during the quarter-century following the 1890 Wounded Knee Massacre. During World War I, however, the United States appealed to Lakota "patriotism" to engage in a near-total and cut-rate sell-off of their cattle to provide rations for American troops fighting in France. After the war, when the Lakota requested assistance in replenishing their herds, the government declined. Lakota grazing lands were then leased by the BIA to non-Indian ranchers, while the Indians assumed a position of permanent destitution. See E. Lazarus, *Black Hills, White Justice: The Sioux Nation versus the United States, 1775 to the Present* (New York: Harper Collins Publishers, 1991), 150–52.

79. Letter, Charles Burke to William Williamson, September 16, 1921; William Williamson Papers, Box 2, Indian Matters, Miscellaneous (I. D. Weeks Library, University of South Dakota). Such articulation of official sensibility was hardly isolated; see *The Commissioners of Indian Affairs, 1824–1977*, ed. R. M. Kvasnicka and H. J. Viola (Lincoln: University of Nebraska Press, 1979).

80. The method was to withdraw federal recognition of the existence of specific indigenous nations, converting large reservations into counties, or incorporating smaller reservations into existing counties. Examples

of legislation enacted pursuant to House Resolution 108, which implemented such practices, include the Menominee Termination Act (Ch. 303, 68 Stat. 250 (June 17, 1954)), Lmanath Termination Act (Ch. 732, 68 Stat. 718 (August 13, 1954), codified at 25 U.S.C. 564 et seq.), and the Act Terminating the Tribes of Western Oregon (Ch. 733, 68 Stat. 724 (August 13, 1954), codified at 25 U.S.C. 691 et seq.).

81. Public Law 959. For details of implementation, see D. L. Fixico, *Termination and Relocation: Federal Indian Policy, 1945–1960* (Albuquerque: University of New Mexico Press, 1986).

82. The U.S. Census of 1900 reported almost no Indians (0.4 percent of the native population) living in cities. A half-century later, the 1950 Census showed that the proportion had grown to only 13.4 percent. With the implementation of coherent federal relocation programs, however, the number mushroomed to 44.5 percent by 1970. Although relocation was geared down during the 1970s, and finally suspended during the 1980s, it continues to have a lingering effect, with the result that the proportion of urban Indians grew to 49 percent in 1980 and to about 52 percent in 1990. See Stiffarm and Lane, *The Demography of North America*, 42 & citations.

83. Ch. 505, 67 Stat. 588 (August 14, 1954), codified in part at 18 U.S.C. 1162 and 28 U.S.C. 1360. For details of implementation, see C. E. Goldberg, "Public Law 280: The Limits of State Law over Indian Reservations," *UCLA L. Rev.* 22 (1975): 535.

84. On resource distribution, see generally M. Garrity, "The U.S. Colonial Empire Is as Close as the Nearest Reservation," in *Trilateralism: The Trilateral Commission and Elite Planning for World Government*, ed H. Sklar (Boston: South End Press, 1980), 238–68. See also *Native Americans and Energy Development II*, ed. J. G. Jorgenson (Cambridge, MA: Anthropology Resource Center/Seventh Generation Funds, 1984).

85. See McDonnell, *The Dispossession of the American Indian*.

86. The IRA was implemented by referenda, reservation by reservation. In instances where traditionals such as the Hopi manifested their resistance to it through the time-honored means of boycotting the proceedings, however, Indian Commissioner John Collier counted their abstentions as "aye" votes. The same method was used with regard to the Lakota Nation, as well as the inclusion of "aye" votes allegedly cast by long-dead voters. Such fraud permeated implementation of reorganization throughout Indian country. See the testimony of Rupert Costo in *Indian Self-Rule: First-Hand Accounts of Indian-White Relations from Roosevelt to Reagan*, ed. K. R. Philip (Salt Lake City: Howe Brothers Publishers, 1986). See also G. D. Taylor, *The New Deal and American Indian Tribalism: The Administration of the Indian Reorganization Act, 1934–45* (Lincoln: University of Nebraska Press, 1980).

87. For further background, see V. Deloria and C. M. Lytle, *The Nations Within: The Past and Future of American Indian Sovereignty* (New York: Pantheon Press, 1984).

88. J. Durham, "Native Americans and Colonialism," *The Guardian*, March 28, 1979. See also T. L. Ammot and J. A. Matthei, *Race, Gender and Work: A Multicultural Economic History of Women in the United States* (Boston: South End Press, 1991).

89. For a somewhat conservative, but nonetheless official acknowledgment of this situation, see U.S. Commission on Civil Rights, *The Navajo Nation: An American Colony* (Washington, DC: U.S. Commission on Civil

Rights, 1976); see also Garrity, "The U.S. Colonial Empire."

90. Primarily at issue are the Navajo reservation (Arizona/New Mexico), Acoma and Laguna Pueblos (New Mexico), Yakima reservation (Washington State), and the Pine Ridge Sioux reservation (South Dakota). For further information—including the 1972 recommendation by the National Institute of Science that the Black Hills and Four Corners regions, the areas of the United States most heavily populated by native people, be designated as National Sacrifice Areas—see W. Churchill and W. LaDuke, "Native America: The Political Economy of Radioactive Colonization," in Jaimes, *State of Native America*, 241–66.

91. This idea has been increasingly fronted during the 1980s by the Council of Energy Resource Tribes (CERT), a federally supported consortium of representatives from IRA tribal councils. See W. LaDuke, "The Council of Energy Resource Tribes: An Outsider's View In," in Jorgenson, *Native Americans*.

92. See U.S. Bureau of the Census, *1980 Census of the Population, Supplementary Reports, Race of the Population by States, 1980* (Washington, DC: Government Printing Office, 1981); see also U.S. Bureau of the Census, *Ancestry of the Population by State, 1980*, Suppl. Rep. PC80-SI-10 (Washington, DC: Government Printing Office, 1983).

93. This argument is advanced rather well in G. F. Seib, "Indians Awaken to Their Lands' Energy Riches and Seek to Wrest Development from Companies," *Wall Street Journal*, September 20, 1979.

94. See U.S. Bureau of the Census, *General Population Characteristics: United States Summary*, PC80-1-B1, Pt. 1 (Washington, DC: Government Printing Office, 1983); see also U.S. Bureau of the Census, *General Social and Economic Characteristics: United States Summary* (Washington, DC: Government Printing Office, 1983) and *1980 Census of the Population, Supplementary Report: American Indian Areas and Alaska Native Villages* (Washington, DC: Government Printing Office, 1984).

95. See U.S. Bureau of the Census, Population Division, Racial Statistics Branch, *A Statistical Profile of the American Indian Population* (Washington, DC: Government Printing Office, 1984); see also U.S. Department of Health and Human Services, *Chart Series Book*, HE20.9409.988 (Washington, DC: Public Health Service, 1988).

96. The quote is taken from E. Galeano, *The Open Veins of Latin America: Five Centuries of the Pillage of a Continent* (New York: Monthly Review Press, 1973).

97. For analysis of the U.S. role in formulating the so-called Nuremberg Doctrine under which the Nazi leadership was tried for violating "customary international law," see B. F. Smith, *The American Road to Nuremberg: The Documentary Record* (Palo Alto: Stanford University Press, 1981). On specific aspects of the German performance in World War II that led to comparison with the earlier American "winning of the West," see A. Dallin, *German Rule in Russia, 1941–1944* (London: Macmillan Publishers, 1957).

98. 60 Stat. 1049 (1946).

99. See A. Ehrenfeld and R. W. Barker, comps., *Legislative Material on the Indian Claims Commission Act of 1946* (Washington, DC, n.d.).

100. For an analysis, see J. J. Vance, "The Congressional Mandate and the Indian Claims Commission," *North Dakota L. Rev.* 45 (1969): 325–36.

101. In 1956, the original ten-year life span of the commission was extended for five years. The process was repeated in 1961, 1972, and 1976. See

U.S. Congress, Joint Committee on Appropriations, *Hearings on Appropriations for the Department of the Interior*, 94th Cong., 1st Sess. (Washington, DC: Government Printing Office, 1976).

102. U.S. Department of Interior, Indian Claims Commission, *Final Report* (Washington, DC: Government Printing Office, 1978).

103. R. Barsh, "Indian Land Claims Policy in the United States," *North Dakota L. Rev.* 58 (1982): 1.

104. Public Law 92–203; 85 Stat. 688, codified at 43 U.S.C. 1601 et seq. For background, see M. C. Berry, *The Alaska Pipeline: The Politics of Oil and Native Land Claims* (Bloomington and Indianapolis: Indiana University Press, 1975).

105. H. Kay Trask, lecture delivered at University of Colorado at Boulder, March 14, 1992 (tape on file with author). For "official" data, see L. Callelora, *The Origin of Hawaiian Land Titles and the Rights of Native Tenants* (Honolulu: Security Title Corporation, 1974).

106. *Sioux Nation of Indians v. United States*, 448 U.S. 371 (1980). For analysis, see S. C. Hanson, "*United States v. Sioux Nation*: Political Questions, Moral Imperative and National Honor," *American Indian L. Rev.* 8 (1980): 459–84.

107. *Western Shoshone Identifiable Group v. United States*, 40 Ind. Cl. Comm. 311 (1977); *United States v. Dann*, 706 F.2d 919, 926 (9th Cir. 1983). For background, see G. T. Morris, "The Battle for Newe Segobia: The Western Shoshone Land Rights Struggle," in *Critical Issues in Native North America*, ed. W. Churchill (Copenhagen: International Work Group on Indigenous Affairs, 1991), 286–98.

108. For details, see P. Matthiessen, *In the Spirit of Crazy Horse* (New York: Viking Press, 1991). Also see W. Churchill and J. Vander Wall, *Agents of Repression: The FBI's Secret Wars Against the Black Panther Party and the American Indian Movement* (Boston: South End Press, 1988).

109. The global study has been completed; see J. R. Martinez Cobo (Commission on Human Rights), *Study of the Problem of Discrimination Against Indigenous Populations, Final Report: Conclusions, Proposals and Recommendations*, U.N./ID no. E/CN.4/Sub.2/1983/21/Add.83 (September 1983). At present, an enhancing study covering the extent and nature of treaty relations between indigenous peoples and various states around the world is being completed by the Cuban representative to the Working Group, Miguel Alfonso Martinez. Meanwhile, a draft Universal Declaration of the Rights of Indigenous Peoples has been prepared, and is in the process of revision prior to its submission to the U.N. General Assembly.

110. As the U.S. Department of State put it in its presentation to the Working Group in 1980 (p. 13): "Actually, the U.S. Government entered into a trust relationship with the separate tribes in acknowledgement . . . of their political status as sovereign national"; quoted in R. Dunbar Ortiz, "Protection of American Indian Territories in the United States: Applicability of International Law," in *Irredeemable America: The Indians' Estate and Land Claims*, ed. I. Sutton (Albuquerque: University of New Mexico Press, 1985), 247–70.

111. This jockeying is well summarized in S. J. Anaya, "The Rights of Indigenous Peoples and International Law in Historical and Contemporary Perspective," in *American Indian Law: Cases and Materials*, ed. N. J. Newton and M. E. Price (Charlottesville: The Michie Co., Law Publishers, 1991), 1257–76.

112. For analysis, see Ortiz, *American Indian Territories*, 260–61.

113. The texts of these instruments may be found in Brownlie, *Basic Documents*.

114. In October 1985, President Ronald Reagan withdrew a 1946 U.S. declaration accepting ICJ jurisdiction in all matters of "international dispute."
The withdrawal took effect in April 1986. This was in response to the
ICJ determination in *Nicaragua v. United States*, the first substantive case
ever brought before it to which the United States was a party. The ICJ
ruled the U.S. action of mining Nicaraguan harbors in times of peace to
be unlawful. The Reagan administration formally rejected the authority
of the ICJ to decide the matter (but removed the mines). It is undoubtedly significant that the Reagan instrument contained a clause accepting continued ICJ jurisdiction over matters pertaining to "international
commercial relationships," thus attempting to convert the World Court
into a mechanism for mere trade arbitration. See U.S. Department of
State, *U.S. Terminates Acceptance of ICJ Compulsory Jurisdiction*, Department of State Bulletin no. 86 (Washington, DC: Government Printing
Office, 1986).

115. The United States declined to ratify the Genocide Convention until 1988,
forty years after it became international law (and after more than 100
other nations had ratified it), and then only with an attached "Sovereignty Package" purporting to subordinate the convention to the U.S.
Constitution (thereby seeking to protect certain aspects of genocidal
conduct). The U.S. stipulation in this regard is, of course, invalid under
Article 27 of the 1969 Vienna Convention on the Law of Treaties, and has
been protested by such countries as Britain, Denmark, and the
Netherlands. Furthermore, the Genocide Convention is now customary
international law, meaning—according to the United States' own Nuremberg Doctrine—that it is binding upon the United States, whether Congress ratifies its terms or not. For further analysis, see L. J. LeBlanc, *The
United States and the Genocide Convention* (Durham: Duke University Press,
1991).

116. The Inouye Committee is following up on the groundwork laid for such
a maneuver by such earlier incorporative legislation as the Indian Civil
Rights Act of 1968 (Public Law 90–284; 82 Stat. 77, codified in part at
25 U.S.C. 1301 et seq.) and the Indian Self-Determination and Educational Assistance Act of 1975 (Public Law 93–638; 88 Stat. 2203, codified
at 25 U.S.C. 450a and elsewhere in Titles 25, 42, and 50, U.S.C.A.). It
should be noted that the latter completely inverts international definitions of "self-determination," providing instead for an Indian preference in the hiring of individuals to fill positions within the federal system
of administering Indian country. Critics such as AIM leader Russell Means
have therefore dubbed it the "Indian Self-Administration Act." For details on the committee itself, see U.S. Senate, Select Committee on Indian Affairs, *Final Report and Legislative Recommendations: A Report of the
Special Committee on Investigations*, 101st Cong., 2d Sess. (Washington,
DC: Government Printing Office, 1989).

117. For the context of this rhetoric, see N. Chomsky, "What We Say Goes:
The Middle East in the New World Order," in *Collateral Damage: The
"New World Order" at Home and Abroad*, ed. C. Peters (Boston: South
End Press, 1992), 49–92.

118. For further information, see N. Chomsky and E. Ahmed, "The Gulf Crisis:
How We Got There," in *Mobilizing Democracy: Changing the U.S. Role in
the Middle East*, ed. G. Bates (Monroe: Common Courage Press, 1991),
3–24.

CHAPTER 13

* This paper was first published, in substantially similar form, in *Law & Sexuality: A Review of Lesbian and Gay Legal Issues*, vol. 1, pp. 9–30, © copyright 1991; all rights reserved. Earlier versions of this paper were presented at the Law and Sexuality Symposium, "The Family in the 1990s: An Exploration of Lesbian and Gay Rights," Tulane University School of Law, October 5, 1990, and at the Fourth Lesbian, Bisexual, and Gay Studies Conference at Harvard University, October 27, 1990. I would like to thank Lisa Duggan, Ruth Colker, Susan Herman, Elizabeth Schneider, Nancy Fink, and Patti Roberts for their insightful comments; Paul Finkelman for his research suggestions; and Teresa Matushaj for able assistance.

1. *Jones v. Hallahan*, 501 S. W. 2d 588 (Ky. Ct. App. 1973); *Baker v. Nelson*, 291 Minn. 310, 191 N. W. 2d 185 (1971), appeal dismissed, 409 U.S. 810 (1972); *Singer v. Hara*, 11 Wash. App. 247, 522 P. 2d 1187 (1974). In two other cases, gay couples have undergone ceremonies of marriage and then sought legal recognition of the marriage to obtain collateral benefits; in each, the court found no legal marriage existed. *Adams v. Howerton*, 673 F. 2d 1036 (9th Cir. 1982), cert. denied, 458 U.S. 1111 (1982); *McConnell v. Nooner*, 547 F. 2d 54 (8th Cir. 1976). In two more recent decisions, courts reached the same result. A New York appellate court denied a right of election against a will to a man asserting that he was the decedent's gay spouse equivalent. *Matter of Cooper*, 187 A.D. 2d 128, 592 N.Y. 2d 797 (1993). And a Pennsylvania trial court refused to grant a divorce to a gay male couple, one of whom argued that they had entered into a common-law marriage, which Pennsylvania recognizes for heterosexual couples. *DeSanto v. Barnsley*, 328 Pa. Super. 181, 476 A. 2d 952 (Pa. Super. Ct. 1984).
2. The primary constitutional claims, based on equal protection and privacy principles, as well as a challenge under a state equal rights amendment, were all pressed in the cases brought during the 1970s. Although the body of decisional law in each of these doctrinal areas has grown since then, the new case law has not lessened the difficulties of a marriage claim on behalf of lesbian or gay couples. The fundamentality of the right to marry as an aspect of personal privacy has been more fully articulated in *Zablocki v. Redhail*, 434 U.S. 374 (1978), but the same right of privacy also has been found not to encompass protection from criminal prosecution for consensual adult homosexual conduct. (*Bowers v. Hardwick*, 478 U.S. 186 (1986)). Since the counsel arguing to uphold the Georgia sodomy law at issue in *Hardwick* conceded during oral argument that even sexual behavior that fell within the definition of sodomy could not be the subject for prosecution if it occurred between spouses, a fascinating legal anomaly would result if a state relied on *Hardwick* to prosecute a married lesbian or gay couple. See 478 U.S. at 218 n. 10; transcript of oral argument at 7–8 (copy on file at the *Law & Sexuality* office).
   Equal protection doctrine as it has been applied to lesbian and gay Americans has also yielded mixed results. Although many courts have refused to invalidate classifications based on sexual orientation, most of the decisions can be read as involving deference to the special authority of the military, national security, or police agencies in personnel matters. See, e.g., *High-Tech Gays v. Defense Indus. Sec. Clearance Office*, 895 F. 2d 563 (9th Cir. 1990) (security clearances); *Ben-Shalom v. Marsh*, 881 F. 2d 454 (7th Cir. 1989) (Army Reserve), cert. denied, 110 S. Ct. 1296 (1990);

Woodward v. United States, 871 F. 2d 1068 (Fed. Cir. 1989) (Navy Reserve), cert. denied, 110 S. Ct. 1295 (1990); *Padula v. Webster*, 822 F. 2d 97 (D. C. Cir. 1987) (FBI); *Dronenburg v. Zech*, 741 F. 2d 1388 (D. C. Cir. 1984) (Navy). Some receptivity to equal protection claims has emerged even within those fields. See, e.g., *Dubbs v. Central Intelligence Agency*, 866 F. 2d 1114 (9th Cir. 1989) (denial of motion to dismiss equal protection claim in security clearance case); *Watkins v. United States*, 847 F. 2d 1329 (9th Cir. 1988) (refusal to bar reenlistment by openly gay male Army sergeant after Army permitted prior reenlistments), vacated and aff'd on other grounds, 875 F. 2d 699 (9th Cir. 1989) (en banc), cert. denied, 111 S. Ct. 384 (1990). Outside of these sensitive areas, courts have ruled favorably on equal protection challenges to discrimination in governmental employments. See, e.g., *Swift v. United States*, 649 F. Supp. 596 (D. D. C. 1986) (denial of motion to dismiss claim of White House staff stenographer allegedly fired because of homosexuality).

An additional constitutional ground, not relied on in prior cases, may be available under the Constitution's protection of the freedom to form intimate associations, a branch of the liberty guarantee of the due process clause. Exclusionary marriage laws could be stricken as violative of the principle that insulates from state infringement "family relationships . . . [that] involve deep attachments and commitments to the necessarily few other individuals with whom one shares not only a special community of thoughts, experiences, and beliefs, but also distinctively personal aspects of one's life." *Roberts v. United States Jaycees*, 468 U.S. 609, 619–20 (1984). The Court identified the attributes of those relationships in terms strikingly similar to the language used by the New York Court of Appeals to accord "family" status to a gay male couple for the purpose of protection from eviction, in *Braschi v. Stahl Associates*, 74 N.Y. 2d 201, 543 N. E. 2d 49, 544 N. Y. S. 2d 784 (1989). Compare *Roberts*, 468 U.S. at 610–20, with *Braschi*, 74 N.Y. 2d at 212–13, 543 N. E. 2d at 55, 544 N.Y. S. 2d at 790.

3. *Baehr v. Lewin*, 852 P. 2d 44 (1993).
4. Note, "A More Perfect Union: A Legal and Social Analysis of Domestic Partnership Ordinances," *Colorado L. Rev.* 92 (1992): 1164.
5. K. Bishop, "San Francisco Grants Recognition to Couples Who Aren't Married," *New York Times*, May 31, 1989, A17.
6. K. Bishop, "Not Quite a Wedding, But Quite a Day for Couples by the Bay," *New York Times*, February 15, 1991, A16.
7. Danish Partnership Act, Danish Act 372, June 7, 1989 (unofficial translation).
8. See Gutis, "Small Steps Toward Acceptance Renew Debate on Gay Marriage," *New York Times*, November 5, 1989, E24; A. Sullivan, "Here Comes the Groom: A (Conservative) Case for Gay Marriage," *New Republic*, August 28, 1989, 20; W. Isaacson, "Should Gays Have Marriage Rights? On Two Different Coasts, the Growing Debate Produces Two Different Answers," *Time*, November 20, 1989, 101; T. Levin, "Suit Over Death Benefits Asks, What Is a Family?" *New York Times*, September 21, 1990, B7.
9. The best exposition of this debate can be found in two companion articles published under the heading "Gay Marriage: A Must or a Bust?": P. L. Ettelbrick, "Since When Was Marriage a Path to Liberation?" and T. B. Stoddard, "Why Gay People Should Seek the Right to Marry," *Out/Look, National Gay and Lesbian Quarterly* 6 (1989): 8. For an account of an earlier version of the debate, see D. Teal, *The Gay Militants* (New York: Stein and Day, 1971), 282–93.

10. Stoddard acknowledges the oppressiveness of marriage in its traditional form, but argues that legalizing lesbian and gay marriage "is . . . the political issue that most fully tests the dedication of people who are not gay to full equality for gay people, and also the issue most likely to lead ultimately to a world free from discrimination against lesbians and gay men." Stoddard, "Gay People," 12.

11. See, e.g., S. A. Scheingold, *The Politics of Rights: Lawyers, Public Policy, and Political Change* (New Haven: Yale University Press, 1974).

12. See, e.g., S. Firestone, *The Dialectic of Sex: The Case for Feminist Revolution* (New York: Morrow, 1970); S. Cronan, "Marriage," in *Radical Feminism*, ed. A. Koedt, E. Levine, and A. Rapone (New York: Quadrangle Books, 1973), 213–21; M. Barrett and M. McIntosh, *The Anti-Social Family* (London: Verso, 1982). For an account of the politics of the early stage of the second wave of feminism, when criticism of marriage was at its height, see A. Echols, *Daring to Be Bad: Radical Feminism in America 1967–1975* (Minneapolis: University of Minnesota Press, 1989).

13. Ettelbrick counterposes "rights" with "justice," arguing that the former may lead to empty victories, and that justice requires that society validate the differentness of lesbians and gay men: "Being queer . . . is an identity, a culture with many variations." Ettelbrick, "Marriage a Path to Liberation," 14. The antimarriage argument was also expressed at the time of the first round of attempts at legalizing lesbian and gay marriage. Writing in 1970, Ralph Hall argued, "Homosexual marriages submitting to the guidelines of so-called conventional rites must be classed as reactionary. . . . [I]t isn't relevant to gay liberation when we start imitating meaningless, bad habits of our oppressors. . . . That isn't our liberation. That isn't the freedom we want." R. Hall, "The Church, State, and Homosexuality: A Radical Analysis," *Gay Power* no. 14, quoted in Teal, *Gay Militants*, 291.

14. See, e.g., S. A. Law, "Rethinking Sex and the Constitution," *U. Pa. L. Rev.* 132 (1984): 955; W. Williams, "Equality's Riddle: Pregnancy and the Equal Treatment/Special Treatment Debate," *N.Y.U. Rev. L. and Soc. Change* 13 (1984/1985): 325.

15. Neither *Baker v. Nelson*, 291 Minn. 310, 191 N. W. 2d 185 (1971), appeal dismissed, 409 U.S. 810 (1972), nor *Jones v. Hallahan*, 501 S. W. 2d 588 (Ky. Ct. App. 1973), occupies more than three printed pages in the published reports. The *Jones* court found simply that "no constitutional issue in involved." 501 S. W. 2d at 590. Although the court in *Singer v. Hara*, 11 Wash. App. 247, 522 P. 2d 1187 (1974), addressed the issues presented, it was equally circular in its reasoning:

> There is no analogous sexual classification [to the racial classification in *Loving*] involved in the instant case because appellants are not being denied entry into the marriage relationship because of their sex; rather, they are being denied entry . . . because of the recognized definition of that relationship as one [that] may be entered into only by . . . members of the opposite sex.

Singer, 11 Wash. App. at 254–55, 533 P. 2d at 1192 (footnote omitted).

16. See A. Swerdlow et al., *Household and Kin: Families in Flux* (New York: McGraw-Hill, 1981); H. G. Gutman, *The Black Family in Slavery and Freedom 1750–1925* (New York: Pantheon, 1976); J. Collier, M. Rosaldo, and S. Yanagisako, "Is There a Family? New Anthropological Views," in *Rethinking the Family: Some Feminist Questions*, ed. B. Thorne and M. Yalom

(New York: Longmans, 1982); M. Ryan, "The Explosion of Family History," *Review of American History* 10, no. 4 (1982): 181, 186–87; J. Bernard, *The Future of Marriage* (New York: World Publishing, 1973), 272–80. In *Jones v. Hallahan*, plaintiffs presented evidence of cross-cultural variability through the testimony of an anthropology professor that women in other cultures, including several African tribal communities, married each other. The trial judge retorted that he was interested only in "this culture," not the cultures of Africa. Teal, *Gay Militants*, 290.

17. E. Kandoian, "Cohabitation, Common Law Marriage, and the Possibility of a Shared Moral Life," *Georgetown L. J.* 75 (1987): 1838 (footnotes omitted).

18. The Kentucky Court of Appeals went the farthest, both in invoking nature and in drawing a complete circle, when it held that

> . . . appellants are prevented from marrying, not by the statutes of Kentucky or the refusal of the County Court Clerk of Jefferson County to issue them a license, but rather by their own incapability of entering into a marriage as that term is defined. A license to enter into a status or a relationship [that] the parties are incapable of achieving is a nullity.

Jones, 501 S. W. 2d at 589.

As the second sentence makes clear, the Kentucky court not only ignores the law's power to command the terms of marriage, to define and therefore to redefine it, but also completely flips the relationship, to the point of casting the law as helpless against the rule of nature. In this configuration, any marriage license that might be granted to the plaintiffs (pursuant to an amended statute, for example) would be a mere "nullity."

19. 388 U.S. 1 (1967).

20. *Baker v. Nelson*, 291 Minn. 310, 315, 191 N. W. 2d 185, 187 (1971) (emphasis added).

21. See *Singer v. Hara*, 11 Wash. App. 247, 255, n. 8, 522 P.2d 1187, 1192 n.8.

22. See *Singer*, 11, Wash. App. at 254, 522 P.2d at 1194.

23. See, e.g., *Malinda and Sarah v. Gardner*, 24 Ala. 719 (1854); *Frazier v. Spear*, 2 Bibb 385 (Ky. 1811); *Girod v. Lewis*, 6 Mart. 559 (La. 1819); *Johnson v. Johnson*, 45 Mo. 595 (1870); *Brewer v. Harris*, 5 Grattan 285 (Va. 1848). Despite the legal prohibition, enslaved persons formed enduring relationships that were recognized within the African-American community as marriages. See Gutman, *The Black Family*, 270–73.

24. See *Perez v. Sharp*, 32 Cal.2d 711 (1948); *Perez v. Lippold*, 198 P.2d 17 (Cal. 1948) (same case).

25. See I. Drummond, *The Sex Paradox* (New York: Putnam, 1953), 361–62. In addition, some states imposed heavier penalties for violation of fornication or adultery laws when partners of different races were involved. See, e.g., *McLaughlin v. Florida*, 379 U.S. 184 (1964).

26. E. De Grazia and R. Newman, *Banned Films: Movies, Censors, and the First Amendment* (New York: Bowker, 1982), 92.

27. See, e.g., J. Younger, "Community Property, Women and the Law School Curriculum," *N.Y.U. L. Rev.* 48 (1973): 211 (describing husband's control over jointly owned property); M. A. Glendon, "Marriage and the State: The Withering Away of Marriage," *Virginia L. Rev.* 62 (1976): 702–703. See generally A. E. Freedman et al., "Sex Role Discrimination in the Law of the Family," in Freedman, *Sex Role Discrimination and the Law: Causes and Remedies* (Boston: Little, Brown, 1975), 561–66.

28. *The First Restatement of the Law of Contracts* (1932), §587, for example, forbade legal enforcement of "[a] bargain between married persons or

persons contemplating marriage to change the essential incidents of marriage." The courts declared void as against public policy because they sought to alter the "essential" elements of marriage a variety of contracts between spouses, including: to permit the wife to choose the marital domicile, *Graham v. Graham*, 33 F. Supp. 936 (E. D. Mich. 1940), and *Sacks v. Sacks*, 200 Pa. Super. 223, 225 (1938); to provide wages to the wife for care she provided to the husband, *Tellez v. Tellez*, 51 N. M. 416, 186 P.2d 390 (1947), or to enforce a contract between the parties to pay the wife for work she performed as a business partner, *Standen v. Pennsylvania R. R. Co.*, 214 Pa. 189, 63 A. 467 (1906); and to end the husband's duty to support his wife, *Kershner v. Kershner*, 244 A. D. 34, 278 N. Y. S. 501 (1935), *aff'd per curiam*, 269 N. Y. 654, 200 N. E. 43 (1936). See Freedman et al., "Sex Role Discrimination in the Law of the Family."

Socially, the consequences of deviance have been considered cataclysmic. Role reversal between husband and wife in African-American families was so debilitating, asserted Daniel Moynihan in 1965, as to underlie what he called "the tangle of pathology" in the black community. L. Rainwater and W. L. Yancey, *The Moynihan Report and the Politics of Controversy* (Cambridge: MIT Press, 1967), 30. See P. Giddings, *When and Where I Enter: The Impact of Black Women on Race and Sex in America* (New York: Morrow, 1984), 325–29 (analyzing the Moynihan report). The phrase "female-headed household" is still widely used as synonymous with social pathology.

29. See *Jones v. Hallahan*, 501 S.W.2d 588 (Ky. Ct. App. 1973); *Baker v. Nelson*, 291 Minn. 310, 191 N.W.2d 185 (1971), appeal dismissed, 409 U.S. 810 (1972); *Singer v. Hara*, 11 Wash. App. 247, 522 P.2d 1187 (1974); see also note 2 above.

30. At least in the abstract, "the test for determining the validity of a gender-based classification . . . must be applied free from fixed notions concerning the roles and abilities of males and females." *Mississippi University for Women v. Hogan*, 458 U. S. 718, 724–25 (1982).

31. See *Kirchberg v. Feenstra*, 450 U. S. 455, 459–60 (1981); *Wengler v. Druggists Mutual Ins. Co.*, 446 U. S. 142, 147 (1980); *Orr v. Orr*, 440 U. S. 268, 293 (1979).

32. See *Stanton v. Stanton*, 421 U. S. 7, 14 (1975); *Reed v. Reed*, 404 U. S. 71, 74 (1971).

33. See L. Weitzman, *The Divorce Revolution: The Unexpected Social and Economic Consequences for Women and Children in America* (New York: Free Press, 1985); N. Hunter, "Child Support Law and Policy: The Systematic Imposition of Costs on Women," *Harvard Women's L. J.* 6 (1983): 1.

34. See *Singer v. Hara*, 11 Wash. App. at 254, 522 P.2d at 1195 (1974).

35. Comparably powerful social inequalities of race and class, which also resonate between spouses, would, of course, remain. This argument does not presume that same-sex relationships are inherently egalitarian.

36. *Singer*, 11 Wash. App. at 254, 522 P.2d at 1195.

37. See M. Felder, "Grounds for Divorce," in *Family Law and Practice*, ed. A. H. Rutkin, 5 vols. (New York: Matthew Bender, 1991), 4:21 (1990 revision by the Honorable J. D. Montgomery) (describing the grounds for divorce); A. Momjian, "Annulment," in *Family Law and Practice*, ed. Rutkin, 5:6, 8–9 (describing the grounds for annulment). Most states recognize that an intent not to consummate the marriage by engaging in sexual relations does form the basis for divorce or annulment, at least if the other party was unaware of that intent. See *Rathburn v. Rathburn*, 138 Cal. App.2d 568, 292 P.2d 274 (1956); *Uniform Marriage and Divorce Act* §208(a)(2); Felder,

"Grounds for Divorce," 4:15, 5:8. However, neither the Uniform Act nor the treatises report infertility as a ground for annulment or divorce. Only one court has ruled otherwise, on grounds of intent rather than incapacity. See *Link v. Link*, 48 A. D.2d 902, 369 N. Y. S.2d 496 (2d Dept. 1975) (holding that secret intention not to have children is sufficient case for annulment). There are an estimated 1 million married couples in the United States who have no children and who are considered infertile. W. D. Mosher and W. F. Pratt, "Fecundity and Infertility in the United States, 1965–88," in 192 *Advance Data from Vital and Health Statistics of the National Center for Health Statistics* (Washington, DC: Government Printing Office, 1990), 1, 5.

38. In cases involving lesbian and gay parents, the fear that children will be exposed to the wrong "role models" is a constant refrain. In affirming a trial court's order removing custody of a daughter from her divorced mother, alleged to be a lesbian, the Missouri Court of Appeals described at length

> ... the evidence ... of [the lover] as a powerful, a dominant personality. She had befriended [the daughter] and had won her affection and her loyalty. She had broached the idea of homosexuality to the child. Allowing that homosexuality is a permissible life style—an "alternative life style," as it is termed these days—if voluntarily chosen, yet who would place the child in a milieu where she may be inclined toward it? She may thereby be condemned, in one degree or another, to sexual disorientation.

N. K. M. v. L. E. M., 606 S. W.2d 179, 186 (Mo. Ct. App. 1980). In *Opinion of the Justices*, 525 A.2d 1095 (N. H. 1987), the New Hampshire Supreme Court (including then-state court judge David Souter) held that legislation forbidding lesbians or gay men from adopting children would be constitutional, stating that "we accept the assertion that the provision of appropriate role models is a legitimate government purpose. . . . [W]e believe that the legislature can rationally act on the theory that a role model can influence the child's developing sexual identity." Ibid., at 1098–99. A similar statute exists in Florida. See Fl. Stat. Ann. §63.042(3) (West 1985). Other custody and visitation cases in which the courts have expressed concern with the impact of lesbian or gay parents as role models include *Jacobson v. Jacobson*, 314 N.W.2d 78, 79–81 (N. D. 1981); *S. v. S.*, 608 S.W.2d 64, 66 (Ky. Ct. App. 1980), cert. denied, 451 U. S. 911 (1981); and *Woodruff v. Woodruff*, 44 N. C. App. 350, 260 S.E.2d 775, 776 (1979). It is notable that the Danish law permitting a form of same-sex marriage expressly forbids lesbian and gay couples from adopting children. See Danish Registered Partnership Act.

39. A *Time*/CNN poll found that 54 percent of respondents agreed that "homosexual couples should be permitted to receive medical and life insurance policies," but 69 percent opposed the legalization of marriage for lesbian and gay couples. Isaacson, "Should Gays Have Marriage Rights?"

40. "Homosexual relationships challenge dichotomous concepts of gender. These relationships challenge the notion that social traits, such as dominance and nurturance, are naturally linked to one sex or the other." S. A. Law, "Homosexuality and the Social Meaning of Gender," *Wisconsin L. Rev.* (1988): 187, 196. Law argues that "disapprobation of homosexual behavior is a reaction to the violation of gender norms, rather than simply scorn for the violation of norms of sexual behavior." Ibid., 187.

41. See R. Robson and S. E. Valentine, "Lov(h)ers: Lesbians as Intimate Part-

ners and Lesbian Legal Theory," *Temple L. Rev.* 63 (1990): 536–37.
42. bell hooks, an African-American feminist, has written of the perspective on family life shared by many women of color:

> [M]any black women find the family the least oppressive institution. Despite sexism in the context of family, we may experience dignity, self-worth, and a humanization that is not experienced in the outside world wherein we confront all forms of oppression. . . . [W]e know that family ties are the only sustained support system for exploited and oppressed peoples. We wish to rid family life of the abusive dimensions created by sexist oppression without devaluing it.

b. hooks, *Feminist Theory: From Margin to Center* (Boston: South End Press, 1984), 32.

43. Indeed, tautologies in judicial reasoning may signal weakness as well as strength. Perhaps the most famous example of a court invoking "nature" to legitimize the construction of gender was the notorious dictum of Justice Bradley in *Bradwell v. Illinois*. Justice Bradley wrote:

> [T]he civil law, as well as nature herself, has always recognized a wide difference in the respective spheres and destinies of man and woman . . . the natural and proper timidity and delicacy [that] belongs to the female sex evidently unfits it for many of the occupations of civil life. The constitution of the family organization, which is founded in the divine ordinance, as well as in the nature of things, indicates the domestic sphere as that which properly belongs to the domain and functions of womanhood.

83 U. S. (16 Wall) 130, 141 (1872). Ironically, the Illinois legislature adopted a statute that eliminated the legal principle upheld in *Bradwell* three years after the Supreme Court ruled. See M. Minow, " 'Forming Underneath Everything that Grows': Toward a History of Family Law," *Wisconsin L. Rev.* (1985): 849. Minow reads Justice Bradley's opinion to reflect his unease with the recognition that "[t]he law itself could change" and with "the vulnerability of his claims of natural and divine authority." Ibid., 844–45.

Similarly, the definitional rationale that has been characterized by each court addressing a gay marriage challenge as transcendent is in fact open to change at any time by the vote of a majority of any state's legislators, as well as by judicial interpretation.

44. See K. London, "Cohabitation, Marriage, Marital Dissolution, and Remarriage: United States, 1988," in 194 *Advance Data from Vital and Health Statistics of the National Center for Health Statistics* 1 (1991): 1.
45. Ibid., 2.
46. Bureau of the Census, U. S. Department of Commerce, "Marital Status and Living Arrangements: March 1989" 1 (1990): 1 (Current Population Reports, Population Characteristics Series P-20, no. 445) (Washington, DC: Government Printing Office, 1990).
47. National Center for Health Statistics, "Advance Report for Final Divorce Statistics, 1987," *Monthly Vital Statistics Report* 38, no. 12, suppl. 2 (Washington, DC: Government Printing Office, 1990).
48. American Psychiatric Association (APA) Task Force on Changing Family Patterns, *Changing Family Patterns in the United States* (Washington, DC: American Psychiatric Association, 1986), 5; C. Scott, "As Baby Boomers Age, Fewer Couples Untie the Knot," *Wall Street Journal*, November 7, 1990, B1.
49. APA, *Changing Family Patterns*, 9.
50. Bureau of the Census, "Marital Status," 2 (Table B). Interestingly, there

has been little long-term change in this figure. In 1960, the comparable numbers were 6 percent for women and 7 percent for men. Ibid.

51. Ibid., 9–10.
52. Criminal laws against cohabitation still exist in 13 states. M. Bernard et al., *The Rights of Single People* (New York: Bantam, 1985), 12. Enforcement, however, appears to be extremely selective and heavily skewed by class and race. A 1978 survey of district attorneys in one of those states (Wisconsin) found that more than 90 prosecutions for violating that state's anticohabitation law had been initiated in the preceding five years. The most common reason, accounting for a third of the prosecutions, was the desire to use the law to exert pressure on a welfare recipient—usually female—either to report income that officials suspected her of receiving from a male cohabitant, or to stop spending part of the welfare allowance to help support the man. M. L. Fineman, "Law and Changing Patterns of Behavior: Sanctions on Non-Marital Cohabitation," *Wisconsin L. Rev.* (1981): 287–90.

In addition, a wide range of benefits that are available to married couples are denied to unmarried couples. For a comprehensive survey, see B. J. Cox, "Alternative Families: Obtaining Traditional Family Benefits Through Litigation, Legislation and Collective Bargaining," *Wisconsin Women's L. J.* 2 (1986): 1.

53. See, e.g., *Hollenbough v. Carnegie Free Library*, 436 F. Supp. 1328 (W. D. Pa. 1977) (upholding firing of unmarried male and female public library employees because of the openness of their relationship), aff'd mem., 578 F.2d 1374 (3rd Cir. 1978), cert. denied, 439 U. S. 1052 (1978).
54. Numerous authors have described how the principles of law discussed herein have developed in response to the legal issues that arise when unmarried couples end a relationship. Of significant usefulness are G. G. Blumberg, "Cohabitation Without Marriage: A Different Perspective," *UCLA L. Rev.* 28 (1981): 1125; Kandoian, "Cohabitation, Common Law Marriage"; and Glendon, "Marriage and the State."
55. *Marvin v. Marvin*, 18 Cal. 3d 660, 557 P.2d 106, 134 Cal. Rptr. 815 (1976), was the case that broke this ground, and other jurisdictions have followed its lead. See *Levar v. Elkins*, 604 P.2d 602 (Alaska 1980); *Carroll v. Lee*, 148 Ariz. 10, 712 P.2d 923 (1986); *Boland v. Catalano*, 202 Conn. 333, 521 A.2d 142 (1987); *Carlson v. Olson*, 256 N. W.2d 249 (Minn. 1977); *Kinkenon v. Hue*, 207 Neb. 698, 301 N. W.2d 77 (1981); *Hay v. Hay*, 100 Nev. 196, 678 P.2d 672 (1984); *Kozlowski v. Kozlowski*, 80 N. J. 378, 403 A.2d 902 (1979); *Beal v. Beal*, 282 Or. 115, 577 P.2d 507 (1978); *Watts v. Watts*, 137 Wis. 2d 506, 405 N. W.2d 303 (1987). In at least one instance, the contract principle has been applied to a gay male couple. See *Whorton v. Dillingham*, 202 Cal. App. 3d 447, 248 Cal. Rptr. 405 (Cal. Ct. App. 1988).
56. *Contra Hewitt v. Hewitt*, 77 Ill. 2d 49, 58, 394 N. E.2d 1204, 1207–8 (1979).
57. This phrase was first employed by the New York Court of Appeals in holding that a household consisting of two surrogate parents and seven foster children was "the functional and factual equivalent of a natural family" for purposes of the zoning law. *Group House of Port Washington, Inc., v. Bd. of Zoning and Appeals of the Town of North Hempstead*, 45 N. Y.2d 266, 272, 380 N. E.2d 207, 209, 408 N. Y. S.2d 377, 379–80 (1978).
58. M. Grossberg, *Governing the Hearth: Law and Family in Nineteenth-Century America* (Chapel Hill: University of North Carolina Press, 1985), 69–78.
59. Courts in North Carolina and Georgia utilized principles of criminal and

evidentiary law applicable to spouses in cases involving de facto marriages between slaves. See *State v. John*, 30 N. C. (3 Ired.) 330 (1848); *William v. State*, 33 Ga. Supp. 85 (1964). See discussion in M. Tushnet, *American Law and Slavery* (Princeton: Princeton University Press, 1981), 15.

60. *Moore v. City of East Cleveland*, 431 U. S. 494 (1977).
61. Blumberg points out that the state is much more likely to treat nonmarital relationships as equivalent to married couples when the result is a disqualification for government benefits. See Blumberg, "Cohabitation Without Marriage," 1138–39. Glendon also found much more of a blurred distinction between married and de facto families in the realm of public, rather than private, law. See Glendon, "Marriage and the State," 711–15.
62. 74 N. Y.2d 201, 543 N. E.2d 49, 544 N. Y. S.2d 784 (1989). The New York State Division of Housing and Community Renewal subsequently promulgated regulations that codify the *Braschi* principles in some detail, for both rent-controlled and rent-stabilized housing units. A preliminary injunction to prevent those regulations from taking effect, brought by a landlords' organization, was denied. *Rent Stabilization Ass'n v. Higgins*, 164 A. D.2d 283, 562 N. Y. S.2d 962 (N. Y. App. Div. 1990).
63. *Braschi*, 74 N. Y.2d at 211, 544 N. Y. S.2d at 788–89, 543 N. E.2d at 53.
64. Ibid., 543 N. E.2d at 55.
65. There have been many proposals over the years for legislation reforming how the law treats unmarried couples; few have ever been enacted. See Kandoian, "Cohabitation, Common Law Marriage," 1854–55; Fineman, "Law and Changing Patterns of Behavior," 317–20, 326.
66. All the domestic partnership laws that have been enacted to date are limited to two-individual partnerships. There is no requirement that the individuals be in a sexual relationship. San Francisco's law, for example, defines domestic partners as "two adults who have chosen to share one another's lives in an intimate and committed relationship of mutual caring, who live together, and who have agreed to be jointly responsible for basic living expenses incurred during the Domestic Partnership." San Francisco Domestic Partnership Act § 2(a) (1990).
67. Ettelbrick, for example, posits the "domestic partnership movement" as a better alternative to a campaign for lesbian and gay marriage. Ettelbrick, "Marriage a Path to Liberation," 17.
68. In addition to New York and San Francisco, some version of domestic partnership law has been adopted in Seattle, Washington; Berkeley, Santa Cruz, and West Hollywood, California; Takoma Park, Maryland; Minneapolis, Minnesota; Ithaca, New York; and Madison, Wisconsin. See District of Columbia's Commission on Domestic Partnership, *Benefits for D. C. Government Employees* (1990), 8–9; W. Lambert, "Domestic Partners of Seattle Workers Get Health Benefits, *Wall Street Journal*, May 7, 1990, B4; American Civil Liberties Union, *Introduction to Domestic Partnership* (1990), 6–7. An excellent analysis of the legal background for enactment of such law can be found in Cox, "Alternative Families."
69. The criteria for recognition of families in the New York State housing regulations (see note 68) also have been criticized for indeterminacy. See editorial, "We Now Pronounce You a Family," *New York Times*, December 15, 1989, A42.
70. The San Francisco system allows persons who meet the definitional criteria for domestic partners to create a partnership either by filing a form with the county clerk or by having a declaration of domestic partnership

notarized and giving a copy to a witness. San Francisco Domestic Partnership Act § 3(a) (1990). In New York, where the benefit established is bereavement leave for employees of the city, partners register by filing a form with the city's Department of Personnel. New York City, N.Y. Executive Order no. 123 § 3, August 7, 1989. New York's version also requires that the partners have lived together for one year or more on a continuous basis before registration. Ibid., § 2.

Another legal device for achieving the same end involves registration by the parties as an unincorporated association. Family diversity advocates in California have recommended the use of this provision of state law for persons living in municipalities that do not have domestic partnership ordinances. See L. Becklund, "The Word 'Family' Gains New Meaning," *Los Angeles Times*, December 13, 1990, A3.

71. In the San Francisco system, if a copy of the partnership declaration was kept by a witness, that person must receive a copy of the notice that the partnership has ended. Only one partner need sign the notice, but it must be sent to the other partner. San Francisco Domestic Partnership Act § 4(b) (1990).

72. Health benefits, in some cases partial coverage, are available to domestic partners under the plans in Seattle, Madison, Berkeley, Santa Cruz, and West Hollywood. Lambert, "Domestic Partners"; ACLU, *Domestic Partnership*. Bereavement leave is included in the New York City, Seattle, Madison, Berkeley, Santa Cruz, and West Hollywood plans. Ibid. Housing-related benefits are covered by New York State regulations for rent-stabilized and rent-controlled apartments, 9 N. Y. St. Reg. 13 (April 4, 1990), and by a city code provision in Takoma Park, Washington, Takoma Park Code, art. 8, § 6-81 (Supp. 1986). The San Francisco system establishes only a registry; it does not itself extend benefits, although it sets the stage for that possibility. San Francisco Domestic Partnership Act (1990). Registered partners can use the partnership as proof of the relationship in attempts to negotiate with private employers and businesses.

73. In Berkeley, Santa Cruz, and West Hollywood, the partners must certify that they are "responsible for [each other's] welfare." See *City of Berkeley Domestic Partnership Information Sheet* (January 1, 1987) and *City of Berkeley Affidavit of Domestic Partnership* (n.d.); West Hollywood, California, Ordinance no. 22 (February 21, 1985) (copies of materials for each city on file at the *Law & Sexuality* office). This provision was based on the 1976 San Francisco bill, the first domestic partnership proposal, which was passed by the Board of Supervisors but vetoed by then-Mayor Diane Feinstein. The primary author of that and subsequent San Francisco proposals, Matthew Coles, has stated that the mutual responsibility provisions were included as a mechanism for balancing the rights and duties aspects of the legislation. M. Coles, telephone conversation with author, January 1991.

74. The San Francisco legislation states the mutual responsibilities in its definitional section. San Francisco Domestic Partnership Act § 2 (1990). It defines the "basic living expenses" for which the partners agree to be responsible as "the costs of basic food and shelter," plus any expenses paid for in part by benefits flowing to the couple on the basis of their status as domestic partners. Ibid., § 2(c). The law provides that by signing a declaration of partnership, the two parties acknowledge "that this agreement can be enforced by anyone to whom those expenses are owed." Ibid., § 2(3). If the partnership ends, the partners can incur no further obligations to each other. Ibid., § 6(b).

75. See F. Olsen, "The Family and the Market: A Study of Ideology and Legal Reform," *Harvard L. Rev.* 96 (1983): 1497; N. Taub and E. Schneider, "Women's Subordination and the Role of Law," in *The Politics of Law: A Progressive Critique,* ed. D. Kairys (New York: Pantheon, 1990), 151.
76. 18 Cal. 3d 660, 557 P.2d 106, 135 Cal. Rptr. 815 (1976).
77. Blumberg argues that the majority of cohabiting heterosexual couples both believe and act as though there is no difference between marriage and cohabitation. She asserts that the failure to treat such couples according to marriage law principles systematically harms cohabiting heterosexual women who, like married women, tend to forgo income opportunities in order to perform domestic labor. She notes that in several of the reported cases, the female partners in a dissolving nonmarital union had sought marriage, but the man had refused. Blumberg proposes that heterosexual cohabitant couples who meet certain durational criteria or who have children be automatically considered as married. Those couples who mutually do intend from the outset of a relationship to avoid the state-dictated terms of matrimony could execute waivers of statutory shares and other specific instruments to achieve the same end, but the burden to act would be on those who wish to opt out of marriage. See Blumberg, "Cohabitation," 1066–70. Kandoian reaches essentially the same conclusion, but would use the principles of business partnerships to achieve that end. See Kandoian, "Cohabitation," 1863–72.
78. Neither Blumberg nor Kandoian mentions lesbians or gay relationships in her analysis. See Blumberg, "Cohabitation"; Kandoian, "Cohabitation."
79. In fact, however, not only are the domestic partnership laws available for use by couples without regard to sexual orientation, but several cities that have adopted such plans report that the majority of the actual registrants are heterosexual couples. See Lambert, "Domestic Partners" (in Seattle, almost 75 percent of participants are heterosexual partners); Mayor's Lesbian and Gay Task Force of Seattle, *The Impact of Domestic Partners Legislation* (1989, n.p.) (more than 80 percent of participants in the Berkeley plan are heterosexual partners; in West Hollywood, however, about 80 percent are same-sex couples).
80. One positive example of changing the framework of reform to include the genuine diversity of interests involved has been suggested by Matthew Coles. In response to concerns that previous versions of domestic partnership initiatives did not addresss the issues of most importance to people of color, Coles has proposed a twin registry system: in addition to the one for couples, a family registry could be added to enhance the usefulness of the concept for households where the unformalized relationship was not between two adults, but existed as a form of unofficial adoption by an adult of a child who was unrelated by blood or marriage, but who was part of a larger, informal community kinship system (Matthew Coles, telephone conversation with the author, January 1991). Advocates in Los Angeles have also sought to frame their efforts in broad, "family diversity" terms, addressing issues of housing, homelessness, child care, family violence, education, disability, and concerns of elders, along with those related to unmarried couples. See Los Angeles City Task Force on Family Diversity, *Strengthening Families: A Model for Community Action* (Los Angeles: Spectrum Institute, 1988). A similar report grew out of the San Francisco campaign to enact a domestic partnership law. See Mayor's Task Force in Family Policy, *Approaching 2000: Meeting*

the Challenges to San Francisco's Families (San Francisco: Office of the Mayor, 1990).

81. The impact of economic class, for example, may be complicated. On the one hand, the moment of marriage (i.e., the wedding) is often a moment of display, or attempted display, of class position, attended by substantial anxiety. Moreover, it is possible that less affluent persons in the lesbian and gay community will be less benefited by the legalization of marriage, because they have less property, and much of marriage law concerns property. However, it is precisely persons with less property who are less likely to have the disposable income with which to obtain the wills, powers of attorney, and other devices that serve as an alternative mechanism for controlling the allocation and devise of property. Domestic partnership laws, as currently drafted, would not supplant that function. Thus, marriage is by far the least expensive (at least in legal costs) and the most easily accessible device by which to ensure that one's partner is the individual who makes whatever decisions might be necessary as to treatment at time of illness or procedures at time of death, as well as to provide that whatever possessions one values pass to that person.

82. F. I. Michelman, "The Supreme Court and Litigation Access Fees: The Right to Protect One's Own Rights—Part I," *Duke L. J.* (1973): 1177.

83. The brief and partial summary presented in this article cannot, of course, do justice to the writing of CLS scholars nor to those of their critics. Two symposium editions of law reviews, from which all of the sources cited in notes 84 and 85 are taken, remain excellent collections of CLS articles in the rights debate: "Critical Legal Studies Symposium," *Stanford L. Rev.* 36 (1984): 1; and "Symposium: A Critique of Rights," *Texas L. Rev.* 62 (1984): 1363.

84. Ideas can "be taken over and falsified immediately, the same way that the appointment of Sandra Day O'Connor is an attempt to falsify the meaning of the women's movement." P. Gabel and D. Kennedy, "Roll Over Beethoven," *Stanford L. Rev.* 36 (1984): 5.

85. A. C. Hutchinson and P. J. Moynihan, "The 'Rights' Stuff: Roberto Unger and Beyond," *Texas L. Rev.* 62 (1984): 1510; S. Lynd, "Communal Rights," *Texas L. Rev.* 62 (1984): 1418–19.

86. A. D. Freeman, "Antidiscrimination Law: The View from 1989," in *Politics of Law*, 96 (recent civil rights decisions by the Supreme Court "can be best understood . . . as reaffirming the myths that normalize inequity as the outcome of impersonal, neutral forces"); R. W. Gordon, "New Developments in Legal Theory," in ibid., 413.

87. "'Law' is just one among many . . . systems of meaning . . . [that] has the effect of making the social world as it is come to seem natural and inevitable." Gordon, "New Developments," 419.

88. See K. W. Crenshaw, "Race, Reform, and Retrenchment: Transformation and Legitimation in Antidiscrimination Law," *Harvard L. Rev.* 101 (1988): 1357 (arguing, inter alia, that CLS critiques have exaggerated the role of ideological constructs and underestimated the power of racial domination and coercion); P. J. Williams, "Alchemical Notes: Reconstructing Ideals From Deconstructed Rights," *Harvard C. R.-C. L. Rev.* 22 (1987): 424 ("This country's worst historical moments have not been attributable to rights-assertion, but to a failure of rights-commitment"); E. Schneider, "The Dialectic of Rights and Politics: Perspectives From the Women's Movement, *N.Y.U. L. Rev.* 61 (1986): 589.

89. Schneider argues that the assertion of rights claims "help[s] women to overcome th[e] sense of privatization and of personal blame [that] has perpetuated women's subordination." Schneider, "The Dialectic of Rights," 626. Crenshaw points out that "[b]ecause rights that other Americans took for granted were routinely denied to Black Americans, Blacks' assertion of their rights constituted a serious ideological challenge to white supremacy. Their demand was not just a place in the front of the bus, but for inclusion in the American political imagination." Crenshaw, "Race, Reform, and Retrenchment," 1365.
90. Schneider, "The Dialectic of Rights," 648–52.
91. Crenshaw, "Race, Reform, and Retrenchment," 1368.

CHAPTER 14

* The author thanks Professors Alan Freeman and Michael Perry for their bibliographic suggestions, as well as Rebecca Sember (Tulane '94) and Sharon Noble (Pitt '95) for their research assistance.

1. R. Colker, *Abortion & Dialogue: Pro-Choice, Pro-Life & American Law* (Indianapolis and Bloomington: Indiana University Press, 1992), 100.
2. See J. B. Nelson, *Embodiment: An Approach to Sexuality and Christian Theology* (Minneapolis: Augsburg Publishing, 1978).
3. Ibid., bookjacket.
4. Ibid., 16.
5. C. Heyward, "Is a Self-Respecting Christian Woman an Oxymoron?: Reflections on a Feminist Spirituality for Justice," *Religion & Intellectual Life* 3 (1986): 45, 46–47.
6. Ibid., 49.
7. Religion is very important to many women in our society. Cherly Preston has summarized the extent of that interest:

    In 1988, three-fourths of American women reported that they considered religious faith the most important influence on their lives. . . . By 1990, that number had dropped, but women still significantly exceeded men in religious activity.

    C. B. Preston, "Feminism and Faith: Reflections on the Mormon Heavenly Mother," *Texas J. of Women and Law* 2 (1993): 337, 340, n. 11.
8. See A. Walker, "Coming Apart," in *Take Back the Night: Women on Pornography,* ed. Laura Lederer (New York: Morrow, 1980), 95, n. 100 (defining "womanist").
9. See generally P. Giddings, *When and Where I Enter: The Impact of Black Women on Race and Sex in America* (New York: Morrow, 1984), 54–55.
10. b. hooks, *Feminist Theory: From Margin to Center* (Boston: South End Press, 1984), 1–2.
11. Giddings, *When and Where,* 305.
12. Ibid., 171.
13. Ibid., 173.
14. *This Bridge Called My Back: Writings by Radical Women of Color,* ed. C. Moraga and G. Anzaldua (Portland: Kitchen Table, 1984).
15. A. Lorde, "An Open Letter to Mary Daly," in ibid., 94–97.
16. Ibid., 95.
17. Ibid., 96. Similarly, the importance of religion or spirituality to making women of color feel included within the women's movement is evident in an anthology of writings by North American Indian women. See *A Gathering of Spirit: A Collection by North American Indian Women,* ed. B.

Brant (Montpelier, VT: Sinister Wisdom Books, 1984).
18. C. Ramazanoglu, *Feminism and the Contradictions of Oppression* (New York: Routledge, 1989).
19. Ibid., 151.
20. Ibid.
21. See Giddings, *When and Where*, 64 (tracing the historical routes of patriarchy within the Black Church in the nineteenth century).
22. Ibid., 312.
23. Nelson, *Embodiment*, 261.
24. Ibid.
25. Ibid., 261–62.
26. A. Y. Davis, *Women, Race & Class* (New York: Random House, 1981), 209.
27. Ibid., 210 (quoting Linda Gordon).
28. Ibid., 215.
29. E. Mensch and A. Freeman, *The Politics of Virtue: Is Abortion Debatable?* (Durham: Duke University Press, 1993), 285, n. 64.
30. Davis, *Women, Race & Class*, 203–206.
31. Colker, *Abortion and Dialogue*.
32. L. Tribe, *Abortion: The Clash of Absolutes* (New York: Norton, 1990).
33. R. Dworkin, *Life's Dominion: An Argument About Abortion, Euthanasia, and Individual Freedom* (New York: Knopf, 1993).
34. Tribe, *Abortion*, 197–228.
35. Ibid., 213–23.
36. Dworkin, *Life's Dominion*.
37. For further discussion of this phenomenon, see R. P. Petchesky, *Abortion and Woman's Choice: The State, Sexuality, & Reproductive Freedom* (Boston: Northeastern University Press, 1990), xii–xvi.
38. Dworkin, *Life's Dominion*, 109.
39. Ibid.
40. Ibid., 13.
41. Ibid., 16.
42. Ibid.
43. D. Roberts, "The Future of Reproductive Choice for Poor Women and Women of Color," *Women's Rights Law Reporter* 12 (1990): 62.
44. See, e.g., *Maher v. Roe*, 432 U. S. 464 (1977); *Harris v. McRae*, 448 U. S. 297 (1980).
45. Roberts, "The Future of Reproductive Choice," 62, quoting Kolbert, "Developing a Reproductive Rights Agenda," in *Reproductive Laws for the 1990s: A Briefing Handbook*, ed. N. Taub and S. Cohen (Clifton: Humana Press, 1989), 8.
46. Feminist Jurisprudence Seminar, Tulane Law School, Spring 1993.
47. Petchesky, *Abortion and Woman's Choice*.
48. Ibid., 331.
49. Ibid., 371.
50. 478 U. S. 186 (1986).
51. Ibid.
52. Ibid., 197.
53. *Bowers v. Hardwick*, 478 U. S. at 211.
54. Nelson, *Embodiment*, 202.
55. M. M. Ellison, "Common Decency: A New Christian Sexual Ethics," *Christianity and Crisis*, November 12, 1990, 352, 355.
56. 881 F. 2d 454 (7th Cir. 1989), cert. denied, 494 U. S. 1004 (1990).
57. Ibid., 464.

58. R. Colker, "Marriage," *Yale J. L. and Feminism* 3 (1991): 321.
59. S. Young, "Breaking Silence About the 'B-Word': Bisexual Identity and Lesbian-Feminist Discourse," in *Closer to Home: Bisexuality & Feminism,* ed. E. R. Weise (Seattle: Seal Press, 1992), 77.
60. *Bi Any Other Name: Bisexual People Speak Out,* ed. L. Hutchins and L. Kaahumanu (Boston: Alyson Publications, 1991).
61. Ibid.
62. B. Blasingame, "The Roots of Biphobia: Racism and Internalized Heterosexism," in *Closer to Home,* ed. Weise, 51–52.
63. hooks, *Feminist Theory,* 68–69.
64. *This Bridge Called My Back,* ed. Moraga and Anzaldua, 121.
65. hooks, *Feminist Theory,* 70.
66. Nevertheless, I do not mean to question the need for various subgroups such as African-American women or lesbians to momentarily separate in order to establish their own sense of needs and priorities. Beverly Smith, for example, criticized separatism as a political movement but nonetheless recognized that "it has some validity in a more limited sphere." See *This Bridge Called My Back,* ed. Moraga and Anzaldua, 121. Barbara Smith recognized that it was legitimate for a lesbian to be a separatist in order to acknowledge "that you really don't need men to define your identity, your sexuality, to make your life meaningful or simply to have a good time. That doesn't necessarily mean that you have no comprehension of the oppressions that you share with men." Ibid. For an excellent defense of the need for African-American women to disassociate from white women, see P. J. Smith, "We Are Not Sisters: African-American Women and the Freedom to Associate and Disassociate," *Tulane L. Rev.* 66 (1992): 1467.

CHAPTER 15

1. See *Campus Life, In Search of Community* 20, a report issued by the Carnegie Foundation for the Advancement of Teaching (Princeton, 1990). Of 355 colleges and universities that answered the Carnegie Foundation's survey in 1989, 60 percent had instituted written policies that included provisions for punishing students found guilty of language offensive to blacks, women, gays, Jews, and so on. Eleven percent of the rest of the responding colleges were working to establish such codes. Ibid., 19. The Carnegie Foundation, itself, finally opposes campus restrictions on speech.
2. See *Doe v. University of Michigan,* 721 F. Supp. 852, 862 (E. D. Mich. 1989). The federal court did allow that some hate speech codes might meet constitutional standards, insofar as they appealed either to the "fighting words" exception to First Amendment protections against criminal prosecution, or to the common law tort of "intentional infliction of emotional distress." "Under certain circumstances racial and ethnic epithets, slurs, and insults might . . . constitutionally be prohibited [under the fighting words doctrine]. In addition, such speech may also be sufficient to state a claim for common law intentional infliction of emotional distress." One of the most well-known and controversial of speech codes, at Stanford University, appeals to the "fighting words" doctrine as grounds for invoking sanctions against speech. As I will later argue, justifications for restricting hate speech are distinct from "fighting words" doctrines, and it would be better to create a new First Amendment exception explicitly recognizing hate speech.

3. See Abigail Adams's famous "Remember the Ladies" letter to her husband John Adams in 1776, for a forthright assertion of the relevance of the principles of liberal democratic theory to the situation of women. See also John Adams's jocular reply to Abigail, nicely complemented by a quite serious letter to a colleague in which he discusses the necessary limitations on the principle of "consent of the people," and particularly why women must be excluded, along with men without property and children. See *The Feminist Papers*, ed. A. S. Rossi (Boston: Northeastern University Press, 1973), 7–15.

   See the U.S. Constitution, Article I, Section 2, for the "Three-Fifths Compromise," whereby three-fifths of the slaves were to be counted for purposes of representation and taxes. See the 1857 Supreme Court decision, *Dred Scott v. Sanford*, in which the original intentions of the Founding Fathers to exclude members of "the enslaved African race" from citizenship and constitutional protection were reaffirmed. Relevant passages from these documents are reprinted in *Racism and Sexism: An Integrated Study*, ed. P. Rothenberg (New York: St. Martin's Press, 1988), 190, 203–206.

4. J. M. Balkin, "Some Realism About Pluralism: Legal Realist Approaches to the First Amendment," *Duke L. J.* (1990): 384.

5. N. Strossen, "Regulating Racist Speech on Campus: A Modest Proposal?" *Duke L. J.* (1990): 484.

6. R. Delgado, "Words that Wound: A Tort Action for Racial Insults, Epithets and Name-Calling," *Harvard C. R.-C. L. L. Rev.* 17 (1982): 157.

7. M. Matsuda, "Public Response to Racist Speech: Considering the Victim's Story," *Michigan L. Rev.* (1989): 2331–32, 2380.

8. C. Lawrence, "If He Hollers Let Him Go: Regulating Racist Speech on Campus," *Duke L. J.* (1990): 432. For the text of the Stanford regulations, see T. Grey, "Civil Rights v. Civil Liberties: The Case of Discriminatory Verbal Harassment," *Social Philosophy and Policy* 8 (1991): 106–107.

9. It is true that a woman or a person of color who is psychologically robust may not be silenced today by hate speech directed at them. But it is quite likely that the effect of their words upon others, when they do choose to speak, has been undermined by the demeaning associations that the act of hate speech evokes.

   Andrew Altman maintains that hate speech functions performatively to actually subordinate its victims. Calling upon J. L. Austin's distinction between a speech act's perlocutionary (causal) effects on the hearer, and the illocutionary force of speech acts that actually do something, Altman claims that hate speech is "a certain kind of illocutionary act, namely, the act of treating someone as a moral subordinate." See Altman's "Liberalism and Campus Hate Speech: A Philosophical Examination," *Ethics* 103 (1993): 310. While this is a useful way of comprehending the power of hate speech, I do not accept Altman's later claim that restrictions upon hate speech therefore target acts of speech-act subordination rather than ideas (ibid., 315). Surely it is simply evasive to suggest that these acts of subordination are not inextricably bound up with particular ideas.

10. As J. M. Balkin points out, "The illusion of content neutrality could only be achieved by viewing certain types of speech as not 'speech'—for example, obscenity, commercial speech, and 'fighting words.'" "Some Realism," 396.

11. A. Giddens, *The Constitution of Society* (Berkeley: University of California Press, 1984), suggests a three-tiered analysis of subjectivity, according to

which we each behave in accordance with a discursive consciousness, a practical consciousness (a habitual, routinized background awareness), and what he terms a "basic security system" (involving degrees of bodily "trust or ontological security" within a social situation) (ibid., 79). Iris Young, citing Giddens, argues that racism, sexism, and homophobia have receded from the discursive level of consciousness where norms of formal equality now prevail, while remaining present within our practical consciousness and our basic security system. See her *Justice and the Politics of Difference* (Princeton: Princeton University Press, 1990), chapter 5.

I think hate speech may be one of those nodal points at which our practical consciousness and our basic security system may be accessible to discursive consciousness, particularly if we are required to acknowledge and critique our desire to engage in hate speech.

12. See *Republic*, Books II, III, IV, trans. P. Shorey, in *The Collected Dialogues of Plato*, ed. E. Hamilton and H. Cairns (Princeton: Princeton University Press, 1961).

13. I use *Twenty Questions: An Introduction to Philosophy*, ed. G. L. Bowie et al. (New York: Harcourt Brace Jovanovich, 1992), which presents the two sides of the controversy very fairly with articles by Ira Glasser and Charles Lawrence (ibid., 492–99).

14. K. Greenawalt, "Insults and Epithets: Are They Protected Speech?" *Rutgers L. Rev.* 42 (1990): 307.

15. See P. S. Mann, *Micro-Politics: Agency in a Postfeminist Era* (Minneapolis: University of Minnesota Press, 1994), for a more extensive analysis of this set of issues.

16. O. Fiss, "Freedom and Feminism," a reading prepared for and presented to the New York University Colloquium in Law, Philosophy and Political Theory, November 14, 1991. Fiss was here discussing the possibility of defending the trafficking provision of the Indianapolis antipornography ordinance written by Catharine MacKinnon against charges that it violated First Amendment rights. Maintaining that the trafficking provision can arguably "be justified on the grounds that pornography silences women," he goes on to distinguish two sorts of silencing dynamics, an ideational and a sociological one. He contends that it is "the social practice" of pornography "rather than any particular book, magazine or film itself" that silences women and "impoverishes public debate" (ibid., 20–22). It is similarly the social practice of hate speech rather than any particular word or idea that oppresses women and minorities today.

17. J. S. Mill, *On Liberty* (New York: Penguin Books, 1984), 68, 136, 97.

18. A. Meiklejohn, *Free Speech and Its Relation to Self-Government* (New York: Harper, 1948), 26.

19. *United States v. Schwimmer*, 279 U.S. 644, 654 (1929) (Holmes, J., dissenting): "If there is any principle of the Constitution that more imperatively calls for attachment than any other it is the principle of free thought—not free thought for those who agree with us, but freedom for the thought that we hate."

20. "A Move to Protect Women From 'Street Harassment,'" *New York Times*, July 2, 1993.

21. Mari Matsuda makes this point about the protection of racist speech. See "Public Response to Racist Speech," 2374–77.

22. Mill, *On Liberty*, 63.

23. See J. S. Mill, "The Subjection of Women," in J. S. Mill and H. T.

Essays on Sex Equality, ed. A. Rossi (Chicago: University of Chicago Press, 1970).

24. D. Dyzenhaus, "John Stuart Mill and the Harm of Pornography," *Ethics* 102 (1992): 545–50. Dyzenhaus argues that Mill might today have supported laws against pornography, insofar as pornography is deemed harmful to women's fundamental interest in autonomy. I think his arguments are even more powerful in suggesting Mill's support for laws against hate speech.

25. Dyzenhaus is quite right that we will understand Mill's ideas better if we integrate his critique of the subjection of women by men into the rest of his theory. The odd thing, however, is that he himself did not integrate it very well. So what we can say is that today he would have been likely to say many of the sorts of things we wish he might have said then.

26. Meiklejohn, *Free Speech*, 24.

27. Ibid., 22, 23, 24, 26.

28. Ibid., 24.

29. See N. Hentoff, *Village Voice*, March 26, April 2, April 9, 1991. In his March 26 column, Hentoff quotes what he terms Hann's "quintessential bigotry." Hann managed to include racist, homophobic, and anti-Semitic epithets in his brief spate of verbal coarseness: "Fuck you, niggers!" "What are you, a faggot?" "What are you, a Jew? Fucking Jew!" Hentoff cites a number of legal experts, among them Nadine Strossen, then president of the ACLU, as supporting an absolute proscription upon the regulation of speech, including such hate speech acts.

30. A more recent controversy at the University of Pennsylvania illustrates some of the complexities of potential hate speech incidents. In this case, some black sorority women were making noise late at night in a dormitory courtyard, evoking shouts of complaint from students trying to sleep or study. Eden Jacobowitz, a freshman, later admitted to calling them "water buffalo," a translation of a Hebrew word, *behayma*, which is a mild epithet for chiding an uncouth individual. The women accused him of violating the university's policy forbidding racial harassment. Eventually the women dropped their charges, but not before this became a national example of the supposed excesses of the "PC" consciousness that would restrict hate speech.

   However, the fact that Jacobowitz had not used any sort of *conventional* racist terminology would have immediately voided hate speech charges had there been a hate speech code of the sort I, as well as many advocates of hate speech regulations, have recommended. See M. deCourcy Hinds, "A Campus Case: Speech or Harassment?" *New York Times*, May 15, 1993.

   Notice, however, that we should take seriously the fact that the black women made charges of racial harassment in response to this phrase. Presumably, their response indicates some experience of racism by black students as a part of everyday relationships on campus. Sanctions against hate speech are but one means to signal the unacceptability of racist or sexist attitudes and behavior that must be opposed on numerous fronts.

31. A. Bloom, *The Closing of the American Mind* (New York: Simon and Schuster, 1987).

32. A. MacIntyre, in *After Virtue* (Notre Dame: University of Notre Dame Press, 1981), maintains that such shared practices and goals are characteristic of traditional moral communities.

33. J. Habermas, *The Theory of Communicative Action*, vols. 1 and 2. (Boston: Beacon Press, 1984, 1987).
34. J. Cohen and A. Arato, *Civil Society and Social Theory* (Cambridge: MIT Press, 1993).
35. S. Benhabib, *Situating the Self: Gender, Community and Postmodernism in Contemporary Ethics* (New York: Routledge, 1992), 38.
36. Ibid., 29.
37. Many people may be puzzled at the idea of having norms of universal respect and egalitarian reciprocity govern academic relations. They may insist that the academy requires relationships of asymmetrical respect and nonreciprocity between students and teachers, insofar as students must trust and respect the greater knowledge and authority of teachers in order for the pedagogical process to function effectively. In order to answer this query, we need merely distinguish between respecting someone as an equal, and regarding her with a universalizable form of respect owed to persons as human beings. It is the latter (Kantian) form of respect that is here being mandated, and that sexism and racism are now recognized to preclude. (Although in Kant's own day there was little recognition of this.)

    Ronald Dworkin has discussed this distinction between being treated with equal respect and being treated equally in "Reverse Discrimination," in *Taking Rights Seriously* (Cambridge: Harvard University Press, 1977). He identifies the right to be treated with equal concern and respect as a basic right of citizens.

    An ideal of egalitarian reciprocity may seem even more counterintuitive in an academic setting, but if read as a mandate of procedural fairness rather than literal quid pro quo behavior, it too has an important role to play in eliminating racial and sexual discrimination. Traditional intellectual hierarchies based upon greater and lesser degrees of wisdom are currently perverted by racist and sexist patterns of domination and subordination that insidiously insert themselves into intellectual relationships, distorting the whole academic fabric. If procedural norms of universal respect and egalitarian reciprocity within all intellectual transactions could diminish the scope of sexism and racism, relationships of cooperation and trust could again flourish between individuals of different degrees of ability and academic status.
38. Proponents of hate speech restrictions today discount slippery slope arguments that have traditionally warned against any regulation of speech on the grounds that it will open the door to ever greater encroachments on First Amendment freedoms. Pointing to the fact that there have always been exceptions to First Amendment rights, they assert that hate speech regulations can be drafted narrowly enough so as to avoid becoming precedents for censors with anti-democratic agendas. See A. Altman, "Liberalism and Campus Hate Speech," 316. A related and more serious problem is the danger of discriminatory applications of hate speech codes. Nadine Strossen points out that during the year in which the University of Michigan speech code was in effect, "the only two instances in which the rule was invoked to sanction racist speech involved the punishment of speech by or on behalf of black students." "Regulating Racist Speech on Campus," 557. Speech code advocates reply that this is merely a consequence of poorly crafted hate speech regulations. Charles Lawrence goes so far as to suggest "an element of unconscious collusion" as

necessary to explain the undue breadth of speech codes like that of the University of Michigan. "It's almost as if the university purposefully wrote an unconstitutional regulation so that they could say to the black students, 'We tried to help you but the courts just won't let us do it'" ("If He Hollers," 477–78, n. 161).

39. K. T. Bartlett and J. O'Barr, "The Chilly Climate on College Campuses: An Expansion of the 'Hate Speech' Debate," *Duke L. J.* (1990): 574. The studies on campus sexism they cite are by R. M. Hall and B. R. Sandler, entitled *The Classroom Climate: A Chilly One for Women* (Project on the Status and Education of Women, 1982); and *Out of the Classroom: A Chilly Campus Climate for Women?* (Project on the Status and Education of Women, 1984).

40. H. Marcuse, "Repressive Tolerance," in *A Critique of Pure Tolerance* (Boston: Beacon Press, 1969), 84–85, 117.

41. Ibid., 100–101.

Contributors

BRUCE A. ARRIGO teaches sociology and criminal justice at Saint Joseph's University (Philadelphia); his work has appeared widely in journal article and book chapter form, addressing issues in the sociology and philosophy of law, crime, and community. His areas of specialization include postmodern feminist jurisprudence, legal semiotics, and critical criminology. He is the author of *Madness, Language, and Law* (Harrow and Heston, 1993).

RAYMOND A. BELLIOTTI is Professor of Philosophy at SUNY Fredonia. He has published numerous articles on ethics and public policy, and is the author of *Justifying Law* (Temple University Press, 1992) and *Good Sex* (University of Kansas Press, 1993).

DENIS J. BRION is Professor of Law at Washington & Lee University School of Law, where he teaches courses in the areas of property and law and economics. He holds a B.S. from Northwestern University and a J.D. from the University of Virginia School of Law. He is the author of *Essential Industry and the NIMBY Phenomenon* (Quorum, 1991) as well as numerous essays on semiotics and the law.

DAVID S. CAUDILL is Associate Professor of Law at Washington & Lee University. He holds a Ph.D. from Vrije Universiteit te Amsterdam. He practiced law for seven years in San Diego and Austin, and is the author of *Disclosing Tilt: Law, Belief and Criticism* (1989), as well as numerous articles in legal theory, law and psychoanalysis, and law and religion.

WARD CHURCHILL, who teaches at the University of Colorado Center for the Study of Ethnicity and Race, is the author of numerous articles on Native American issues in politics and law; a collection of his essays, entitled *Struggle for the Land* (Common Courage Press), appeared in 1992.

RUTH COLKER, Professor of Law at the University of Pittsburgh, is the author of numerous articles in law and religion, and of *Abortion and Dialogue: Pro-Choice, Pro-Life & American Law* (1992).

STEVEN JAY GOLD has taught at Carleton College, Iowa State University, and Southern Connecticut State University; he now lives in Los Angeles. He holds a Ph.D. in philosophy from the University of California at Santa Barbara. He is the author of numerous articles on social and political theory, Marxism, Foucault, and applied ethics and is the editor of two books: *Moral Controversies: Race, Class and Gender in Applied Ethics* (Wadsworth Publishing, 1993), and *Paradigms in Political Theory* (Iowa State University Press, 1993).

NAN D. HUNTER, now Assistant General Counsel in the U.S. Department of Health and Human Services, was formerly a law professor at Brooklyn Law School and the Director of the American Civil Liberties Union Lesbian and Gay Rights Project.

DAVID INGRAM is a Professor of Philosophy at Loyola University of Chicago. He is the author of *Habermas and the Dialectic of Reason, Critical Theory and Philosophy,* and *Reason, History, and Politics* (forthcoming), as well as co-editor of *Critical Theory: The Essential Readings.*

PATRICIA S. MANN, Assistant Professor of Philosophy at Hofstra University, is the author of *Micropolitics: Agency in a Post-Feminist Era* (Minnesota University Press, 1994). She is on the editorial boards of *Hypatia* and *Social Text* and is the author of numerous publications in social and political theory.

DRAGAN MILOVANOVIC is Professor of Criminal Justice at Northeastern Illinois University; he is also the Honors Coordinator of the university. He has published numerous articles and several books in the field of criminal law employing Marxian theory, semiotics, chaos theory, and psychoanalysis; his recent book is *Postmodern Law and Disorder* (Deb. Charles Publishers, 1993).

JEFFREY REIMAN is William Fraser McDowell Professor of Philosophy at The American University in Washington, D.C. He is the author of *In Defense of Political Philosophy: A Reply to R. P. Wolff's "In Defense of Anarchism"* (Harper & Row, 1972), *The Rich Get Richer and the Poor Get Prison: Ideology, Class, and Criminal Justice* (Wiley, 1979, 1984; Macmillan, 1990), *Justice and Modern Moral Philosophy* (Yale, 1990), and over forty articles in moral, political, and legal philosophy.

THOMAS W. SIMON received his Ph.D. from Washington University and his J.D. from the University of Illinois. He has been admitted to the bar in the District of Columbia, Illinois, and Maryland. His most recent publication is *Democracy and Social Injustice* (Rowman & Littlefield).

PATRICIA SMITH, J.D., Ph.D., University of Arizona, is Associate Professor (philosophy) at the University of Kentucky. She is the editor of *Feminist Jurisprudence* (Oxford, 1992) and of *The Nature and Process of Law* (Oxford, 1993) and author of numerous articles on responsibility, legal process, feminism, and action theory.

CARL SWIDORSKI is Professor of Political Science at the College of Saint Rose in Albany, New York. He has written on the role of the U.S. Supreme Court as a legitimating institution, labor law, and New York State constitutional law. Currently, he is working on a book on the Warren Court and the politics of corporate liberalism.

INDEX

Abortion controversy, 238–46
Athusser, L., 41, 52–53
Apel, K. O., 159
Aristotle, 142
Arrow, K., 149–50

Benhabib, S., 268
Bisexuality, 246–54
Brenkman, J., 52–53

Chaos Theory, 181–86, 193
Criminal Law, 103. *See also* Marx, K.
  & Marxism
Critical Legal Studies, 45–47, 140,
  152–55, 164, 166–69, 231. *See also*
  Horwitz, M.; Kennedy, D.;
  Unger, R.
Critical Race Theory, 29–30. *See also*
  Delgado, R.; Lawrence, C.;
  Matsuda, M.
Cohen, G. A., 32–37
Constitutive critique of law, 39
Contractualism, theory of, 141–47
Crenshaw, K. W., 29, 232

Dahl, R., 69–70, 150
Dahl, S., 93–94
Delgado, R., 257
Democracy, 67–71, 141–52, 160–61
Dewey, J., 149
Downs, A., 149
Dworkin, R., 240–43

Elster, J., 36
Equal Protection doctrine, 75–77

Feminism, 43, 73–75, 78–82, 89–107,
  224–25, 230. *See also* Dahl, S.;
  Friedan, B.; Gilligan, C.; Irigaray,
  L.; MacKinnon, C.; Minow, M.;
  Smart, C.
Feminist theology, 234–35
First Amendment (freedom of
  speech), 263
Foucault, M., 37, 89, 91–92
Frank, J., 23–25

Frankfurt School Critical Theory, 48
Freud, S., 47–50
Friedan, B., 236

Gabel, P., 50–53
Gay rights. *See* Lesbian and Gay
  rights
Gilligan, C., 90, 97–98
Gramsci, A., 163

Habermas, J., 159
Hate Speech codes, 255–71
Hobbes, T., 142–44
Horwitz, M., 145, 186–87

Ideology, 9, 35, 45–47. *See also* Marx,
  K., & Marxism
Injustice, theory of, 60–72
International Law, (colonialism):
  Great Britain, 201–04; U.S. treaties
  with Native Americans, 204–206,
  216–18
Irigaray, L., 90, 94–97

Justice, theory of, 55–60. *See also*
  Rawls, J.

Kennedy, D., 154–55

Labor Law, 155–57, 169–75
Lacan, J., 41–44, 49–51; clinical
  analysis, 50; feminism, 43; law,
  43–44; *Schema L*, 42
Langer, S., 101
Lawrence, C., 257
Legal Process, 193–98
Legal Realism, 23–25
Lesbian and Gay rights, 246–54;
  Bowers v. Hardwick, 247–49;
  domestic partnership laws, 229–31;
  "rights" controversy, 231–32;
  same-sex marriage, 221–22,
  225–26
Lindblom, C., 150
Littleton, C., 77–79
Locke, J., 143
Lukes, S., 65

MacKinnon, C., 25–27, 78, 81–82, 90, 98–100
Marcuse, H., 48, 270–71
Marriage Law, 223–24, 227–29
Marshall Doctrine (Native American relations; Marshall, J.), 207–16
Marx, K., and Marxism: Agency, (human freedom), 38–41, 115; Alienation, 3–4; Base/Superstructure, 5-8, 18–19, 39–40; Capitalism, 117–20; Contingency of law, 15–17, 21–23; Criminal law; 125–35; Critique, nature of, 112–13; Determinism, 6–7; Dialectical Method, 9–10; Economics, *See* Base/Superstructure; Empiricism, 115–16; Exploitation, 4–5; False consciousness, 8–9, 17 (law); Fetishism (of law), 10–13; Functional Explanation (of law), 13–15, 19–21, 32–37; Idealism, 127–28; Ideology, 120–25; Instrumental Perspective, 38–40; Morality, 111, 135–37; Positivism, 127–28; Radicalism, 114; Rule of Law, 12–13; Structural perspectives, 39–41
Matsuda, M., 257
McLellan, D., 46
Meiklejohn, A., 264–65
Mill. J. S., 261–62, 264
Minow, M., 79–81, 84
Murray, E., 90–91, 99–102

Native American Law (discrimination, treaties), 200–20
New Deal legislation, 167

Newton, I. (Newtonian world-view), 181–86, 193

Parsons, T., 32–33
Pashukanis, E., 39–41, 125, 134–35
Persian Gulf War (Kuwait, Iraq), 219
Petchesky, R., 244–46
Plato, 259
Pluralism, theory of, 150–52
Powerlessness, 65–67

Racism in law (discrimination, civil rights), 175–77; race and feminism, 236–38, 244
Rape: law of, 85, 87, 105, 107
Rawls, J., 59, 151
"Rights" controversy, 231–32
Rousseau, J. J., 146–47

Sampford, C., 179–80, 192
Smart, C., 89, 92–93
suffering, 62–64

Taub, N., 79, 81
Thompson, J., 46
Title VII litigation, 82–84. *See also* Equal Protection doctrine
Tort Law, 186–92
Tribe, L., 240

Unger, R., 27–29, 103, 152–54
Utilitarianism, (Bentham and Mill), 147–49

Weber, M., 152
Weinreb, E., 179–80, 192
Welfare rights, 157–58
Wheelright, P., 101
Will theory, (contract law), 144
Williams, J., 83
Williams, W., 79, 81
Woodhull, W., 104